PATRICK HENRY
AND HIS WORLD

Patrick Henry by Thomas Sully.
From the Colonial Williamsburg Collection.

PATRICK HENRY
and
HIS WORLD

by George F. Willison

Doubleday and Company, Inc. Garden City, New York, 1969

To

Malcolm and Esther

LIBRARY OF CONGRESS CATALOG CARD NUMBER 65-13976

PRINTED IN THE UNITED STATES OF AMERICA

Preface

Patrick Henry was one of the most brilliant, most influential, and most controversial Americans of his day—or of any other day.

Everybody knows his "give me liberty or give me death" phrase, but little else about Henry and his accomplishments.

He was, beyond question, the greatest American orator of his time, and perhaps one of the great of all times. "Call it oratory or what you will," Jefferson once said, "but I never heard anything like it. He had more command over the passions than any man I ever knew."

To some of his contemporaries, Henry was merely a demagogue, shifting position every time the wind changed, playing upon the passions of the people for his party's or his own advantage. To many more Americans, particularly in the days leading up to the Revolution, he was a "forest-born Demosthenes," an eloquent and trumpeting voice leading them out of the wilderness to liberty, justice, democracy, and independence. These contradictory views of Henry have long been argued, but can never be reconciled.

Henry was much more than a matchless orator. He was a practical and almost matchless leader in the day-to-day workings of politics, exerting an influence paramount in Virginia and extending beyond to the farthest reaches of the country.

Henry's was a highly significant and dramatic career from the day in 1765 when, at the age of twenty-nine, he emerged unheralded from the backwoods and, rather shabbily dressed in rough country clothes, startled the elegant, bewigged, and beribboned Grandees in Virginia's sedate House of Burgesses by offering his explosive Stamp Tax Resolutions. Henry was the youngest and newest member of the House, having taken his seat only ten days before, and veterans among the Burgesses looked at him askance as a troublemaking upstart.

When Henry succeeded, after "most bloody debate," in having most of his resolutions adopted, this even more startled and disturbed the Grandees, scions of "long-tailed families," who had governed Virginia in accord with their almost baronial interests for generations. With one shot, Henry knocked down the hitherto unchallenged domination of the Long Tails. A most eloquent new voice resounded in the land.

In Jefferson's opinion, shared by most others, Henry "gave the first impulse to the ball of Revolution." Almost overnight, he became "the Noble Patriot," our first national hero—"the idol of his country beyond any man who ever lived," observed Jefferson, who added later: "It is not now easy to say what we should have done without Patrick Henry."

The great George Mason, author of our Bill of Rights, said that though Henry was overwhelming as an orator, that was "the smallest part of his merit. He is, in my opinion, the first man upon this continent, as well in abilities as public virtues."

To John Adams, Henry was a man "of deep reflection, keen sagacity, clear foresight, daring enterprise, inflexible intrepidity, and untainted integrity, with an ardent zeal for the liberties, the honor, and felicity of his country and his species," and his contributions to the Patriot cause would never be forgotten.

At Red Hill, where Henry died and was buried, his marble gravestone bears this inscription carved long ago:

"His fame his best epitaph."

There is a deep irony here. His fame has faded away, has gone into almost total eclipse.

It is time, I think, to have another look at Henry, his strength and his faults, what he represented, what he achieved and what he failed to achieve, and the many forces, both personal and general, that enabled him to rise so rapidly from obscurity to play such an important role in founding the nation and shaping its beginnings.

I wish here to thank the American Council of Learned Societies for a grant that helped finance completion of this book. My thanks also go to my good and accomplished friend, Mr. Charles Swick, who read the script with care and made many helpful suggestions, and to my severest and best critic, T.H.W., who did all of the hard work, as on my previous manuscripts, in preparing the copy of this book for press.

South Hill GEORGE F. WILLISON
October 6, 1967

Contents

The distinctions between Virginians, Pennsylvanians,
New Yorkers, and New Englanders are no more.
I am not a Virginian, but an American.

PATRICK HENRY*

He was the idol of the country beyond any man
who ever lived.

THOMAS JEFFERSON

* From Henry's speech, the opening speech from the floor,
at the First Continental Congress, Philadelphia, September, 1774.

I
A Day to Remember

. . . he left all of us far behind.

—THOMAS JEFFERSON

It was hot and muggy; but that was not unusual for a late spring day in Tidewater Virginia which is flat, low-lying, often very humid.

The date—May 29, 1765.

The place—Williamsburg, capital of colonial Virginia, an unusually attractive but ordinarily rather sleepy country town of perhaps a thousand people, white and black, free and slave, about half and half.

Here, in the Capitol, a handsome two-storied steep-gabled Queen Anne brick structure at the foot of the Duke of Gloucester Street, the House of Burgesses—the lower half of the colonial legislature—was in session.

With the main items on the agenda disposed of, the session was droning to a close. The Hall of the House of Burgesses, a small but impressive chamber modeled in its arrangements on the British House of Commons, had a somewhat empty look and deserted air, being not even half filled. Only 39 of 116 members were in their seats. The others—two thirds of the Burgesses—had packed up and gone home, on the assumption that nothing of importance would come up in the last few days of the session.

On the basis of experience, a quite reasonable supposition.

But how false it proved to be in this instance. And what a surprise the absentees had when they heard the news about what decisions had been taken in the House after their departure—news that was, for most of them, unpleasant and very disturbing.

As anticipated by the absentees, the Burgesses still at their desks in Williamsburg went along about as usual, following the normal routine of doing nothing but tie up loose odds and ends of minor legislation. With the weather oppressive and nothing of moment on the agenda, the House was in a listless and inattentive mood as it plowed through the chore of winding up dull last-minute business.

To anyone viewing the scene and sensing its tone and tempo, it would have seemed that this was an unlikely place and a still less likely time for a sudden great explosion, for a dazzling display of forensic fireworks of immense consequence in the history of the country.

The daring proposals and fiery debate on that day struck a spark in all the colonies, doing as much as anything to kindle the flames that soon blazed up with a roar in the American Revolution and lighted the way, through smoke of battle, to Independence.

It is curious that Independence was finally won not far from here, some ten miles away at Yorktown where Lord Cornwallis surrendered late in October, 1781. In a strange way, and after much doubt and hardship, the Revolution had come full circle, almost to the very point where it started.

But to keep first things first, back now to the relatively few Burgesses still at their desks in Williamsburg late in May, 1765.

Nothing disturbed the drone of their proceedings until, to almost everybody's surprise, a motion was made that the House should review what Virginia had already done and consider what further steps should be taken to make the strongest possible protest against the "infamous" Stamp Act, which was soon to go into effect unless effective action were promptly taken to stop it. The motion to reopen the question passed, quite unexpectedly, and heated discussion began with the House sitting as Committee of the Whole.

The Stamp Tax had first come up six months before, late in 1764. At that time the House had been full and dominated by a large conservative majority led by Tidewater Grandees—Randolphs, Byrds, Carters, Robinsons, Harrisons, Burwells, Ludwells, Carys, Nelsons, and others whose vast clan-like families had built fortunes on huge grants of public land, on tobacco and the sweat of "shoals" of slaves.

These Tidewater lords did not like the Stamp Act, under which, for the first time, a tax was to be levied directly upon the colonies for the acknowledged purpose of raising revenue for the British Treasury, to be spent as Parliament directed. Such a direct tax, they said, was a new and most unwelcome departure in British imperial policy. It violated rights and privileges the colonists had enjoyed since the beginning of settlement. It would upset the friendly relationship that had grown up between the Mother Country and the colonies–a rather free and easy relationship that had proved to be generally acceptable to all.

But the Grandee leaders, intensely loyal to Britain by commercial and financial interests, and to the Crown by long royalist family tradition–many of their ancestors were Cavalier refugees from Charles I's shattered forces–saw to it that the Burgesses did not go beyond passing some mild resolutions taking exception to the Stamp Tax.

Drawn up in three parts, the objections took the form of an Address "to the King's most excellent Majesty," assuring him of Virginia's "firm and inviolable attachment to your sacred person and government"; a Memorial to the House of Lords, "the fixed and hereditary guardians of British liberty"; and a Remonstrance to the House of Commons against an act that would impair the "most desireable connexion between Great Britain and her colonies, supported by such a happy intercourse of reciprocal benefits."

The Stamp Tax was ill-conceived, the Burgesses unanimously agreed. It was a "long & hasty stride" into an unexplored field that vitally concerned not only Virginia but all the colonies.

But in speaking out about the Stamp Tax, the Burgesses hastily added, they wished, as loyal and "ever loving" subjects of the Crown, to avoid "the least Disposition to any sort of Rudeness."

It was this adulatory tone, at times almost obsequious, that increasingly tried the patience of younger and less conservative members of the House. If Virginia had constitutional and inalienable rights, let her assert them forthrightly–not beg for them on bended knee.

These less conventional and more radical Burgesses came, for the most part, from the westerly counties–from the higher rolling lands of the Piedmont. They spoke for the small planters and frontiersmen of that section who did not necessarily identify their interests with those of Tidewater lords. All along the frontier, in Virginia and in all the colonies, a new and more democratic spirit was stirring. In pioneer communities where people lived by hard toil and most men were their own masters, a new equalitarian society was evolving—one in which there were no marked distinctions in wealth and social status. Depending on his energy and abilities, one man was as good as any other, and none was disposed to bow to the pretensions and *obiter dicta* of their self-styled "betters."

It was this spirit which animated the group that, taking advantage of the premature departure of so many "aristocratical" Burgesses, succeeded in persuading the House to take up the whole matter of the Stamp Tax for reconsideration.

As debate opened, the first member to get the floor was a young roughly dressed backwoods lawyer—Patrick Henry, from Louisa, a Piedmont county. Not only was he the youngest of the Burgesses, but also the least experienced, having first taken his seat in the House less than ten days before as the result of a special election.

Who was this brash young upstart now presuming to launch and lead debate on a great State matter about which he knew nothing?

Though the newest member of the House, Henry was known, at least by name, to some of the Burgesses. He had won more than local renown as "the people's advocate" about eighteen months before when, at a trial in the hamlet of Hanover Courthouse, he had won a surprising victory in the celebrated Parsons' Cause. During the trial Henry had stigmatized King George III as a "tyrant" for vetoing a "salutary law" adopted by the House at a time of financial crisis for the relief of impoverished debtors.

Some six feet tall, trim and lithe, obviously very much alive, Henry was not a handsome man, but personable and engaging. His manner toward all men, from the humblest to the highest, was quiet, friendly, and unaffected. Though in sharp contrast to the bright silks, satins, and generously powdered wigs of "gentlemen," Henry's simple country clothes became him, being in character. He was always his own man.

In opening debate, Henry knew exactly what he was going to propose. On a blank page torn from an old law book, he had written out seven rather short resolutions. Keeping his own counsel, he had shown these to only two of his friends in the House, both of whom were tingling with excitement as Henry immediately got the floor and rose to speak. He was calm and collected. After making a few bows to the officers and members of the House, Henry came directly to the point. He drew his paper from a pocket and began reading his resolutions, slowly, in a clear resonant voice:

> *Resolved,* That the first adventurers and settlers of this, his Majesty's colony and dominion brought with them and transmitted to their posterity . . . all the privileges, franchises, and immunities that have at any time been held, enjoyed, and possessed by the people of Great Britain;
>
> *Resolved,* That these privileges, franchises, and immunities have been confirmed [by two royal charters];
>
> *Resolved,* That taxation of the people by themselves or by persons chosen by themselves . . . is the distinguishing characteristic of British freedom, . . .
>
> *Resolved,* That [Virginians] have uninterruptedly enjoyed the right of being thus governed by their own Assemblies in the article of their taxes and internal policy . . .

No exception could be taken to any part of this. It was good Virginia doctrine dating back to 1624. But conservatives in the House were getting nervous and restive. They did not like the tone and drift of the resolutions, suspecting that they were a prelude, as they were, to something else.

Conservatives tried to close debate, arguing that the same ground, more or less, had been covered in the protests earlier sent to London. Nothing more should be done until they had a reply from London. (They would never get a reply, for the head of the British ministry, Lord George Grenville, author of the Stamp Act, had scarcely glanced at the colonial protests before dumping them in the wastebasket.)

After much discussion, Henry's first four resolutions were adopted, but by only the scantiest of margins. Then came what the conservatives had feared:

> *Resolved,* therefore, That the General Assembly* . . . have the only and sole exclusive right and power to lay taxes and impositions upon the inhabitants of this colony. . . .

Here was something new! That the British government, acting

---

* Composed of two legislative bodies—the lower House of popularly elected Burgesses and an upper chamber, the Governor's Council, its twelve members appointed by the Crown on the recommendation of the royal governor. For some time, Council members had been Virginians, chosen from the ranks of the Grandees. The lower House was the more powerful and usually had its way.

through Parliament, had no right to tax Virginians, for the "only and sole exclusive" right to do so rested in the colonial Assembly, particularly in the House of Burgesses where all money bills originated. This was a bold challenge to British authority that many shied away from. It would end any hope of patching up the current quarrel, for it introduced an entirely new question. When Henry's resolution came to a vote, it barely passed—by one vote. When the tally was announced, Attorney General Peyton Randolph, a Grandee leader, was overheard growling to himself:

"By God, I would have given five hundred guineas* for a single vote!"

But conservatives had yet to hear the worst. Their concern and anger rose as Henry went on to read his sixth and seventh resolutions:

> *Resolved,* That . . . the inhabitants of this colony are not bound to yield obedience to any law or ordinance whatever, designed to impose any taxation whatsoever upon them, other than the laws and ordinances of the General Assembly aforesaid:
>
> *Resolved,* That [anyone maintaining the contrary] by writing or speaking . . . shall be deemed an enemy to his Majesty's colony.

There was an uproar. As debate raged, a crowd gathered in the wide doorway that opened into the House chamber, which did not yet have a public gallery. In the crowd, listening intently to every word spoken in what he described as a "most bloody debate," stood a tall, sandy-haired, freckle-faced, and rather awkward young man of twenty-two—Thomas Jefferson. A recent graduate of the College of William and Mary in the town, he was still in Williamsburg studying law in the office of an older friend, George Wythe, the colony's finest legal scholar.

By reason of birth and a considerable inheritance, Jefferson might have become a Grandee, having the most aristocratic connections, such as to the Randolphs, his mother being one. But he had already advanced to the views that, in time, made him world-famed as "the friend of the Common Man."

---

* As the price of votes went in Virginia, this was very high. It amounted to £525, the equivalent in real value (purchasing power) of some $15,000 today. As a rule, an ordinary Virginia voter could be bought by buying him a dram (25¢) in the nearest tavern.

Jefferson and Henry had met five years before at a gay Christmas house party given by the Dandridges, rich and rather distinguished friends of Henry, who lived in the back country not far from Hanover Courthouse where Henry was then residing. Jefferson was not much impressed with Henry at their first meeting, finding him to be solely interested in dancing and making jokes and refusing, in the spirit of the holiday, to be drawn into any serious conversation. But now, as he followed the "bloody debate," Jefferson was all admiration, saying that Henry in defending himself and his views spoke "as Homer wrote, . . . with torrents of sublime eloquence." Though sympathetic with his views, even Jefferson must have winced, as almost all did, when Henry sharply remarked at one point:

"Tarquin and Caesar had each his Brutus; Charles the First, his Cromwell; and George the Third . . ."

"Treason!" cried the Speaker of the House. A great many took up the shout till the chamber rang and echoed—"Treason!" Waiting for the din to subside, Henry quietly resumed:

". . . and George the Third may profit from their example. If that be treason, make the most of it."

For two days, May 29 and 30, the acrid debate went on. On May 29, it may be remarked, Henry was celebrating his twenty-ninth birthday—and celebrate it he certainly did to his enduring renown. On the first day of debate in the Committee of the Whole, all seven of Henry's resolutions appear to have been accepted. Next day, the matter was brought to the floor of the House sitting in formal session for final decision. At this session, it appears that the inflammatory sixth and seventh resolutions were not brought up.* A day later, the House reversed its vote on the controversial fifth resolution about the Assembly's "only and sole exclusive right" to tax Virginians.

In the end, therefore, only the first four of Henry's resolutions were officially adopted. Even so, the "Young, hot, and Giddy" members of the House, as they were called by Francis Fauquier, the royal governor, had won a momentous and quite unexpected victory, one that shook to its foundations the political power of the conservatives who had dominated Virginia without challenge for so long.

Condemning the resolutions as "rash heat," the governor dissolved the House of Burgesses. But this too late; the damage had

* The course of the extended debate, as reported, is not entirely clear, a point to be discussed in detail later.

been done. Copies of all seven of Henry's resolutions had already gone out to other colonies, creating the impression that all of them had been adopted.

This false impression was fostered by some witless censorship on the part of Joseph Royle, editor-publisher of the *Virginia Gazette*. A high Tory in his views, an ardent royalist, Royle was so incensed and outraged by the whole business that he decided not to give it a single line in his columns, which was a serious error. Had he reported the relatively mild resolutions finally passed, he would have kept the published record straight and dissipated the notion that all seven of Henry's resolutions spoke officially for Virginia.

These resolutions, from first article to last, first appeared in print late in June, about a month after the Williamsburg debate, a copy of them having come into the hands of the *Newport Mercury*. Soon, the Rhode Island legislature adopted a series of strong resolutions, following Henry's in pattern and sometimes word for word. The *Mercury* item was quickly picked up and reprinted by papers in Boston and elsewhere. Widely circulated and read not only in newspapers but in handbills, the "Virginia Resolves," as they were called, stirred up animated discussions everywhere—in country kitchens, town shops, city mansions, village halls, churches and meeting houses, taverns, and wherever people met.

Massachusetts had earlier suggested that the colonies send delegates to a general conference on the best ways of organizing resistance to the Stamp Act. The response to this was very cool until publication of Henry's resolutions became the "signal for a general outcry."

Here was the tocsin for which many had been waiting. In Massachusetts, the royal governor noted, things had been very quiet "till an account was received of the Virginia Resolves." Then, said he, all was "bedlam." Other royal governors remarked with some anxiety the sudden change in the political climate as Americans began talking louder and asking themselves a central question:

If Virginia—the oldest, largest, richest, and traditionally most loyal and royalist of the colonies—was prepared to take the lead in resisting British "tyranny," why should her sister colonies hesitate to follow? The answer was: They shouldn't. And they began organizing associations to boycott British goods and to take other measures to force repeal of the Stamp Tax.

As author of the Virginia Resolves which inspired the colonies and set them moving, Henry became almost overnight a popular idol, "the Noble Patriot," our first national hero–the first whose fame leaped over confining provincial barriers to spread through city, town, and countryside all along the seaboard from Maine to Georgia.

Years later, when assessing the relative influence of American leaders on the eve of Independence, it was Jefferson, always in the vanguard himself, who said of Henry:

"He left all of us far behind . . . He gave the first impulse to the ball of Revolution . . . He was the idol of the country beyond anyone that ever lived."

II
A Hard School

. . . a mere child of Nature.

—William Wirt

Henry left Williamsburg immediately after the vote on his resolutions, not waiting for the end of the session which carried over another day before Governor Fauquier, denouncing its "rash heat," dissolved the House of Burgesses, virtually telling its members to go home and mind their own business, particularly to refrain from "giddy" opposition to British policy as laid down by Parliament and the Crown.

On his departure from Williamsburg, Henry can have had no idea of the great stir his "Virginia Resolves" would soon be causing in all the colonies. Later, there would be loud cheers for him in Williamsburg. But there were none for him now as, accompanied by a friend, he walked slowly up the Duke of Gloucester Street, "clad in a pair of buckskin breeches, his saddle bags over his arm, leading a lean horse." Swinging up into the saddle, he headed for home—a ride of eighty miles or more—to join his wife Sarah and their three children, the eldest being ten. Though young in years, Henry had married early and was already an "old" family man.

As he rode along dusty roads and trails—many mere wagon tracks winding around fields and bogs and through the woods—

Henry must have mused a bit, and perhaps have been amused more than a bit, as he looked back with his characteristic "half smile" on his past life. His had been a zigzag course that had led him to so many defeats. Now the wheel of fortune had suddenly turned, and he had come up in the world–so far, and so fast. There was an irony here that did not escape Henry.

Five years earlier, "the Noble Patriot" had been a nobody–so poor, so at loose ends, so without prospects, that he and his family had taken shelter in a roadside tavern owned and operated by his father-in-law, John Shelton. The latter, an active and fairly prosperous planter, had more interests than the tavern to occupy him, and it appears that the Henrys, in return for room and board and perhaps a nominal salary, managed the establishment for him, taking care of the needs of those who stopped for lodging, food, and drink at this backwoods hostelry in the tiny community of Hanover Courthouse.

Ordinarily, business was dull. But when the county court was sitting in the small but attractive brick courthouse just across the road, the tavern was filled up, and particularly the bar, with judges, lawyers, clients and their friends, witnesses, and some of the curious who came just to see what was going on, hoping an exciting trial might come up. Excitements in rural Virginia were few and far between, and always welcome as a relief from the monotony of lonely country life.

As *maitre d'hôtel,* and occasional barkeeper, Henry did rather well. This success must have pleased him, for he had tried his hand at several things and been a signal failure in all. Gay, witty, and amiable, Henry was well liked. Always friendly and a good conversationalist, he liked to talk and loved to exchange tall tales and ribald stories with anyone at all.

"I own myself a democrat," said Henry in later years, and he always was, never putting on airs. Even at the peak of his power, his manner remained simple, direct, and sympathetic. So long as a man was interesting and had something serious or amusing to say, Henry did not give a rap about his social status, or his financial status either.

But except as a pleasant companion, adept at mixing good flips and rum punch in the tavern, young Henry had made no mark for himself as yet, not even in his obscure hamlet. If he thought about the matter at all–as he obviously did in view of later developments–

it must have seemed to him that his prospects for making a place for himself in a larger world were very dim indeed.

As a youth, Henry had enjoyed—"enjoyed" is hardly the term, better to say had been exposed to—more and better schooling than most sons of the "common Sorte" in Virginia. This advantage he owed to his father, John Henry, one of very few men of college education in the back country.

Those who pioneered the ever westward moving frontier were not, for the most part, "eddicated folk." Though short on "book larnin'," they had other knowledge and skills of more immediate practical use, such as where to look for deer and other game, and how to cultivate corn and the wild strawberry, and where and how to dig a well.

Henry's father had been born in Scotland, in Aberdeenshire, in the parish of Foveran, up-coast about fifteen miles from the ancient city of Aberdeen.* It is not known just when he was born, but probably in 1704 or 1705. Nor is it known where he got his early schooling. It may have been at home or at a local school, perhaps the small parish school. At any rate, he proved himself to be a likely scholar and against strong competition won a highly-prized scholarship or bursary. In 1720, he entered King's College, one of Aberdeen's two celebrated colleges.**

The Henrys, it appears, were a literate and rather literary clan, given to scholarly pursuits. John Henry's older and favorite brother, Patrick, had preceded him at King's, taking his M.A. there and becoming a Church of England clergyman, later migrating to Virginia. One of their cousins, David Henry, went up to London as a journeyman printer and became a chief contributor and later the editor of *The Gentleman's Magazine,* one of the more widely read periodicals of the day.

John Henry's mother was sister of a respected historian and eminent divine, the Reverend William Robertson, who became Moderator of the Assembly of the Anglican Church in Scotland, principal

---

* For an exhaustive and at times rather exhausting account of Henry antecedents, see *Patrick Henry: The Making of a Patriot* (1957), by Robert Douhat Meade. By his wide research in Britain, the latter has unearthed hitherto unknown facts about the ancestry and background of the Henrys.

** King's College, founded in 1494, and Marischal College (1593) became affiliated in 1860 to form Aberdeen University. Carrying on the long tradition of its component colleges, the university is noted for its high scholastic standards.

of the University of Edinburgh, and historiographer to His Majesty in Scotland.

The Henrys and related families, as David Henry once observed in his magazine, were "more respected for their good sense and superior education than for their riches."

At King's College, young John Henry, aged fifteen or sixteen, went through the rigorous and really Spartan regimen usual in Scottish schools. They were known then, as ever since, for their exacting thoroughness and strict discipline, not only moral but intellectual. No college of the day offered elective courses. Everybody at King's "took" Latin, Greek, ancient and more recent history, mathematics, geography, philosophy, and theology.

Of these studies, theology (Christian, of course, and no other) was principal and most esteemed, for all colleges were still primarily theological seminaries, having been founded as such. Their chief concern was to train clergy who would be tolerably competent to perform their doctrinal and other duties in whatever church they happened to belong to—whether Church of England, Roman Catholic, Presbyterian, Lutheran, or whatever.

For curious historical reasons, Aberdeen and the surrounding area constituted an Anglican (Church of England) enclave in almost wholly Presbyterian Scotland. This had influence upon the education and thought of John Henry and his son Patrick.

Regular reading and study of the Bible were common practice in the literate families of the day. Bible discussion was not only a duty, but something of a pastime, raising all kinds of interesting arguments and speculations.

If the Henrys had been Presbyterians, as almost all the area Scots were, they would have used the dull and wooden Geneva ("Breeches") Bible as did Calvinists everywhere. But being Anglicans—or Episcopalians, as we now say—they read and studied the magnificent King James Version of the Bible, put together by brilliant scholar-poets and issued in 1611, one of the towering literary monuments in our language. Patrick Henry's speeches and writings contain many echoes of passages from the wonderfully eloquent and poetic King James Version.*

In 1724, after four years of study, John Henry left King's College,

* We now have "improved" versions of the King James. All are limp and lame. They have no lift, no sing. In their translation and interpretation of terms, they may be more "correct" academically, but who cares? They have entirely lost the fine Elizabethan swing in the verse.

but without a degree. Why he failed to receive a degree is not recorded. Perhaps he failed to pass some important final examination. Whatever the circumstances, he was now out in the world and on his own. As with so many young men of the time, his eyes turned toward the New World, and he decided to try his fortune there where opportunity, in the form of free land, seemed to beckon.

Early in 1727, a raw young immigrant in his early twenties, John Henry was in Williamsburg. There he obtained a patent to 400 acres of undeveloped land to the west, in Hanover County. Because of Britain's desire to stimulate settlement, such land could be had, in blocs totaling thousands of acres, at no cost at all, subject to later payment of an annual quitrent of two shillings per hundred acres. As applications went, Henry's was a very modest one, no doubt because he had yet to learn how Virginia land-grabbers worked, which was on a large scale, as will be seen.

Going to Hanover County, young John Henry joined the household of Colonel John Syme, also from Aberdeenshire and probably a kinsman. There would seem to have been some correspondence between the two before Henry decided to come to Virginia and try his luck in remote Hanover County.

The Symes lived in a substantial house on Studley Farm, a plantation of several hundred acres planted to tobacco and cultivated by a half dozen slaves. Henry was not a hired hand, but a member of the family. What he did to earn his keep is not clear. In the beginning, he cannot have been very helpful. Things were so foreign to his background and training. He knew little about farming in general, and less about the particulars of growing tobacco. Later, when a planter himself, he never showed much interest in farming and was never very successful at it.

But Henry, as he gained experience, evidently made himself useful at Studley Farm, probably directing affairs when Colonel Syme was away, as he frequently was, for he had other properties and varied interests elsewhere.

This was apparently a pleasant and profitable arrangement all around. But it ended abruptly four years later, in 1731, with the sudden premature death of Colonel Syme. After an appropriate interval, Henry married the young widow, Sarah, who became, again after a proper interval, the mother of Patrick Henry.

And what a personable and charming woman she was by all accounts. One day, in 1732, while still in mourning and wearing weeds, Widow Syme had a quite unexpected visitor—a most elegant and distinguished gentleman, Colonel William Byrd II, perhaps the grandest of contemporary Grandees. An accomplished man of the world, at home in the most fashionable circles abroad, long a power in Virginia affairs as one of the Governor's Council, Byrd was enormously rich, perhaps as rich as anyone in Virginia, or in any of the colonies.

More interestingly, he loved literature, music, and art; had collected as large and fine a library as any in America; was a gifted writer himself. Of even more interest today, he was a great gossip and kept secret diaries written in code—diaries that have been found, deciphered, and published.

At the moment, Byrd was building a new mansion for himself and family at Westover—an elaborate and beautiful brick manor house, classic of its kind, which still stands overlooking the James River about twenty-five miles below Richmond. Westover had long been the seat of the vast Byrd empire that, in its scattered portions, contained some 180,000 acres embracing the entire tract on which the town of Richmond was soon built (1737), to enrich the family further.

Being in Hanover County on business, with night coming on and no public accommodations available along the lonesome roads, Byrd inquired of one of his men about quarters. The latter suggested a possibility and guided him. Riding up the tree-lined lane that led to Studley Farm, Byrd dismounted, went to the door, knocked, introduced himself, and was invited in.

If Widow Syme entertained any notion—and she apparently did—that this handsome and well-groomed gentleman had come to court her as an "heiress," she was soon disillusioned. Byrd explained the reason of his coming very simply: Could he arrange to have dinner and lodging for the night? This was quickly arranged according to the hospitable custom that prevailed in the back country where public accommodations were scarce, and usually pretty wretched and fly-specked—certainly, not fit for a Byrd.

Sarah Syme welcomed her unexpected guest very cordially, as Byrd noted in his diary, and once preliminaries were over, "brightened up into an unusual cheerfulness and Serenity." Byrd also noted that she seemed "not to pine too much" for her late husband, and that she was "a portly, handsome Dame, . . . much less reserved than most of her countrymen." This, he added, "became her well and set off her other agreeable qualities to good advantage."

The evening, though it lacked a romantic note, passed very pleasantly. Conversation at dinner was easy, even gay, as the hostess and her beaming guest "tost off a bottle of honest Port, which we relished," said Byrd, "with a broiled chicken. . . .

"At nine, I retired to my devotions [and diary] and slept so sound that fancy itself was stupified, else I should have dreamed of my most obliging landlady."

What he would have dreamt if his "fancy" had not failed him is easy to imagine. Byrd always had a bright and eager eye for the fairer of the fair sex. Whenever he met a charming and handsome woman, he was very fond, so he confided to his diary, "of sweetening my lips with saluting the Lady."

Next morning, Byrd enjoyed a hearty breakfast, washed down with cups of steaming tea, which he found "altogether as great a help to discourse as the juice of the grape." The day being Sunday, "the courteous Widow invited me to rest myself there that good day. . . ."

Though pleased and flattered, the colonel declined the invitation and even begged off from accompanying his attractive hostess to church, offering the gallant excuse that her charms were so great they would certainly distract him from his devotion.

As Byrd was never noted for devotion to his devotions, he was evidently anxious to get away early for his ride of forty miles or more to Westover to see how work on his great new house there was progressing.

Though she never knew what Byrd confided to his diary about her and was unaware that he was keeping notes on his visit, Widow Syme would doubtless have been flattered had she known how much she had impressed the discriminating and widely traveled lord of Westover.

Sarah had been born about 1710, the oldest child of Isaac Winston and his wife, Mary Dabney. Both the Winstons and the Dabneys were "old" Virginia families in the sense that they had been established in the colony for several generations, having come in the 1660s when the tide of immigration began to rise. They were not recent arrivals like Colonel Syme and John Henry. Though not rich, they were prosperous planters in what would now be called the middle bracket and had already made a respected place for themselves in community life and local political affairs. His Winston and Dabney connections would later be useful to Patrick Henry in his personal and public life.

After their marriage, John Henry and Widow Syme continued living at Studley Farm. She was holding this in trust for a son and only child by her first marriage, John Syme, Jr., later a man of some prominence in the colony, who served a number of times as a Burgess and in other offices.

The Henrys' first child was William, named for Sarah's favorite brother, William ("Langloo") Winston—said by some to be "sort of a wild Indian . . . a Buckskin . . . a Long Knife," who liked to go off into the woods for weeks at a time to live and hunt with the Indians to whom he was very attached.

On May 29, 1736, the Henrys had a second infant, christened Patrick Henry. He was named for his father's older brother, the Reverend Patrick Henry, who had migrated from Scotland to Virginia and recently, on his appointment as rector of St. Paul's, the local Anglican parish, had become a rather near neighbor. The rector no doubt officiated at the christening of his nephew and namesake.

After two sons, the Henrys had a succession of daughters who kept coming, and coming, until there were nine. This made for a sizable family. But it was not as large as many others of the day—or of a later day. In time, Patrick Henry himself would sire seventeen children and, at his death in his early sixties, would have more than sixty grandchildren.

All of the colonies were eager to increase their populations as fast as they could, both by encouraging immigration and by home production, so to speak. Nothing better attests the virility and fertility of our colonial forebears than this tombstone in an old Connecticut "burying ground":

Here lies the body
of Mrs Mary, wife of
Dr John Buell, Esq.
She died Nov. 4th
1768. AEtatis 90
Having had 13 children
107 Grand Children
274 Great G. Children
22 Great G. G. Children
416 Total
336 survived her.

This was enough to people a new frontier county.

In his early years, Patrick Henry appears to have been a run-of-the-mill urchin, doing what average youngsters always do and presenting familiar problems. No one noted anything unusual about him. At the age of five or six, he was sent to school. This was not just a matter of course. Throughout the colony, particularly in the back country, schools were few, and competent schoolmasters scarce. Most sons of the "common sort" had no formal schooling at all, receiving only such instruction as could be offered them at home by their parents, many of whom were more or less illiterate.

Tidewater lords and richer planters elsewhere solved the school problem by bringing tutors into the household to instruct their children—but only the boys, not the girls. Virginians of every rank agreed with the Pilgrim Fathers and almost all others of the day that "female education" was a "vaine & idle thing"—at best, a silly affectation; at worst, a threat to the *status quo,* the "natural" order of things.

The world was still a jealously guarded male world, and its masters intended to keep it so. They were appalled at what "heresies" might creep in if those of the "other sex" ever got the idea that life for them might be something more than learning from their mothers a few social graces and how to cook, sew, spin, wash, dust, sweep, churn butter, tend the kitchen garden, and bear children—frequently.

The women of Virginia, wrote a friendly English traveler, the Reverend Andrew Burnaby, were, "generally speaking, handsome, though not to be compared with our fair countrywomen in England. They have but few advantages, and consequently are seldom accomplished. This makes them reserved, and unequal to any interesting or refined conversation.

"They are immoderately fond of dancing, and indeed it is almost the only amusement they partake of . . . Towards the close of an evening, when the company is pretty well tired with country dances, it is usual to dance jigs; a practice originally borrowed, I am informed, from the Negroes.

"These dances are without method or regularity; a gentleman and a lady stand up, and dance about the room, one of them retiring, the other pursuing, then perhaps meeting, in an irregular fantastical manner.

"After some time, another lady gets up, and then the first lady must sit down, so being, as they term it, 'cut out.' The second lady acts the same part which the first did until somebody cuts her out. The gentlemen perform in the same manner."

Burnaby also noted that Virginia girls arrived at maturity very early. "Some are marriageable at eleven, many at thirteen, and the generality at fourteen or fifteen years of age." Another British visitor, a Scotsman, Lord Adam Gordon, observed that Virginia girls made "excellent wives" and were, "in general, great Breeders. It is much the fashion to marry young, and what is remarkable in a stay I have made of near a month in the Province, I have not heard of one unhappy couple."

The "public schools" of the time were not public schools in our sense of the word. All were private schools run by hungry parsons or even hungrier pedagogues hoping to make a modest living from the fees they charged. Such schools were public in the sense that they were open to the children of all parents who had the desire and means to pay tuition fees. Such fees, in general, were not high, but beyond the reach of most families.

In spite of early efforts by Jefferson and others to set up a democratic educational system in the Old Dominion, it was not until 1870, five years after the Civil War, that Virginia first established a free public school system worthy of the name.

The young Henry sons, William and Patrick, were sent to a public school, a "common English school," established somewhere near Studley Farm. The schoolhouse was probably makeshift, perhaps a rough log cabin. In any case, as in the celebrated Little Red Schoolhouse of later years, there was a single classroom seating a dozen or more restless youngsters of different ages, at various levels of study. While some recited, others studied—or whispered, or giggled, or started some commotion—as the distraught schoolmaster tried to maintain some semblance of order so he could get on with recitations.

If it was like others, the Henrys learned little more at their "common English school" than how to read, write, "cyfer," and endure a deal of switching, paddling, and even flogging. Corporal punishment at the time was not merely incidental, but quite systematic, being highly regarded as the very essence of learning. Almost everybody agreed that "ye wretched boys"* had quite literally to

* They were "young vipers!" hissed that great breather of hell fire, the Reverend Jonathan Edwards, a long-suffering schoolmaster and later a college president. "Yea!" he exclaimed, "infinitely more hateful than vipers to God."

Edwards was also a philosopher and had plainly come to the opinion that God had made a mistake in creating some of His creatures. In addition to "ye wretched boys" and vipers, Edwards might have extended his list of undesirables to include yellow jackets and tent caterpillars.

have the hell beaten out of them if they were ever to come to any good.

When about ten, young Patrick was withdrawn from this school, and could not have been unhappy about it. He had not liked reading, rereading, and reciting mechanically from a few dull and dog-eared textbooks. Nor had he liked, as he never would, heavy-handed discipline to enforce conformity in all things.

He preferred other things, much more pleasant and quite as profitable for a youth, such as roaming the fields and woods, learning birdsong, fishing in Totopotomy Creek near by, or stretching out in some quiet sunny forest glade to daydream. Young Patrick would certainly have agreed with George Bernard Shaw, who once remarked: "School was to me a sentence of penal servitude."

Patrick Henry was, in a sense, "out of school" all his life, being always something of a truant, a confirmed nonconformist. He persistently went his own way, often against good friendly advice. This course led him into difficulties at times, especially when he was younger. But he concluded in later years that his troubles had not hurt him, had even helped him, for "adversity toughens manhood. . . . The best men always make themselves."

There was always in Henry something of Huckleberry Finn, Mark Twain's immortal. Neither of them was much given to books, acquiring their learning from observation and experience. They much preferred to live life than read about it. Like Huck, Pat (as his mother called him, even when he was grown) shied away from merely "nice" people with their hollow formalism, solemnities, timidities, and want of curiosity, wit, and humor. Both had a taste for good "low" company where there was warm companionship, easy give-and-take, and a lively sense of fun.

Henry would have loved floating down the Mississippi on a raft with Huck, Nigger Jim, and those two monumental frauds, the Duke of Bilgewater and the Lost Dauphin, "Looy the Seventeenth." And how he would have laughed during the performance at an Arkansas town of their hastily concocted melodrama, "The King's Cameleopard, or the Royal Nonesuch, ! ! !" at the conclusion of which the two had to take to their heels with all speed to escape the sheriff and a lynch mob. Henry would have helped them get away, and had another laugh.

Above all, Henry was like Huck in being essentially a "loner." There was nothing of Tom Sawyer in him; he was never an "organization man." This, as will be seen, was at once his greatest strength and his greatest weakness in his political career. Though his enormous popularity and influence carried the greatest weight, he never organized a party around him as he could easily have done. His was a personal following.

If young Pat, on leaving the "common English school," entertained the notion that he would now be free to roam at will, that notion was quickly dispelled. His father immediately took him in hand and opened a school at Studley Farm, with himself as teacher, recruiting some neighborhood boys to join the class. His schoolmaster fees provided a small but welcome addition to John Henry's income, for he was not doing so well as a planter. Further to augment his income, the elder Henry took surveying jobs from time to time.

What subjects Patrick studied under his father's tutelage, how much he applied himself, what progress he made in his studies, are questions that cannot be answered authoritatively. All accounts of these years are secondhand, and they differ widely. Patrick Henry talked and wrote very little about himself, leaving lamentably few records about his personal life. He did not keep a diary or make notes about himself and his activities as so many of eminence have done. Seemingly, he was content to let his life speak for itself.

Questions arising from Henry's diffidence in regard to his personal affairs were not much clarified by William Wirt, his first biographer, who in 1817, almost twenty years after Henry's death, published an extraordinary mishmash entitled *Sketches of the Life and Character of Patrick Henry*. Though very unreliable as to fact and preposterous in its style, this is an important book, going through many editions. It remained the chief and almost only source of information about Henry for decades. It has colored, and discolored, much that has been written about Patrick Henry down to our own day. Wirt's portrait of Henry, particularly in his younger days, is ridiculous.

In one of the first of many ludicrous scenes, Wirt tells us that Patrick was "coarse, his manners uncommonly awkward, his dress slovenly . . . his aversion to study invincible, and his faculties almost benumbed by indolence. . . . [He] could not support the confinement and toil which education required. . . .

"When the hour of his school exercises arrived, Patrick was scarcely ever to be found [one wonders whether his father-teacher was asleep, or what]. He was in the forest with his gun, or over the brook with his angle-iron . . . No persuasion could bring him to read or work. On the contrary, he ran wild in the forest like one of the aborigines of the country."

Soon, suddenly, somewhere, somehow, he acquired "Shakespeare's genius," but in the beginning Patrick was "a mere child of Nature," according to Wirt, "and Nature seems to have been too proud and jealous of her work to permit it to be touched by the hand of art."

This is pure Wirt, so to speak, though some may prefer another word. But what a pretty picture it is—Mother Nature and her sprites, perhaps soaring somewhere aloft, jealously watching over Nature Boy until, "coarse . . . awkward . . . slovenly," and virtually illiterate, he comes bounding out of the forest magically possessed of all the arts and strewing golden words about as thousands cheer—and the author hastily snatches up his pen again and the page is simply awash with purple prose.

More to the point on Patrick's earlier years is an account left by a boyhood friend, Samuel Meredith, later his brother-in-law. The long close relationship between them may have somewhat colored Meredith's view, but it has far more substance than that of Wirt, who had never known Henry, had never seen him or heard him speak.

There was nothing remarkable about young Henry, so Meredith recalled. In appearance, he was neither "uncouth or genteel." In disposition, he was "very mild, benevolent, and humane. . . . He interested himself much in the happiness of others, particularly his sisters, . . . whose advocate he always was when any favor or indulgence was to be procured from their mother." Though he liked being with people and indulging in amusements, he was "quiet and inclined to be thoughtful. . . . He was fond of reading." Also, as true throughout his life, he was "remarkably fond of his gun."

Henry's salient characteristic, as noted by Meredith and others, was "his invariable habit of close and attentive observation. . . . From his earliest years, he was a close observer of everything of consequence that passed before him. . . . Nothing escaped his attention."

In his studies under his father, young Patrick "acquired a knowledge of the Latin tongue, and a smattering of Greek. He became well acquainted with the Mathematics, of which he was very fond. At the age of fifteen, he was well versed in both ancient and modern History."*

---

* Writing on Henry, Wirt had Meredith's notes before him. But he chose to ignore them; they did not fit into his "child of Nature" thesis.

When he was fifteen, Patrick's schooling ended. Whatever his other accomplishments, it was evident that he was not cut out to be a scholar. Nor had he showed much interest or aptitude in farming; nor had his brother William.

With two sons approaching manhood, John Henry had a problem. How best to get them started toward earning a livelihood? One possibility was to run a country store. Starting from small beginnings, many merchants in Virginia were thriving; a few had become quite prosperous. A number of the merchants came from Scotland, and John Henry had friends among them. He doubtless consulted some of these on what he should do to carry out the plan he had in mind—to set up his sons in a business of their own.

Before that was done, it was evident that they had to learn something about the mercantile business—where to buy goods, what merchandise was most in demand, how to keep books, and related things. To advance this aspect of their education, Patrick and William were apprenticed to serve for a year as clerks in a country store. Where the store was, who ran it, is not known. A typical country store of the day was, as Colonel Byrd described it, "a place where the way of dealing . . . is for some small merchant or peddler to buy a Scots pennyworth of goods, and clap 150 per cent on that" as the price to customers. Complaints about exorbitant prices for shoddy goods were frequent.

After their apprenticeship, presumably having learned something about stocking goods, pleasing customers, and keeping books, Patrick and William embarked on an enterprise of their own, financed by their father. Their store appears to have been some miles from Studley Farm, in the northeastern corner of Hanover County, on the Pamunkey River where rather brisk water traffic supported some small communities which seemed to offer possibilities of trade.

The teen-aged Henrys' venture in commerce failed. The reason, according to Wirt, was that neither of them paid much attention to business. Patrick was forced to become "principal Manager" because his older brother William led a "wild and dissipated" life. And Patrick's management was "most wretched. . . . Left to himself, all of his indolence returned." He found the "drudgery of retailing and of bookkeeping . . . intolerable." When he should have been tending store, he locked up to go fishing or hunting.

While expressed with Wirt's usual extravagance, this may have been true in part. Seventeen-year-old Patrick may well have found bookkeeping exasperating because, knowing so little about it, it baffled him. And certainly, he must have been bored beyond measure to sit all day long in a lonely country store hoping that a handful of customers would turn up to buy something more than a small bag of salt or perhaps a few needles and some yard goods to be made into dresses or diapers.

But the main cause of failure lay elsewhere. The young storekeepers were too generous in extending credit to customers in the neighborhood. It was general business practice at the time for planters to charge purchases and let the indebtedness carry over until fall when their tobacco crop was sold, at which time accounts were settled.

If crops were bad or if tobacco prices fell too much, the planters' store debts, in whole or in part, had to be carried on the books till the next harvest.

The youthful Henrys did not have the capital to carry large unpaid balances. Had they been older, harder of heart, wiser in the ways of the world, they would not have allowed such balances to pile up until they became a crushing burden. After a year or more of profitless operation, the store had to be closed.

Patrick and William returned home, but home was no longer Studley Farm. Their mother had been holding Studley in trust for her first son, John Syme, Jr. The latter, having come of age, wished to have this part of his inheritance. Under an amicable arrangement, the Henrys moved out.

A man of many enterprises, like his father, Syme soon decided to improve Studley Farm by building two large stables and a racetrack there, and began importing blooded stallions to improve the breed of horses in the colony. This promised to be an interesting and profitable business, for Virginians were very interested in horses for riding, hunting, and racing. On one occasion, Syme advertised in the *Virginia Gazette* the stud services of his Sampson, sired by Morton's Old Traveler out of an imported hunting mare, specifying the cost of such services as "covering at 12s., sixpence 'a leap,' or 40s. the season."

As the Henrys had lived at Studley Farm for more than twenty years, all their children being born there, it must have been a rather painful wrench for all the family to leave familiar scenes and loosen close ties with old neighbors.

Moving westward in Hanover County, from Tidewater to the Piedmont, they established themselves at Mount Brilliant, a small plantation of several hundred acres that John Henry had bought.

Standing on high ground with fields sloping away from it on every side, the house was larger than that at Studley Farm, providing more ample space for eleven children, all of whom were at home, including the two oldest, William and Patrick, whose store had "broke" them.

Soon, William left, moving westward into Fluvanna County to farm a sizable tract given to him by his father. However "wild and dissipated" he may have been in his younger years, as Wirt averred, William did rather well as a small planter and became a man of some power and influence in local affairs, serving in a number of county offices and several times representing Fluvanna in the House of Burgesses.

And young Patrick soon left home, too, after his marriage to Sarah Shelton. The two had probably known each other since childhood, for the Sheltons lived at Rural Plains only a few miles from Studley Farm. While keeping store and after his family's removal to Mount Brilliant, Patrick evidently had managed to see Sarah frequently. They had fallen in love and were married in the fall of 1754.

The bride's father, John Shelton, was a prosperous planter and the owner-operator of the tavern at Hanover Courthouse. Her mother was Eleanor, daughter of William Parks, a man of some distinction in early Virginia.

Parks had been appointed as the colony's first public printer and opened its first bookshop. Later, he became editor-publisher of the *Virginia Gazette,* a weekly founded in 1736, the year of Henry's birth. The *Gazette,* reporting news at home and abroad and read by everyone of consequence in the colony, remained Virginia's only newspaper for decades, down almost to the Revolution.

The parents of the bridal pair appear to have been not too happy that the marriage occurred when it did.* Sarah was only sixteen; Patrick, just over eighteen, seemingly without prospects and unable to shoulder family responsibilities. As a member of the Henry family remarked about the attitude of Patrick's parents, it was "not that they objected to Sarah, for she was dear and sweet, but they felt Patrick over-young to set rocking the cradle that rocked almost continuously until he was well nigh into his grave."

Little is known about Sarah, who remains a shadowy figure. She is said to have been an attractive girl, with blonde hair and a fair

---

* There is a hint in the records that the formalization of the union was hastened by an untoward development.

complexion. She had six children by Patrick, and patiently bore with him as he struggled through many hardships to an ultimately triumphant career, which she was not to share for long, due to a premature and tragic end.

As young Sarah's dowry, John Shelton gave Patrick six Negro slaves and 300 acres cut off from a corner of his large Rural Plains estate. On this tract, which Henry called Piney Slash, there was a house, perhaps a tenant farmer's house, into which the young Henrys could move immediately, furnishing it no doubt with bedsteads, tables, chairs, pots, pans, and other things donated by their families and friends.

Henry worked hard to make Piney Slash a profitable tobacco plantation, taking great pains in the tedious business of planting, cultivating, leafing, worming, and curing the "filthy weed" upon which the livelihood of most Virginians depended. In spite of his best efforts, Henry was hard pressed, as an uncle noted, "to provide even a scanty support for his family." His success as a planter was marginal. Mother Nature, it appears, had not cut out her "child of Nature" to be a tiller of the soil.

After less than three years at Piney Slash, the Henrys were burned out in a fire that destroyed their house and almost everything in it. For a time they occupied the overseer's house, an oversized cabin, but soon moved into more ample and congenial quarters in the Shelton tavern at Hanover Courthouse, where they lived for many years.

It appears, as noted earlier, that Henry took over the day-to-day management of the tavern for his father-in-law who lived not far away on his Rural Plains plantation. Though doing well enough, Henry was restless. He wanted to be on his own, to be his own master, free of dependence on others.

Selling a few of his Piney Slash slaves to provide the necessary capital, Henry decided to establish his own business enterprise and chose, of all things, to have another try at being a country merchant, opening a small store near Hanover Courthouse.

But times were bad. The French and Indian War had begun and was causing hardship. The 1758 Virginia tobacco crop was a disaster because of adverse weather, necessitating emergency legislation that led to much litigation, in the course of which young Henry first made a name for himself as a lawyer.

Henry, as a storekeeper, was again too lenient in extending credit. Charge accounts piled up and up; fewer and fewer paying customers came in. For a period of many months, his receipts totaled less than £40 [$1,200],* most of which went to pay for goods on the shelves that he had obtained on credit, so there was no profit.

Business steadily went from bad to worse. After a year or so, the store had to be closed. Its books were decidedly in the red, which left Henry, if not actually in bankruptcy, at least heavily in debt and worse off than before.

Well, where to turn? Now, what to do?

---

* Monetary sums throughout have been roughly equated with the real value—i.e., the purchasing power—of the 1967 dollar. During this century, particularly since the 1930s, the dollar has been sharply depreciated many times. In terms of living costs—i.e., purchasing power—its value has declined more than 10 per cent since the late 1950s.

III
At Shelton's Tavern

. . . very attentive to his guests . . .

—A WINSTON COUSIN.

In looking about for something to do that might provide independence and a livelihood for a growing family, Henry, now twenty-three, made a fortunate decision. He came to his choice, it almost seems, by a process of osmosis—as if he "had it in his bones all the time" and had only to probe deep enough to discover a born talent.

That may be. But a series of highly fortuitous circumstances helped in putting him on the road to fame and fortune. It is idle, but interesting, to speculate on what his career might have been:

If Henry had succeeded in his first venture as a storekeeper and settled down to become a reasonably prosperous country merchant with few interests beyond the people and gossip of the neighborhood;

If the young Henrys had made a go of their Piney Slash plantation, and the house there had not burned down on them one night;

If Henry's kindly father-in-law, John Shelton, had not invited the destitute young Henrys to move into his roadside tavern;

If that tavern had stood elsewhere than just across the road from a county courthouse.

Tending bar at the Hanover Courthouse tavern, it turned out, had its advantages. It opened vistas to puzzled young Henry that he might otherwise not have glimpsed at all. It became his first school of law as he listened to the conversations and arguments going on among the judges, lawyers, litigants, witnesses, and others interested in cases being heard across the road. And he had a personal interest in the local county court, for his father was one of the eight judges or "Gentlemen justices of the peace" as they were titled.

To be a county judge did not necessarily indicate that one had been a lawyer or had any training in jurisprudence. John Henry had none, as was true of the majority of county judges in the colony. But legal learning, though desirable, was not a prerequisite for the office because the county courts—the center and arm of local government—had more than judicial duties to perform, being entrusted with many important executive and administrative functions. To most Virginians, the county court was "government;" the higher authorities at Williamsburg seemed far away.

When sitting in judicial capacity, the courts probated wills, recorded deeds, heard civil suits involving not more than 25s. [$38.00] or 200 pounds of tobacco, and tried criminal cases except those in which the penalty might be death. More important cases were heard in Williamsburg by the General Court, the highest judicial body in the colony.

In their other functions, county judges were responsible for building and maintaining roads and bridges, supervising ferry services, regulating official tobacco warehouses, licensing taverns and checking to see that they did not charge more than the ceiling prices set for their services. The county court also made up the tax rolls and was responsible for collecting taxes due to the colony and to the county. Quite as important, the judges sat as the board of elections, making all necessary arrangements for holding an election, seeing to it that only qualified voters had a voice and that their votes were correctly counted and reported. Also, the judges were empowered to pass ordinances on matters not covered, or inadequately covered, by acts of the General Assembly.

If responsibilities were conscientiously performed, as was usually but not always the case, a county judgeship was a time-consuming job for which judges received no salary or other compensation, not even expenses incurred in carrying out their duties. Yet the office was eagerly sought for. Its social prestige was high and provided an avenue to political preferment and advancement, leading into the

House of Burgesses, or the Governor's Council, or some remunerative provincial office.

County judges were not elected, but appointed by the royal governor. As the appointment was for life, it was virtually impossible to weed out the lazy, the incompetent, or even the notoriously corrupt.

When a vacancy occurred in their ranks, the judges drew up a list naming three persons who, in their opinion, were the best qualified to fill the vacant post and submitted the list as recommendations to the royal governor. The latter, with the advice of the Governor's Council, then selected one from the list of three for appointment. Every county court was thus, in effect, a self-perpetuating body, and it kept its ranks closed.

Those recommended and appointed as judges came from those who were regarded as "the best people in the country"—coming from the rich landed gentry or from less rich but nevertheless prominent county squires, which had been the English governing pattern for centuries. Poorer freeholders were not yet prepared to challenge class rule by Virginia's "better" families.

Court Days were always gala occasions in every county and were attended by people from all around the neighborhood. Court sessions were held on regular schedule—in Hanover County, the first Thursday in every month, at which time the ordinarily somnolent hamlet of Hanover Courthouse took on a more spirited air.

But the big times came when the county courts held their Quarter Sessions—in March, June, September, and December—when the more important cases were heard. Spending most of the year on isolated farms, Virginians liked nothing better than a good lively lawsuit containing a spice of scandal and in which opposing counsel clashed loudly and fiercely. That provided a good show and gave country people an opportunity to socialize, renew old acquaintances, and make new ones. Besides, there were many special amusements and entertainments.

All Court Days, but particularly Quarter Sessions, had the carnival air of a county fair. Horses were raced along the roads or in neighboring fields, with bets running high. Traveling troupes of acrobats and jugglers put on performances several times a day. There were cockfights, prizefights, and "wrastling" matches. A favorite pugilist among local strong men was "Fighting Jack" Harris, one of Henry's first law clients.

"Generally speaking," an English traveler noted, "the young men are gamblers, cock-fighters, and horse jockies. To hear them converse, you would imagine that the grand point of all science was properly to fix a gaff and touch with dexterity the tail of a cock while in combat."

A Court Day offered other "fun." Groups could—and did—collect to taunt and shout coarse jibes at those sentenced to stand in the pillory, sit in the stocks, or be lashed at the whipping post, these being the usual punishments for those unlucky enough to be caught and convicted of such minor indiscretions as getting "inordinately" drunk, cursing too profanely and obscenely in public, punching an obnoxious neighbor on the nose or "slandering" his perhaps equally obnoxious wife, raiding a chicken coop to provide an evening fry, beating up a spouse "with unnecessary violence," or "prophaning" the Sabbath.

The line on this last, though not so tightly drawn as in Puritan New England, was nevertheless a tricky tightrope. One could be fined, or put in the stocks, or both, for plowing a field or doing other weekday chores on the Sabbath. But one could also be punished for taking it too easy and becoming too merry in celebrating the Holy Day as a holiday, as was the custom in England and on the Continent.

Court Days were also a time for business. Local planters and merchants settled their accounts. There was a lot of sharp horse-trading. Lands, houses, cattle, and other livestock were sold, bought, or swapped. Negro slaves, often in chains, were placed on the auction block and held there as prospective buyers came up to examine their eyes, teeth, arms, legs, and bodies—as if they were so much livestock, as they were at the time, and of considerable value.

A healthy strong tractable young slave, male or female, brought as much as £50 [$1,500]. No doubt it was over the Hanover Courthouse auction block that Patrick Henry sold a few "blacks" from his Piney Slash farm to provide the capital needed to embark on his second disastrous storekeeping venture.

On Court Days, other business attracted more general interest and attention. Itinerant merchants arrived in brightly painted wagons to hawk their wares from the tail gate, offering all kinds of "bargains" in tools, saddles, harness, kitchenware, glassware, bolts of woven goods, and other things. Poor peddlers came on foot, bearing on their backs a large bag stuffed with lighter goods—pins and needles (always in great demand), cheap laces, ribbons, printed cotton yard goods to be fashioned into dresses, soft flannels to be cut up for diapers.

As the social center of Hanover Courthouse, Shelton's tavern filled up with men–some with their families–who wanted food, drink, and beds for the night if the ride home was too long to be accomplished before dark.

Tavern keepers paid £50 [$1,500] a year for a license requiring them to provide "good, wholesome, and cleanly lodging and diet for travelers, and stableage, fodder, and provender or pasturage." County courts laid down regulations on maximum prices to be charged. Ceiling prices in the Hanover area generally ran:

"Rum, the gallon, eight shillings [$12.00]; Virginia brandy, six shillings; Punch or Flipp, the quart, with white Sugar, one and three pence; with brown Sugar, one shilling; . . . a hot Dyet [meal], one shilling; a Lodging with clean Sheets, six pence [75¢]; Oats, the gallon, six pence; Pasturage, the day, six pence per head . . ."

How far such ceiling prices were observed cannot be ascertained. But the rule was certainly far better observed than another that forbade taverns to have "a billiard table, a backgammon table, cards, dice, and other instruments of various games" for the pleasure and enticement of patrons seeking a bit of excitement and a chance to gamble. Every Virginia tavern, as contemporary accounts agree, was plentifully supplied with "instruments of various games," as was no doubt true of Shelton's tavern.

Another rule laid down the law that, on Sundays, tavern keepers were not "to suffer any person to tipple or drink any more than necessary." This was such an elastic phrase that any tavern keeper and a steady patron could amiably agree on a broad definition of what was "necessary," not a bit more, and certainly not a bit less.

Shelton's tavern, a long, L-shaped, two-storied frame structure, somewhat altered and a bit enlarged down the years, still stands. Known now as Hanover Inn, it still serves the needs of neighbors and of travelers passing by. Until fairly recent years,* the old taproom remained much as it was two centuries ago when young Patrick Henry was host there and making patrons happy as he served them potions of various kinds:

Mint juleps and "bombos," a toddy served either hot or cold,

---

* In 1953, part of the inn was transformed into a small theater which presents everything from Shakespeare to Becket. The old taproom is now the theater lobby.

compounded of rum, sugar, nutmeg, and spring water; plain rum, or hot buttered rum on frosty nights; brandies, Virginian and imported; cordials–blackberry, cherry, and other flavors–powerful and pungent native apple jack; beer, usually brewed on the premises or in the neighborhood. Groups of friends seated around a table, talking and laughing, might call to Henry to uncork and bring over another bottle of imported wine–Madeira, Canary, claret, sherry, port, or a good solid red Burgundy.

Young Henry, far from regarding his bar duties as a chore or a bore, evidently enjoyed them, for he was sociable by nature, and often in a very gay mood.

A young Winston cousin, who used to drop in occasionally to enjoy a dram or two and have a chat, later recalled that Henry was "very active and attentive to his guests, and very frequently amused them with his violin, on which he played very well."

Henry, it appears, had learned by himself how to play the violin when in his teens, at a time when he was more or less housebound by a minor injury, perhaps incurred in some more reckless feat of derring-do during one of his forest jaunts. He later tried his hand at the flute and harpsichord. But the violin remained his favorite instrument, and all his life he loved to fiddle, to the pleasure of many and to the especial delight of his children.

One wonders what Henry played for guests in the tavern–country tunes and lively jigs, no doubt, for Henry liked to dance, perhaps while sawing on the fiddle held under his chin. And on occasion, in earlier years, he must have accompanied his guests when they lustily sang "God Save the King," as glasses were raised in toast after toast to His Sacred Majesty, followed by cheers and resounding huzzahs that shook the rafters. None of the colonies was as royalist as Virginia.

When tending bar, as his Winston cousin noted, Henry was usually "clad in an Ozna* Shirt Jump, Jacket and Trousers of Ozna or checks, . . . [and] very often Barefooted."

In regard to his bartending days it should be remarked now rather than later that Henry, unlike so many of his contemporaries, was not "a drinking man." He did not like hard liquor, such as rum, whisky, and other "strong waters," seldom drinking them. Nor had

---

* "Ozna" is from Osnabrück, a German town (in Hanover) renowned for its linens, particularly of the heavier and coarser kinds. A "shirt jump," evidently, was a pullover–something like our modern T-shirts.

he much of a taste for wine. He preferred beer, sending to Scotland in later years for special barley seed, and arranged to bring over "a Scotch brewer and his wife to cultivate the seed and make small beer."

When he was governor, disturbed by the increase in drunkenness during Revolutionary War years, Henry shocked and chagrined many by offering guests at State dinners and other official functions only his own home brew, recommending that all hosts likewise serve nothing but small beer. But this was one of Henry's "reforms" that got little public or private support. People in general—both aristocrats and the "common sort"—much preferred rum punch, flips, bombos, wines, and their own homemade whisky, or "corn likkor," which was known as mule, from its "kick."

Years later, after Patrick Henry's death and long after he and Henry had become estranged both politically and personally, Jefferson observed very condescendingly, and in a rather unpleasant manner:

"Mr. Henry began his career with very little property. He acted, as I have understood, as barkeeper in the tavern at Hanover CT [Courthouse] for some time. He married very young, . . . got credit for some little store of merchandise, but soon failed." Jefferson later strengthened his derogatory remarks in telling Daniel Webster, with evident malice, that Henry was "originally a barkeeper."

Jefferson was being patrician here, looking down his Randolph nose at Henry—no "gentleman," no matter how poor his circumstances, would descend to tending bar in a public house.*

As Jefferson well knew when he wrote, Henry was not "originally" a barkeeper. He had first tried his hand at storekeeping, then at tobacco farming, then at storekeeping again. His duties at Shelton's tavern gave him interim employment and security while he was looking about for something else to do.

Yet in a sense, though not in the sense he intended, Jefferson was right. Henry's career did begin in the taproom at Shelton's tavern, and in the courthouse across the road. There he first became acquainted with and interested in the law as a profession, what it involved, how it was practiced, the men who practiced it, and what were the tricks of the trade, so to speak.

A career in the law seemed to offer possibilities. Even obscure

---

* For some strained and rather amusing "explanations" of Henry's barkeeping days, see Appendix A (pp. 481–82).

backwoods lawyers, as Henry observed, made enough to support themselves and their families in reasonable comfort, and enjoyed being their own masters, deciding what they would or would not do, with their success depending on their own independent individual efforts.

In Virginia, lawyers had come far up in the world since 1645 when the House of Burgesses forbade anyone to set up as a lawyer, declaring that all those then practicing law were "unprincipled pettifoggers," interested only in stirring up trouble and conflict for their own profit, or were just plain "frauds," not knowing what they were talking about.

Though that ban had been lifted soon, lawyers were kept under strict supervision and regulation. All had to take an examination to qualify for a license. No exorbitant fees were to be charged; a maximum was set for every form of legal action. Lawyers found guilty of malpractice had their licenses revoked.

By Patrick Henry's time, the legal profession had become very respectable and increasingly powerful in all Virginia affairs, public as well as private. The roster of barristers included the names of Randolphs, and Carters, and Byrds, and other Grandees. If Henry succeeded in entering the rather exclusive legal fraternity, he could hope to better his social and economic station in life.

Then, too, there was the matter of applying evenhanded justice, an important consideration throughout Henry's life. It was notorious that many plainly guilty of offenses escaped punishment because of their family influence and money. Too many of the innocent, particularly among those too poor to engage competent legal counsel, became trapped in the labyrinthine mazes of the law and got hurt unjustly. A lawyer might, if he chose, become "a People's Advocate."

In pondering the possibilities of the law as a career, Henry certainly considered the fact that, unlike becoming a planter or a storekeeper, he could set up as a lawyer with no other capital than a good mind able to grasp what it wanted. A lawyer's office was "under his hat," so to say, and Henry never had any doubts about the quality of his mind. Nor did those who knew him at this time. or encountered him later. He had immense powers of concentration. Though he never read much, he had a most retentive memory, never forgetting what he found significant, provocative, or amusing in what he read, storing up knowledge for ready use on occasion.

In one field, Henry already was and would always remain a profound student. His subject was people—in the flesh, in the "raw," and not as mirrored or shadowed on the printed page. He viewed them in the round, from all angles—from the back as well as the front.

Whereas Jefferson, somewhat reserved and aloof, liked mankind in the abstract, Henry liked "man" as man, in every facet of individuality. He liked talking with people of all kinds, being at once a good talker and a good listener—a rare combination. Wherever he was, on a stagecoach, at an inn, in a courthouse, he would pick up a conversation with strangers and remarked in later life that he had never talked with anyone without learning something of value and interest, if only a new ribald joke. Henry had, in superlative degree, "the common touch."

As he took stock of himself in considering a new career, Henry was certainly aware that he had other attributes of great use to success as an advocate. He spoke well, had a love for words, knew how to put them together, had a fine ear for the sounds and rhythms of speech, and possessed a sense of style—a style that became more and more distinctively his own, quite unmistakable. He had a wonderful voice, low and resonant, rich in overtones and undertones, usually quiet and always in complete control. Any number of persons testified to its "magic."

While his were not the "refined" elaborate manners of the aristocratic school, Henry was always known for having good manners in the proper sense of the term. With all persons, he was considerate and polite, showing everyone due courtesy and respect. He did not have one manner for a poor backwoods neighbor and another for a visiting Grandee. Almost without exception, people liked him and found him charming, even those who violently disagreed with his opinions. As Henry had discovered for himself in the courtroom across the road, charm stood an advocate in good stead, especially when addressing a jury.

Whatever his calculations about prospects of success in a new career, Henry decided that study of the law might open a way out of the narrow world in which adversity had cornered him.

IV
To Williamsburg

. . . much resembles a good Country Town in England.

—LORD ADAM GORDON

Wishing to be a lawyer was one thing. How to become one was another. There was as yet no law school in all the colonies; nor would a beginning toward that end be made for another twenty years.* Even if there had been such a school, poverty would have prevented Henry from attending.

For generations, in Virginia and other colonies, richer families with sons aspiring to practice law had been sending them to London to get training in the celebrated Inns of Court. Sons of the less wealthy studied—or in the phrase of the day "read"—law in the office of some local attorney of reasonable competence agreeable to taking them on as unpaid apprentices or as junior law clerks at a meager salary.

Henry, for reasons unknown, chose a very difficult and unusual course. He would "read" law by himself, be his own tutor, and instruct himself in all the intricate mazes of the law.

Perhaps egotism led him to this decision. But that is doubtful,

* The first professorship of law in the country was instituted in Virginia, at Williamsburg in 1779, at the College of William and Mary, with the distinguished legal scholar George Wythe appointed to the chair.

though Henry always had unshaken confidence in his ability to master by himself any subject in which he was seriously interested. Or it may be that no attorney of recognized competence kept a full-time office at Hanover Courthouse or in the immediate vicinity. But this, too, is doubtful.

It seems more probable that, to support himself and his family, Henry felt obliged to continue his duties at Shelton's tavern while he was studying law.

In any case, Henry "read" law by himself, secluding himself as much as possible while doing so, letting only a few people know what he was doing. From his father he obtained the "use of a few old Law books," one probably being a volume dealing with Virginia statutes, a *Digest of the Virginia Acts,* which John Henry, as a county judge, would have had for reference. From a friend Patrick Henry borrowed a book from which he could learn how legal documents—pleas, writs, declarations, wills, deeds, mortgages, and other formal papers—were drawn up and filled out. In the broad field of English Common Law, the basic law in all the colonies, Henry applied himself to *Coke upon Littleton,** the first of four volumes collectively entitled *Institutes.*

By all accounts, this was the extent of Henry's law library as he began studying by himself for a legal career. He could well have used some suggestions and advice, but he evidently solicited none. According to his lifelong friend, Samuel Meredith, his study of the law was not known "to any of his friends until he consulted his friend John Lewis [a respected country lawyer] as to his fitness to commence practice, who encouraged him to apply for a license."

It was while he was more or less secretly studying law, late in 1759, that young Pat Henry and even younger Tom Jefferson first met, as briefly noted before, at a lively Christmas party held at the mansion of Colonel Nathaniel West Dandridge.

---

* The works of Sir Edward Coke (1552–1634)—"dusty old Coke," Jefferson called him—constituted the lawyers' Bible of the day, being supplanted later by Blackstone, the first volume of whose *Commentaries on the Laws of England* appeared in 1765.

While studying law, Jefferson wrote: "I do wish the Devil had old Coke, for I am sure I never was so tired of an old dull scoundrel in my life."

Yet in later years Jefferson much preferred the libertarian views of "old Coke," England's first Lord Chief Justice, to what he called the Tory "sophistries" of Sir William Blackstone (1723–1780), and those of the philosopher-historian David Hume (1711–1776), who sought to destroy what he called the "plaguy prejudices of Whiggism."

The Dandridges were people of consequence,* perhaps the first of the kind that young Henry had known. The colonel was descended from the blue-blooded West family, which gave Virginia one of its first and worst governors, Lord de La Warr (Delaware). Other Wests had been governors in the colony.

Dandridge's wife was Dorothea, daughter of Alexander Spotswood, one of the best of the royal governors, serving from 1710 to 1722 and initiating many much-needed administrative reforms. The Burgesses so liked and appreciated him that they appropriated £2,000 to build him a Governor's Mansion or "Palace," as it was soon known. Taking great interest in this project, which became one of Williamsburg's showplaces, Spotswood personally supervised every detail in the construction of this large handsome structure that Patrick Henry would one day occupy.

When Spotswood learned he was to be relieved of office because his administrative and fiscal reforms had alienated so many powerful land-grabbing tax-evading Grandees, the governor took a leaf from their book and went into the land-grabbing business, granting to himself, by very devious and dubious means, a patent to a vast tract of almost 90,000 acres along the frontier in what became Spotsylvania County.

There, with skilled workers brought from Germany, Spotswood set up an ironworks to manufacture utensils of various kinds, a new industry in the colony, and built a beautiful manor house, Germanna. Here Spotswood lived for almost twenty years, enjoying his "enchanted castle" with its spacious living rooms "elegantly set off with Pier glasses," with its marble fountain and terraced gardens. The splendors of Germanna impressed even that connoisseur of life in high style, Colonel William Byrd II of Westover, who on a visit admired the elegant "Pier glasses" and other things and also noted: "two tame deer run familiarly through the house."

Spotswood's daughter Dorothea and her husband did not live in such ducal splendor. But the Dandridge house was spacious, had its elegancies and refinements, and was a popular social center for the gentry of Upper Hanover.

Somehow, though still a nobody, young Henry had come to the attention of the Dandridges, who were somewhat older than he and proved to be very sympathetic and helpful to him. Steadily involved

---

* George Washington's rich wife, Martha, was a Dandridge, being the colonel's niece.

in lawsuits about one thing or another, Colonel Dandridge became one of the first and among the more frequent of Henry's law clients. In time, Henry would come into the family as a son-in-law, marrying young Dorothea Spotswood Dandridge after the tragic death of his first wife.

At the Dandridges' Christmas house party in 1759, said Jefferson, he met Henry "in society every day, and we became well acquainted, altho' I was much his junior, being then in my seventeenth year, and he a married man. . . .* His passion was fiddling, dancing, and pleasantry. He excelled at this last, and it attached everyone to him."

Jefferson found that Henry's "manners had something of the coarseness of the society he had frequented." But the Dandridges and their guests obviously did not. But what was worse in the eyes of the already serious-minded young Jefferson was that Henry declined to be drawn into any serious "conversation which might give the measure of his mind or information."

There was plenty of opportunity for such conversation, said Jefferson, for one of the guests was "a Mr. John Campbell, . . . a man of science [who] often introduced conversations on scientific subjects." In the holiday spirit of the occasion, Henry went on with his dancing, fiddling, and pleasantries, being not the slightest bit interested in hearing Mr. Campbell dilate on "scientific subjects," or in having seventeen-year-old Jefferson probe his mind in a desire to take its "measure."

How long Henry studied in preparing for his bar examinations cannot be determined. One of his closest friends said that he studied "not more than six or eight months." Another close friend said only one month, declaring that Henry had told him so himself. Another said six weeks, during which time Henry devoted himself to "reading of such books as he could borrow, with other assistance."

In any case, however long he studied, it was not long enough, as soon became apparent, most painfully to Henry himself.

Early in 1760, with a wintry chill still in the air, Henry saddled up and rode off on his first long journey out of the back country, bound for Williamsburg where he was to face his bar examiners and, hopefully, become a licensed attorney. His saddlebags no doubt contained a "few old law books" into which he could dig to refresh his memory on points that might be put to him by his examiners.

---

* Henry was about seven years older.

To Henry, who had never been far from the hamlet of Hanover Courthouse, its uneventful rural quiet seldom broken except at court time, the town of Williamsburg, though small itself, must have seemed a very metropolis, bustling with life, offering many unfamiliar sights and sounds, facilities and excitements. There was even a theater in the town, one of the few in the colonies.

Though its permanent residents numbered only a thousand or so, the town had charm and was impressive with its tree-lined streets, its many fine houses with lawns and gardens around them, its shops of many kinds along the Duke of Gloucester Street, and its two handsome government buildings—the Governor's Palace and the Capitol. It was also a college town, the seat of the College of William and Mary, the second oldest in the colonies.

The capital of colonial Virginia since 1699,* after Jamestown had burned down for the third time and been abandoned, Williamsburg remained the largest town in the colony until the 1740s when the port of Norfolk began to boom and soon surpassed it in population. But Williamsburg retained its pre-eminence as *the* town in Virginia, its political, social, and intellectual center.

Williamsburg of the day impressed far more sophisticated visitors than young Henry. A widely traveled British army colonel, aristocratic Lord Adam Gordon, journeying north from Florida to New England, stopped to enjoy Williamsburg for a time and found it to be much like a "good Country Town in England," adding:

"The situation of Williamsburg has one advantage which few or no places in these lower parts have, that of being free from mosquitoes. . . . There are many good Houses in Town. . . . The people are well bred, polite and extremely civil to Strangers."

His lordship admired the "very handsome Statehouse" (the Capitol), the "handsome and commodious Governor's House" (the Palace), and the college buildings. Of the Virginians he had met and in whose houses he had been entertained, he remarked that all of them lived very well:

"Their provisions of every kind is good; their Rivers supply them with a variety of Fish, particularly Crabs and Oysters. Their Pastures afford them excellent Beef and Mutton, and their Woods are stocked with Venison, Game, and Hogs . . . their Madeira Wine excellent,

---

* First known as Middle Plantation, the small settlement on becoming the capital was renamed Williamsburg to honor King William III (Prince of Orange), who came to the throne as joint sovereign with his wife, Queen Mary, after James II had been deposed in 1688.

almost in every house. Punch and small Beer brewed from Molasses is also in use, but their Cyder far exceeds any cyder I ever tasted at home. It is genuine and unadulterated, and will keep good to the age of twelve years or more"—no doubt in the form of hard cider or apple jack.

Lord Gordon also noted that the breed of horses in Virginia was "extremely good, and in particular those that they run in their carriages, which are most from thorough-bred Horses and country Mares. They all drive six Horses, and travel generally from 8 to 9 Miles an hour, going frequently sixty Miles to dinner"—which almost necessarily required them to stay on overnight. Their hosts would have liked this, for plantation life was usually rather lonely.

There is the story of rich planters coming down to the road, stopping the stagecoach, and inviting its occupants to come up to the house and enjoy its hospitality as long as they cared to. Anything was better than isolation and boredom, the same day-to-day unbroken routines for weeks and even months on end.

A quiet rural village most of the year, "in a manner deserted," Williamsburg became "Devilsburg," in young Jefferson's phrase, at "Publick Times." These occurred when the General Court held sessions twice a year and the House of Burgesses usually assembled. At such times, known as the Season, the town filled up and was "crowded with the gentry of the country," many of whom brought along their families and a number of retainers, temporarily doubling or tripling the population.

During the Season, always a gay and boisterous affair, Grandees came wheeling in along the Duke of Gloucester Street in highly ornamental coaches, with a Negro servant or two in bright livery sitting high on the box and skillfully driving at a fast pace two- or three-span of spirited horses, all closely matched in size and color. Lesser gentry came in on saddle, riding a high-stepping mare or gelding. Out of curiosity and to enjoy the carnival, others came by what means they could—by stagecoach, in creaking farm wagons, astride balky mules, or on foot.

All inns and places of public accommodation were filled and roaring, with men "hurrying back and forth from the Capitoll to the taverns, and at night Carousing and Drinking in one chamber, and box and Dice in another."

The Season offered diversions and entertainments to suit almost any taste—plays at the theater, Punch and Judy shows, acrobatic acts and other performances by itinerant troupes, prizefights, wrestling matches, horse races, footraces, cockfights, dinner parties, and elaborate balls that went on all night. The high light of the Season came with the traditional Governor's Ball at the Palace, to which everybody who was anybody schemed to obtain an invitation.

More than one English visitor observed that the Season at Williamsburg was scarcely inferior in fashion and gaiety, and in extravagance, to the fabulous Season in London, the talk of all Europe.

Young Henry arrived in Williamsburg in off-Season, missing its excitements, exuberances, and entertainments. Even so, he cannot have been bored. There was so much to interest and impress him, including several things of very special personal interest.

The axis of Williamsburg was the broad, straight, sandy, and tree-lined Duke of Gloucester Street—or The Street, as Williamsburgers called it—dusty in summer, miry in winter, traveled up and down by men on horseback, by carriages, an occasional stagecoach, and rough farm wagons and carts drawn by mules in jangling harness. There were "well kept sidewalks" for pedestrians—elegantly attired gentle folk and ragged Negro slaves, handicraftsmen from local shops wearing leather aprons, poorer farmers in linsey-woolsey and yarn caps, "buckskins" from the backwoods, romping college boys, and now and again painted Indian chiefs of the Cherokee tribe and others, come with the hope—usually futile—of trying to straighten out problems raised by palefaces in their ever increasing aggressive encroachment on lands reserved for the Indians by solemn treaty.

Such treaties, for the most part, were not worth the paper they were written on, being constantly violated by land-hungry colonists and especially by those who hoped to make a fortune, as many did, in real estate speculations on land to which they had no right except their self-asserted claim to it.

At one end of the mile-long Duke of Gloucester Street, facing the thoroughfare, stood the Capitol, "the best and most commodious pile" in the colonies, a large handsome two-storied H-shaped building constructed of beautiful pink brick. From its high steep-gabled roof rose a slender white cupola topped with the arms of Queen Anne, in whose reign the Capitol was built, being completed in 1705.* Around the building was a low wall, also of pink brick,

* Burned in 1747, the building was restored a few years later, with several notable additions, including the western portico that Jefferson admired so much.

enclosing the Capitol Yard with its well kept lawn and many flower beds.

On the ground floor of the building was the small but impressive Hall of the House of Burgesses, patterned in its arrangements on those of the British House of Commons. The Burgesses followed the Commons as closely as possible in rules, procedures, parliamentary usages, and almost everything else, including a taste for elaborate and often long-winded speeches that never got to the point at all.

Upstairs, on the second floor, was an oval chamber where the twelve-member Governor's Council met and the General Court, the highest judicial body in the colony, held its sessions. The Capitol also provided committee rooms and offices for higher colonial authorities—the secretary of state, the treasurer, and others.

If Henry, his mind occupied with other things, was not particularly interested at the moment in the Capitol and its workings, he soon would be and would there enjoy the first of many great triumphs.

At the other end of The Street, facing down the thoroughfare, stood Main, the principal building of the College of William and Mary, built in 1699. On the small campus were two smaller structures—the Brafferton Building (1723), planned to serve as an Indian school, and the President's House (1732).

Down the years, Main has lost its name, becoming known as the Wren Building because it was "first modeled" by the great English architect, Sir Christopher Wren, designer of St. Paul's Cathedral and other magnificent buildings in London, as well as in Oxford and Cambridge.

But Virginia planters, not entirely pleased with Wren's "model" of the college building, decided that it could be improved. As a consequence, Wren's design was "adapted to the Nature of the Country by the Gentlemen there." To try to "improve" on Wren took quite a bit of presumption, but the design was "adapted" without ruinous results.

Chartered in 1693, with a grant from the Crown of £2,000 [$60,000], the receipt of certain taxes, and 20,000 acres of land, the college opened its doors in temporary quarters the next year. The staff consisted of a president, a "writing master," and an usher. Like all colleges of the day, William and Mary was denominational in its character and interests, being a Church of England institution, with the Bishop of London as chancellor ex-officio. Most of its staff were reverends chiefly interested in expounding the Anglican credo.

In 1705, Main (the semi-Wren Building), then the college's only facility, was gutted by fire and, in want of public or any support, was not fully restored for almost twenty years, not till 1723. Shortly after, William and Mary was described by one of its professors as a "college without a chapel, without a scholarship, and without a statute [i.e., without authorization to award degrees]; a library without books, comparatively speaking . . . ."

By 1760, when Jefferson enrolled, things had generally improved. The college had about eighty students and a small but distinguished staff. Even so, Jefferson had criticisms and complaints.

The college was "filled with children," he said, meaning that most students were just beginners in studying Latin, Greek, ancient history, mathematics, philosophy, and other subjects they should have been introduced to in lower schools. Worse, students were treated like small children, being under the constant surveillance and hard discipline of their schoolmasters.

In particular, Jefferson objected to the religiosity into which all instruction had been cast by the terms of the royal charter and of various endowments. The college, in his judgment, "was just well enough endowed to draw out the miserable existence to which a miserable constitution has doomed it."

Midway between the college and the Capitol, set far back from the Duke of Gloucester Street in the beautiful Palace Green, sat the imposing Governor's Mansion. Knowing that it had been built by Governor Alexander Spotswood, father of his good friend, Mrs. Dorothea Spotswood Dandridge, Henry must have taken more than a second glance at the Palace, little dreaming at the moment that in not too long a time he would be occupying the Palace himself and there be married to another and younger Dorothea Spotswood Dandridge, and that one of their children would be christened Alexander Spotswood Henry.

Among the many shops along The Street, Henry certainly took particular notice of one, the office and the printing shop of the *Virginia Gazette*. This weekly, the colony's only newspaper down almost to the Revolution, the single source of local and general news, had been founded in 1736 (the year of Henry's birth) by his wife's grandfather, William Parks.* The latter for some years was both publisher and editor, writing most of the columns himself.

In his shop, Parks also opened the colony's first good bookstore, importing important works from London and the Continent, for as yet there was no general book publishing business in the colonies.

Established with a subsidy from the House of Burgesses and the governor, the *Gazette* was a semiofficial publication, quoting or giving summaries of the more important acts of the General Assembly and the pronouncements, proclamations, and such things by the governor. While the weekly carried some local news, it dealt mainly with happenings abroad, especially with decisions taken in London affecting the interests of the colonies in general, and of Virginia in particular. Virginians of consequence read the *Gazette* regularly to keep informed of what was going on in the world. Shelton's tavern, like most taverns, probably had a subscription to provide copies for its patrons.

And among the establishments along The Street, or close by on side streets, were the town's numerous inns and taverns—Purdie's, Wetherburn's, Charlton's, the King's Arms, Mrs. Vobe's on York Road, and other hostelries of less fashion and repute. Wetherburn's was noteworthy for its fine punch, based on strong arrack rum which came from India and the Dutch East Indies and was flavored with Oriental fruits and herbs.

This popular punch played a part in the life of the Jeffersons. In 1736, in exchange "for Henry Wetherburn's biggest bowl of Arrack Punch to him delivered," William Randolph of Tuckahoe sold to Peter Jefferson, whose wife was a Randolph, a 400-acre tract to the west in what became Albemarle County. There the elder Jefferson built Shadwell, the birthplace of his son Thomas.

But the tavern of the town was the Raleigh, at the lower end of the Duke of Gloucester Street, not far from the Capitol. On a pediment over the main doorway stood a leaden bust of Sir Walter Raleigh, who had given Virginia its name in honor of the celebrated Virgin Queen, the great Elizabeth I, whose lover he probably was at the time.

Raleigh Tavern, with its popular taproom and its beautiful Apollo Room—the center of much revolutionary planning in later years—

---

* The *Gazette* was the ninth oldest newspaper in the country. Others had previously been established in Boston (two), Newport, New York (two), Philadelphia, Annapolis, and Charleston, South Carolina.

was the rendezvous of the great, the near-great, and the merely fashionable. Henry may have taken a peek into the Raleigh to see how things were done there, particularly in the taproom, for he had what might be called a semiprofessional interest in bartending; he might perhaps have hoped to pick up an idea or two for use at Shelton's.

But, certainly, Henry did not enter the Raleigh. In his rough country clothes, he would have been very conspicuous among the assembled periwigs and their expensively gowned ladies. Besides, he probably did not have a spare sixpence in his pocket.

If Henry was lonesome in Williamsburg, as doubtless he was, he knew at least one person in town, a student at the college—Tom Jefferson, whom he had met a few months before at the Dandridge Christmas party. He evidently looked him up at the college, for Jefferson later said that at this time Henry told him that he had been studying law for six weeks. Which would seem to settle that matter unless Jefferson was wrong, as he so often was in his septuagenarian recollections about Henry.

V

From Bar to Bar

. . . if your industry be only half equal to your genius, I augur that you will do well . . .

—John Randolph

Quite as impressive as Williamsburg in young Henry's awed eyes—and he was never one to "awe" easily—were the four very distinguished and elegant gentlemen, all eminent barristers, who had been named to examine him on his knowledge of the law and decide whether he would be "an ornament to the Bar," or not.

The four were not only well established and respected lawyers, but also leaders in public life, serving at various times as prominent members in the House of Burgesses. They would soon become Henry's friends, but his first meeting with them was very painful and almost ended in disaster.

In Virginia at the time, bar examiners did not sit as a board. Nor were written examinations generally used. Rather, each examiner individually interviewed the applicant for a license. No license was issued unless at least two of the examiners agreed to sign.

None of Henry's prosperous well-groomed examiners, all of them owning fine houses in town, was much taken with the general appearance of the roughly dressed young aspirant from Hanover Courthouse. After his long ride on horseback and his stay in some small cheap Williamsburg inn or boardinghouse, Henry may have been more disheveled than usual. He was, in his younger years, always a bit careless about his appearance, paying little or no attention to his clothes—except that he was, said a friend, "unusually attentive in having clean linen and stockings."

Nor were any of Henry's examiners at all impressed with his knowledge of the law. He was first interviewed by the eminent legal scholar, George Wythe. Largely self-educated, Wythe was a man of wide knowledge and interests, and was a remarkable teacher. Many Virginians of note—Thomas Jefferson, James Monroe, U. S. Chief Justice John Marshall, Henry Clay, among others—gratefully acknowledged the deep debt they owed Wythe for the schooling they had from him not only in the law, but in history, philosophy, political theory, and other fields. Jefferson admired and loved Wythe more than any man in his life, repeatedly extolling his "most affectionate friend" for his "superior learning, correct elocution, and logical style of reasoning."

In his examination by sharp-minded Wythe, Henry evidently did very badly, revealing great ignorance of the law. While Wythe was libertarian in his political and social views, he was very patrician in manner. There was no one, it was said, who could express more courtesy with a bow. It was no doubt with such a bow that he dismissed the bewildered and unhappy young Henry, having told him that he "absolutely refused" to sign his application for a license to practice law.*

Henry was next interviewed and questioned by Robert Carter Nicholas, one of a numerous clan made very wealthy by Robert "King" Carter (1663–1732), land-grabber extraordinary, who died possessed of more than 300,000 acres, having meantime bestowed hundreds of thousands of acres on sons, grandsons, sons-in-law, and more remote in-laws and relatives.

An accomplished lawyer with perhaps the most lucrative practice in the Old Dominion, later a judge in the High Court of Chancery and in the Court of Appeals, Robert Carter Nicholas found Henry's knowledge of legal matters sadly deficient and was about to end the interview when Henry appealed to him, asking for an opportunity to prove himself. A kindly man, deeply religious and a devout

* Jefferson is the authority for this, as well as for the statement in regard to Robert Carter Nicholas that follows. How far Jefferson can be trusted here is uncertain. He wrote contradictory accounts about Henry's difficulties with his bar examiners.

churchman, charitable in his sympathies, Nicholas listened to Henry and "on repeated importunity" agreed to sign his license, but only on Henry's promise that on his return to Hanover Courthouse he would dig in, do his homework, and really learn some law.

That Henry did his homework well is attested by the fact that eleven years later, when Nicholas decided to give up his large private practice, the best in Virginia, he turned it over to Henry.

The other two examiners were Randolphs—Peyton and his younger brother John, sons of Sir John Randolph, the only native-born Virginian to be knighted, being so honored for having served long and well as attorney general (King's Counsel) in the colony.

To anticipate developments a bit, there is good reason here to say several things about the later careers of Peyton Randolph and his brother John. Graduates of the College of William and Mary, both had gone to London to study in the famed law institutions there—Peyton, at the Inner Temple; John, at Gray's Inn. On his father's death, Peyton had been appointed by the Crown to succeed him as attorney general. Intensely loyal to the King in the Randolph family tradition, it was he who led the conservatives as they tried in that "most bloody debate" to defeat Henry's "treasonable" Stamp Tax resolutions.

But as Virginia and her sister colonies became more restive and sharper in their complaints about British "tyranny," Randolph changed his position and moved rather rapidly into "rebel" ranks. Elected as speaker of the House of Burgesses in 1766, he resigned as attorney general and devoted the rest of his life to forwarding the "Patriot" cause, throwing in his lot with the often turbulent Sons of Liberty.

A large and handsome man, well spoken and extremely gracious in manner, Randolph was, so a contemporary described him, "an honest man; has knowledge, temper, judgment, and above all, integrity—a true Roman spirit." He also had an extraordinary talent for negotiation, for conciliation, for bringing about working agreements among men holding widely divergent views.

At meetings of the discontented in Virginia, whether in a small select committee or at a large public rally, Randolph was usually chosen to preside, for he was liked and trusted by all. He was eminently fair in his rulings from the chair and knew how to expedite business by avoiding procedural wrangles and keeping debate on the main issues. In the years leading up to the Revolution, he played an important role in acting as an "honest broker" between hesitant moderates and the "firebrands" led by Henry, Jefferson, and Richard Henry Lee.

In 1774, Peyton Randolph received the signal honor of being elected unanimously as president of the First Continental Congress. At the Second Continental Congress the next year he was again chosen unanimously to preside. Had he not suddenly died, he would almost certainly have presided over the Third Continental Congress in 1776. In that case, he would have been a signer of the Declaration of Independence—and, without question, the first signer.

So that today, in requesting someone's signature on a document, instead of asking for his "John Hancock," we might be saying, "Would you put your Peyton Randolph down here?" Fame—or want of it—so often hangs on such thin threads of circumstance.

In 1766, on Peyton Randolph's resignation as attorney general to become speaker of the House of Burgesses, his brother John, six years his junior, was appointed by the Crown to succeed him. A brilliant lawyer, the younger Randolph was also deeply interested in literature, music, painting, and the arts in general. He especially liked music, doing some composing, playing exceptionally well on the violin—young Thomas Jefferson, a relative, himself an excellent musician, bought one of Randolph's fine old Italian violins. Randolph was not merely a verbal but a hard-working, dirt-digging enthusiast about gardens and flowers, writing an interesting and useful *Treatise on Gardening.*

As attorney general in the colony, John Randolph could not publicly identify himself with the views of his brother Peyton and those who were ever more sharply challenging imperial policies and organizing associations and other popular movements to resist British "tyranny." Nor, in his private views, did he have much sympathy with the patriot cause.

In the family tradition, John Randolph remained a staunch Loyalist, and Royalist. On the other hand, he had no desire to come into direct and perhaps violent conflict with members of his family, friends, neighbors, and a large part of his countrymen. This faced him with a hard decision.

Early in 1775, with the outbreak of armed hostilities obviously approaching, Randolph made his decision. He reluctantly tore up deep roots in Virginia and, with his wife and two daughters, sailed for Britain. The decision was doubly painful, for it broke up his immediate family. His only son, Edmund, aged twenty-two, not sharing his father's views but rather those of his uncle Peyton, chose to stay behind in Virginia, later going on to become one of General Washington's aides, a governor of Virginia, our first United States Attorney General and our second Secretary of State, succeeding Jefferson on the latter's resignation in 1794.

Landing in England, John Randolph lived the rest of his life there as an American Tory exile. But he never forgot Virginia, loving it to the last, making a dying request that he be buried there. A daughter carried out his wish, bringing back his remains to Williamsburg where they were placed near his brother Peyton's and his father's in the Randolph vault in the chapel of the College of William and Mary.

Ironically, it was this Tory exile-to-be who was chiefly instrumental in putting worried young Henry on the road to advancement and to becoming the leader of the "rebel" forces that Randolph found so objectionable and led him to abandon his homeland. In a sense, Henry forced him into unhappy exile.

As bar examiners, Peyton and John Randolph seem not to have been in a hurry to interview Henry and come to a judgment on his qualifications. Both were very busy men deep in both public and private affairs. There are intimations that they had decided it was not worthwhile to talk with Henry at all; by all appearances, the applicant seemed to be so unpromising.

It was entirely due to a misapprehension that John Randolph asked Henry to come for an interview. Somehow, Randolph had got the impression that Henry already had the two signatures he required on his license–though, in fact, he had only one, and that given reluctantly by Nicholas "on his promise of future reading."

Laboring under this misapprehension, Randolph may have felt, being always a very gracious and courteous person, that the least he could do was to receive the supposedly successful candidate, test his knowledge a bit, and welcome him into the legal fraternity.

The interview had not gone very far before Randolph saw clearly "the erroneous conclusion which he had drawn from the exterior of the candidate. With evident marks of increasing surprise (produced no doubt by the peculiar texture and strength of Mr. Henry's style, and the boldness and originality of his combinations), he continued the examination for several hours,"* with eager and anxious

---

* This quotation and the paragraphs that follow are based on what Henry later told his close friend, Judge John Tyler, who wrote out almost immediately an account of their conversation. The judge was the father of John Tyler (1790–1862), tenth President of the United States.

young Henry doing his best to impress Randolph. Both men were relatively young, Randolph being in his early thirties, nine years older than Henry. But in their training and background they were worlds apart.

Randolph first questioned Henry on municipal law and there "soon discovered his deficiency." He then asked questions on other subjects—the law of nations, the laws of nature, the policy of the feudal system, and general history, "which last he found to be his stronghold." All of this must have abashed a twenty-four-year-old with little systematic education.

Then turning to the English Common Law, Randolph raised various points and asked Henry to discuss them. The latter did so, with Randolph cutting in repeatedly, taking exception to Henry's interpretations, "drawing him out by questions, endeavoring to puzzle him with subtleties, assailing him with declamations, and watching continually the defensive operations of his mind."

How could Henry's mind be anything but "defensive" under a barrage of questions, exceptions, and declamations by one of the most brilliant lawyers in the colony. After considerable discussion, Randolph said:

"You defend your opinions very well, Sir, but now to the law and the testimony." He then led Henry into his office and, "opening the authorities," said:

"Behold the force of natural reason; you have never seen these books, nor this principle of the law; yet you are right and I am wrong; and from this lesson you have given me (you must excuse my saying it), I will never trust to appearances again.

"Mr. Henry, if your industry be only half equal to your genius, I augur that you will do well, and become an ornament and an honor to your profession."

With John Randolph willing to sign his license, Henry now had the two signatures he required. Whether Peyton Randolph later interviewed Henry and agreed to sign is not clear, though possibly he did. Saying that he had been told so by the two Randolphs, who were kinsmen and close friends, Jefferson wrote:

"Peyton and John Randolph, men of great facility of temper, signed his license with as much reluctance as their dispositions would permit them to show, . . . acknowledging he was very ignorant of law, but that they perceived him to be a young man of genius and did not doubt he would soon qualify himself."

In brief, Henry obtained a license not so much to practice law, of which he was then "very ignorant," as to exercise his "genius," of which he had given only a flash. To grant a license on such subjective opinions and not by objective standards was to make bar examinations seem to be somewhat whimsical and a bit ridiculous.

In any case, no matter how obtained, Henry now had a license to set up as a lawyer and rode back to Hanover Courthouse elated, to hang out his shingle on Shelton's tavern, where he and his family continued to live for five years.

As an office, the tavern had obvious advantages. It was readily accessible to those needing legal aid in cases being tried in the courthouse just across the road. It enabled clients to enjoy more social amenities than available around the offices of most country lawyers. While doing, as he had promised, some much needed homework in the mysteries of the law, Henry began looking about hopefully for clients.

When bar business of that nature was slow, as it was bound to be in the beginning, he could help earn his keep by continuing to lend a hand at Shelton's bar, no doubt finding time on many occasions to take out his violin and pleasure himself and his guests with some lively fiddling.

Henry's immediate family, his many relatives, and friends helped him by directing their legal business his way. His father, his father-in-law, and his mother-in-law were among his first clients. Other early clients included members of his mother's family—Winstons and Dabneys—and his half brother, John Syme, Jr., who was an enterprising planter and land speculator, and ever in litigation, bringing suit or being sued. Henry's friend, Colonel Nathaniel West Dandridge, gave him several cases to handle.

Henry's first large account came from Patrick Coutts, of the prosperous firm of "Coutts & Crosse, Merchants," in the young and growing town of Richmond not far away. Coutts was a Scot, from the "old country," no doubt one of John Henry's friends. But for reasons of friendship, it is highly doubtful that Coutts would have entrusted some of his important affairs to a young lawyer who had just hung out his shingle.

One of Henry's early cases involved Major Thomas Bolling, a descendant of Pocahontas ("Princess Rebecca") and John Rolfe, and thereby of Virginia's native "royal" blood, coming down from Powhatan, whom the English had dubbed "Imp. [Emperor] Virginiae."* Henry prosecuted a suit for damages against Major Bolling for "improper use" of a stallion. The charge was not as shocking as it sounds. The major, it appears, had "abused" the stallion by allowing him to run free and satisfy his desires without properly crediting his owner with stud fees.

In another case, Henry represented his cousin, John Winston, in a suit for slander. Winston averred that one Spencer "did utter, publish, and declare aloud" that he (Winston) was a "hog-stealer." This slanderous libel, said Winston, had brought him into "much contempt & Danger" and quite destroyed his peace of mind. For his sufferings and impaired reputation, the complainant sought £500 [$15,000]. The jury thought this excessive and, in spite of Henry's earnest and eloquent pleadings, awarded the "injured" Winston only £20 [$600].

Henry soon extended his practice from Hanover into Louisa and other neighboring counties. Sessions of county courts in various areas were arranged on a staggered schedule so that lawyers might travel from courthouse to courthouse to represent clients. The schedule in the Hanover area was: Spotsylvania County, first Tuesday of every month, and Hanover, first Thursday; King and Queen, second Tuesday, and Caroline, second Thursday; Essex, third Tuesday, and King William, third Thursday.

During 1760, having been actively in practice for perhaps half the year, Henry represented some 60 clients in 176 civil cases. For his services in these cases, and "for advice, and for preparing papers out of court," Henry charged his clients with fees totaling £123. 13. 3. But of this sum, as his fee books show, he managed to collect less than half–about £49 [$1,470]. His clients and collections did not increase much the next year.

Then occurred a sharp rise in the number of cases placed in his hands and in the amount of fees he managed to collect. In 1763, his fourth year of practice, he represented about 160 clients in almost 500 cases, charging fees aggregating £660 [$19,800]. But during the year he was paid only a third of this, slightly more than £225 [$6,750].**

To Henry, his 1763 income represented a princely sum, quite literally a fortune. It was certainly not large as Virginians' fortunes

* President Woodrow Wilson's second wife was a Bolling.

** Of his unpaid accounts, Henry could reasonably expect to collect a half or more within a year or two. Among his larger debtors were a number of friends and relations, including his half brother John Syme.

went, but was far larger than any that he or any of his young friends had known. He was moving up in the world and establishing himself in his own right.

No longer would he have to be dependent on the bounty and favors of others. After much floundering and struggle, having surmounted many obstacles, some self-made, some because of circumstance, he had succeeded in becoming his own master at the age of twenty-seven. He was now quite able to provide for himself and his own, free to direct his life as he chose, happy to be in the position of being able to help those who had so generously helped him —in particular, his father and his father-in-law, both of whom were having financial troubles, being sued for nonpayment of debts.

Times were hard in Virginia for several reasons, but principally because the price of tobacco kept falling, and the whole economy rested on tobacco. In 1758, in a suit brought by merchants, a court judgment for £365 [$11,000] was handed down against John Shelton; next year, a judgment for almost £100 [$3,000] was handed down against John Henry; both were involved in other suits.

The prestige and income from a growing law practice pleased Henry, of course. But as yet there was nothing at all noteworthy about his legal career. His was the customary run-of-the-mill practice of an obscure young country lawyer, dealing with such minor matters as debt collections, damage suits, mortgage papers, deeds, drawing and executing wills, out-of-court settlements on disputes of various kinds, and defense of those charged with misdemeanors and other less serious breaches of the law.

Nothing of any consequence, however, was coming his way, and it seemed that things might go on like this for some time, until he had made more of a name for himself as a lawyer. After all, he was just a beginner, having practiced for little more than three years.

But the "big case" that lawyers are always looking for was suddenly upon him. To his surprise as much as to anybody's, it was literally dropped into his lap when a friend, an older lawyer, turned over to him a case that had no support in point of law and seemed utterly hopeless.

Whatever his deficiencies, Henry never lacked hope. Nor did he ever want courage. He would dare anything, as in going to Williamsburg to take his bar examinations after six weeks' study and succeed in obtaining a license to practice his putative "genius," which was now about to flash for the first time.

VI
Two Penny Law: The Parsons' Cause

. . . the more sober part of the audience were struck with Horror . . .

—The Reverend James Maury

On December 1, 1763, an unusually large number of people converged on Hanover Courthouse from miles around, even from adjoining counties, to attend a trial of wide interest not only locally, but throughout the colony—and even in London.

The question at issue seemed simple enough. It dealt with claims for back salary made by Church of England clergymen. But the issue was not simple at all. It had wide ramifications and concerned almost everybody—most of all, taxpayers and tithe payers.

In Virginia, as in Britain, the Church of England was the official church, the Established Church, enjoying powers, rights, and privileges not enjoyed by any other church, its greatest right and privilege being that it was tax-supported. Tithes to support the Establishment—to pay the salaries of its ministers, to build and maintain Anglican churches and parsonages—were levied on all taxpayers whether they chose to worship in the Anglican church or not. This was becoming an increasingly sore point as Virginia began filling up with more and more Presbyterians, Quakers, Baptists, Methodists, and other non-Anglicans.*

Though not strictly enforced, except on occasion against non-Anglicans—the nonconformists, the Dissenters—the law required all Virginians to take communion in an Anglican church at least twice a year. No nonconformist minister could conduct services of any kind unless he had gone to Williamsburg to be questioned there on his beliefs, his moral character, his loyalty to the Crown, and had there obtained—as if he were a ferry-operator—a license to preach, signed by the governor.

Presbyterians were willing to accept the licensing law. But Baptist, Methodist, Quaker, and other dissenting ministers refused to obey it as a matter of principle, declaring that they stood in no need of a license "to preach the Word of God." Many unlicensed preachers were jailed and fined; their meetings were often forcibly broken up not only by the sheriff and his men, but by groups of hostile bigoted neighbors, often led by belligerent Anglican parsons who regarded "itinerant" preachers as so many poachers on their exclusive preserve.

Dissenters were largely centered in the Piedmont, there being few among Tidewater lords and their dependents. Under the influence of the Great Awakening, an historic revivalist movement that affected all Protestant churches, there was rapidly growing in Hanover and the westerly counties a spirit of religious revolt that in not too many years would succeed in disestablishing the Establishment and toppling the Anglican church from its privileged position as the State church.**

Though never a Dissenter, Patrick Henry was always very friendly toward the prosecuted and persecuted nonconformists, doing much to aid them in their troubles, as will appear.

1. State Church

Purportedly, Virginia had been founded for religious reasons. The merchant adventurers who owned the First Virginia [London] Com-

* Theoretically, all the colonies were officially Anglican in credo, being part of the see of the Bishop of London. But the writ of the bishops of London did not run in Puritan New England where the Anglican rite was not tolerated, and it was ignored in other colonies, such as Quaker Pennsylvania.

** Though it had been partially effected during the Revolution, the formal separation of Church and State in Virginia did not occur until 1785 with the passage of Jefferson's Act for Establishing Religious Freedom.

pany declared time and again that their "principall & maine end" was to carry the Christian Gospel to the Indians and thus "recover out of the armes of the Divell a number of pore and miserable souls wrapt up unto death in almost *invincible ignorance.*" The adventurers were eager, they said, "to add our myte to the Treasury of Heaven."

They were also eager to add a mite or two, or more, to the company treasury. They could at once "plant" religion and make some money, which to them seemed a good arrangement all around. From the Indians they would buy "the Pearles of Earth and sell to them the Pearles of Heaven"—a usual imperial pattern.

But the Indians, "those naked slaves of Hell," were not much interested, being quite content with their gods, as most of us are, and turned a deaf ear to those bringing them "the Glad Tidings of Salvation," particularly when these harbingers of "Eternal Joy" were ruthlessly and bloodily pushing them out of their homelands and cheating them outrageously on every possible occasion, as starkly revealed in the accounts of Captain John Smith and his contemporaries.

Having no reason to like or trust the white aggressors, the Indians seemed to be so spiritually "benighted" that a parson of the early days, the Reverend Jonas Stockden, took to publicly proclaiming his version of the Gospel.

There was no use, he said, in trying to convert the "horrid Salvages" by such gentle means as education. He had a few students, and when they were questioned about such awe-full mysteries as the Godhead, the Trinity, the Holy Ghost, and the Virgin Birth, he got only "derision and ridiculous answers."

Nor was there any use in trying to win them with gifts, he concluded: ". . . till their Priests and Ancients have their throats cut, there is no hope of conversion." With such doctrine being openly preached, the Indians had good reason to be skeptical and uneasy.

Virginia ministers were chosen and sent out by the Bishop of London. Those sent over were not, for the most part, distinguished for character, learning, talent, or zeal. Almost no Anglican clergyman with a good parish in England wished to exchange the comforts of home for a rude and precarious life along the frontier. Virginia became a bag into which to toss incompetent gentlemen of the cloth.

The House of Burgesses early noted that too many of the parsons foisted on the colony "paddled in factions and State matters, being such as wore black coats and could gabble in a pulpit, roar in a tavern, exact from their parishes, and rather by their dissoluteness destroy than feed their flock."

Ministers, said the Burgesses, "shall not give themselves to excess in drinking or riott, spending their tyme idellye by day or night playing at dice, cards, or any other unlawfull game." Rather, they should "at all tymes convenient, . . . heare and reade somewhat of the Holy Scripture, or occupie themselves with some honest study or exercise." Always they should keep "in mynd that they ought to excell all others in puritie of life."

For the better ordering of church affairs in Virginia, the Bishop of London decided in 1689 to appoint a new officer with the title of commissary, who was to act as a central administrator and general superintendent. He was to prevent scandals and abuses in the church. Theoretically, he was empowered to remove from office any incompetent parson or any whose public or private life was deemed a disgrace to the cloth. But his actual powers were rather weak.

As the first commissary, the Bishop of London appointed the Reverend James Blair, an energetic and learned man,* soon to be instrumental in founding the College of William and Mary, a Church of England institution.

The commissary was distressed by the want of grace among so many of the Virginia parsons. So was his lordship, the bishop, who in 1727 ordered Blair to call a convocation at Williamsburg of all Anglican clergy in the colony, declaring that "nothing was such a great disservice to Religion as the leaving of so many Parishes destitute of ministers, and the Supplying so many with indifferent ones, either as to their ministerial talents or good life."

The bishop commanded those at the convocation to report, in writing, the acts and names of fellow parsons known to them "personally" as leading unchristian and dissolute lives. Not wishing to compromise their friends and colleagues, and perhaps incriminate themselves, all of them signed statements that they did not "personally" know any parsons who were "evil livers."

Other people evidently had a wider acquaintance and knew a number of "evil livers." An endowment in one parish had been established to pay the rector an extra stipend for preaching "four quarterly sermons yearly against the four reigning vices, . . . atheism and irreligion, swearing and cursing, fornication and adul-

---

* Like Patrick Henry's father, Blair had been born in Scotland and had his training at King's College, Aberdeen.

tery, and drunkenness." To collect the stipend, a later rector conscientiously preached the required quarterly sermons as his parishioners snickered behind their hands or burned with indignation at his hypocrisy, for the reverend was notoriously addicted to the "reigning vices," particuarly the last two.

Then there was the parson who organized and became president of the local Jockey Club and spent most of his time ministering to his stable of horses, racing them on every occasion for large bets, and when sober enough, riding to hounds. Even as he lay dying and his mind was wandering, he was still "hallooing to the hounds."

Another parson, when deep in his cups, liked to go about insulting and beating up those vestrymen in his parish whom he found to be especially objectionable. Though this treatment was a bit rough, it was understandable, for vestries could be very exasperating, given to constant carping and criticism of the incumbent minister, for good cause or bad.

Vestrymen in particular, parishioners in general, were often hard to please. If a parson appeared to lack zeal, he was considered "undesireable." On the other hand, if he became too pointed in his observations on the morals and spiritual failings of his flock, he fell into disfavor for being "overzealous." How to steer an acceptable middle course always posed a problem.

2. The Great Awakening

Religious life in Virginia and other colonies was quite shaken up in the 1740s by the spirited enthusiasm of a widespread revivalist movement known as the Great Awakening.

It started in England, inspired and led by a Church of England clergyman, the Reverend George Whitefield, a man of great eloquence and deep convictions and by all accounts a most persuasive evangelist. He was so eloquent, it is said, that he could reduce audiences to tears merely by pronouncing the word "Mesopotamia."

However that may be, Whitefield had powers enough to make a deep impression on two old skeptics, not to say cynics–the Earl of Chesterfield and Benjamin Franklin. Being in London, the latter went to hear one of his sermons. Going to scoff, Franklin remained to pray, being so touched that he emptied his "pocket into the collector's plate, gold and all." It was never easy to separate "Poor Richard" from a gold sovereign.

Whitefield rejected the dry sterile formalism of the Anglican church, its aristocratic bias and social snobbery, its want of interest in the problems and concerns of the "lower orders." He decided, however, to remain in the Church and not become a Dissenter as his friend and co-worker, the Reverend John Wesley, had done in founding Methodism.

With the aim of reforming the Church from within and injecting new life into it, Whitefield journeyed widely through Britain preaching to people wherever he could find them, weekdays and Sundays, talking to them in the coalfields, on the docks, in poor factory towns, on village greens, in prisons.

Thousands gave him tumultuous ovations because he brought to them what they had been thirsting for—a sense of identity, with each having a soul worth saving. He excited them; he gave them a taste of brimstone, hellfire, and damnation to shake them up. He held huge audiences spellbound for hours as he called on them, one and all, young and old, to "come to the Light," live by their faith, give up their sins and publicly repent of them, which they did with moans, groans, and shouts of joy—Hallelujah! They called themselves the "New Lights," or the "Come-outers," and there was certainly no love lost, either Christian or otherwise, between them and those whom they dubbed the "Old Lights."

In 1745, in one of seven visits to America, Whitefield stopped in Virginia and was invited to come to Hanover County where a number of "reading houses" had been established, inspired by one Samuel Morris, a small planter and occasional bricklayer, who had interested friends and many others in religious discussion and speculation.

Accepting the invitation to preach in Hanover County, Whitefield politely wrote to the Reverend Patrick Henry to announce his coming and ask if he might use St. Paul's Parish church for services. This placed young Patrick's uncle in a quandary.

He had no use at all for "New Lights." Yet, Whitefield was not a "notorious heretic," not a Dissenter, but a renowned Church of England clergyman in good standing, even if that standing was low in the eyes of his ecclesiastical superiors who scowled at his "enthusiasm," especially when exercised in huge "tumultuous" open-air meetings before crowds of 20,000 or more. It was the view of the Archbishop of Canterbury and of those down the chain of hierarchical command that good Anglicans should worship sedately, take communion once a month in the quiet parish church, and keep far away from newfangled notions about spreading the Gospel through meetings in fields, prisons, and such places.

The Reverend Patrick Henry could not very well refuse a fellow Anglican clergyman's request to use St. Paul's, especially since the commissary himself had granted Whitefield permission to preach at Williamsburg in the Bruton Parish church. Not knowing what to do, the rector decided to temporize and try to find a way out. He wrote a rather impudent letter to inform Whitefield that if he would come to the parsonage for an interview, then it could be decided whether or not it was "proper" to grant his request for the use of St. Paul's.

Brushing off the suggestion that he submit to being questioned about his character and tenets of faith by an obscure country parson, Whitefield replied with the simple announcement that on Sunday next he would preach in the parish—if not in the church, then in the churchyard. As the "Great Awakener" was determined to come, the Reverend Henry hastily capitulated and opened the doors of St. Paul's. But the nervous rector made one request—that Whitefield include in his service "some use of the Book of Common Prayer, etc."

Giving assurance that he always did so, Whitefield came and delivered a thundering sermon in St. Paul's, making a second address to the large overflow crowd in the churchyard. More people attended out of curiosity perhaps than from any serious interest in Whitefield's doctrinal views. His mere presence was attraction enough. After all, it was not every day that people in the backwoods had an opportunity to hear a great orator renowned on both sides of the Atlantic. Virginians in general, scantily supplied with reading matter, loved to listen to a good speaker, whether they agreed with his opinions or not.

Whether young Pat Henry, aged nine, attended Whitefield's services in his uncle's church is not known. But his mother Sarah, who had charmed Colonel William Byrd II as "Widow Syme," no doubt did. She appreciated good sermons, had an interest in religion, and was not a traditionalist in her views. In her family there appears to have been a bit of a Dissenting streak. About this time her father, Isaac ("Bald Ike") Winston, a highly respected planter, got into trouble before the General Court and drew a fine because "unlicensed" religious meetings had been held in his house.

During his visit, Whitefield preached rousing sermons to large audiences in other parts of the area. These, and Samuel Morris' "reading houses," and the increasingly numerous "unlawful" meetings of

Baptists and others, aroused considerable religious "enthusiasm" in Hanover and adjoining counties. This led, in turn, to the coming of another eloquent and distinguished preacher, the Reverend Samuel Davies, who arrived in Hanover in 1747, two years after Whitefield's brief visit.

A young man of twenty-two, born in Pennsylvania, trained for the Presbyterian ministry, Davies went to Williamsburg to obtain a license to preach as a Dissenter. After some strong objections, raised principally by Attorney General Peyton Randolph, he acquired a license and came to reside in Hanover County where he soon organized seven active and growing congregations.

As the Reverend Patrick Henry viewed it, Whitefield's short visit was bad enough, but Davies' permanent ministrations in the neighborhood were anathema. Rector Henry complained to the commissary that such a person as Davies should never have been allowed to come into the county and upset St. Paul's parish, that he was an upstart, an unwelcome intruder, another of those "pretended" ministers who made such a nuisance of themselves "by holding numerous Assemblies, particularly of the Common People, upon a pretended religious account."

It must have shocked—indeed, insulted—the irate rector that his sister-in-law, Sarah Henry, preferred Davies' sermons and services to his own. On Sundays, while the Henrys were still at Studley Farm, she would drive to the Fork Church, or to the Providence Church, to hear Davies preach, "riding in a double gig, taking with her young Patrick, who, from the first, showed a high appreciation of the preacher. Returning from church, she would make him give the text and a recapitulation of the discourse." As a relative remarked, "she could have done her son no greater service."

A learned man, ranging widely in his "discourse" into matters both secular and divine, Davies opened a whole new world to young Patrick Henry. The latter learned from him the powers of speech and the art of speaking—the organization of thought, the use of language, the music of words, the use of restrained gesture and of clear and measured enunciation. Henry always regarded Davies as the greatest orator he ever heard, which was high praise from one who became one of the greatest himself.

Davies remained in the Hanover area during Henry's formative years, until 1759, when he departed to succeed the Reverend Jonathan Edwards, that great breather of hellfire, as president of the College of New Jersey, the original unit of Princeton University.

Princeton appears to have been a rather unhealthy spot at the time, especially for college presidents. Edwards had been in office little more than a month when he died of smallpox; Davies, a little more than a year when he died of pneumonia.

3. Two Penny Law

Under a law passed in 1696, all Anglican ministers received a salary of 16,000 pounds of tobacco a year, collected under the direction of the vestry in each parish. For the support of the parish Establishment, not only to pay salaries but to build and maintain churches and parsonages, the vestries levied a tithe, or tax, on all males, free or slave, aged sixteen or more. Masters paid tithes for each male slave in that age group.

Considered in terms of salary, there were two kinds of parishes —"Orinoco" and "sweet-scented," so called for the kind of tobacco predominantly grown in each. Parsons preferred the "sweet-scented" because that variety of tobacco brought better prices.

A parson's income fluctuated as tobacco prices rose and fell. There was no general complaint about this, for there was a rough equity here. When the planters prospered, so did the parsons. When tobacco prices fell, incomes shrank in roughly the same ratio.

Then came a threat of economic-financial crisis. In 1755, it appeared that because of adverse weather conditions, principally drought, Virginia was going to have a very small tobacco crop. This raised many serious problems. The colony's economy was based on the "filthy weed," as James I termed it—or "on smoke," in Charles I's phrase. But "on smoke" the Virginia planters had succeeded in building a highly profitable trade. Tobacco had a ready market in Britain, and funds realized from its sale there were used to buy and bring back necessaries and luxuries.

In the colony, tobacco was not only a valuable commodity but served as a medium of exchange. Business transactions, in large part, were negotiated in terms of tobacco. For some years the price of tobacco had averaged about two pence a pound. But if the 1755 crop turned out to be as short as expected, the resulting scarcity would cause tobacco prices to rise suddenly and steeply, to the disadvantage of those who had obligations to pay in terms of tobacco. Everybody was worried, particularly the poorer people.

To anticipate possible hardship, the House of Burgesses proposed a measure called the Option Act, under which taxes, debts, fees, and other obligations could be paid either in tobacco or in money, "as best suited"—meaning, whichever was cheaper.

Furthermore, when translating tobacco terms into money terms, tobacco was to be arbitrarily rated at two pence a pound, far less than its anticipated market price. The Two Penny Law applied only to payment of taxes, debts, and other contractual obligations. Tobacco could be sold in the open market for whatever price it might bring.

The proposed Option Act aroused an immediate outcry from the parsons, who proceeded to make themselves widely unpopular. They were so ill-advised as to be publicly jubilant about the impending scarcity, regarding it as the sign of a benign "Providence," for it might double or triple their incomes by enhancing the value of the 16,000 pounds of tobacco they received each year as salary.

Their golden dreams vanished with the introduction of the Two Penny Law. That law, they protested, was "unfair" to them. When tobacco prices fell, their incomes suffered, and the General Assembly never did anything to help them.* And now when, "in the course of Providence," they might enjoy a bit of profit and "be set free of debt, or be enabled to buy a few books," they were to be denied their "just expectations and lawful rights." Theirs was a "peculiar case," they said. When other men's incomes fell, they could go out and find odd jobs to do. Parsons could not do so because of the "dignity and sacred character" of their calling.

The Reverend Patrick Henry joined about a dozen prominent parsons in publishing a denunciation of the proposed Two Penny Law as "a breaking in upon the Establishment, an insult to the Royal Prerogative and contrary to the liberty of the subject, as well as to natural Justice & Equity."

While the Two Penny Law was still under consideration, the parsons asked that a delegation of them be received by the House to speak on the matter. This was a reasonable request, and ordinarily would have been granted. But all of the Burgesses—even those opposed to the Option Act—were blazing mad at some of the parsons' spokesmen and refused to receive any of them.

A leader in the protest, the Reverend Mr. Rowe, professor of divinity at the College of William and Mary, went about Williamsburg

* Nor, for that matter, had the Assembly ever done anything to help planters and others hurt when tobacco prices fell. The parsons plainly thought themselves entitled to special status.

asking in public how many Burgesses, and which ones, ought to be hanged. No one but a "scoundrel" would think of voting for the Two Penny Law. If any such came to him to take communion, he would turn them away.

Outraged, the Burgesses, all of them Anglicans, threatened Rowe with jail for contempt of the House. When the latter hastily apologized, he escaped imprisonment and got off with nothing more than a sharp censure. But this incident and other rather similar ones were not soon forgotten. The parsons were, to say the least, tactless.

After the Two Penny Law had passed, parsons waited on Governor Dinwiddie and more or less peremptorily insisted that he veto the measure. Though Dinwiddie did not like the bill, he declined to act, saying "I do not want to have the people on my back." It is plain that, whatever the parsons' arguments and objections, the bill had wide popular support, even being favored by Grandees sitting in the House or on the Governor's Council.

Having failed to persuade Governor Dinwiddie to act, the parsons' leaders went over his head and petitioned the Crown to strike down the Option Act. Under the law, no substantive enactment of the General Assembly was valid until it had been signed by the King. Assembly measures were reviewed by the Board of Trade, then by the Privy Council, and finally passed on with recommendations to the King to approve or disapprove.

Often it was a year or two, sometimes three or four, before Virginians knew whether a General Assembly enactment was law or not. This caused troublesome uncertainties on matters requiring immediate decision. The Assembly had recently asked if minor legislation on local matters could be put into effect without waiting for royal sanction. No! came the flat reply from the Crown.

Well, there was a way of avoiding uncertainty and delay in the existing emergency. First, the Two Penny Law was passed without the usual suspending clause, under which a measure had not the force of law until signed by His Majesty. Second, the Option Act would run for only ten months, until the next tobacco harvest was in, by which time the crisis presumably would be over.

If word later came that the King disapproved of the measure, the point would be largely academic. The law would have lapsed and be no longer on the books. Meantime, it would have served its emergency purpose. By the time word arrived that the King had pronounced the Two Penny Law to be "no law" the point was doubly academic. Not only had the law lapsed; it had not been used.

Contrary to every expectation, the 1755 tobacco crop turned out to be a good one. There was no shortage. Obligations were met in the usual way. Quiet was restored, and it seemed that the Two Penny issue was dead and buried.

But three years later, in 1758, Virginia faced another acute tobacco shortage. In spite of the King's veto of the first Two Penny Act, the Assembly passed another, again without the suspending clause. This one was to run for twelve months. Again the parsons raised a loud protest, and again went over the heads of colonial authorities in making appeals to the Privy Council and to the King asking for "justice."

In appealing to the Crown to strike down the Two Penny Law once and for all, the parsons were on sound constitutional ground. But they were getting deeper into a damaging political position in seeking intervention from London. In Virginia and all the colonies there was a rising desire for more home rule, for a larger measure of self-government in their internal affairs. Even some of their strongest supporters felt it very unwise of the parsons to keep calling for British intervention in a matter of domestic concern.

This time, the Two Penny Law was used, for the need was great. The 1758 tobacco crop was a disaster. Times were hard; taxes had gone up to help pay for the French and Indian War. While in effect, the Option Act relieved distress and measurably helped most Virginians, leaving only the parsons dissatisfied and still grumbling.

More than a year after the lapse of the Option Act, word arrived that the King, in stronger terms than before, had ruled that the second Two Penny Law, like the first, was "no law." This encouraged the parsons in the hope that they could collect back pay on their 1758 salaries. Again they appealed to London, asking the Privy Council for counsel on how they should proceed. The Council advised them to bring damage suits, individually, in the Virginia courts, adding that if they did not get satisfaction there, they should again appeal to the Council and the King.

A suit brought before the General Court in Williamsburg was dismissed on a legal technicality, whereupon the plaintiff appealed to the King to overrule the decision of the General Court as he had the enactments of the General Assembly. Three suits were brought in the county courts. The first two were inconclusive; in one, the parson was awarded some damages; in the other, none at all. In the third case, filed in Hanover County, young Patrick Henry was to enjoy his first great triumph and make a name for himself as "the People's Advocate."

4. The Parsons' Cause

The Hanover County suit, filed on April 1, 1762, three years after the lapse of the Two Penny Law, was brought by the Reverend James Fontaine Maury, rector of Fredericksville, a large parish that lay largely in neighboring Louisa County.

Unlike so many of his misfit colleagues, the Reverend Maury was a distinguished and highly respected man, sincerely religious, exemplary in his public and private life. He was also a learned man in many fields. Interested in education and also in increasing his income (he had twelve children), he had established and was conducting an excellent classical school for older boys, having as pupils a number of teen-agers who went on to notable careers. The most brilliant and scholarly of his students was young Tom Jefferson, who studied at Maury's school for two years before leaving to enter the College of William and Mary.

Maury was, said Jefferson, "a correct classical scholar"—so "classical," indeed, that he gave to his slaves such names as Cato, Clio, Ajax, Scipio, and Cicero. Jefferson also remembered him as being "an harassed if not unhappy man," worried about money, and inveighing against the inequities and iniquities of the Two Penny Law.

Hoping to get back pay on his 1758 salary, Maury first applied to his parish vestry, which declared itself powerless to do anything. He then applied to the two collectors of tithes in the parish, Thomas Johnson and Tarleton Brown. When they said the matter was beyond their authority, Maury decided to bring court action, choosing to file suit not in Louisa County where he lived, but in Hanover County, which he was entitled to do because a small part of his parish lay in that county.

Why Maury made this choice is a mystery. He certainly knew that Hanover County had been a center of Dissenters and "New Lights" for almost twenty years, ever since Whitefield's momentous visit in 1745 and the beginning of the Reverend Samuel Davies' long pastorate in 1747. He certainly knew that he had not endeared himself to Baptists, Presbyterians, and "New Lights" by recently publishing a blast against them. If he did not know, he would soon find out.

After nineteen months' delay caused by legal formalities, Maury's suit came to trial at Hanover Courthouse on November 3, 1763. To represent him as plaintiff, Maury had engaged able counsel, a devout Anglican, Peter Lyons, later a distinguished judge in the higher courts. The trial was brief, with Patrick Henry participating in no way except perhaps as an interested observer, for his father, John Henry, was presiding on the Bench. Having heard the arguments, the judges handed down their decision, agreed with the King that the Two Penny Law was "no law," and never had been. The plaintiff was therefore plainly entitled to recover any damages he had suffered under the "no law."

The decision delighted Maury, of course, and there was general rejoicing among the parsons in the colony when they heard of it. Here was the first clear unequivocal decision in a Virginia court on the question–a decision that could be effectively cited as precedent in parsons' suits brought elsewhere. The road, at last, seemed clear.

To conclude the Maury case, all that remained to be done was for the judges to call a special session and impanel a petit jury to determine the amount of damages to which Maury was entitled. That seemed to present no problem beyond simple mathematics; i.e., to figure the difference between what Maury had been paid under the Two Penny Law and what he should have received on his tobacco if sold at then prevailing market prices.

The defendants in the suit, the two Fredericksville parish collectors, Thomas Johnson and Tarleton Brown, had been represented by John Lewis, an experienced country lawyer. Not seeing much to do in view of the court's decision, Lewis decided to withdraw as counsel for the defense and handed the case over to his young friend, Patrick Henry. Let him try to do what he could with it.

With the second trial set for December 1, Henry had little more than three weeks in which to prepare whatever arguments he could develop in defense of an apparently hopeless cause. For that purpose, he did not have to dig into law books and come up with citations on statutory or constitutional questions. The point of law on the Option Act had been decided by the Hanover Court. There was no use in arguing that. Other grounds would have to be found for argument.

In preparing his case, Henry consulted no one, keeping his own counsel. How he evolved his argument is not known. But it is evident from what he later said that he had read and very thoughtfully pondered a pamphlet published in Williamsburg in 1760, "A Letter to the Clergy of Virginia," written by Richard Bland, a Tidewater Grandee, a veteran and very influential member of the House of Burgesses, an accepted authority on legal and constitutional matters.

A tireless scholar, Bland had "something of the look of the musty old Parchments which he handleth and studieth much," said a friend. Because he knew so much about the colony from its beginning, had delved so deeply into its history, he was known to some as "the Virginia Antiquarian." But there was nothing antiquarian about his lines of thought.

His "Letter" dealt with the parsons' loud protests against the Two Penny Law. As principal author of that law, he advised the parsons to cease their clamor about it. It was true, he admitted, that the King had declared the law invalid. In ordinary course, the King's instructions ought to be obeyed. But in times of extreme emergency, there was a higher law, and that was the right of the people to take what steps they thought necessary to assure their safety and welfare. Echoing John Locke's *On Civil Government,** Bland had written:

"As *salus populi est suprema lex,* where Necessity prevails, every Consideration must give Place to it, and even these [royal] Instructions may be deviated from with impunity." This was "so evident to reason and so fundamental a Rule in the *English* Constitution," said Bland blandly, "that it would be losing of time to produce Instances of it." Patrick Henry accepted and would soon brilliantly apply the principle that "the safety of the people is the supreme law."

On December 1, 1763, the hamlet of Hanover Courthouse filled up with a large crowd—country squires and humbler people—interested in hearing the *finale* of an important case that could affect them all. If Maury won his suit for damages in any substantial amount, they would have to be taxed to pay the damages.

Those attending the trial included a score of parsons from many parts of the colony. All were in a confident mood, looking forward to enjoying Maury's triumph, which would be theirs, too. They would be vindicated and might collect some back pay as well.

According to an account written years later, the Reverend Patrick

---

* Locke had written to justify the Glorious Revolution of 1688 which had deposed James II, the last of the wrongheaded and always arbitrary opinionated Stuarts. In arguing about government in general, Locke theorized about its sources of authority, its legitimate powers, the social-compact obligations between the ruler and the ruled, and the "inalienable" right of the people to resist tyranny and oppression.

Henry would certainly have agreed when Jefferson said: "Locke's little book is perfect as far as it goes."

Henry, Jefferson, John Adams, Sam Adams, and others would soon go much farther.

Henry came from his parsonage at Mount Pleasant nearby and had just stepped from his carriage when he was spied by young Henry who hastened over and asked his uncle not to attend the trial.

"Why so?" asked the rector.

"Because, Sir, . . . I fear that I shall be too much overawed by your presence to be able to do my duty to my clients; besides, Sir, I shall be obliged to say some hard things of the clergy, and I am very unwilling to give pain to your feelings. . . ."

"Why, Patrick, as to your saying hard things of the clergy, I advise you to let that alone; take my word for it, you will do yourself more harm than you will them.

"As to my leaving the ground, I fear, my boy, that my presence could neither do you harm nor good in such a cause. However, since you seem to think otherwise, and desire it of me so earnestly, you shall be gratified."* With that, he wheeled about and drove home, and was thus spared hearing some uncommonly harsh things about the clergy.

Proceedings began with a rather heated argument about jury selection. When ordered by the Court, the sheriff set about rounding up twelve "honest men and true" to sit in the jury box. He first went into "a public room"—perhaps the taproom in Shelton's tavern—where some "Gentlemen" were present, and talked with one of them. When the latter begged off, the sheriff talked to no more of the "Gentlemen," Maury complained, but went "among the vulgar Herd." Getting a look at the list of prospective jurors, Maury protested to the sheriff:

"These are not such jurors as the Court directed you to get. I have never before heard of but one of them."

Maury and his counsel, Peter Lyons, then complained to the judges, at which point Henry rose to insist that those on the sheriff's list were "honest men, and therefore unexceptionable." The judges agreed, and those selected were "called to the Book, and sworn."

If Maury and Lyons had been better acquainted with the neighborhood, they would almost certainly have been sustained in challenging some of those placed in the box. At least three of them were well-known Dissenters or "Anglican New Lights"—Samuel Morris, founder of the revivalist "reading houses;" George Dabney, a New Light and Henry's cousin and friend from boyhood; and Roger

---

* This story, sounding a bit apocryphal, came from Samuel Meredith, who wrote that he was with Henry while talking with his uncle.

Shackelford, who had been up on charges of allowing a Dissenter to preach in his house.

As the trial opened, the many visiting parsons were smiling. They had been given places of honor up front, being seated on either side of the judges on the dais, facing the crowded benches in the courtroom.

Peter Lyons rose majestically. Irish-born, speaking with a charming brogue, a large and imposing man, tall and broad and round, Falstaffian in his dimensions, weighing almost 300 pounds, he was "renowned for his refined politeness." Disappointingly for the crowd, which had come to see fireworks, Lyons had not much to say, merely submitting various documents as evidence on matters that no one contested:

That a parish levy had been ordered for the year in question; that the levy had been made; that the defendants, Johnson and Brown, had collected it; that they had paid Maury his salary under the Two Penny Law; that if he had been paid at the rate of the market price of tobacco, he would have received three times more; that, in view of the recent court decision, he should have been paid at the market rate.

Rising for the defense, Henry submitted a signed receipt showing that Maury had been paid £144 for his 1758 salary, and sat down—to the amazement of everybody, judges and all.

Was that all he was going to say and do? If so, the trial was as good as over. The crowd was disappointed. Why had anybody bothered to come at all?

Rising again to make a final argument and plea for his client, Lyons pointed out to the jury that under the Two Penny Law the Reverend Maury had been paid £144; but for that "no law," he would have received about £450; that the jury should therefore award him back pay for some £300 [$9,000]—a sizable sum.

Lyons would have been wise if he had rested his case here. Instead, he went into a long "highly wrought" speech in praise of the Anglican Establishment in general, extolling all of its works, its tender concern for the souls and welfare of the common people, the zeal of its clergy, their charity and fine Christian character. The Establishment merited the respect and support of all.

If Henry had prayed for it, he could not have asked for a better opening for his attack.

Rising slowly, Henry made a bow to the Bench where his father was presiding and, walking with his characteristic slight stoop, sauntered toward the jury box. The courtroom was quiet and expectant, with everybody wondering what he was going to say. After all, what could he say? Everything relevant, it seemed, had already been said.

To get one view of an historic scene, let us sail aloft with Wirt in his big hot-air balloon:

> The array before Mr. Henry's eyes was now most fearful. On the bench sat more than twenty clergymen, the most learned [?] men in the colony . . . The courthouse was crowded with an overwhelming multitude . . . But there was something still more disconcerting than all this; for in the chair of the presiding magistrate sat no other person than his own father [his "own" father, imagine that!]
>
> And now came on the first trial of Patrick Henry's strength . . . Curiosity was on tiptoe . . . No one had ever heard him speak [he had been speaking in a number of courts for almost four years now, though never before such a large and interested audience].
>
> He rose very awkwardly, and faltered much in his exordium [Henry always had trouble with his "exordium," as Wirt liked to call a speaker's opening remarks]. The people hung their heads at so unpromising a commencement; the clergy were observed to exchange sly looks with each other; and his father is described as having almost sunk with confusion from his seat."

But the embarrassments of the people and of Henry's father were "of short duration," Wirt assures us, and soon gave way to feelings of a very different character:

> For now were those wonderful faculties he possessed, for the first time, developed; and was first witnessed that mysterious and almost supernatural transformation of appearance, which the fire of his own eloquence never failed to work in him.
>
> For as his mind rolled along, and began to glow from its own action, all the *exuviae* of the clown [!] seemed to shed themselves spontaneously.

Henry's posture became "erect and lofty"; his countenance shone with "nobleness and grandeur"; he was "graceful, bold, and commanding" in his every attitude and gesture.

> There was lightning in his eyes which seemed to rive the spectator . . . In the tones of his voice, but more especially in his emphasis, there was a peculiar charm, a magic . . .

> Add to all these, his wonder-working fancy, and the peculiar phraseology in which he clothed his images; for he painted to the heart with a force that almost petrified it.
>
> [People] began to look up; then to look at each other with surprise, as if doubting the evidence of their senses; then, attracted by some strong gesture, struck by some majestic attitude, fascinated by the spell of his eye, the charm of his emphasis, and the varied and commanding expression of his countenance, they could look away no more, . . . all of their senses listening and riveted upon the speaker, as if to catch the least strain of some heavenly visitant[!] . . .
>
> The mockery of the clergy was soon turned into alarm . . . As for his father, such was his surprise, such his amazement, such his rapture, that forgetting where he was, and the character he was filling, tears of ecstasy streamed down his cheeks.

All of this, said Wirt, left the jury "completely bewildered." And well it might if the "heavenly visitant" performed as described. Getting back down to earth, this is what happened at the trial. And it was dramatic enough without any splashes of purple prose.

According to "good little Mr. Maury," Patrick Henry "harangued" the jury for an hour and confused the issue by bringing up "points as much out of his own depth, and that of the jury, as they were foreign from the purpose."*

On a strictly legalistic basis, Henry's points were out of order, "foreign from the purpose," which was only to determine the amount that Maury should receive in back pay on his 1758 salary.

Henry chose to discuss the matter on other grounds. The Two Penny Law, he said, was

> a law of general utility and could not, consistently with the original compact between the King and the people, stipulating protection on the one hand and obedience on the other, be annulled. The King, by disallowing acts of this salutary nature,

---

* This paragraph and those that follow are based on a long letter written by Maury to a fellow parson twelve days after the trial. He wrote, it is obvious, from notes made either at the trial or a few days later. Though his account has evident bias, it is, for the most part, fundamentally credible. In his letter Maury noted:

"You will observe I do not pretend to remember his [Henry's] words, but take this to be the sum and substance . . . of his labored oration."

> from being the father of his people, degenerates into a tyrant and forfeits all right to his subjects' obedience.

Hearing this, "the more sober part of the audience were struck with horror," according to Maury. Peter Lyons jumped to his feet and called with "honest warmth" to the Bench:

"The gentleman has spoken treason."

Lyons remarked his astonishment "that their Worships could hear it without emotion or any other mark of dissatisfaction." Far from being called to account, Henry was allowed to go on, so Maury complained, "in the same treasonable & licentious Strain without interference from the Bench—nay, even without receiving the least exterior token of their Disapprobation."

What was quite as bad, said Maury, "One of the jury, too, was so highly pleased with these doctrines that, as I was afterwards told, he every now and then gave the traitorous Declaimer a nod of Approbation." Henry next attacked the State Church in its entirety:

> The only use of an Established Church and clergy in society is to enforce obedience to civil sanctions and the observance of those which are called duties of imperfect obligation. When a Clergy ceases to answer these ends, the Community have no further need of their Ministry and may justly strip them of their appointments.
>
> The Clergy of Virginia in this particular instance of their refusing to acquiesce in the law in question have been so far from answering that they have most notoriously counteracted those great ends of their institution.

Far from being honored as "useful members of the State," Virginia parsons should be regarded as enemies of the community:

> We have heard a great deal about the benevolence of our reverend clergy.*
>
> But how is this manifested?
>
> Do they manifest their zeal in the cause of religion and humanity by practising the mild and benevolent precepts of the Gospel of Jesus Christ? Do they feed the hungry, or clothe the naked?
>
> Oh no, Gentlemen. Instead of feeding the hungry and cloth-

---

* Referring to Peter Lyons' "highly wrought" speech about the virtues of the Establishment.

> ing the naked, these rapacious harpies would, were their powers equal to their will, snatch from the hearth of their honest parishioner his last hoe-cake, from the widow and her orphan children their last milch cow,* and the last bed—nay, the last blanket—from the lying-in woman.

Court proceedings were interrupted at this point. The score of parsons seated up front, facing Henry, flushed with anger and began talking animatedly among themselves. Were they going to sit there and quietly endure such insults?

Suddenly, they rose and moved to depart as a body. As they stalked down the aisle toward the door, trying to act as dignified as possible, there must have been many a smile and perhaps some audible snickers among the "vulgar Herd" on the crowded benches in the courtroom. Perhaps Henry had trouble repressing a smile as he watched the red-faced "black coats" making for the door.

Resuming, Henry began talking specifically about the plaintiff, "good little Mr. Maury." However good he might be as a person and exemplary as a parson, he should not be given any "countenance, protection, or damages."

Rather, he should be punished "with signal severity" for his presumption in daring to challenge the "salutary" Two Penny Law. Such an example should be made of him "as may hereafter be a warning to him and his brethren not to have the temerity, for the future, to dispute the validity of such laws authenticated by the only authority [the General Assembly] which can give force to laws for the government of this colony."

In conclusion, Henry pointed out to the jury that it was under no legal compulsion to award any damages at all. That matter was entirely within its discretion. He added that, in his opinion, the plaintiff was not entitled to any damages. If the jury decided otherwise, then let the damages be merely nominal—not more than a farthing [5¢].

After a final plea by Peter Lyons, the jury retired and returned five minutes later with its verdict. Technically, Henry lost the case. The jury did not follow his recommendations. It decided that the Reverend Maury was entitled to damages, and also that a farthing was not enough. It upped the award and made it one penny [20¢].

This was a mockery, and it was meant to be. The parsons might have the King's law on their side. But as others had accepted the

* If Henry actually used this widow-orphan tag, it was unworthy of him.

emergency restrictions of the Two Penny Law with good grace, the parsons were not to be considered a "peculiar case."

The verdict dealt Maury and his counsel a stunning blow. Lyons was on his feet to protest to the Bench that the verdict was contrary to the evidence, that the case should be returned to the jury. When the judges declined to do that, Lyons demanded that a new trial be ordered. The judges again declined to act, observing that if Maury wished, he might appeal the case to the General Court in Williamsburg.

There was talk of doing this, but nothing came of it. Also, Maury and his friends "more than hinted" that they were going to bring charges of treason against Henry. They went so far as to round up witnesses willing to testify that during the trial Henry had denounced the King as a "tyrant." But nothing came of this, either.

The Parsons' Cause was as good as dead, but it continued to be pressed elsewhere, through appeals to the Privy Council. The item remained on the Council's agenda for another four years, until 1767, when the Council decided to drop it, quietly, on technical grounds.

The members of the Council had more important things to think about in American affairs than the complaints of a few score Virginia parsons in a case almost ten years old. There was trouble enough without reviving controversy about the Two Penny Law. There had been an explosion about the "infamous" Stamp Tax, and now Americans in all the colonies were organizing to resist payment of the "execrable" Townshend duties.

While the question about the official status of the Church of England in Virginia had not been directly raised in the trial at Hanover Courthouse, that question was implicit in the proceedings. Though few realized it at the moment, the Establishment had been given notice that its days as a privileged tax-supported semi-feudal institution were numbered.

VII
Getting Out the Vote

. . . old habits were too deeply rooted to be suddenly reformed.

—JAMES MADISON

Henry's unexpected "moral" victory in the Parsons' Cause brought him acclaim in many quarters, especially among friends and neighbors. At the end of the trial, the crowd in the courtroom surrounded him and, "in spite of his own exertions and the continued cry of Order from the sheriff and the Court, bore him out of the courthouse and, raising him on their shoulders, carried him about the Yard, in a kind of electioneering triumph."

And then, no doubt, carried him across the road to Shelton's to stand him on a chair or table, or perhaps on the bar, to celebrate the occasion as the noisy happy crowd drank toast after toast to "the People's Advocate" and forced him to listen dutifully to many long-winded speeches in his praise by those whose tongues "good old John Barleycorn" had loosened.

To this dramatic scene, Maury added an interesting but not very plausible detail. When court adjourned, Henry hurried over and, according to Maury, "apologized to me for what he had said, alleging that his sole view in engaging in the cause and in saying what he had, was to render himself popular. . . .

"You see, then, it is so clear a point in this person's opinion that the ready road to popularity here is to trample under foot the interests of Religion, the rights of the Church, and the prerogatives of the Crown."

As reported, this incident is most unlikely. If there is one thing that can be stated categorically in the light of everything we know about Henry, it is this—that in the sense of the term as used by Maury, Henry never "apologized" to anybody.

It may well be, however, that Henry made it a point to approach Maury to tell him not to take personally the attacks he had made on the parsons in general. Henry well knew that "good little Mr. Maury" was certainly not one of those whom he had described as "rapacious harpies" nesting in the Establishment and preying on the body, soul, and substance of the people.

In his personal feelings and responses, Henry was always notably courteous and friendly toward those whom he opposed in public debate. It would have been considerate and only fair of him in this instance to say something conciliatory to a worthy man whose promising case he had so suddenly and completely shattered, and to assure him that he had not been motivated by any personal animus against him.

Maury's remarks have another interesting aspect—a most ironic one. Maury plainly did not realize the implications of what he was saying when he growled his complaint that a "ready road to popularity" was "to trample under foot the interests of Religion [Anglicism], the rights of the [Established] Church, and the prerogatives of the Crown." Maury, his fellow parsons, and few others yet realized how "ready" that road would soon be.

Whether Henry deliberately courted popularity or not, he now enjoyed it—with a very stimulating effect on his law business. During the next year, he gained many new clients and was now practicing in some ten westerly counties. His steadily rising income made him relatively well-to-do, so that he could now start thinking of leaving Shelton's tavern, where he and his growing family had lived for more than six years. From his father he acquired a sizable tract of cleared land along Roundabout Creek, in neighboring Louisa County, and began making plans to build a house there.

Late in 1764, a year after the Parsons' Cause, Henry was in Williamsburg again for his first visit since taking his bar examinations almost five years before. He had been retained by his old friend, Colonel Nathaniel West Dandridge, to draw up, present, and argue a petition to the House of Burgesses in which the colonel complained that he had lost his seat in the House because of his opponent's illegal electioneering practices.

With an election coming up, Dandridge had announced that he would not seek re-election as a Burgess. Two candidates immediately presented themselves. One was Colonel James Littlepage; the other, a Samuel Overton, who had run for the office before. Littlepage seemed certain to win until Dandridge, changing his mind, announced that he would run again. After a campaign embittered by personalities, Littlepage won by a narrow margin.

Dandridge immediately challenged the validity of the vote, protesting in a petition to the House that Littlepage should not be seated because he had violated the law against using "undue influence" in soliciting votes. The House referred his petition to its Committee on Privileges and Elections, a most important standing committee always composed of seasoned and eminent Burgesses.

On his arrival in Williamsburg, Henry wandered about town like a lost soul, according to a thirdhand account first published by Wirt and still much quoted. Knowing nobody, according to this account, Henry haunted the halls of the Capitol, "dressed in very coarse apparel, . . . so very plain and ordinary in appearance" that no one bothered to inquire, or even to wonder, what brought this backwoodsman to town.

> He was ushered with great state and ceremony into the room of the Committee, whose chairman was Colonel [Richard] Bland, . . . and scarcely was he treated with decent respect except by the Chairman. . . . No one knew anything about him.

This is more of Wirt's "child of Nature" rubbish, as a moment's thought about the known facts makes clear. Henry had previously met and talked with two members of the Elections Committee—Peyton Randolph and George Wythe, who had been his bar examiners some five years before.

Both certainly had some acquaintance with Henry's subsequent career. Unquestionably, Randolph knew of Henry's argument in the Parsons' Cause, for it was his business as attorney general to know, seeing that the verdict at Hanover Courthouse vitally affected similar suits filed in other parts of the colony—suits in which he might have to take a hand.

And George Wythe, a scholar who always kept himself informed about recent court decisions, must have had his attention and curiosity aroused by the verdict in the Parsons' Cause and by Henry's arguments in defeating it. He may well have thought, as others did, that the jury's verdict was a good political decision but that, on legalistic and constitutional grounds, it was bad law.

The chairman of the Elections Committee, Colonel Bland, had good reason to know something about Henry. As a chief author of the Two Penny Law, Bland had spiritedly defended it in his "Letter to the Clergy," using arguments that Henry later echoed. If he had not previously met Henry, or corresponded with him, Bland certainly knew Henry at least by name and reputation, and perhaps took the occasion of their present meeting to congratulate him on giving the Parsons' Cause a lethal blow.

Furthermore, as to Henry being alone in Williamsburg and knowing nobody, it is likely that Colonel Dandridge came with him. Indeed, it would have been strange if he did not. Having been to the trouble and expense of filing a complaint and gathering evidence to support it, he had several good reasons for coming down from Hanover.

First, that he might talk with his many friends among the Burgesses and seek to gain their interest and influence in his behalf. Second, that he might be on hand to take his seat immediately if the Elections Committee decided in his favor.

If Dandridge did not come down from Hanover, he certainly sent letters to his Williamsburg friends telling them of Henry's mission and asking them to assist in forwarding his cause. Henry may have been carrying letters of introduction to some of the more influential Burgesses. It is sheer fantasy to picture Henry arriving in Williamsburg as an unrecognized nobody or that he appeared before the Elections Committee "cold," as the phrase goes.

The Committee was the most distinguished and sharp-minded group that Henry had yet addressed. To its members he presented Dandridge's detailed complaint and argued that Littlepage should not be seated because he had "flagrantly" violated the law that no candidate, "directly or indirectly," should give "money, meat, drink, present, gift, reward, or entertainment . . . in order to be elected."

Committee hearings on the Dandridge complaint brought out interesting details on the electioneering process in Virginia at the time. For one thing, the complaint charged that Littlepage had used "undue influence" in quite literally buying off a rival candidate, Samuel Overton. So long as he and Overton were the only candidates, Littlepage evidently had confidence that he would easily win the election.

But Dandridge's announcement that he had changed his mind about retiring and would run again for the House of Burgesses changed the picture entirely. Votes might be so split that Dandridge would win.

To strengthen his position, Littlepage went to Overton to offer a deal. If Overton withdrew from the race, Littlepage would reimburse him for all the expenses he had incurred in the campaign—and also for the expenses he had incurred in an earlier unsuccessful campaign.

If Overton withdrew, Littlepage agreed to pay him £75 [$2,250] under a written agreement which carried this proviso—Overton was to receive only £50 if "Mr. Henry" ran and was elected.*

The deal required that Overton not only withdraw from the race but go out and actively campaign for Littlepage. This was done satisfactorily, it seems, for Overton was duly paid his bounty of £75. Littlepage made no attempt to deny this deal. There was written evidence against him.

Littlepage was charged with using "undue influence" and demeaning elections in another respect. Candidates for the House, with few exceptions, were "gentlemen," members of richer and older county families. The code among them was that no candidate should go out among the people and personally solicit their votes (shades of our modern handshakers, baby-kissers, blintz-eaters, bubble-top automobilists, and performers on TV, radio, and screen).

Nor were candidates to make any promises to anyone. They did not discuss issues; they had no platform; they did not run on their political views, but on their characters, personalities, and the strength of their family and social connections.

Colonel Littlepage, it appears, had not acted like a "gentleman," for he had gone out all around the county, knocking on doors and soliciting support. Worse, in the eyes of respectable Anglicans, he had paid particular attention to such people as Baptists, Quakers, Presbyterians, and other Dissenters not too happy about the *status quo*. And even worse, he had raised an issue and stirred popular agitation about it, proposing a reform in the tobacco warehouse inspection system.

This system, the anchor of the colony's economy, had been es-

---

* The "Mr. Henry" presumably was young Patrick. It may refer to his father John, however, though the latter had never run for elective office. If the reference was to the younger Henry, as is likely, it reveals that he had become a significant political figure in Hanover County as a result of the popularity he had won as the "People's Advocate" in the Parsons' Cause.

tablished by law in 1731 at a time when the price of Virginia tobacco was declining calamitously, in large part because the average quality of its tobacco had fallen off, thus reducing its value in overseas markets, especially in Britain.

Under the law, licensed tobacco warehouses were established at convenient points along navigable waters where tobacco could readily be loaded for shipment abroad. Each warehouse had two inspectors, and no tobacco could be exported until it had been examined and graded by these inspectors, who had the right to order the burning of bad tobacco to keep it off the market because of its depressing effect on prices.

At first, many planters loudly complained about this law, wishing to sell their tobacco where and how they pleased, as they always had done. But complaints soon died down, for within two years the price of export tobacco more than doubled, and tobacco exports constituted the planters' profit and balance of payments against their usually large debits in Britain.

Planters had their hogsheads of cured tobacco carried or rolled to the nearest warehouse where the hoops and staves of each hogshead were removed and the contents left standing—on an average, some 800 pounds of pressed tobacco. After the tobacco had been sampled and graded, it was put back in the hogshead which was then marked with the name and brand—many were like a cattle brand—of the owner, the grade and net weight of the tobacco, and other pertinent particulars.

The two inspectors then gave the planter a signed receipt, or certificate, for each hogshead accepted and held in the warehouse. This was like having money in the bank, and tobacco certificates, or notes, were readily bought and sold, becoming a chief medium of exchange, being accepted as legal tender in payment of taxes and certain other obligations. The warehouses, indeed, were the only "banks" in Virginia, and the "tobacco money" issued by them was preferred to the colony's usually depreciated paper currency.

During his campaign, Littlepage had inveighed against the warehouse system. He did not object to it as such, but to its administration and management. He shared with many other planters, both large and small, a feeling that merchants, looking for a bargain, exercised too much influence on the inspectors when they were sampling and grading tobacco. Merchants were interested in downgrading all tobacco, even the best, so that they could buy it cheaper.

Littlepage had gone about saying that he intended "to serve the

People that's now so injured by the damned Inspecting Law," because the merchants had "so great influence on the Men called Inspectors," who allowed the merchants "a View or Review on the Tobacco," even after it had passed first inspection.

Littlepage had a remedy for this. In every county having a warehouse, the inspectors were appointed by the county court. They held office "during good behavior," which usually meant for life. They were beyond any popular control. Littlepage proposed a change. Inspectors should not be appointed but elected, and he campaigned by promising that, if sent to Williamsburg, he would do his best to effect this "necessary" reform.

In replying to Dandridge's charge that he had violated the rule against making campaign promises of any kind, Littlepage demolished that by submitting proof that on election day, "just before the Poll was opened, he publickly and openly declared, in the Court House, before a great Number of People, that he did not look upon any of the Promises he had made to the People as binding on him, but that they were all void."*

Dandridge also charged Littlepage with having used "undue influence" in another way. The use of alcoholic and other refreshments and entertainments in virtually buying elections was an old English custom early transplanted in Virginia and all the colonies.

In England, there were scores of "Rotten Boroughs," or Pocket Boroughs, as they were also called. These were well named, for they were literally in the pocket of nobles, squires, and local nabobs. The lords of the manor told "their" people how to vote, which they did unless they wished to get into serious trouble about rental of fields, renewing a lease on a house, and such things. But lords of the manor were usually gracious enough to offer their "free" voters some recompense for bothering to go to the polls—rounds of drink, perhaps, or an open-air feast.

In larger constituencies with a sizable and rather free popular vote, elections to choose a representative to the House of Commons were always a riot. At Westminster, Oxford, and Liverpool there was "beer and mob rule;" at Winchelsea and Rye, "oligarchy and wine rule."

Candidates for a seat in the House of Burgesses at Williamsburg

---

* Many candidates in our day are equally facile in repudiating campaign promises, but not "publickly and openly," and certainly never before the polls are opened. They prefer to sneak off later in a cloud of double-talk.

did not have to buy too many votes. Half the male population could not vote—Negro and Indian slaves and white indentured servants. And, of course, no woman could vote. Nor could all adult freemen because of a property qualification. The franchise was limited to those freeholders owning fifty acres of undeveloped land, or twenty-five acres of developed land with a habitable house on the premises. But as land could be had almost for the asking, particularly in the westerly counties, this property qualification was not too restrictive, and a candidate for office had a sizable number of voters to round up and "influence" if he hoped to get elected.

The use of "influence" in various forms to secure votes—virtually buy them—caused so many disputes and scandals that the Burgesses passed a law against using "undue influence," stating that no candidate should, "directly or indirectly, give money, meat, drink, present, gift, reward, or entertainment . . . in order to be elected." Any successful candidate found guilty of such practices should be unseated by the House.

In his complaint, Dandridge charged that Littlepage, in "flagrant" violation of this law, had been unduly generous in providing meat, drink, and entertainment in his desire "to get out the vote." Every candidate always had a problem in rounding up voters pledged to his support.

In every county, there was just one polling place—in the county courthouse. This entailed a long journey, as much as forty or more miles, for some who wished to cast a ballot. Elections were conducted at some convenient place inside the courthouse. There, behind a large table, sat the election board—the sheriff, with a few ranking county judges on either side. At the ends of the table sat the candidates with their clerks, or "writers," seated nearby. These "writers" kept track of the votes cast. When the weather was warm and pleasant, the table was often moved outside and placed in a shady spot on the courthouse green.

Voters were not registered, but they could be challenged either by the election board or by the candidates as to their qualifications to vote—age (twenty-one), length of residence in the county, and proof of ownership of property of the required minimum. Voters came forward, one by one, to announce for all to hear their choice among the candidates. Everybody knew how each man had voted, and this established a certain sort of honesty in elections. If a voter had accepted meat and drink from one candidate and then voted for another, he was not apt to be offered "refreshments" again, being written off by all as unreliable and "corrupt."

It should be emphasized that the Burgesses were the only popularly elected officers in the colony, which accounts for the relatively large turnout at such elections. Here, Virginians had their only opportunity to speak out by voting for one candidate or another. They had no voice in selecting other government officers.

The Crown appointed the governor and the Governor's Council, which also sat as the General Court, the colony's supreme court. The governor appointed the county judges who, in turn, chose the sheriff, clerk of the court, assessors, tobacco warehouse inspectors, road supervisors, constables, and other lesser county officials. The House of Burgesses symbolized the only form of representative government in the colony, which gave it great strength and influence.

On the eve of the Hanover election, Littlepage had learned that some of his friends were planning to stay home, excusing themselves by saying that it was "too cold weather to go so long a way (it being above twenty-five miles) to the election." Littlepage changed their minds by inviting them to come on the day before the election to spend the night at his house near Hanover Courthouse. A dozen or more appeared, some of them "pretty merry with Liquor," and were warmly welcomed by their host, "though their Entertainment was not more than usual with him."

The company spent a pleasant day and evening together, talking, eating, and drinking, chiefly hard cider. Next day, "some of them drank Drams in the morning, and went merry to the Court House."

Outside the polling place, so the charge ran, Littlepage was equally generous in entertaining other friends, or almost any voter at all. "One Grubbs, a Freeholder," came staggering across the courthouse green loudly announcing that "he was ready to vote for anyone who would give him a Dram." Littlepage's friends evidently got to him before Dandridge's and obtained his promise to vote "right" by buying him a dram, probably in the bar at Shelton's, which always did a very brisk business on election days, even better than on Court Days. When tending bar in earlier years, young Henry in pouring or mixing drinks must have taken an innocent hand in "swinging" many a vote. He was not naïve in such matters.

On hearing the charges against him, Littlepage replied that Dandridge had done some "entertaining," too. This could not be denied and Henry, as the complainant's counsel, chose to ignore it.

What voters liked to find close to the polls was a big and constantly replenished bowl of good strong rum punch, or neat whisky from a barrel, or applejack, wine, beer, or anything else elevating. Along with drinks, cookies and ginger cakes were usually to be had by reaching out a hand. At more elaborate "entertainments," voters were offered tasty bits carved from a barbecued bullock, or from a roasted pig, or from fowl turned a golden brown on the spit. Whoever won an election, "old John Barleycorn" always took a beating, suffering "greatly in the fray," as one unsuccessful candidate observed.

The custom of treating, which all candidates followed in one form or another, some more subtle than others, raised moral and even more perplexing legal problems for the Burgesses. It was certainly a candidate's privilege to entertain his friends if he wished. But what if he entertained them and others "in order to be elected"? There was a fine line to be drawn here, and how was it to be drawn? This question constantly stretched the wits of the House and its Elections Committee.

A leading Burgess, the always sedate and rather conservative Edmund Pendleton, had recently asked, somewhat rhetorically, "if the people were willing to sell their liberties for a bottle of rum."

The "people" could not answer directly, but any number of them felt strongly that if they went to the trouble of going to the polls to vote for a particular candidate, he might at least have the grace to offer them a bit of "refreshment."

A question of reciprocity, even a matter of pride, was involved here. Candidates, almost without exception, were "gentlemen." Being of the squirearchy, the gentry, members of the "better" county families, they had very little to do with the average freeholder except at election time when the latter's vote counted. As they went to the polls, freeholders expected to be courted, to be treated as friends and equals at least for a day. This was, in a sense, their assertion of democracy; their votes did have some weight in the direction of public affairs.

A candidate's failure to offer his supporters proper "entertainment" was regarded as a "want of respect," as an indication of "pride, or parsimony." Voters did not favor stingy candidates who, having ample means to afford it, failed to provide near the polling place something in the line of a "barrel of whisky, . . . knocked in the head," with plenty of tin or iron dippers available.

Whatever the moral and legal questions involved, the simple fact was that a candidate, if he hoped to win, had to do some appropriate entertaining, as learned from experience by George Washington, Thomas Jefferson, James Madison, John Marshall, and many more, including Patrick Henry not long after he appeared before the Elections Committee to argue Dandridge's complaint.

Washington first ran for the House of Burgesses in 1755. He was already something of a popular hero. But in spite of that, he was defeated, largely because he did not do what was expected of him in the way of social amenities. When he ran again in 1758, he won handily, having instructed his agents to see to it that the customary rites on election day were well performed.

His agents did nobly. At a cost of £50 [$1,500], they supplied persuadable voters with 50 gallons of toddy, 28 of rum, 46 of beer, 34 of wine, and some of other things–in all, 160 gallons. As Washington received 361 votes, the amount of free drink represented an average of more than a quart and a half of "good cheer" per voter, and this seems to have been satisfactory.

Later, in first running for the House of Burgesses, young James Madison, always a bit prissy, decided to conduct another kind of campaign, one wholly free of the "corrupting influence of spirituous liquors and other treats," because treating was "inconsistent with the purity of moral and republican principles." He would show "by example," he said, how to establish "a more chaste Mode of conducting elections in Virginia."

Running on "purity" principles, Madison was roundly defeated by an opponent who made his appeal to voters in the traditional manner. To his chagrin and disillusionment, Madison learned that eligible freeholders decidedly preferred free rum to any newfangled notions about "chastity" at the polling place. When he ran again, he triumphed because he followed the example of other successful candidates in "swilling the Planters with bombo," ruefully observing that "old habits were too deeply rooted to be suddenly reformed."

One thing can be said for old Virginia electioneering. Open-minded voters were offered something more substantial, relaxing, warming, and inspiring than stale speeches on the "issues" by narrowly partisan candidates mouthing windy platitudes at insufferable length.

As all candidates were "swilling the Planters," the members of the Elections Committee could not take too seriously Dandridge's complaint that Littlepage should be unseated because he had been overgenerous in his hospitality, that he had used "undue influence" in achieving his end–that is, "in order to get elected."

Speaking in Dandridge's behalf, Henry, according to an account quoted by Wirt, "distinguished himself by a copious and brilliant display on the great subject of the rights of suffrage, superior to anything that had been heard before within those walls."

However that may be, the members of the Elections Committee were not at all impressed. They recommended, and the House agreed, that Dandridge's complaint should be dismissed as "frivolous & vexatious." To express their further displeasure with the evidence and presentation of the complaint, the Burgesses ordered Dandridge to pay costs.

Henry's first venture into political matters was certainly not a success, but he would be back soon to become master of the House almost overnight.

VIII
First Alarm

No tax appears to me so easy
and equitable as a stamp duty . . .
—LORD GEORGE GRENVILLE

While of no great moment in itself, the Dandridge case was important in Henry's career because it took him to Williamsburg at a time when the town was buzzing with talk about an alarming new development.

Word had come from London that the British ministry, headed by Lord George Grenville, intended to impose a new tax on all the colonies. It was not merely a new tax, but a new kind of tax. It would affect almost everybody, and raised a constitutional question of serious concern to the Burgesses as guardians of Virginia's legal rights and traditional privileges.

A year before, early in 1763, Britain had emerged triumphantly victorious from a great war waged in many parts of the globe, the Seven Years' War. That conflict, which caused a mighty shift of empire, had been precipitated on the American frontier by a rash act taken by a young Virginia militia officer, Lieutenant Colonel George Washington, aged twenty-two. The fighting grew out of conflicting claims by Britain and France to the vast midland of the continent. The land belonged to the Indians, of course, but European monarchs never allowed that thought to disturb them as they elaborated their imperial designs for expanding their domain and revenues.

Under a 1612 charter, James I had "graciously granted" Virginia an immense strip of territory 400 miles wide and extending westward from the Atlantic "to the Other Sea"—an area of some 1,200,000 square miles, though at the time no one realized its immensity. The "Other Sea" was presumed to be the fabulous South Sea, which the English thought to lie only a few hundred miles inland.

Later, in 1633, King Charles I carved a large chunk out of Virginia and bestowed it as a semi-feudal fief on a Court favorite, George Calvert, first Baron of Baltimore, who proceeded to found a colony which he named Maryland in honor of the Queen. Virginians were furious about this high-handed business, bitterly complaining that it was an invasion of their charter. When the King blandly asked them to help Baltimore's people in getting settled, a leading Virginia planter threw his hat to the ground, jumped on it, and angrily exclaimed, "A pox on Maryland!" Relations between the two colonies remained very strained for decades.

Still later, in the early 1660s, Charles II took a large slice of Virginia territory along its southern boundary and bestowed it on a Court favorite, Lord Berkeley, who named his principality Carolina in honor of the King, Carolus Rex Secundus.

Even with these substantial subtractions, Virginia still had at least paper claims to a vast territory which, if extended westward to the Mississippi, included all of what is now West Virginia and Kentucky, and roughly the southern half of the present states of Ohio, Indiana, and Illinois.

For more than a century Virginians showed surprisingly little curiosity about the colony's lands to the westward. In early years, a few exploring expeditions were sent out, primarily in the hope of finding gold or the South Sea. But these expeditions never penetrated far beyond the Fall Line, the great geologic fault that sharply divides low-lying tidewater lands from higher rolling piedmont country all along this part of the seaboard.

In 1668, more than sixty years after the founding of Jamestown, Governor Sir William Berkeley led a small mounted exploring party out of Jamestown to look for "gold mynes" and "for ye finding out of the ebbing and flowing of ye waters behind the mountains in order to make a discovery of the South Sea." Berkeley and his men were easily discouraged about prowling the wilderness and, after a short time, turned back, "because of rain."

Except for individual fur trappers and Indian traders, who kept what they learned to themselves, not wishing to see the wilderness opened up and developed, there was little westward exploration until 1716 when, with great fanfare, Governor Alexander Spotswood rode out of Williamsburg at the head of a troop of some fifty "Gentlemen," all resplendently dressed and riding spirited mounts—the romantic and highly romanticized "Knights of the Golden Horseshoe."

Riding along leisurely, galloping off in small parties to hunt deer and other game, stopping occasionally to compete in horse races and other sports, the Knights wound their way on trails over the Blue Ridge Mountains and came down into the fertile Valley of Virginia, veined by the beautiful Shenandoah River, a southern tributary of the Potomac.

Here, on the banks of the river, Governor Spotswood "buried a bottle with a paper inclosed, on which he writ that he took possession of this place in the name of and for King George the First of England." A diary kept by one of the sportive Knights continues:

"We drank the King's health in champagne, and fired a volley; the Princess's name in Burgundy, and fired a volley; and all the rest of the Royal Family in Claret, and fired a volley. We drank the Governor's health, and fired a volley. We had several sorts of liquors, viz: Virginia red wine, Irish usquebaugh,* brandy shrub, two sorts of rum, champagne, Canary, cherry punch, cider, etc."

The Knights, enjoying themselves along the way, taking time out for a hunt or two, wound their way back to Williamsburg where they were honored at a great banquet and fashionable "entertainment" in the Governor's Palace, at public expense. Each of these "intrepid" explorers received, in the form of a pin or a badge, a miniature gold horseshoe studded with jewels, presented to them by Governor Spotswood, who took one for himself.

This showy business was not quite as silly as it sounds. Many Grandees shared Spotswood's opinion that what Virginia most needed for social stability was the establishment of an heraldic aristocratic order, and the first of such orders might be "the Transmontane Order of the Knights of the Golden Horseshoe."

---

* Usquebaugh comes from the Celtic, *uisge beatha,* or water of life. So from Irish-Scottish *uisge* (water) comes "whisky," by a magic transformation.

This idea was stillborn. Most Virginians laughed at it. When the College of Heralds in London heard of it, they sharply reminded Spotswood that knighthoods were not self-created, but only bestowed by the Crown.

Not long after the Golden Horseshoe expedition to the banks of the Shenandoah, the fertile Valley of Virginia began to be occupied by settlers. These were, for the most part, small farmers. Some were Virginians from Tidewater or the Piedmont. But most came from Pennsylvania, being German and Scotch-Irish by birth or descent, with some Welsh Baptists and English Quakers among them. These people brought new blood strains and new views into the colony. In general, they were Dissenters, hostile to the Anglican Establishment, and paid as little attention to the royal governor at Williamsburg as they dared.

By the middle 1740s, settlements had been pushed westward to the foot of the Allegheny Mountains. Some more enterprising Virginians now began looking beyond the mountains, speculatively eyeing the vast Virginia territory there that could be profitably exploited.

In 1749, some larger planters, with rich London merchants as partners, organized the Ohio Company and obtained a grant to 600,000 acres in the upper reaches of the Ohio River watershed. About the same time, Dr. Thomas Walker, a friend and neighbor of the Jeffersons, organized the Loyal Land Company and obtained a grant to 800,000 acres.

Meantime, the French, coming down from Canada, had moved in behind the Alleghenies and laid claim to the whole mid-continent, from the Alleghenies to the Rocky Mountains. Along the Great Lakes and the Ohio and Mississippi Rivers they had built a number of small forts which served also as trading posts, where they sold Indians the goods they wanted in exchange for valuable furs, a profitable trade.

The French did not disturb the Indian pattern of life. As a consequence, they got on very well with most Indian tribes, far better than the English, who seemed possessed by only one idea—drive out the Indians, take over their hunting grounds, and divide these up among white "proprietors," meantime having exterminated as many of the "aborigines" as possible. This, to our disgrace, became American practice and policy as the frontier swept westward to the Pacific.

"The only good Indian is a dead Indian," said our now honored pioneers, and this was not merely a phrase, but a principle of action.

There was never a more ruthless imperialist and white supremacist operation than our expansion westward in accord with what some, who should know better, call "manifest destiny."

It seemed to Virginians and others interested in the Ohio Company, the Loyal Land Company, and others that "manifest destiny" required the removal of French forces and influence in the wilderness beyond the Alleghenies. The governor of Virginia, Robert Dinwiddie, financially interested in the Ohio Company, was decidedly of that opinion and commissioned young George Washington to go into the Ohio country to command the French to cease their "encroachments" there, and get out.

Late in 1753, in frosty weather, Washington and an aide mounted their horses and set off on a 600-mile ride along wilderness trails to have a parley with the French. Finding the French commander of the area at Fort LeBoeuf, Washington delivered Governor Dinwiddie's ultimatum, to which the commander replied that the French had an "absolute design to take possession of the Ohio and, by God, they would do it!"

On his way back to Virginia, Washington kept his eye out for strategic sites which might be fortified to resist French "intrusion" into the Ohio country. Reporting to Dinwiddie, he particularly recommended a most strategic spot, on high ground, where the Allegheny and Monongahela Rivers join to form the Ohio. The governor liked the recommendation and immediately sent out a party of workers who were to build with all speed a fort there at the Forks of the Ohio, in what is now Pittsburgh.

1. French and Indian War

To protect the workers dispatched to the Forks, Dinwiddie next sent out a regiment of militia under the command of Colonel Joshua Fry, a large shareholder in the Loyal Land Company. Along the way, Fry learned that the French had attacked the workers, driven them off, and taken over the half-built fortification, which they enlarged and strengthened, naming it Fort Duquesne.

Colonel Fry, stricken with illness and dying, ordered two companies to press forward with all speed under the second in command, Lieutenant Colonel George Washington. Carrying out orders, Washington advanced to Great Meadows, about forty miles southeast of Fort Duquesne, where his troops threw up some weak breastworks. Learning that a French-Indian reconnoitering party was in the vicinity, Washington personally led a surprise night attack, killing ten of the party and capturing the rest—about a score. The dead included the French commander, the Sieur de Jumonville. The killing of this prominent French knight caused something of a sensation in all the chancellories of Europe.

The shot fired here, without warning and with no attempt at parley, was truly the shot heard round the world, bringing on a great war that had repercussions almost global. As remarked in England at the time by Sir Horace Walpole, historian and diarist: "The volley fired by a young Virginian in the backwoods of America set the world on fire."

Young and inexperienced, evidencing none of the balance and sound judgment that marked his later years, Washington had acted very rashly, for vastly superior forces from Fort Duquesne now came down upon him. Anticipating attack, he had holed up at Great Meadows, hastily building a crude redoubt there, appropriately naming it Fort Necessity.

After a siege lasting only a day, having suffered heavy losses, Washington had to capitulate, accepting the generous terms offered by the French. He and his surviving men were allowed to march off, as Washington rather proudly reported, "with all the honours of war, . . . with our drums beating and our colours flying."

But this was not an auspicious start for what became one of the world's most illustrious military and political careers.

The ministry in London decided that if British claims to western lands were going to be worth a sixpence, the French had to be driven out of Fort Duquesne. The task was assigned to General Edward Braddock, who was given two regiments of seasoned British regulars taken from garrison towns in Ireland. It was thought that these troops, having successfully kept the spirited and turbulent Irish in check, would have no trouble at all in putting French and Indians in their places.

After a conference with four colonial governors in Virginia, in the six-year-old town of Alexandria, Braddock proceeded up the Potomac with a sizable force. It consisted of some 1,400 Redcoats, plus about 700 Colonials and Indian mercenaries, the latter being under the command of Washington, who had recently been promoted and was now a colonel.

General Braddock, like so many of his counterparts before him and since, regarded the military manual as his Bible. He did everything by the book. If Fort Duquesne was to be taken, speed was essential to effect surprise and success. But in plunging into the wilderness, Braddock ordered his columns to follow the prescribed order of march—an order designed for European conditions. Worried by the slow progress being made, Washington remarked with exasperation:

"I find that, instead of pushing on with vigor, without regarding a little rough road, they are halting to level every molehill, and to erect bridges over every creek."

Finally reaching the Monongahela River, Braddock encamped within ten miles of Fort Duquesne. As no signs of the enemy had been seen, he assumed the fort had been abandoned and could be occupied without resistance. Next morning, Washington cautioned him that no sign of the enemy was a bad sign, and ominous, suggesting that he should take the lead with his forces, many of them experienced woodsmen, to scout the neighborhood and occupy the woods ahead.

Scornfully rejecting this advice, detailing Washington and his men to bring up the rear, Braddock sent a column forward, led by a select detachment of 300 resplendent Redcoats under the command of Colonel Horatio Gates.* By noon, this detachment was halfway to Fort Duquesne and swinging along a road through an open wood where there was an undergrowth of tall grass.

Nothing had aroused any apprehension. Everything was quiet until, quite suddenly, soldiers in Gates' advance guard began dropping to the ground from French bullets and Indian arrows hitting them from all sides—from the front, from both flanks, even from the rear. The bewildered European-trained Redcoats raised their muskets but could find no targets to shoot at, except at heads bobbing up in the tall grass or out from behind tall trees—here, there, everywhere.

Braddock hurried up with his main force, followed by Washington and his Colonials. Used to bushfighting, Washington's men immediately broke ranks and literally took to the woods, followed by some more discerning British soldiers, who hoped to take the French and Indians from the rear.

But Braddock would have none of that. It was not according to the book. He ordered his troops to keep massed together and lined up for battle in the form of a hollow square, which offered a fine

---

* Gates later settled in Virginia, joined the Revolutionary cause, and served under Washington as a major general.

stationary target for the attackers. With deadly aim, the French and Indians concentrated on picking off British officers, who could easily be distinguished because they were on horseback and offered such shining targets in their brilliant uniforms.

Whatever his other qualities, Braddock was consistent, persistent, and brave. He remained in the very center of the melee. He had a horse shot out from under him once, twice, three times, and was on his fourth, still shouting absurd commands, when a shot hit him in the chest and he tumbled to the ground with a serious wound, soon dying after being carried to the rear, remarking along the way:

"Who would have thought it! We shall know better how to deal with them another time."

The action lasted only three hours and resulted in complete rout, total defeat. More than half the British and Colonials were killed or seriously wounded. Casualties ran very high among the officers. Only seventeen out of eighty-five escaped death or serious injury. Washington was lucky enough to be the only one on horseback not to be hit or even scratched.

As the army turned tail to flee in wild confusion, Washington organized his force as a rearguard and did his best to fend off the pursuing enemy bent on picking off stragglers, sniping constantly.

Braddock's disastrous defeat along the Monongahela, in the Battle of the Wilderness fought in the summer of 1755, had many repercussions. All Britons, from the King down, were dumbfounded. The French Court, of course, was jubilant. Other European courts studied the debacle to see what national advantage could be gained from it. All agreed that the British reverse was the opening battle in a tremendous struggle for empire, and that fishing in troubled waters might bring some prizes.

Among American colonists, the response was mixed. Certainly, none wished to see an increase in the power and territorial control of the French-Indian alliance. On the other hand, Braddock's resounding defeat might teach the Mother Country a lesson. The haughty British might cease showing such open contempt of the colonists and their opinions, perhaps going so far as to listen to experienced American advice in certain matters, such as the necessity of "bushfighting" on occasion. In commenting on the blow to the prestige of British arms, Benjamin Franklin spoke the thoughts of many in observing:

"This whole transaction gave us Americans the first suspicions that our exalted ideas of the prowess of British regular troops had not been well founded."

In the beginning, the French and Indian War went very badly for British-Colonial forces, which met defeat after defeat, with only a few minor successes. Their rout and losses at Ticonderoga, New York, were almost as disastrous as in the ambush along the Monongahela. The military situation began to improve after 1757 when William Pitt, the "Great Commoner," became head of the British ministry and threw into the task of winning the war his enormous abilities and energies.

Meantime, in the spring of 1756, Britain and France had formally gone to war—with Prussia lined up with Britain; Austria, with France. Later, Spain declared war on Britain, principally with the aim of retaking Gibraltar which the British had seized in 1704. In spite of heavy British war commitments on the Continent, on the high seas, and as far away as India, Pitt sent reinforcements to America, where the tide of battle began to turn.

In 1758, Washington and his Colonials took over Fort Duquesne, or what remained of it after the French had blown up the fort before retreating northward. Fort Niagara and other French outposts fell, one by one. Quebec was taken in 1759. Next year, at Montreal, the French governor general of Canada surrendered himself and his forces. This ended major fighting in the French and Indian War, though skirmishes with the Indians continued all along the frontier from Maine to Georgia.

The Treaty of Paris, signed early in 1763, ended the Seven Years' War from which Britain emerged victorious as the mightiest power in the world. She had countered the French in India. She had acquired East and West Florida from Spain. Of particular interest to her colonials, Britain took over Canada and the territory claimed by France west from the Allegheny Mountains to the Mississippi.*

Pleased to have French power removed, eager to expand and exploit an immense tract of virgin territory no longer in dispute (except with the Indians, the rightful owners), Virginia and other colonies claiming lands to the west received a rude shock when King George

---

* France also ceded to Spain her claims to lands west of the Mississippi, a vast ill-defined and almost wholly unoccupied territory known as Louisiana. Later, Napoleon snatched it back from Spain and then in 1803 sold it for $11,250,000 to President Jefferson in the Louisiana Purchase, probably the best real estate deal in all history. It doubled the area of the United States without any conflict or bloodshed.

II proclaimed that the country beyond the Alleghenies was closed to settlement. Those few already settled there were commanded "forthwith to remove themselves."

As the reason for this, the home government declared that the action had been taken to preserve peace in the area by preventing whites from encroaching on Indian lands—a laudable aim. But another reason was operative, though it could not be publicly declared. Britain hoped to confine the colonists to the Atlantic seaboard. It intended to discourage westward migration, for if the colonists got too far inland, this would tend to weaken their political and commercial dependence on the Mother Country. As the Board of Trade had pointed out to the Privy Council in recommending action on policy involving

". . . that principle which was adopted by this Board, and approved and confirmed by his Majesty immediately after the Treaty of Paris, namely, the confining the western extent of the settlements to such a distance from the seacoast as that those settlements should lie within the reach of trade and commerce of this kingdom, whereby also will be facilitated the exercise of that authority and jurisdiction which is conceived to be necessary for the preservation of the colonies in a due subordination to and dependence upon the Mother Country."

If closing western lands to settlement was a blow, particularly to Virginia, all colonies soon suffered a worse one.

While Britain had gained rich spoils from the Seven Years' War, she had also incurred heavy expenses. The national debt had greatly increased, which pointed to the necessity of higher taxes. The great nobles and lesser country gentry, who between them controlled Parliament, groaned at the prospect of having to pay higher land taxes, a chief source of revenue. As the colonies enjoyed the protection of Empire, why should they not help pay the cost of their "keep"?

It seemed to Parliament that this was a very reasonable and sensible idea. The whole Empire, which had grown up in a haphazard fashion, should be reorganized, reformed, and given more efficient and productive machinery. Under a uniform policy, the colonies should be brought more effectively under the control and the immediate direction of London.

Britain began her reform program by ordering much stricter enforcement of the Navigation Acts, and of the trade laws that narrowly restricted American commerce, at least in theory, if not in practice.

Evading the trade laws, all American seaports, including Norfolk, Virginia's largest town, had been thriving on a widespread profitable smuggling system to the detriment of the Royal Treasury, and to the mounting indignation of British merchants and manufacturers who held, under the trade laws, a virtual monopoly in American markets. Increasing use of writs of assistance—a kind of general, unspecified, "illegal" search warrant employed to track down and seize smuggled goods—created much friction, especially in Boston, Providence, and Newport, all of which were heavily engaged in contraband trade.

Parliament also passed a new Sugar Act that highly incensed the northern colonies—Massachusetts and Rhode Island, in particular. The act threatened their highly profitable and most obnoxious triangular rum-slave-molasses trade.

But the heaviest blow came when Parliament adopted a resolution that "it is just and necessary that a revenue be raised in his Majesty's dominions in America for defraying the expense of defending, protecting, and securing the same," a proposal affecting all the colonies.

2. Stamp Tax

Just how this revenue was to be raised was still an open question, though many in Parliament leaned to the view that "it may be proper to charge certain stamp duties upon them."

The head of the ministry, the Prime Minister,* Lord George Grenville, rather favored the stamp tax. It would be easy to administer and inexpensive to collect. It was not a new or strange form of levy. Britons had been paying stamp duties for years without much complaint about the principle of the tax or the amount of the duties. As such duties constituted a time-tested part of the kingdom's fiscal structure, why not place a stamp tax on the colonies to raise revenue from them? It might be an almost painless way of raising money without arousing contentions and complaints.

Lord Grenville was not doctrinaire about his stamp tax proposal. He wished to be conciliatory. Unlike so many of the Tory courtiers around George III, he had no desire to get into heated arguments with the colonists about their "traditional" rights and "pretended" privileges. What he wanted to obtain was some revenue as simply as possible and with the least commotion.

---

* To avoid repetition of such long phrases as "head of the ministry" or "chief of the administration," the term "Prime Minister" will be used henceforth in these pages, though that term did not become an official title until later.

Able and honest, but quite unimaginative, Grenville approached the question almost wholly from a fiscal and administrative point of view, not comprehending at all the political implications involved. A man of business, he drove to the point, being very meticulous about minor detail and always a bit pedantic, as once remarked by George III, who likewise had a passion for minute detail and was always somewhat pedantic himself. Said the King of his Prime Minister with marked exasperation:

"When he has wearied me for two hours, he looks at his watch to see if he may not tire me for an hour more."

Whether pedant or not, Grenville decided against making an attempt to ram the stamp tax down the colonists' throats. Rather, he would be suave and diplomatic; he would bring them into the discussion and offer them an alternative:

"It is highly reasonable," he informed the colonies, that they "should contribute something toward the charge of protecting themselves, and in aid of the great expense Great Britain has put herself to on their account. No tax appears to me so easy and equitable as a stamp duty . . .

"If the colonists think of any other mode of taxation more convenient to them, and make any proposition of equal efficacy with the stamp duty, I will give it all due consideration."

If Lord Grenville hoped to cozen the colonists into swallowing what they described as "this gilded pill," he was soon disillusioned. His bland invitation to the colonies to express some ideas about how they preferred to be taxed was an attempt to confuse the issue and gloss over the main point, the heart of the matter. They had no wish to discuss whether a stamp tax would be "easy and equitable." They declined to "think of any other mode of taxation more convenient to them." That was irrelevant.

No form of internal and direct tax, imposed on them by Parliament, was "convenient to them." Any such tax should be opposed as a matter of principle. The colonies had their own long-established "constitutional" ways of raising revenue for their own needs and imperial purposes. Those ways had worked well enough, and should not be disturbed by any newfangled "revolutionary" notions about reform.

As early as 1623, four years after being established, the House of Burgesses sitting at Jamestown had quite clearly stated its position: that no one should "lay any taxes or impositions upon the colony, their lands, or commodities other way than by the authority of the

General Assembly, to be levied and employed as the said Assembly shall appoint." This doctrine was declared time and again in Virginia, and was echoed in other colonies. It had become generally accepted that only the general assemblies in the various colonies could directly tax residents in their respective jurisdictions.

At Williamsburg in 1753, the royal governor, Robert Dinwiddie, decided on his own initiative to charge a sizable fee for signing land grants and stamping them with the official seal–a sort of stamp tax. The Burgesses immediately protested that this was "illegal and arbitrary, . . . an Infringement of the Rights of the People, and a grievance highly to be complained of," a plain violation of traditional practice. Retreating before widespread uproar, Dinwiddie went back to signing and sealing land grants without charging a "stamp" fee.

Now, a general and quite explicit stamp tax had been proposed–and this time, for the first time, on the initiative and with the authority of the governing British ministry. To Virginia, as to almost all the colonies, this seemed objectionable not only for what it was, but for what it presaged. One direct internal tax could lead to a second and a third, or even more.

Here, in an American phrase, was the "first alarm," and it led the colonists' leaders to begin thinking seriously about what might happen in all fields and how they could best defend their position. Lord Chancellor Northington had quite frankly laid out Britain's position.

"The colonies," said Lord Northington, "are become too big to be governed by the laws that they at first set out with. They have therefore run into confusion, and it will be the policy of this country to form a new plan of laws for them."

It was not the colonies that had "run into confusion," as events proved, but the home government–a continuing confusion that in little more than a decade cost Britain the better part of her Empire.

Faced with a new situation that threatened their traditional "liberties," the colonies did not quite know what to do. All were agreed, however, that they should protest any measures for direct taxation imposed on them by the British Parliament in which they had no representation.

Colonists had other points of contention with Britain. One concerned slavery. At Williamsburg in 1757, Richard Henry Lee had delivered before the Burgesses an indictment of the whole institution. In particular, he urged that strong measures be taken to stop any further importations of slaves from Africa, or from the British, Spanish, and French West Indies, which were busy markets in this vicious trade.

Lee's proposal had considerable support, even among Grandees who used "shoals" of slaves on their plantations. They preferred, they said, to replenish the supply from their own stock, without introducing any additional workers and breeders. The colony had repeatedly sought to halt or, at least, curtail the slave trade, less for "moral" reasons than from fear of slave insurrections. In some colonies, slaves constituted up to half the population, a cause of continuing apprehension.

But efforts by Virginia and other colonies to curb the slave trade were always thwarted. The Crown had a private as well as a public interest in the business through the Royal African Company, founded in 1662, with the Duke of York (later James II) as president and King Charles II as a principal stockholder. Royal governors received strict instructions to be most vigilant in protecting and forwarding the Royal African Company's lucrative and hideous traffic.

To discourage all such traffic, some colonies sought to impose custom duties on imported slaves. But this "interference" with royal business was sharply struck down in 1731 when the Crown ordered all royal governors to veto any and all acts imposing any restraints.

There was another forced importation that particularly infuriated Virginians—the colony's obligation under law to accept prisoners shipped out from jails in the United Kingdom.

Almost from the founding of Jamestown, prisoners had been dumped in the colony at command of the Crown. In 1670, Virginia succeeded in putting a stop to this. But a half century later, in 1717, Parliament forced the colony to open its doors again to those convicted of certain offenses. Banishment from the Kingdom became a regular form of punishment, with Virginia as the chief receptacle for what it called "scum & scruff" from the streets of London and other places.

Many of these prisoners were merely poor unfortunates, first offenders, caught in making off with a loaf or two of bread, or a warm coat, or a pair of shoes, to relieve their desperate needs. But among these were some hard-case criminals, and this certainly did not improve the colony's repute. In an angry article published in 1751, the *Virginia Gazette* blazed out against Britain:

"Thou art called our Mother Country. But what Mother ever sent Thieves and Villains to accompany her children? In what can Britain show a more Sovereign contempt for us than by emptying their jails into our settlements—unless they would likewise empty their Jakes* on our tables!"

But protests had no effect. From the 1720s to the mid-1770s, some 20,000 "jail-birds" were transported to Virginia. These included, as Virginians remarked, a number of profligate women "from the Bridewell [a prison], from Turnbull Street [London's brothel center], and such like places of education." In his lively novel *Moll Flanders* (1722), Daniel Defoe described the shipment of that celebrated trollop to Virginia for her trumperies, and her adventures there.

Virginia remained Britain's chief penal colony down to the Revolution when a change had to be made. Britain then chose Australia where she established noisome prison camps at Botany Bay and other places. To be transported to Botany Bay was, in the first days of settlement, virtually a death sentence.

Forced importation of slaves, forced acceptance of British convicts, closure of the trans-Allegheny country to settlement were all in the minds of the Burgesses as they met in Williamsburg late in 1764 to consider Lord Grenville's proposed stamp tax and his "honey-drip" suggestion that they might wish to propose an alternative as a "more convenient" way of contributing revenue to the Royal Treasury.

The Burgesses, after considerable discussion of Grenville's proposals, decided that they would register their objections in a Remonstrance to the House of Commons, a Memorial to the House of Lords, and an Address to the King.

All of these were mild in tone, as briefly noted before.

The King was assured that Virginians, as "dutiful and loyal subjects," had "a firm and inviolable attachment to your sacred person and government." Therefore, they entreated him to be "graciously pleased to protect the people of this colony in the enjoyment of their ancient and inestimable right of being governed by such laws, respecting their internal polity and taxation, as are derived from their own consent, with the approbation of their Sovereign . . . a right which as men, and descendants of *Britons,* they have ever quietly possessed."

The proposed stamp tax was "a long & hasty stride" into a new and uncharted field of great concern to the colonists, and should not

---

* Bedroom chamber pots.

be taken. If the Crown needed more revenue from the colonies, there was a customary and accepted way of going about this.

Let the King, as before, inform the colonies about what revenue from them was needed, indicating the amount desired and expressing the "royal desire" that such money would be appropriated by the thirteen provincial legislatures.

The colonies had always been very quick and generous—so they said, but others disagreed—in satisfying the "royal desire," and they would continue to be generous, they said, in appropriating funds "in the usual constitutional manner," but not at the dictate of Parliament.

Speaking in a somewhat apologetic manner, the Burgesses added that in registering their protest against what Britain proposed, they wished to avoid "the least Disposition to any sort of Rudeness."

Protests along similar lines were voiced by other colonies. None was stronger than Virginia's; many were weaker. All had a moderate tone, being designed to persuade the British ministry to change its mind. This was not beyond reasonable hope. After all, schemes to tax the colonies directly had been contemplated before and been abandoned after "due consideration."

Some thirty years before, a proposal had been made to the head of the ministry, the great Sir Robert Walpole, "that the duties of stamps upon parchment and paper in England be extended by Act of Parliament to all the American plantations."

The shrewd and politic Walpole dismissed this with a smile: "I will leave *that* to some of my successors who have more courage than I have, and are less friends to commerce than I am." Walpole went on to explain his colonial policy:

"It has been a maxim with me, during my administration, to encourage the trade of the American colonies in the utmost latitude," even to the point of winking at their persistent violations of the Navigation Acts and trade laws, for if by such trade "they gain £500,000 [$25,000,000] a year, I am convinced that, in two years afterwards, full £250,000 of this will be in his Majesty's Exchequer," through the colonists' necessary purchase of British goods to the enrichment of home manufacturers and merchants.

Thus, "as they increase their foreign trade, more of our produce will be wanted. This is taxing them more agreeably to their own constitutions, and ours."

More recently, during the French and Indian-Seven Years' War, the Prime Minister, William Pitt, had expressed high displeasure with the colonies for what he regarded as their inexcusable delays and halfhearted actions in appropriating funds to help prosecute the war, declaring that something had to be done about the colonies' powers to hold up necessary supplies. He had come to the decided opinion that, after the war, steps should be taken to raise revenue in America by taxes imposed by Parliament, thus bypassing "procrastinating" colonial legislatures.

In 1759, Pitt wrote to Williamsburg to sound out Governor Fauquier on the advisability of such a move. The governor—"the ablest man who ever filled that office," said Jefferson—liked Virginians and got on very well with them. Knowing how they would react, Fauquier cautioned Pitt that if any such move were taken, it would meet with determined opposition and could even provoke considerable popular commotion. Taking this sound advice, Pitt dropped his idea.

There was reason to hope that Lord Grenville, having read and pondered the colonies' objections to his tax scheme, might prove himself to be as wise and circumspect as Pitt and Walpole. Meantime, with their protests off to London, there was nothing to do but wait to see what happened.

Little did the colonists suspect what summary and even contemptuous treatment their petitions would receive from the King, the Lords, and the Commons.

IX
"Treason!"

Tarquin and Caesar had each his Brutus;
Charles the First, his Cromwell;
and George the Third . . .

—PATRICK HENRY

Returning home from Williamsburg after Dandridge and he had lost their appeal to the Elections Committee, Henry busied himself with the usual run of duties. He made the rounds of courthouses in neighboring counties where he had cases pending or other legal matters to tend to. His law practice kept growing, and his income accordingly.

Henry bought from his father a tract of several thousand acres along Roundabout Creek, in adjoining Louisa County.* He contracted to have a house built there for himself and family. No doubt Henry often rode over into Louisa County to see how work was progressing at Round Top, as he named his place.

Henry had other things on his mind. The two Burgesses from Louisa County were brothers, William and Thomas Johnson, of a prominent family, liberal in their views, friends and clients of Henry. In the spring of 1765, William Johnson decided to resign to accept

---

* This was probably a paper transaction, a part payment on loans that Patrick had made to his father, who was frequently in financial straits.

another post, and Henry decided to run for his seat. Though not yet a resident of Louisa County, Henry owned the requisite amount of property to be a voter and officeholder there.

A writ for a special election was issued, and Henry campaigned in the good old Virginia fashion, seeing to it that his "friends" were shown proper respect and provided with becoming "entertainment." Henry noted in his account book after the election:

By Waggoning punch etc. to Louisa	£1. 0. 0
By 1 Loaf Sugar 15/	.15
By 28 Galls. Rum @ 5/	7. 0. 0
	£8.15. 0*

The punch no doubt helped, but Henry must have exercised all of his persuasiveness and personal charm to succeed in inducing forty-one of his Hanover County neighbors and friends, also eligible to vote in Louisa, to journey many miles to vote for him at the county courthouse.

Winning the election, Henry took his seat in the House of Burgesses on or about May 20, 1765, for on that day he was assigned to the Committee for Courts of Justice. Nothing of moment came to the floor until a few days later when a motion was offered for the establishment of a Public Loan Office, "from which monies might be lent on public account, and on good landed security, to individuals."

This seemed like a good idea, and innocent enough. It appeared that the bill, favored by the Grandees, would pass unopposed, without discussion or debate, until the newest and youngest of the Burgesses, Patrick Henry, rose and attacked the proposal as bad public policy.

Not yet having the slightest suspicion about the real intent of the proposal, Henry argued that it would lead to favoritism and many abuses. He addressed the Burgesses "in that style of bold, grand, and overwhelming eloquence for which he became so justly celebrated afterwards," said Jefferson, who heard the debate.

Much to the surprise of everybody—and of the Grandees, especially—the majority in the House agreed with Henry, voted down the proposal, and thus the Public Loan Office "was crushed at birth."**

* Something like $270 today, which was considerably less than the £50 ($1,500) that Washington laid out for liquor in his first successful campaign, or the £75 ($2,250) that Littlepage had paid to buy off a rival candidate.

** This issue, important in its political and social ramifications, will be discussed later in connection with another matter—a great scandal, "a chasm in the public coffers."

The long-reigning conservatives received an even ruder shock only a few days later, and again at the hands of that "upstart" Henry.

One subject was on everybody's mind, but nobody wanted to talk about it—at least, not publicly or officially. The Stamp Tax suggested by Lord Grenville was now law, having been passed by Parliament and signed by the King, and was to go into effect in five months, on November 1.

In announcing his purpose, Grenville had earlier informed the colonies that he would take "under due consideration" any alternative they might offer as a substitute for the Stamp Tax. By the time Grenville was ready to proceed, he had received only one petition—that from Pennsylvania, presented to him by Benjamin Franklin, the colony's resident agent in London.

The petition stressed the point that Pennsylvanians had always been loyal subjects and were quite willing to help pay the costs of Empire, but in the old traditional way. Let the King make known to them his "royal desire" for funds—and for how much, and for what purpose. The provincial legislature would then consider the matter and no doubt make a generous grant, as it had always done. Franklin argued the practicality and realism of this approach.

How much money was the Stamp Tax supposed to raise? asked Franklin. At the highest estimate, about £60,000 [$1,800,000] a year, it was answered. Well, said Franklin, far more money could be raised—much more easily, without any fuss or contention—if the individual provincial legislatures were requested to appropriate funds in the long-accepted manner. They would make a "free" grant toward making up the sum requested.

The British ministry headed by Lord Grenville was much less interested in raising revenue, it is plain, than in raising a question of "principle": Britain had the right to tax the colonies in any form it saw fit. Americans were quick to challenge that thesis. The colonies were not prepared to accept an "internal" tax of any kind levied upon them in London by a Parliament in which they had no representation.

Grenville had his bill introduced in the Commons early in 1765. The particulars of the tax schedule were spelled out in fifty-five articles.

Virtually "every skin or piece of vellum or parchment, or sheet or piece of paper, . . . engrossed, written, or printed . . ." had to bear a stamp—legal documents of all kinds, mortgages, transfers of property, land grants, wills, testaments, marriage licenses, liquor licenses, preachers' licenses, college diplomas, appointments to public office, customs receipts, and similar things. Every copy of printed materials—newspapers, handbills, advertisements, calendars, almanacs, pamphlets, and general publications—had to bear a stamp.

And as if to make sure of missing nothing that might annoy the colonists, Virginians in particular, there was to be a 1s. tax on a pack of cards; 10s. ($15) on a pair of dice. Some "moral" distinction between the queen of diamonds and "snake eyes" seems to have been drawn here.

On the floor of the House of Commons, there was no debate at all on the specific items in the Stamp Act. Only a few rose to question the principle and wisdom of such a measure, the lead being taken by Colonel Isaac Barré. A distinguished army officer, the colonel had served in America during the French and Indian War, being one of General James Wolfe's chief aides. Knowing the colonists, liking them, understanding their views, and respecting their independent spirit, Barré warned that there would certainly be trouble if the Grenville ministry persisted in its course.

Charles Townshend, later the author of Acts even more infuriating than the Stamp Tax, answered with an angry attack on Barré personally and on his libertarian political views. There can be little doubt that brilliant but shallow Townshend spoke for most of the British ruling class in asking loftily and scornfully:

"And now, will these Americans, children planted by our care, nourished by our indulgence until they are grown up to a high degree of strength and opulence, and protected by our arms—will they now grudge to contribute their mite to relieve us from the heavy weight of that burden which we lie under?"

Colonel Barré, having heard the arguments of Townshend and others, rose to make a forceful and prophetic reply:

> *They planted by your care!* No, your oppressions planted them in America. They fled from your tyranny to a then uncultivated and inhospitable country. . . .
>
> *They nourished by your indulgence!* They grew by your neglect of them. As soon as you began to care about them, that care was exercised in sending persons to rule them in one department or another, . . . to spy out their liberties, to misrepresent their actions, and to prey upon them—men whose behavior on many occasions has caused the blood of these sons of liberty* to recoil within them. . . .

---

* The more active Patriots in the colonies, liking this phrase, picked it up and soon began styling their organizations the Sons of Liberty.

> *They protected by your arms!* They have nobly taken up arms in your defense and have exerted a shining valor amidst their constant and laborious industry for the defense of a country whose frontier was drenched in blood while its interior parts yielded all their little savings for your emolument. . . .
>
> The people, I believe, are as truly loyal as any subjects the King has—but a people jealous of their liberties. . . .
>
> And believe me—remember I this day told you so—that the same spirit of freedom which actuated that people at first will accompany them still—but prudence forbids me to explain myself farther.

When debate was resumed at the second reading of the bill, influential London merchants doing business in the colonies submitted a petition in opposition to the measure. Anticipating trouble, they feared—with prescience, it turned out—that the colonies in protest might start a movement to stop buying British goods and delay payments on their accounts. The merchants had the strong support of the very influential and vociferous London authorities—the Lord Mayor and many of the aldermen, who were having their own conflicts with Parliament and the Crown on the matter of proper representation in the Commons and related questions.

Under a procedural rule in the Commons, once a money or tax bill had been introduced, no petitions either for it or against it could be officially received and considered. The merchants' petitions therefore did not come to the floor.

Meantime, petitions of protest from Virginia and other colonies had arrived. In spite of cogent pleas by Colonel Barré and others that the colonies' petitions be received and discussed, the House declined to waive the rule.

Perhaps Grenville and his friends had rushed introduction of the measure just so this would happen to curtail debate and avoid any discussion of thorny "constitutional" issues. In any case, by a majority of better than five to one, the Stamp Act was passed by the Commons, quickly approved by the House of Lords, and signed by the King on March 2, 1765.

"The sun of liberty is set," said Benjamin Franklin, writing from London to a friend in the colonies. "You must now light the lamps of industry and economy."

The friend, closer to the feelings of the people and therefore less pessimistic and quiescent, replied that Americans under the circumstances would be lighting more than the lamps Franklin spoke of.

The land would soon be blazing with torches in great demonstrations to rally the people in defense of their imperilled "liberties."

Henry saw the necessity of torchbearers and felt he was now in a position to light a torch officially, in the name of a whole colony. It was worth at least a try.

After Henry's defeat of the Public Loan Office scheme, nothing of importance remained on the agenda of the House of Burgesses. The one subject uppermost in the minds of all was not on the agenda. That was the recently enacted Stamp Act. There was a conspiracy of silence about it. No one wanted to touch it. There was an unspoken consensus that it would be better to let the matter go over to the next session, by which time many perplexing questions might be clearer.

With the session drawing to a close, with only minor matters to be taken up, two thirds of the Burgesses—almost all belonging to the conservative majority—decided to pack up and go home. It was later said that their premature departure was prompted by fear that, somehow, the Stamp Tax question might be brought up for discussion and debate.

Conservatives wanted to keep away from that, not yet knowing what position they should take. They did not like the measure, of course. No one did. But it was one thing to object to the measure when it was merely a proposal. It was something else again to know what to do now that the Stamp Act was on the books. Should they reconcile themselves to it with what grace they could, and counsel the people to accept and obey it? Or should they counsel some kind of organized protest and resistance? That would open them to the charge of being disloyal subjects of the Crown, or even seditious rebels. It was a painful dilemma for the conservatives, and most of them preferred not to face it at the moment.

On May 29, 1765, only 39 of the 116 members of the House were in their seats. At least half of these were non-Grandees from the middle and upper counties. If anything was going to be done, Henry decided, now was the time to strike when conservative ranks were so depleted.

The chamber was quiet, with nothing much going forward, when young Henry rose—it was his twenty-ninth birthday—and offered a motion that the House should take under consideration what Virginia had done, and what it should now do, about the Stamp Tax. To everybody's surprise—perhaps as much to his as anyone's—the motion was carried, and the House resolved itself into a Committee of the Whole for preliminary and rather informal discussion and debate.

Henry again was the first to get the floor, with the Burgesses expectantly waiting to hear what this new raw member from the backwoods was going to say on a matter of the highest policy, which presented as critical a problem as any Virginia had faced since its founding more than a century and a half before.

Henry had prepared himself very well to lead the debate. He had carefully thought out what he planned to propose and the line of argument that he would use in defending his position against the violent attacks that he anticipated would come his way.

Beginning quietly, as he always did, Henry made some pleasant and conciliatory remarks before moving quickly and adroitly to his subject. After his brief preamble, he drew from his pocket a piece of paper, a blank page torn out of an old law book, on which he had drafted a series of resolutions for consideration of the House.

Henry prized what he did on this occasion above any other action or triumph of his life. On his death there was found, lying beside his will, a sealed document bearing this inscription:

"Inclosed are the resolutions of the Virginia Assembly in 1765, concerning the Stamp Act. Let my executors open this paper."

On one side of the paper Henry had put down the text of the first five of the seven resolutions he offered. On the other side he had written:

> The within resolutions . . . formed the first opposition to the Stamp Act, and the scheme of taxing America by the British Parliament. All the colonies, either through fear, or want of opportunity to form an opposition, or from influence of some kind or other, had remained silent. I had been for the first time elected a Burgess a few days before; was young, inexperienced, unacquainted with the forms of the House and the members that composed it.
>
> Finding the men of weight averse to opposition and the commencement of the tax at hand, and that no person was likely to step forward, I determined to venture; and alone, unadvised, and unassisted, . . . wrote the within.*

No one ever made a more successful and far-reaching first "venture." Henry could scarcely have expected to do as well as he did.

* For comments on questions raised about Henry's authorship of the Stamp Tax Resolutions, see Appendix B (p. 483).

But here, as he was to do so often again, he anticipated events and, with a sure intuition about the thoughts and desires vaguely disturbing others, had the genius to evoke them, shape them, and give them telling voice for the first time.

Only two of his colleagues in the House—George Johnston of Fairfax County and John Fleming of Cumberland, both of whom were, like himself, younger members from the westerly counties—had seen what Henry had written on the paper which he now unfolded and began to read slowly, quietly, deliberately in a low resonant voice that vibrated through the chamber:

> *Whereas,* the honourable House of Commons in England have of late drawn into question how far the General Assembly of this colony hath power to enact laws for laying of taxes and imposing duties, payable by the people of this his Majesty's most ancient colony: for settling and ascertaining the same to all future times, the House of Burgesses of this present General Assembly have come to the following resolves:
>
> 1. *Resolved,* That the first adventurers and settlers of this his Majesty's colony and dominion brought with them and transmitted to their posterity, and all other his Majesty's subjects since inhabiting in this his Majesty's said colony, all the privileges, franchises, and immunities that have at any time been held, enjoyed, and possessed by the people of Great Britain;
>
> 2. *Resolved,* That by two royal charters granted by King James the First, the colonists aforesaid are declared entitled to all the privileges, liberties, and immunities of denizens and native-born subjects, to all intents and purposes, as if they had been abiding and born within the realm of England . . .

Here, Henry was referring to specific terms in the original Virginia charter of 1606 and in the Great Charter of 1619 which had given the colony, among other things, the right to a considerable degree of self-government to be exercised through its General Assembly.

Decisions taken by the lower house, that of the Burgesses elected to represent the planters' interests, could be disapproved and thrown out by the upper house, the Governor's Council, appointed by the Crown. If a measure was approved by both houses of the Assembly, it was still subject to veto by the royal governor, or by the Lords of Trade, or by the Privy Council, or by the Crown itself.

Even with such limitations, Virginians prized what they called their "inalienable rights," and Henry went on to specify some of them:

> 3. *Resolved,* That the taxation of the people by themselves or by persons chosen by themselves to represent them, who can only know what taxes the people are able to bear and the easiest mode of raising them, and are equally affected by such taxes themselves, is the distinguishing characteristic of British freedom, and without which the ancient constitution cannot subsist;
>
> 4. *Resolved,* That his Majesty's liege people of this most ancient colony have uninterruptedly enjoyed the right of being thus governed by their own Assembly in the article of their taxes and internal policy, and that the same hath never been forfeited or any other way given up, but hath been constantly recognized by the kings and people of Great Britain . . .

Except for the phrasing and rather challenging tone, there was nothing new in this. It was old and accepted Virginia doctrine, stated over and over again, ever since 1623.

Yet, many of the Burgesses were uneasy, not liking the drift of Henry's argument. This ground, they felt, had been more or less covered in the petitions sent to London earlier.

True, Grenville had not even acknowledged receipt of their petitions; he had gone ahead with his stamp tax which was soon to go into effect. Notwithstanding, it would be prudent not to make another pronouncement until some explanation had been received from London.

Over considerable opposition, the appearance of which seems rather surprising, these innocuous resolutions were adopted in the end, one after the other, but each by a very narrow margin. Henry's next resolution generated great heat and violent opposition:

> 5. *Resolved,* therefore, That the General Assembly of this colony have the only and sole exclusive right and power to lay taxes and impositions upon the inhabitants of this colony; and that every attempt to vest such power in any person or persons whatsoever other than the General Assembly aforesaid has a manifest tendency to destroy British as well as American freedom. . . .

Here was something radically new—the assertion of the Assembly's "only and sole exclusive" right to lay all taxes "whatsoever" upon

Virginians! It was at this point that, as Henry declared in his testament, "violent debates ensued." They would become more violent on Henry's additional proposals:

> 6. *Resolved,* That his Majesty's liege people, the inhabitants of this colony, are not bound to yield obedience to any law or ordinance whatever, designed to impose any taxation whatsoever upon them, other than the laws or ordinances of the General Assembly aforesaid;
>
> 7. *Resolved,* That any persons who shall by writing or speaking assert or maintain that any person or persons have any right or power to impose or lay any taxation on the people shall be deemed an enemy to his Majesty's colony.

This last resolution was, in effect, an act of proscription. It would have virtually precluded free discussion of the issue involved—as was true, in a lesser degree, of the previous resolution. Both of them were extreme and, from any balanced point of view, ill-advised.

Yet, by an ironic turn of circumstance, resulting from the shortsightedness of an ultra-conservative, these last two resolutions, though not formally adopted by the House, did as much as anything to arouse the passions of the people in all the colonies and spark the Revolution.

How this happened is curious. The course of the debate, in its entirety, is not reported anywhere. But reasonable conjectures about it can be made from what is known.

In the light of what soon occurred, Henry evidently offered all seven of his resolutions to the House sitting as Committee of the Whole, precipitating violent all-day debate. Toward the end of the day, the House ceased sitting as Committee of the Whole and went into regular session. John Robinson, speaker of the House, resumed the chair and Attorney General Peyton Randolph, as chairman of the Committee of the Whole, made a report which was entered in the Journal of the House:

> May 30, Mr. Attorney, from the committee of the whole House, reported, according to order, that the Committee had considered the steps necessary to be taken in consequence of the resolutions of the House of Commons of Great Britain, relative to the charging certain stamp duties in the colonies and plantations in America, and they had come to several resolutions thereon, which he was ready to deliver in at the table.

For two days, first in committee and then in the House, debate raged in what Henry called a "long and warm contest." Not only were his resolutions sharply attacked, but the author of them was violently denounced and personally vilified. "Many threats were uttered, and much abuse cast on me," said Henry who answered both political and personal attacks with great spirit, stoutly and eloquently defending himself and his position in that "most bloody debate" as it was described by Thomas Jefferson. Aged twenty-two at the time, a recent college graduate and already deeply interested in public affairs, Jefferson was standing in the wide doorway of the Hall of the House of Burgesses, listening intently to every word spoken in the noisy, bitter, tiring debate, during which Henry sharply remarked, as noted before:

"Tarquin and Caesar had each his Brutus; Charles the First, his Cromwell; and George the Third . . ."

At this, the speaker of the House, a grand Grandee, the most powerful man in the colony, shouted, "Treason!"—a shout picked up by many more until the chamber echoed treason! treason! treason! When the clamor subsided, Henry resumed, quietly:

". . . and George the Third may profit from their example. If this be treason, make the most of it."*

Throughout the debate, said Jefferson, Henry spoke "as Homer wrote, . . . with torrents of sublime eloquence." In later years, having heard all of the great orators of his day, Jefferson described the overpowering effect of Henry's words, voice, and manner:

> Henry spoke wonderfully. Call it oratory or what you please, but I never heard anything like it. He had more command over the passions than any man I ever knew . . . It was his profound knowledge of human nature and his manner of speaking more than the matter of his orations.

In the doorway crowd listening to the debate was a stranger, a visitor from France, whose presence in the crowd was not noted by anyone there; at least, no one said anything about him for the record, and his name has been lost. Presumably in the employ of his government, the Frenchman evidently was traveling through the colonies to

* Some scholars have suggested that this last sentence was added by Henry's first biographer, William Wirt. That may be so, but it is unlikely. In its terseness, the sentence sounds far more like Henry than Wirt, who was given to labyrinthian Byzantine prose. If Wirt had decided to add something, it would have been at least a paragraph of elaborate nonsense.

study and make a report on various technical and scientific matters. In his journeys from place to place, he kept a day-by-day journal of what he did, what he saw and heard. His unsigned journal suddenly came to light in Paris in fairly recent years. Found in the archives of the Service Hydrographique de la Marine, it was published in 1921 by the *American Historical Review* as "Journal of a French Traveler."

The Journal is a unique document in many respects—for one thing, it contains the only account we have of the debate as written on the spot, and not out of recollections in later years, when memory is apt to be faulty.

The Frenchman arrived in Williamsburg on May 30 and immediately went to the Capitol where he joined the crowd standing in the House doorway and there listened to "very strong debates" on the floor (it was the second day of debate). His Journal for that day records, in somewhat broken English:

> Shortly after I Came in, one of the members stood up and said he had read that in former times Tarquin and Julus had their Brutus, Charles had his Cromwell, and he Did not Doubt but some good american would stand up in favour of his Country.

It was at this point that Speaker Robinson raised the cry of "Treason!" against Henry, adding rather angrily that he was "very sorry to see that not one of the members of the house was loyal Enough to stop him, before he had gone so far." After this interruption, proceeding resumed:

> The Same member stood up again (his name is henery) and said that if he had afronted the speaker, or the house, he was ready to ask pardon, and he would show his loyalty to his majesty King G. the third, at the Expense of the last Drop of his blood, but what he had said must be atributed to the Interest of his Country's Dying liberty which he had at heart, and the heat of passion might have lead him to have said something more than he intended; but, again, if he said anything wrong, he beged the speaker's and the house's pardon.* Some other Members stood up and backed him, on which that afaire was dropped.

Or so that author thought in concluding his journal entry for the day. Henry thought so, too, for at the end of debate that day he

* For comments on the Frenchman's other remarks, see Appendix C (p. 484).

saddled up and left for home. Both were mistaken, as the Frenchman discovered the next day, May 31: "I returned to the assembly today, and heard very hot Debates still about the Stamp Duties." The "afaire" was not over.

What happened that day was interesting and unusual. Henry, it is plain, had assumed that, after the action taken by the Burgesses, Governor Fauquier would immediately dissolve the House and send its members packing. But that was not the case. On Henry's departure, the head of the Anglican Church in Virginia, the Reverend William Robinson, still boiling mad about the Parsons' Cause, reported to the Bishop of London:

> Mr. Henry, the hero of whom I am writing, is gone quietly into the upper parts of the country to recommend himself to his constituents by spreading treason and enforcing firm resolutions against the authority of the British Parliament . . .
>
> He blazed out in a violent speech against the authority of Parliament and the King, comparing his Majesty as a Tarquin, a Caesar, and a Charles the First, and not sparing insinuations that he wished another Cromwell would arise.
>
> He made a motion for several outrageous resolves, some of which were passed and again erased as soon as his back was turned.

This last statement is only partly true. As soon as Henry's "back was turned," an effort was made to have all of his resolutions "erased," but it was only partially successful. It seems plain that Speaker Robinson, Attorney General Peyton Randolph, and other Grandees had waited on Governor Fauquier and persuaded him not to dissolve the House immediately, but to let the session run over another day so that they, with Henry out of the way, might see what could be done about erasing or at least toning down the Stamp Tax Resolutions already on the books.

The governor agreed to extend the session for a day, and the next morning Jefferson was in the Capitol where he found a friend and relative, the venerable Colonel Peter Randolph, a member of the Governor's Council, seated at a table and hurriedly thumbing through the records, assisted by clerks and friends. With Jefferson standing beside him, looking over his shoulder, Randolph explained that he was seeking "a precedent for expunging a vote of the House," saying he was pretty sure that some such action had been taken while he was clerk of the House.

Armed with some sort of dubious precedent, the conservative leaders, in control of the House that day, moved to knock down all of Henry's resolutions. When this general assault failed, they concentrated their attack on the controversial fifth resolution about the Assembly's "only and sole exclusive right" to tax Virginians. The vote on this, which had passed by a majority of only one, was now reversed, and the resolution stricken from the Journal of the House. That accomplished, the governor dissolved the House and reported to his superiors in London:

> On Friday, the 31st, there having happened a small alteration in the House,* there was an Attempt made to strike all the Resolutions off the Journal. The 5th, which was thought the most offensive, was accordingly struck off, but it did not succeed as to the other four.
>
> I am informed that the Gentlemen [Henry and his colleagues, John Fleming and George Johnston] had two more resolutions in their pockets, but finding the difficulty they had in carrying the 5th, which was by a single Voice, and knowing them to be more violent and inflammatory, they did not produce them.
>
> The most strenuous opposers of this rash heat were the Speaker [John Robinson, soon to be disgraced in a shocking financial scandal], the King's Attorney [Peyton Randolph, soon to join the Patriot cause in an eminent capacity], and Mr. George Wythe [Jefferson's close friend and law tutor], but they were overpowered by the Young, hot, and Giddy members.
>
> In the Course of the debates I have heard that very indecent language was used by a Mr. Henry, a young lawyer, who had not been a Month a Member of House, who carried all of the young members with him.

The governor was critical not only of the "rash heat" of the younger members, but of the conduct of the older staid conservative members. If the latter "had done their Duty by attending to the end of the Session," instead of packing up and going home prematurely, they could have blocked any attempt to bring the Stamp Tax ques-

* A "small alteration" indeed! It was a major alteration brought about by the fact that Henry and some of his friends had gone home on the assumption that the debate was over, with victory secured—and the debate would have been over had it not been for the conniving of the Grandees and the governor.

tion to the floor, in which case there would have been no acrimonious and explosive debate.

It was more than whispered at the time that many of the older conservative members had left the House early, not because of any careless neglect of duty, but because they feared that consideration of the Stamp Act would come up in one form or another. They did not like the Stamp Act, to be sure. No one did. But it was one thing to protest against it when it was merely a proposal. It was quite another thing to oppose it and organize resistance against it now that the tax law was on the books, and soon to go into effect. Conservatives in Virginia, as in other colonies, wanted to wait and see how the wind was blowing. They had no desire at the moment to stand up and be counted in support of one side or the other. It seemed to them prudent to lie low for a time.

Striking Henry's fifth resolution from the House Journal no doubt helped make the official record look better, particularly when reviewed in London. But it really accomplished nothing because of a curious chain of circumstances.

The editor-publisher of the *Virginia Gazette,* ultra-royalist Joseph Royle, had been so roiled with the entire Stamp Tax proceedings that he decided he would not dignify them by giving them any space—not a word—in his columns. He would blank out the whole thing, saying that he would give no countenance to "treason." As a consequence, the public in general had no accurate account of what the Burgesses had and had not done.

Meantime, copies of all seven of Henry's resolutions had gone out and were circulating and, in want of any public notice to the contrary, were accepted everywhere as being what the Virginia legislature had officially decided to say not only about the Stamp Tax, but about American "rights, privileges, and immunities" in general.

How copies of all seven of Henry's draft resolutions got out as representing what action the Virginia legislature had taken is not altogether clear. But in the light of what happened, this seems to be a reasonable surmise.

All of Henry's resolutions must have been proposed and debated on May 29 when the House was sitting as Committee of the Whole. The committee must have recommended the adoption of all the resolutions, not only the controversial fifth, but the "violent and inflammatory" sixth and seventh. Recommendations of the Committee of a Whole were almost always adopted by the House, for the committee consisted of the whole membership of the House. How members voted in committee was an almost sure indication of how they were going to vote in the House when it took up any question for formal debate and decision.

If all of Henry's resolutions had not been recommended by the Committee of the Whole, virtually assuring adoption by the House, Henry and his followers would not have dared to do what they did. On the afternoon and evening of May 29, after debate in the committee, they hurriedly transcribed and sent out to other colonies a number of copies of the Stamp Tax Resolutions, all seven of them, as if these had already been officially approved by the House, which they had reason to believe would accept them.

In any case, copies of all seven of Henry's draft resolutions were in the mails—or off by special courier, perhaps—before the House took formal action the next day. A copy soon reached Philadelphia; another appeared in New York, where the document was handed about "with great privacy." It was regarded as so seditious, if not treasonable, that no printer could be persuaded to put it in type, fearing to be fined or jailed, or maybe suffer worse.

Another copy, forwarded from either Philadelphia or New York, came into Rhode Island, always liberal in its views since it was founded by "that heretic," the great Roger Williams. This copy fell into the hands of the editor-publisher of the *Newport Mercury*. A nephew of Benjamin Franklin, the editor liked the document and the spirit it reflected, saying that it was "of an extraordinary nature" and "might not be disagreeable" to readers. On June 24, about a month after the "bloody debate" in Williamsburg, the *Mercury* gave to the world for the first time Henry's resolutions in their original form.

The item in the *Mercury* was quickly picked up and reprinted by newspapers in Boston and all along the seaboard. "The people of Virginia have spoken very sensibly," commented the *Boston Gazette*. A distinguished Massachusetts judge exclaimed as he lay dying: "Oh! those Virginians are men; they are noble spirits."

Publication of Henry's bold resolutions proved to be the tocsin for which many had been waiting. People in general had been rather apathetic about the Stamp Tax, but now the subject was on every tongue. "The general Dissatisfaction at the Duties laid by the Stamp Tax," observed Governor Fauquier, ". . . breaks out and shews itself on every trifling occasion." The royal governor in Massachusetts, Francis Bernard, reported the situation to London:

> Two or three months ago, I thought that this people would submit to the Stamp Act. Murmurs were indeed continually heard, but they seemed to be such as would die away. But the publication of the Virginia Resolves* proved an alarm bell to the disaffected.

That bell was soon sounding far and wide, as Henry recalled:

> The alarm spread throughout America with astonishing quickness, and the ministerial party were overwhelmed. The great point of resistance to British taxation was universally established in the colonies.

Conservatives angrily denounced the Virginia Resolves as spurious. They were, but who cared? People found that the Resolves expressed their feelings about the Stamp Tax and their determination to resist "tyranny." Agitation became general, nor was it only verbal. Those trying to block action against the Stamp Tax were often rather roughly handled.

Before the Virginia Resolves appeared, Massachusetts had suggested a general conference of the colonies to discuss the question of united action. This suggestion met with a very cool reception at first. The New Jersey legislature replied that its members stood "unanimously against uniting on the present occasion." Other colonies were, at best, lukewarm. This cool attitude was suddenly changed by the Virginia Resolves, which became "the signal for a general outcry over the continent," as noted with serious concern by General Thomas Gage, British commander-in-chief in America.

At New York, early in October, a Stamp Act Congress convened, with nine colonies represented–Massachusetts, Rhode Island, Connecticut, New York, New Jersey, Pennsylvania, Delaware, Maryland, and South Carolina. No delegates came from Virginia, New Hampshire, North Carolina, or Georgia because the royal governors there refused to call general assemblies at which official representatives could be duly chosen.

The Stamp Tax Congress did nothing startling, merely going over familiar ground. In its "Declaration of Rights and Grievances," it repeated the arguments that the Stamp Act was "unconstitutional," that it had a "manifest tendency to subvert the rights and liberties of the colonists," that only the colonial legislatures had the right to

* The term "Virginia Resolves" will hereafter be used to indicate all of Henry's as published, and not just the four adopted by the House of Burgesses.

levy direct taxes on their people, that the Stamp Tax should be repealed, at which time the colonists would be happy to return to loving obedience as loyal subjects of the Crown.

While these arguments did not much advance the colonial case, the Congress was useful in showing that some measure of united action was possible—a precedent to be followed.

Plans for the administration of the Stamp Tax, soon to go into effect, had been laid out. In each colony the Crown would appoint a master of stamps. The post carried a salary of £300 [$9,000] a year—not big as political plums went. But as selling stamps and keeping books entailed little work, which could be performed by a few clerks, the job was really a sinecure, a handout, a bit of patronage for bestowal on the right people.

Lord George Grenville nursed, among other illusions, the notion that he could make his Stamp Tax more palatable if Americans were named as stamp masters and made responsible for administration and enforcement. That would be a friendly and neighborly arrangement, and it would certainly do no harm if Americans of position and influence were given a personal interest in defending the Stamp Tax against its critics. Some Americans were approached about the job and happily accepted appointment.

The idea seemed to be a good one, but it turned out to be a very bad one and caused great commotion. Americans could understand how some haughty British "foreigners" would be willing to accept appointment. But that some of their "Fellow Slaves" were willing to lend a hand in fastening "iron chains of bondage" on them was inexcusable, insufferable, monstrous.

A native Virginian, Colonel James Mercer, came from London carrying in his pocket a commission appointing him to be stamp master in the colony. Arriving in Williamsburg, he was surprised to find himself hanging in effigy and his father blasting away against the "stamp tyranny" in the *Virginia Gazette.*

With the General Court about to sit, the town was crowded, and Mercer's appearance brought it to a state of high excitement. A number of men, many of them prominent political and business leaders, gathered in a coffeehouse to consider the situation. After some discussion, raising a shout of "One and all!" the group came streaming out of the coffeehouse to go in search of the stamp master. Mercer took to his heels and hurried to the Palace to place himself under the protection of Governor Fauquier, who described the scene in a report to London:

> This Concourse of people I should call a Mob, did I not know that it was chiefly, if not altogether, composed of Gentlemen of property in the Colony, some of them at the Head of their Respective Counties, and the Merchants of the Country, whether English, Scotch, or Virginians, for few Absented themselves.

Mercer submitted his resignation to the governor, who declined to accept it, saying that he had no authority to do so. Mercer then thought it best to face the scowling crowd to make a solemn pledge that he would not exercise his commission, which set off a great demonstration. That night, with bells tolling and torches, flares, and bonfires lighting up the town, Williamsburg enjoyed a splendid "entertainment," with many toasts to Liberty, to the Sons of Liberty, even to the cooperative stamp master. Though something of a hero for the moment, Mercer still felt uneasy and took the first opportunity to sail for England—"on business."

The colonel got off more easily than stamp masters in other colonies. Several had their houses assaulted, broken into, and despoiled by unruly crowds in an ugly mood, often inflamed with drink. In Maryland, Sons of Liberty waited on one Hood, the colony's stamp master, and demanded his resignation. Not wishing to surrender his commission to an easy and rather lucrative job, Hood fled. Men were sent after him and tracked him down in New York, where they "persuaded" him to write a letter of resignation and forced him to sign it under oath before a magistrate.

By November 1, when the tax went into effect, all stamp masters had resigned. No stamps were sold, and none ever would be. This raised legal and business problems of a perplexing nature.

Under the law, no legal document, no business contract, no receipt for payment of debt, no ship clearance paper, no marriage license, no death certificate, no will, or any such document was valid unless it bore the prescribed stamp. With no stamps on sale, and with people determined not to buy any even if they were available, the courts in Virginia and elsewhere suspended judicial proceedings. This curtailed the practice of Henry and other lawyers, who handled only such matters as might be settled without the use of stamped papers. This caused a disruption in public and private affairs, threatening such anarchy that the courts after a time resumed normal proceedings, ignoring the stamp law, hoping that their proceedings would later be validated, as they were—or at least, they were not challenged or reversed.

But the refusal to buy stamps had less effect than the colonists' refusal to buy any more British goods. This boycott struck the imperial system where it hurt most—in the pocketbook. New York merchants instructed their agents in Britain not to ship them any more goods till the Stamp Act was repealed. Merchants in Boston, Providence, and Philadelphia did likewise. Large public meetings passed resolutions that lawyers should not represent British creditors against American debtors, that debts owed in Britain should not be paid until American "grievances" had been redressed.

Women joined the boycott movement. They gave up buying imported fineries and dressed themselves in woolen or other homespun. In Boston, it was almost worth a butcher's life to offer a lamb chop for sale. Lambs were not to be slaughtered. They were to be allowed to grow up into mature sheep which could be sheared to provide more wool to be woven into cloth on domestic looms, and lessen dependence on Britain.

Trade with the Mother Country declined steeply, falling some £500,000 [$15,000,000] during the five months after agitation began. To the clamor of the colonists were now added the loud groans of British merchants, manufacturers, and bankers, who had been hard hit. The voice of these powerful interests carried immeasurably more weight in government councils and the House of Commons than the irritating and "incessant" gripes from overseas.

The situation, both politically and economically, had obviously become serious. Everybody agreed that things could not go on as they had been going. Either British authority had to be asserted by enforcing the Stamp Act unreservedly, or the Stamp Tax had to be repealed.

As it was, the mighty British Lion was cutting a pretty sorry figure with his cubs literally spitting in his face, and defying him to do anything about it.

X

Some Private Concerns

. . . he thought his property
was not worth more than £1,500.
—JUDGE EDMUND WINSTON

On his return to his home in Hanover Courthouse after the Stamp Tax debate, Henry was widely and wildly acclaimed as "the Noble Patriot." The French visitor who had recorded in his Journal what he thought he heard in the debate at Williamsburg traveled into Hanover County a few days later. There he heard a great deal "about the Noble Patriot Mr. henery, who lives in the county; . . . the whole Inhabitants say publicly that if the least Injury was offered to him, they'd stand by him to the last Drop of their blood. Some of them muter betwixt their teeth, let the worst Come to the worst, we'l Call the french to our sucour."

Henry had almost eighteen months at home to devote to his private concerns because Governor Fauquier had no desire to issue a call for the election of a new House of Burgesses. He well knew that his life would be happier and less complicated if he had no Burgesses around, particularly at a time when Virginians were "so heated as to shut up all avenues of Reason," adding that the "colonies reciprocally inflame each other, and where the Fury will end I know not." Fauquier, as governor, found this situation disturbing and distasteful, for personally he liked the Virginians and disliked being at odds with them.

During his year and a half absence from Williamsburg, Henry found plenty of things to occupy his mind and his time. His greatest concern was about the house being built for him and his family in Louisa County.

Late in 1765 or early the next year, the Henrys moved into their new house, Round Top, leaving Shelton's tavern where they had lived since 1757 when the house on their Piney Slash farm had burned down. Round Top was a modest house, not remotely approaching the size and elegance of the seignorial mansions built along the Potomac, the James, the York, and elsewhere by Tidewater Grandees —Washington's Mount Vernon, Mason's Gunston Hall, Stratford Hall of the Lees, Tuckahoe and other Randolph manor houses, Westover of the Byrds, and Robert Carter's fabulous Nomini Hall, which had some thirty rooms and a private chapel.* Henry would soon own a "big house," but as yet could not afford one.

A story-and-a-half structure built of hand-hewn lumber, Round Top had four rooms, none too ample space for a family of six. When the Henrys moved in, the interior of the house was still unfinished. Henry later had some of the rooms lathed and plastered. Downstairs, there were two rooms and a kitchen. Upstairs, under the sloping roof, there was an attic, a long room running the length of the house. Lighted by dormer windows, this large room probably served as the bedroom and playroom of the children, and could be used on occasion to bed down an overflow of overnight guests.

Back of the house were outbuildings and the usual plantation facilities—the family privy, the overseer's cabin, slave quarters, tobacco sheds, a stable for horses and a barn for cows, carriage and wagon sheds, a blacksmithy, a well house, and almost certainly a large pigsty. Liking pork, Virginians ate a lot of it and took great pride in their piggeries, taking pains to improve the breed of their porkers. Hickory-smoked Virginia ham was a great delicacy then, as now.

The house sat pleasantly on high ground, with fields sloping away from it on all sides. Though planted largely to tobacco, the fields were also planted to wheat and other grains. Nearby were roads to

---

* For a charming account of life at a "big house," see *Journal and Letters, 1767–1774*, by Philip Vickers Fithian, who in 1773 came from Princeton to Nomini Hall to tutor the Carter children.

market towns, including Richmond, a young raw town founded by Colonel William Byrd II in the 1730s.

Though never very successful as a farmer, Henry appears to have recognized some of the problems faced by Virginia planters. Many of them wished to end their almost complete dependence on tobacco as a money crop. Prices for the "weed" kept sliding down. Also, tobacco quickly depleted the soil. Some planters began experimenting with hemp, indigo, and other crops to provide another source of income and to check soil depletion, which was becoming an increasingly serious problem on all but virgin lands. Henry experimented with hemp and other crops; with what success does not appear.

Round Top was a lonesome place, and all of the Henrys must have occasionally missed what was, comparatively, the bustle of life at Hanover Courthouse and in Shelton's tavern, particularly on monthly Court Days. Still, Round Top represented an achievement, a new independence, and was a pleasant spot where the children could run freely in fields and woods. And Henry, remembering his own happy carefree childhood, allowed the children to run freely, even wildly.

While Henry was now a planter, his main business continued to be in the law. Though rather out of the way, Round Top was not too inconvenient a place from which to make a round of county courthouses in the area as occasion required. His triumph as "the People's Advocate" in the Parsons' Cause and as "the Noble Patriot" in the Stamp Tax debate spread his name and fame, and brought him more clients and larger cases, and larger fees.

But a good law practice was nowhere as remunerative in those days as now. The size of legal fees for services of every kind was strictly limited by law, and the limit was kept moderate. In acting for the defense in the Parsons' Cause, Henry charged only 15s. [$22.50], and had to wait more than a year before that was paid. From 1765 through 1767, Henry handled 1,205 cases and managed to collect sizable fees. Though far more successful than most young country lawyers in Virginia, Henry was not getting rich, but he was richer than ever before and his income was climbing.

Henry realized, along with Washington and many others, that the way to fortune in Virginia, as it had been from the beginning, was to acquire as much land as possible by purchase or by government grant and to hold such lands not necessarily for development, but for speculative purposes. Some day, westward-moving settlers might buy them.

Though Tidewater and much of Piedmont Virginia had been staked out, western land in vast expanses could still be acquired easily in Patrick Henry's day. To stimulate settlement, Virginia had early decreed that any responsible freeman could apply for a grant to unclaimed land, on which he had to pay a very small quitrent of 2s. [$3.00] a year per 100 acres. Many planters obtained thousands upon thousands of acres in this way—the foundation of most Grandee fortunes. The law, though good in itself, was exploited by land-grabbers who acquired huge holdings which they retained for future use or speculation.

Under another act, known as the "head-right" law, anyone at the expense of shipping in white indentured servants was entitled to receive for himself fifty acres of unclaimed ground for each such servant. This law, too, was subject to grave frauds and abuses.

Lists showing import of servants were padded. Certificates of transportation were used again and again. Clerks in the county courts and in the office of the secretary of the colony in Williamsburg carried on a brisk under-the-counter sale of spurious head-rights. Faked certificates could be purchased, as everybody knew, "at very easy rates," for as little as 1s. [$1.50] each. That was considerably cheaper than transporting a servant at an average cost of £5 [$150].

On one occasion, Philip Burwell, secretary of the colony, brought in forty servants, which entitled him to 2,000 acres. He added a cipher in making out to himself a patent for 20,000 acres. This was public knowledge, but no one said anything, for the irascible secretary was a dangerous man to cross.

None of the land-grabbers* had quite the zeal of Robert Carter, agent of the English lords who were proprietors of the Northern Neck, a tract of 5,000,000 acres that stretched along the south bank of the Potomac River from Chesapeake Bay to the Alleghenies. Helping himself to the Northern Neck, Carter granted to himself and his sons and his grandsons some 90,000 acres in one year alone and died possessed of more than 300,000 acres. The proprietors tolerated this because "King" Carter dominated the Governor's

---

* The biggest land-grabbers, of course, were the European monarchs—English, French, Spanish, and Portuguese—who took over the entire Western Hemisphere as theirs by "divine right" and divided it up among themselves, parceling out portions of it to their favorites.

Council and vigorously defended their interests there, exercising almost as much actual power as the royal governor.

More than 1,000,000 acres of the Northern Neck proprietorship were inherited by Thomas Lord Fairfax, Washington's young friend and neighbor and his first patron. It was Fairfax who gave young George, aged sixteen, his first job, engaging him as a surveyor to lay out the town of Winchester along the Shenandoah River and later the town of Alexandria along the Potomac.

"Honest" George no doubt surveyed conscientiously and ran proper lines. But many surveyors did not, practicing all kinds of "knaveries." Frequently they ran no lines at all, merely describing properties by a few natural boundaries, always making "sure to allow large measure so that the persons for whom they surveyed might enjoy larger tracts of land than they were to pay quitrents for."

The annual quitrent of 2s. per 100 acres was not burdensome on owners of lands in cultivation. But if paid on vast tracts of idle and undeveloped lands, it was costly. Land-grabbers found a way of getting around that by "concealing" hundreds of thousands of acres in their possession.

No surveyor interested in future employment, either private or public, reported the actual acreage of unoccupied lands held by members of the Council, the Burgesses, and other Grandees.

Nor did sheriffs, being so overawed by the "richer sort of inhabitants, some holding forty, fifty, and sixty thousand acres, . . . that they take their accounts as they themselves would have them," dare summon such persons to court and challengs their quitrent rolls.

In the 1720s, finding "very great abuses" in the rent rolls, Governor Alexander Spotswood proposed that lands on which no quitrents had been paid for three years should be confiscated. There was an immediate outcry in the Governor's Council and the House of Burgesses, many of whose members were notorious land-grabbers and tax-evaders. Using their influence to have him unseated, these powerful tax delinquents pilloried Spotswood as a public enemy for daring to make his proposals. Defeated by the Grandees, the governor decided to join them and indulged in some land-grabbing tax-evading business of his own, becoming a very rich man.

Henry's beginnings as a propertied man and land speculator were necessarily modest. He still owned the 300-acre Piney Slash farm that was part of his wife's dowry. More recently he had acquired the 1,700-acre Roundabout plantation from his father. Both of these were "solid properties," as the phrase went, meaning that, in large part, they had been cleared and were under cultivation. But they were deemed to be not enough to "provide a sufficient competence."

Henry soon acquired another larger property that was not at all "solid," but sheer wilderness, buying it from his father-in-law, John Shelton, who seems to have shared with Henry's father a penchant for running into debt and having to be bailed out.

Sued for nonpayment of a considerable debt, Shelton had a court judgment handed down against him. Among other properties, Shelton owned some 3,400 acres in the wilds to the southwest, along the Holston River. He feared that the sheriff might take possession of these lands and sell them at public auction "for a trifle" to satisfy the court judgment against him. He therefore asked Henry to sell the property for him in the hope of acquiring sufficient funds to pay off the court judgment and other debts.

Henry decided to have a look at the Holston River lands himself, taking with him a small party that included his older brother William. If William had ever been "dissolute," in Wirt's phrase, he was so no longer. A reasonably prosperous planter on the lands that his father had given him in Fluvanna County, William had become quite respectable, representing the county now and again in the House of Burgesses and holding other offices.

The Holston River property consisted of three adjoining tracts which, according to the surveyor's report, had been laid out about twenty years before. But Henry and his party had the greatest difficulty in finding any marks or corners to define boundaries. Only one tract could be located definitely. Perhaps lines on the two other tracts had never been run, which meant that the paper boundaries might be challenged and lead to protracted law suits. Also, the Cherokee Indians had claims under treaty to a slice of the property.

But even "under that risque," Henry decided to purchase the 3,400 acres, partly to help his father-in-law who was "greatly distressed for money," partly because he regarded the Holston lands as a good investment. To do this, he had to take out a heavy mortgage, a document which Jefferson signed as a witness.

Henry also became deeply involved in a land deal of far greater dimensions. All of the trans-Allegheny country taken from France at the conclusion of the French and Indian-Seven Years' War had been closed to settlement, as noted before, by a royal proclamation, which had been inspired in part by a desire to preserve peace on the frontier by preventing white settlers from moving in and taking over lands which the Indians owned not only by natural right but by negotiated treaties.

But white intrusion continued. To discourage this, Governor Fauquier issued in 1766 a proclamation warning Virginians against "trespassing beyond the Mountains." Such trespassers would receive no protection from the colony, the governor announced, and could expect no aid of any kind if they were attacked by the exasperated Indians. All intruders into the forbidden lands should get out and if they valued their scalps, they would be wise to do so immediately.

But none of this discouraged the Ohio Company, the Loyal Land Company, and other big speculators in wild western lands. They were intent on grabbing as much as possible, proclamations or no proclamations.

A new grandiose scheme was dreamed up by Jefferson's friend and neighbor, Dr. Thomas Walker, chief organizer of the Loyal Land Company which had dubious claims to 800,000 wilderness acres in the rich Ohio River valley. Walker's new enterprise was even more ambitious, aimed at obtaining rights to an immense area farther west, vaguely described as lying "on the waters of the Mississippi."

Buying shares in this new enterprise, Henry became most interested in promoting it. A Captain Fleming had been engaged to have a look at the distant domain and select "some such spot as would be proper for the first company of adventurers to begin execution of the scheme." Urging speed, Henry wrote to Fleming recommending that he keep a diary:

> Even the trees, herbs, grass, stones, hills, etc., I think ought to be described. The reasons I wish you to be so particular is that a succinct account of your Journal may be printed in order to invite our countrymen to become settlers. . . . To view that vast forest, describe the face of the Country & such of the rivers, Creeks, etc., as present themselves to view is a work of much Trouble, hazard & fatigue, & will in my Judgement intitle you to the favourable notice of every gentleman engaged in the Scheme.

The scheme came to nothing, and Henry turned to more familiar pursuits. He was not to make his fortune from the boundless tract that lay just south of the junction of the Ohio and Mississippi rivers, in what is now western Kentucky.

While Henry was not rich, he was doing well enough, and better each year. In 1769, nine years after he became a lawyer and started his way up in the world, he spent an evening with a cousin on his mother's side of the family, Edmund Winston, later a distinguished judge, who made a note on their conversation:

> . . . he thought his property was not worth more than £1,500 [$45,000], adding that if he could only make double that sum, he would be entirely content.

XI
Scandal

. . . a chasm in the public coffers.
—EDMUND RANDOLPH

Late in 1766, a recently elected House of Burgesses met in Williamsburg. The House had not been in session for eighteen months, not since Governor Fauquier had dissolved the previous House for its action on Henry's Stamp Tax Resolutions.

The governor, happy to be relieved of the presence of the House, enjoying relative peace and quiet, not wishing more fiery debate, was in no hurry to issue a call for new elections. He doubtless would have continued to postpone the call, had his hand not been forced by a sudden death–that of Speaker-Treasurer John Robinson.

This created a serious problem, a need for immediate action. Virginia could get on for a while without a speaker of the House, particularly since the House was not in session. But the colony needed a new treasurer at once if confusion and even chaos were to be avoided. The nub of the problem was this: The Burgesses chose the treasurer. It was therefore Governor Fauquier's sad necessity to call for new elections so that the Burgesses might fill the post and keep financial affairs in order.

Reluctantly, the governor issued a proclamation calling for elections. As was required by law, Fauquier had the proclamation printed and posted in all county courthouses and other public buildings, had it published in three successive issues of the weekly *Virginia Gazette,* and ordered it to be read during services in all Anglican churches on three successive Sundays. The governor wrote to London about the impending election:

"The cool old Members by their great Steadyness and moderation will, I am in great hopes, regain that Lead in the House which they formerly had, but at present it is lost."

His high hopes about the "cool old Members" regaining leadership in the House were dashed. When the new House met, observers noted many unfamiliar younger faces in the chamber. Many of the "cool old" Burgesses had been replaced, most of them being among those who had vigorously opposed the Stamp Tax Resolutions, or those who had gone home early to avoid participation in the debate, not yet wishing to stand up and be counted on the issue. Some of these, sensing the tide of popular opinion, chose not to run for re-election, feeling certain the vote would go against them. Many of those who chose to run were roundly defeated—a fact that aroused anxiety in Governor Fauquier and others. The people were "sour," said Fauquier, and almost any question became "a Matter of heat and Party Faction."

Louisa County had returned Patrick Henry as one of its two delegates, along with his friend and client, Richard Anderson, a substantial planter with liberal views. Hanover County had chosen Henry's half-brother, John Syme, as one of its representatives. John Fleming and most of Henry's more ardent supporters in the Stamp Tax debate had been returned to the House by larger majorities than before. A brilliant youngish aristocrat, Richard Henry Lee, now one of Henry's friends and invaluable allies, again represented Westmoreland County, as he had for some years.

The first order of business in the House was to elect a speaker. The loss of John Robinson was bemoaned by all. He had come to be regarded as a permanent fixture in the chair which he had occupied with distinction for almost thirty years. As speaker, Robinson had early won, and to his death retained, the respect and the affection of the Burgesses, even of those who strongly opposed his conservative political views. But Robinson was never doctrinaire. He was always fair handed in guiding proceedings in the House. His rulings from the chair were seldom challenged and rarely reversed by a vote on the floor. A man of very different political views, liberal

Edmund Randolph spoke an almost unanimous opinion in saying of Speaker Robinson:

> When he presided, the decorum of the House outshone that of the British House of Commons. He stated to the House the contents of every bill, and shewed himself to be a perfect master of the subject. When he pronounced the rules of order, he convinced the reluctant . . . In the limited sphere of colonial politics, he was a column . . . The thousand little flattering attentions which can be scattered from the Chair* operated as a delicious incense.

As a person, Robinson enjoyed equal respect and affection. A rich and powerful Grandee, having the highest social and financial connections as a member of one of Virginia's older families,** a man "of cultivated mind and polished manners," he was generous, pleasantly spoken, and most gracious at all times.

One young man never forgot Robinson's charm and tact. In 1759, Colonel George Washington, not yet thirty, took a seat in the House for the first time. As Washington had just returned from leading a very successful campaign in the French and Indian War, the House passed a resolution highly praising him for his achievements and many services. Wishing to express thanks, Washington rose and, never much of a speaker, was stumbling along most painfully and in a very embarrassing manner when Speaker Robinson cut in and said gently, with a smile:

"Sit down, Mr. Washington. Your modesty surpasses your valor, and that is beyond any language at my command."

As Governor Fauquier said with no exaggeration, Robinson was "the darling of the country." As a veteran member of the House, he was always more than ready to share his knowledge and experience with new members who came to him to acquaint themselves with parliamentary procedures and the special rules of the House.

---

* Such as naming members to sit on important committees, etc., and allotting other distinctions and favors.

** The Robinsons belonged to what Governor Robert Dinwiddie had acidly called the "long-tailed families"; i.e., those with a long pedigree, at least in Virginia. The term "Long Tail" came to be applied, often derisively, to the established landed "aristocracy"—a "pseudo-aristocracy," living on entails and primogeniture, said Jefferson, one of the longer "Long Tails" himself, an ancestor having settled in Virginia before 1619 and been a member of the first House of Burgesses.

Some House rules were very special indeed. At this time, subject to minor modifications now and again, the rules contained some articles of particular interest in the light of legislative practices and procedures today.

No Burgess was to be absent without prearranged official leave unless he was suddenly too sick to attend, and he had to submit proof of illness. Otherwise, he lost his *per diem* pay and could even be fined, as many were.

A member getting the floor was to rise and stand by his seat, "confining himself strictly to the Point of Debate" [what an admirable rule!]. Nor was he to use "indecent and disrespectful Language." No one was to speak more than twice on a question without the permission of the speaker, and such permission had to be approved by a vote of the House. There was to be no long-winded filibustering.

While a vote was being taken, no member was to "entertain private Discourse, stand up, walk into, out of, or across the House, or read any printed Book." That is, there should be no last-minute lobbying and no blatant display of disinterest.

No member was to vote on a question in which he was "immediately interested"—meaning one in which he had a financial or other personal interest. Unless so disqualified, every member present had to vote. Abstentions were not allowed. Everybody had to stand up and be counted.

No committee was to conduct business "during divine service." And there was to be no chewing of tobacco "during a session of the House or Committee of the Whole." Evidently, it was permissible to "chaw" tobacco in the meetings of smaller committees, and at public hearings.*

With the election over, Governor Fauquier reported to London that there were two leading contenders for the vacant speakership in the House—Attorney General Peyton Randolph and Richard Henry Lee. Randolph, backed by the conservatives, had the discreet support of the governor, who did some quiet electioneering. Fauquier went about whispering praise of Randolph for opposing the "late hot virulent resolutions [Henry's] which brought on the dissolution,"

---

* Until fairly recent years, a polished brass spittoon, frequently and expertly used, was the very hallmark of a legislator, or a ward heeler, or any politician aspiring to public office. The larger and more shiny the spittoon, the bigger the politician. With the disappearance of this badge of rank, people have found it increasingly difficult to distinguish one politician from another.

saying that the attorney general possessed all of the "good qualities" of John Robinson, "his late most intimate friend."

The opposing party first supported Richard Henry Lee, another of a most remarkable generation of Virginians, as brilliant a generation of leaders as any society of comparable area and population ever produced. Born to wealth and position, Lee had been educated at home by a fine tutor engaged by his father to run a family school at Stratford Hall for Richard Henry and his five brothers—Philip Ludwell, Thomas Ludwell, Francis Lightfoot, William, and Arthur, all of whom made names for themselves.

Their school day began at seven in the morning. After a break for breakfast, work went on till another break for midday dinner, after which study was resumed till five in the afternoon. What Patrick Henry would have thought of such a regimen can be imagined.

An eager and apt scholar, Richard Henry Lee was sent abroad to continue his studies, living some time in England and France. Returning home, he was given a large section of the vast Lee estate and there erected a large house, Chantilly, named for a beautiful French chateau in which he had stayed.

Entering political life early, Lee was elected in 1757, at the age of twenty-five, to represent rich Westmoreland County in the House of Burgesses, being continued at that post where he rapidly became very influential and effective. Because of his wide range of knowledge, he "required no preparation for debate," as his friend Edmund Randolph observed. "He was ready for any subject as soon as it was announced."

As a speaker, Lee commanded great eloquence, being known to his contemporaries as the "Cicero of the age" and ranked next to Henry, "the forest-born Demosthenes." A tall, spare, and very distinguished-looking man, having a fine head and a pronounced Roman profile, Lee had a maimed right hand, "which he kept covered with a black silk bandage neatly fitted to the palm of hand, but leaving the thumb free." But this disability was not noticed when he was speaking, and "his gesture was so graceful and so highly finished that," so his friend Randolph said, he could have acquired it only by practicing before a mirror.

His oratorical style differed markedly from Henry's. He did not have the latter's torrential rhetoric, or his sudden and dazzling "flashes of mind." Rather, Lee's style was what Wirt and others called "chaste." He spoke softly, precisely, and directly to the point, drawing upon his learning for apt citations and for allusions to or quotations from ancient classics to make an analogy and illuminate a point. His speeches flowed strongly and evenly, like a sparkling stream in a mountain meadow, broken here and there by a swift ripple, but there was no roar or dashing of spray as of waters pouring over a high craggy waterfall. But Lee was always listened to with attention and respect, even by those who disagreed with his views.

The Lee family ranked with the Randolphs as the first of the first families of Virginia (now the self-styled F.F.V.). Though born to the purple, Richard Henry Lee did not believe in the oligarchical rule of "aristocratical" men, nor in the dominance of the "opulent."

"I own myself a democrat," Patrick Henry once said. Richard Henry Lee might have said the same. He became, along with Henry and others, a "firebrand" in the House, especially during the Stamp Tax troubles.

Being known as a radical was a disability in seeking the speakership. Also, Lee was rather young, being thirty-four at this time, four years older than Henry. No doubt after a caucus, Lee, Henry, and their friends decided that they should unite behind some older, more conservative, yet acceptable candidate who might win needed votes among the moderates, and they found their man, one of the Grandees–Richard Bland, a wary, old, experienced veteran at the bar and in the house.

Bland had strongly supported the Two Penny Law and certainly applauded Henry's triumph in the Parsons' Cause. On the other hand, he strongly opposed Henry's resolutions on the Stamp Tax question. Bland had just published and circulated a pamphlet, "An Inquiry into the Rights of the British Colonies," in which he developed the argument that the colonies were "no part of the Kingdom of England," but were united with the British Empire solely through allegiance to the Crown. The colonies had the right to go their own way in most matters, particularly in directing and managing their "internal" affairs.

Though it seems to be a contradiction in terms, Bland truly was, as some characterized him, "a conservative revolutionary." Jefferson once described how Bland's train of thought proceeded and always landed him in a dilemma that many another liberal has faced in a revolutionary situation:

> He would set out on sound principles, pursue them logically till he found them leading to the precipice which he had to

> leap, start back alarmed, then resume his ground, go over it again in another direction, be led again by the correctness of his reasoning to the same place, and again back out, and try other processes to reconcile right and wrong, but finally left his reader and himself bewildered between the steady index of the compass in his hand and the chasm to which it seemed to point.

Even so, Jefferson added, "there was more sound matter in his pamphlet than in the celebrated 'Letters'* which were truly but *ignis fatuus,* leading us from true principles."

Peyton Randolph was nominated for the speakership by an able, powerful, and rather crusty Grandee, Colonel Archibald Cary, known to some as "the old Bruiser," with whom Henry would later have some sharp clashes. Lee, with Henry seconding, placed Bland in nomination. The vote went to Randolph, who continued to be speaker till his death some ten years later. While he performed his duties very well, he proved to be a sore disappointment to many of his supporters, for he soon moved out of conservative ranks to join Henry, Lee, Washington, George Mason, and others in supporting the Patriot cause.

With Randolph installed in the chair after a very formal and rather elaborate ceremony, the House was ready to take up the next order of business—electing a new treasurer. Richard Henry Lee was instantly on his feet, got the floor, and made a motion, strongly supported by Henry in a seconding speech, that henceforth the offices of speaker and treasurer were not to be held by anyone at the same time, as Robinson had held them for some thirty years.

British authorities had rather frowned on the Robinson arrangement, but tolerated it as a roundabout way of compensating the speaker for performing the special duties and responsibilities of his position. The speaker received no other compensation than that of every other Burgess—a per diem allowance of 10s. [$15.00] when present in the House and an equal allowance for every day spent

---

* Referring to the "Letters from a Pennsylvania Farmer to the Inhabitants of the British Colonies" (1767), written by John Dickinson, a Quaker and rich Philadelphia lawyer, who remained a reconciliationist to the last, hoping to patch up the quarrel with Britain. As a member of the Third Continental Congress, he opposed the Declaration of Independence. But once it was adopted, he showed his quality and mettle by enlisting, at the age of forty-four, as a private in the Continental forces, later rising to become a brigadier general.

in traveling to and from Williamsburg to attend legislative sessions.* These allowances did little more than pay expenses, if that.

On the other hand, the treasurership paid rather well. Treasurers worked on a commission basis, receiving 2.5 per cent of collections made on taxes and assessments levied on the colony as a whole. Out of his commission, the treasurer had to provide himself with whatever was necessary for the performance of his duties. As the expense was slight, limited to keeping a small office and employing a few clerks to keep accounts, prepare vouchers, receipts, and such things, the treasurer pocketed most of his commission.

Under this arrangement, Treasurer Robinson had been paying Speaker Robinson his salary "as a recompense for his Service in that Station, the Advantages and profitts arising from the Speakership being very inconsiderable and inadequate to the great Trouble and Attendance of that Office."

Now Lee and Henry moved to break up this arrangement. Henry's first speech in the House had been made on a Treasury matter. He had been seated about a week when the Burgesses took up a motion to establish a Public Loan Office, "from which monies might be lent on public account, and on good landed security to individuals."

This seemed to be a good idea, even to experienced and sharp-eyed Richard Bland. Idle money in the Treasury could be put to work to provide capital for developing Virginia's economy. That would attract more settlers. Interest from the loans might even help to reduce taxes, something ever to be desired.

The scheme appeared to be public spirited and innocent enough. Supported by the Grandees, the measure was on the point of passage with scarcely a word of debate when Henry rose to make his first speech in the House. Older members must have smiled rather contemptuously as this "ignorant" young rawbones from the back country took it upon himself to address himself to a high matter

---

* Then as now, it appears, legislators were given to padding their travel and expense accounts. In coming down from the back country, Henry could easily have made it to Williamsburg in two days. But after each House session, he usually put in a voucher for six days of travel each way, twelve days in all, entitling him to £6 [$180]–not much, but three times what he was legitimately entitled to. Against this, however, should be reckoned the loss of income he suffered because he had to suspend his law practice, sometimes for many weeks, while attending in Williamsburg.

of public finance. What could he possibly know about it? All would soon be listening to him most intently.

Having as yet no slightest suspicion about the real intent of the bill, Henry opposed the Public Loan Office proposal as bad public policy on principle and proceeded to attack the scheme with "bold, grand, and overwhelming eloquence," as remarked by Jefferson, who heard the debate!

> Henry laid open with so much energy the spirit of favoritism on which the proposition was founded, and the abuses to which it would lead, that it was crushed in its birth. He carried with him all the members of the upper counties, and left a minority composed merely of the aristocracy of the country.
>
> From this time his popularity swelled apace,* and Mr. Robinson dying the year afterward, his deficit was brought to light and discovered the true object of the proposition.

The Lee-Henry motion to divorce the speakership and the treasurership made many members of the House "very nervous," and for understandable reasons, as soon became apparent. In arguing for the divorce, Henry denounced the arrangement tolerated under Robinson as "a dangerous system," lending itself to favoritism, corruption, and use of "undue influence." Henry did not yet know how true he spoke.

The bill to separate the two offices passed the House, 68 to 29. Henceforth, no one was to be both speaker and treasurer at the same time, which ruled out the nomination of Speaker Peyton Randolph, whom many would have been happy to see play a dual role. As treasurer, the House chose a veteran Burgess, a man of the highest integrity, respected by all, a moderate in his political views, Robert Carter Nicholas.

That done, Henry took the floor again and made a motion, seconded by Lee, that a select committee be named to look into the state of the treasury "with the utmost precision" and make a report as soon as possible. Previously, a small committee of the House had been named each year to examine and report on Treasury affairs. In the light of what was soon revealed, these committees can have

* It was only a few days after this that Henry struck the "aristocracy" an even more stunning blow with his Stamp Tax Resolutions. Seldom can a freshman member of any legislative body have won two such surprising and signal triumphs within ten days of taking his seat.

made only the most perfunctory examination of Treasury matters—if, indeed, they made any examination at all. They did not ask to see an audit of the books. Being friends of his, and not wishing to be nosey, they had probably taken Speaker-Treasurer Robinson's word for it that everything was all right in the fiscal office.

Henry's proposal to set up a select committee made many in the House, and on the Governor's Council and elsewhere, more nervous than before. But there was little open opposition to Henry's bill, which passed, and a committee of eleven was named, with Richard Bland as chairman and Henry and Lee as members. Edmund Pendleton, who knew more about Robinson's private and public affairs than anyone, was soon added to the committee.

After Robinson's death about six months before, it had become immediately apparent to his wife and to close friends that there was something seriously wrong with his personal and public accounts. Robinson had died without naming executors of his estate. His widow appealed to an old family friend, Colonel Peter Randolph, a member of the Governor's Council and chiefly responsible for having the House reverse itself on one of Henry's Stamp Tax Resolutions, the controversial fifth.

Randolph agreed to serve as an administrator of the estate and wrote to Edmund Pendleton, another of Robinson's close friends. As Pendleton was at home in Caroline County, Randolph hastily dispatched a letter by special courier, imploring Pendleton to aid in seeing what could be done to salvage something from the tangled affairs of Robinson "whose humanity and good nature have been the only inducement in his acting in a manner that must inevitably reflect on him. For God's sake," exclaimed Randolph, "refuse not this favor, and give me an answer by the bearer."

Pendleton could not well refuse. From rather humble beginnings, he had come far up in the world, greatly assisted along the way by Robinson, who had befriended him as a young man, opened many doors for him, and pushed him forward. Pendleton agreed to act, undertaking a burdensome task that occupied much of his time for the rest of his life.

It took some seventy years and hundreds of court actions to straighten out the mess left by the late treasurer whom Governor Fauquier, in a funerary encomium, had so recently extolled for "his great integrity, assiduity, and ability in business."

To assist them as executors, Randolph and Pendleton enlisted the aid of Peter Lyons, whom Henry had so belabored as Maury's counsel in the Parsons' Cause. But almost the entire burden of administering the estate fell upon Pendleton. Peter Randolph was not of much help and soon died. Lyons was frankly not much interested, always regretting that he had become involved. "This is a sad business," he remarked later, "and I often wish I had been sick the day I ingaged in it"—in modern Goldwynese, he should "have stood in bed."*

After a month's work, the select committee looking into Treasury affairs submitted findings, and its report dropped like a bombshell, causing "a ferment" throughout the colony. The committee found that Robinson had dipped into the Treasury for more than £100,000 [$3,000,000]—not that he had pocketed that sizable sum or used it to his financial advantage, but rather to help his friends.

Always affable and accommodating, Robinson had fallen into the practice of using Treasury funds to make loans to Grandees and larger planters. Many of these were deeply in debt, partly because times were rather hard, but more because of extravagance in their manner of life. Such loans, for the most part being personal loans, had been made without securing any specific collateral, and all were "free" loans, not bearing any interest charges. One of the richest men in the colony, Robinson made himself personally responsible for the repayment of such loans, thinking his estate large enough to absorb any losses incurred on these transactions.

But by 1765, at the time of the Stamp Tax debate, Robinson had come to realize that most of the borrowers were bad risks, that they could not repay their loans for a long time, if ever. It was to cover his Treasury deficit and protect his debtor friends that the proposal had been made to establish a Public Loan Office, designed to shift unauthorized "loans" from private to public account and thus legitimatize them, a scheme that Henry struck down with one blow.

The discovery of Robinson's freehanded use of public funds caused quite as much shock as if in our time plutocratic Andrew Mellon, Secretary of the Treasury in President Harding's administration, had been found doling out public funds as interest-free unsecured "loans" to his millionaire friends among bankers and industrial magnates, as well as to members of the Cabinet and the Congress.

The first estimate of Robinson's deficit, revealing "a chasm in the

---

* Curiously, Lyons later bought Studley Farm, Henry's birthplace, and established himself there. In 1775, a fire in Lyons' office-library at Studley destroyed many important Robinson papers, which made confusion worse confounded.

public coffers," was startling. Quite as disturbing was the select committee's discovery that Treasury accounts were in almost hopeless disorder. On some loans he made, Robinson had scratched a few words on odd scraps of paper, which were scattered all around. On other loans, as was later discovered, there was not even a scrap of paper to note the transaction. Ledgers were incomplete and inaccurate on tax collections and other matters. Many Treasury records were missing, perhaps never having been made.

Dismayed by all this, eager to make sure that the public interest would not again be violated, the Burgesses demanded that Robinson's executors—Peter Randolph, Edmund Pendleton, and Peter Lyons—place themselves under bond for £250,000, equal to half of the colony's public debt.

Robinson had left a large estate—several fine mansions, more than 20,000 acres of good land, some 400 slaves, and many personal belongings of value. But he also left £30,000 of personal debts, plus the £100,000 he owed the Treasury. The value of the estate, though large, was judged to be barely sufficient to pay debts. In short, Robinson had died insolvent, or nearly so.

This raised a question. If the entire estate were to be liquidated immediately to pay debts, Robinson's family would be left with little or nothing. To protect the family, and partly for reasons to be considered in a moment, Pendleton and his fellow executors petitioned the Burgesses to argue that selling all of the estate should not be done at once. It would be to the best interests of all to proceed more slowly. If that were done, so they assured the House, Robinson's debt to the Treasury could be paid in three years.

Resting on this assurance, the Burgesses agreed. At the same time, however, they decreed that 5 per cent interest a year should be charged against the Robinson estate on the public money the treasurer had "received and misapplied."

To make collections for the Robinson estate, the executors could have gone to court and taken action for repayment against those who held Treasury "loans." They chose not to do this for several reasons. One was to protect their friends, even members of their families. As Pendleton well knew, immediate court action would force many of the grandest of the Grandees into bankruptcy, or at least into selling sizable parts of their properties. Those owing money to the Robinson estate on Treasury "loans" should be given time to work off their debts.

Besides, court action would reveal a secret—the names and the amount of debt of those who had received Robinson's favors. Many of these favorites were Tidewater lords and preferred, at least in this, to remain anonymous. Perhaps because he had received and still owed above £1,000 [$30,000] in Treasury "loans," and his brother John about £500, and some of his law clients many times more, Pendleton decided from the start not to disclose the identity of those who had enjoyed Robinson's largesse. He kept his secret by successfully fending off the repeated insistence of Patrick Henry, Richard Henry Lee, and other Burgesses that the House and the public had the right to know who was involved, and for how much.

Deciding to use persuasion instead of law as a means of collection, Pendleton published in the *Virginia Gazette* several appeals to conscience. The first made the plea that as Robinson had "from a goodness of heart and benevolent disposition peculiar to him, . . . advanced large sums of money to assist and relieve his friends," the latter should "in honour and gratitude, . . . pay immediately what they owe, without further trouble or application; and even cheerfully sell their own estates to discharge it, rather than suffer the estate of their friend to be distressed for the payment of their debts."

This plea, made in 1766, produced very little. Collections for the year totaled only £2,000. The debtors, it was plain, were not willing "cheerfully," or otherwise, to sell their estates unless they had to. This was not a shining example of *noblesse oblige*.

Not too discouraged, Pendleton decided to take another tack in publishing a plea in the *Gazette* the next year. Delinquent debtors should come quickly forward and do their utmost to save that "distressed family, and to consider that if they neglect doing it, Mr. Robinson's innocent infant children will be left without a home, or a single slave to make them a single morsel of bread. Surely, if they have any humanity, they will shew it on this occasion."

And what kind of a life could the Robinsons lead without a "single" slave to make them a "single" morsel of bread! Obviously, they could not make out at all. This appalling prospect apparently moved a few tender hearts, for collections during the year rose to £6,000.

But money continued to come in slowly, and only in driblets. At the end of 1769, by which time Robinson's accounts with the Treasury were to have been cleared under Pendleton's delayed-payment plan, the debt was larger than ever, having grown because repayments did not even cover accumulating interest charges.

At this point, the House ordered that a start be made toward selling off the Robinson estate within four months. Pendleton saw to it that Mrs. Robinson was able to retain considerable property, including sufficient slaves to provide bread for her and her children. But the larger part of Robinson's baronial estate was auctioned off and sold, parcel by parcel, and a very choice parcel Patrick Henry managed to buy "at a bargain."

Even the sale of the estate, however, did not pay off the Treasury debt. That matter was not finally settled until 1781, and in a way that was virtually a swindle. At long last, the debt was cleared by what Pendleton called "a lucky operation of paper money," the last payments being made in depreciated colonial paper bills "not worth oak leaves."

Though the identity of most of them was not known at the time, and would not be known till almost two centuries later,* those favored by Robinson with Treasury loans represented the top crust of the First Families of Virginia, bearing such F.F.V. names as Randolph, Byrd, Carter, Cary, Burwell, Braxton, Mercer, Fitzhugh, Churchill, and many another of the pedigreed "Long Tails." Robinson had "loaned" more than £37,000 [$1,100,000] to his friends among the Burgesses, and almost £16,000 to members of the Governor's Council.

The largest aggregate loan had been made to a long-time friend, a member of the Council, Colonel William Byrd III, who was rapidly dissipating a great inherited fortune, perhaps the largest of its day in Virginia. In 1766, his debt to Robinson stood at £14,921 [$450,000]. Even when the loans were being made, it was not a secret that Byrd's finances were in a "desperate" state because of his neglect of business and his passion for gambling for the highest stakes at cards, with dice, or in any form.

Byrd was obviously "not good pay," and it pained Pendleton to discover that this was true of many other debtors among the most exalted Grandees. Pendleton himself owed £1,020 [$30,500]. When calling on Robinson's debtors to come forward "cheerfully" and pay up, he was evidently not thinking of himself, for he never paid. In 1780, he canceled his debt, writing it off as payment for his services as administrator. This was legitimate, and he was certainly not overpaid for all of the time, trouble, and expense he had spent in such services.

---

* For an excellent and fascinating account of the whole Robinson affair and its wide ramifications, see a splendid biography, *Edmund Pendleton* (1952), by David John Mays.

Robinson had loaned himself £8,085 [$240,000] which he used to invest, along with Colonel Byrd and Governor Fauquier, in a speculative lead-mining venture. But with this single exception, he apparently did not use Treasury funds for his own enrichment. Certainly, he derived no profit from illicit transactions that left him more than £100,000 in debt.

One may well believe what was said of Robinson by his successor as treasurer, scrupulous and meticulous Robert Carter Nicholas. After seven years in office, having examined all accounts, Nicholas declared that he had "abundant reason to believe" that Robinson had acted rather "from a mistaken kind of humanity and compassion for persons than any view to his own private emolument."

Still, that does not excuse his abuse of public office. Nor does it really explain how he, with all his experience, fell into the folly that cost him so much and involved his Grandee friends in great worry and embarrassment. The scandal struck the "aristocratical" party a stunning blow from which it did not soon recover. Its members never regained the political power, the deferential respect, the almost unquestioned social prestige and financial position they had enjoyed for generations.

By killing the Public Loan Office scheme at birth, by their joint action in opening up the scandal that so glaringly revealed how the "aristocracy" manipulated public affairs in Virginia to advance group and personal interests, Patrick Henry and Richard Henry Lee greatly strengthened the popular forces moving toward revolutionary change.

XII

"Good King George"

. . . the best King that any nation was ever blessed with.

—BENJAMIN FRANKLIN

While "a chasm in the public coffers" was nothing to cheer about, Virginia along with her sister colonies had very good news to celebrate.

The Stamp Act had been repealed.

Rising opposition to the Act on both sides of the Atlantic had come to a head early in 1766. The widespread boycott of British goods had seriously affected powerful economic interests at home. These began sending to Parliament a stream of petitions strongly urging that the stamp plan be abandoned because it was hurting business. Members of the House of Commons might airily brush aside the colonies' complaints and their arguments about their constitutional rights, but it was something else again when rich British merchants, manufacturers, shipowners, bankers, and others began pouring in complaints about their "grievances." To such complaints, Parliament was disposed to listen.

In urging immediate repeal of the Stamp Tax, these business interests argued that the law was as good as dead anyhow. Not a stamp had been bought in the colonies. As Americans had already effectively "repealed" the law, it might as well be taken off the books, for it was quite useless, merely a nuisance interfering with British trade.

Lord Grenville, author of the Stamp Act, had fallen from the King's good graces and was succeeded as prime minister by the leader of a Whig faction, Lord Rockingham, rather libertarian in his views but ineffectual as a leader—"that nothing Rockingham," Sir Horace Walpole described him. He was so uncertain of himself and so diffident that he almost never spoke in Parliament even when he and his measures were under the heaviest attack. On one occasion when he rose to defend himself and his administration, the King—perhaps with tongue in cheek—hastily wrote him a note to congratulate him on his rare courage.

Under mounting pressure, eager to stop the clamor both in the colonies and at home, Rockingham and his Cabinet agreed that the Stamp Tax should go and took steps to accomplish this. The question, when it came to the floor of the Commons, provoked the longest and angriest debate in almost a century. Nothing like it had been heard since 1688 when Parliament was debating whether or not to depose James II, last and worst of the Stuart kings.

Still proud of his brainchild, Lord Grenville stoutly defended the Stamp Tax and called for its strictest enforcement, by arms if necessary. He had the vociferous support of the Court party, the King's Friends, and of some in the Whig factions. It was the unanimous opinion of the seventeen Lords of the Bedchamber, who had the King's ear at all times and who, among them, controlled a tenth of the members in the Commons, that no slightest concession should be made to the colonies on the Stamp Tax, and that continued resistance to it should be speedily crushed with fire and sword.

That, too, was the opinion of a most powerful royal personage, the King's uncle and a chief adviser, the Duke of Cumberland, who had brutally ravaged Scotland in suppressing the last Jacobite uprising. He strongly urged a similar sanguinary course against American "rebels."

In the prolonged heated debate, the strongest voice on the other side was that of William Pitt, "the Great Commoner," a man of great eloquence and commanding presence. Because of sickness, Pitt had been absent from the House for a time, but now unexpectedly appeared to deliver a thundering speech, telling the Commons:

> You have no right to tax America . . . This House represents the commons of Britain. Here we give and grant what

> is our own. But it is unjust and absurd to suppose that we can give and grant the property of the commons of America.
>
> This constitutional right has ever been exercised by the commons of America themselves, represented in their own provincial assemblies; and without it, they would have been slaves.

Which is what Henry, along with others, had been saying, and which he had incorporated as Virginia doctrine in his Stamp Tax Resolutions.

> We are told that America is obstinate, that America is almost in open rebellion . . . I rejoice that America resisted!*

If three millions of His Majesty's American subjects had been "so dead to all the feelings of liberty," they would have been "fit instruments to make slaves of all the rest of us."

The Stamp Tax, Pitt concluded, should be abandoned "absolutely, totally, and immediately." Furthermore, the reason for doing so should be clearly and explicitly stated—that such a tax, or anything similar, was based on "erroneous principle."

During the debate, to quiet the fears of those anxious to preserve the profits and perquisites of Empire, Pitt went out of his way to give unqualified support to the most important part of Britain's exploitative colonial system:

> Let the sovereign authority of legislative and commercial control, always possessed by this country, be asserted in as strong terms as can be devised . . .
>
> We may, and they [the colonists] are willing that we shall, bind their trade, confine their manufactures, and exercise every power except that of taking money out of their pockets without their consent . . .
>
> I would not suffer even a nail for a horseshoe to be manufactured in America.

Americans were not as "willing" as Pitt supposed to have Parliament "bind their trade, confine their manufactures" for the benefit of those at home growing rich on British monopoly commerce. That point would come up later, but was not at issue now.

In proposing action on the Stamp Tax, the Rockingham administration carefully refrained from raising any question about "constitutional" rights. A change should be made not as a matter of

---

* No wonder the King angrily denounced Pitt as the "trumpet of sedition."

principle, but as a practical matter, for "continuance of the said Act would be attended with many inconveniences, and may be productive of consequences greatly detrimental to the commercial interests of these Kingdoms."

At length, at three in the morning of February 22, 1766, after an acrimonious and tempestuous last-day debate that went on for fifteen hours, the House of Commons decided to abandon the Stamp Act by a vote of 275 to 167. Most reluctantly the House of Lords concurred, and the Act expired.

With typical English indirection, as in so many political affairs, the change was effected not by passage of a bill to repeal the Stamp Tax, but by defeat of a motion that it should continue in effect and be enforced at all costs, even at bayonet point if required. The Stamp Tax remained on the books, but nothing more was going to be done about it. It was to be allowed to lapse, to become a dead letter, which amounted actually, if not formally, to repeal.

News of the vote occasioned joyous popular demonstrations throughout the kingdom, particularly in the ports and larger commercial and manufacturing centers. Celebrations throughout the colonies were even more joyous. Church bells rang out the happy tidings; cannon boomed; huge bonfires blazed day and night. Large crowds marched along town streets and around village greens, singing and shouting. Taverns from Maine to Georgia resounded to cheers, laughter, and rousing toasts to the "Sons of Liberty, Triumphant."

Before abandoning the Stamp Tax, Parliament had passed a Declaratory Act to cover its retreat. The Act was designed, read its preamble, "for the better securing the dependency of His Majesty's dominions in America upon the Crown and Parliament of Great Britain," and went on to declare Britain's right "to bind the colonies and people of America . . . in all cases whatsoever."

Colonial leaders took note of this, but were not bothered about it at the moment. So long as the declared right remained theoretic, and was not put into practice, there was no point in raising a somewhat academic argument about it. What immediately mattered was that the colonies by concerted action had won a signal victory—their resistance had scuttled the "infamous" Stamp Tax.

Nowhere was this victory more joyously celebrated than in Virginia, where resistance had begun when Patrick Henry introduced and the Burgesses adopted most of his Stamp Tax Resolutions. News of the victory was celebrated at Williamsburg with "a ball and elegant entertainment at the Capitoll," with Governor Fauquier attending. No doubt there were festivities at Hanover Courthouse, centering in Shelton's tavern. Perhaps Henry was present to be again saluted as "the Noble Patriot," for Hanoverians had become very proud of "Pah-trick," as his friends and neighbors called him.

Virginians of all classes were so delighted with the turn of events that when the House of Burgesses met, a motion was made that a stone obelisk be set up to commemorate the "death" of the Stamp Tax, and that a statue of George III be erected. Other colonial assemblies entertained similar resolutions.

Proposals for specially honoring the King at this time reflect a curious illusion that persisted for some time. It was presumed that His Majesty had helped bring about repeal. Down almost to Independence, nothing could shake the notion of most Americans that "good King George" was their friend, that he understood and sympathized with their aims and aspirations, that he patiently considered their complaints and even found some merit in their "constitutional" arguments.

With few exceptions, Americans accepted a simple thesis—and how simple-minded it was—to account for their recent troubles. The young inexperienced King had been misled by the machinations of "wicked" old ministers forced on him by a "corrupt" Parliament. If only he could shake himself loose from these "master devils" and do what he desired, all would be well. The colonists would quickly return to being, what they had always been, "humbly obedient servants." Time and again, they professed their utter loyalty to George III, their "sacred" Sovereign Lord, even when violently resisting measures taken in his name.

This American thesis was a strange misreading of the nature of the power structure and of the fierce power struggle going on at the time in Britain, which was having a constitutional crisis of its own. Many of the King's ministers were "wicked" enough, to be sure, but they were not the ogres that, on this side of the Atlantic, they were made out to be. Their chief fault lay in their want of political judgment and their sheer incompetence. But Americans missed the main point about them—or chose to ignore it.

Most of them—and all of the worst—were the King's own choice, his current Court favorites, put in office and kept there as long as possible to work his will and carry out his personal policy. The King strongly favored the Stamp Tax and was grieved by its repeal, later attributing all subsequent troubles to the failure to enforce it with all strength from the start. If resistance had been promptly smashed, he maintained, Americans would never again have dared to beard the British Lion.

At the time of repeal, George had been king for six years, since 1760, when he ascended the throne at the age of twenty-three, being a year younger than Henry, two years younger than John Adams, five years younger than Washington and six years older than Jefferson. All of these were more or less of an age, so that there was no conflict here between an older and a younger generation.

The young and inexperienced King was resolved from the start to exercise royal powers to the full—powers that had been allowed to erode for a half century during the reigns of his forebears, George I and George II. During their reigns, the great Whig nobles through their control of Parliament had taken to governing the kingdom almost as they pleased. From failure to use it, the royal prerogative had become dusty and tarnished. That prerogative—the right, theoretically at least, of a sovereign to rule without any restriction—was to be brought out of the closet, polished up, and restored to its former bright luster.

British parliamentary democracy, in its slow evolution, owes much to George I and George II; not for anything they did, but precisely for the things they signally failed to do. They did not tend to business as British sovereigns, having their chief interests elsewhere.

George I was fifty-four when he succeeded to the throne in 1714 at the death of Queen Anne. The Queen had died childless—or "without issue," in elegant officialese. George had been, and remained, Elector (hereditary monarch) of Hanover, one of many small constantly quarreling German principalities. That he was a man of little ability and no distinction at all did not matter. He was "legitimate," standing next in line of succession to the Crown as grandson of deposed James II.

So far as he had any public interest at all, the new King confined himself to German affairs. He visited England as seldom as possible, hating its climate, loathing its food and drink, disliking its people, finding the islanders "uncongenial." He spent most of his time in his Hanover castles, dabbling in petty German politics when not enjoying himself with a long line of billowy German mistresses, each of whom was generously pensioned off at British expense when her day of favor was over. George I had little interest in the British Crown except as a source of gold to provide more luxurious extravagances and heighten his prestige among the small German princes who were always maneuvering and conspiring against one another.

The King knew no English, and did nothing about that. His British ministers knew no German, and were too proud to learn. Consequently, communication between them was difficult and spasmodic. But nobody was displeased. The King went his way in Germany; the governing Whig nobles went theirs in Britain, ignoring the Crown.

George II (1683–1760) was, as a British sovereign, somewhat of an improvement on his father. Though largely German in his interests and viewpoint, he visited London more frequently, could speak a bit of broken English, and did not exercise himself so exclusively in the royal bedchamber—though he, too, had a fickle passion for plump, blonde, compliant *Deutsche damen.*

Occasionally, he put his mind to business, but in the manner of a junior clerk or an apprentice bookkeeper. Fascinated by detail, a stickler for having unimportant things done just right, he did not bother much with larger matters, principally because their significance was lost on him. He preferred checking his money accounts, the cash in hand, getting out his gold pieces and counting them over and over, one by one, day after day. As remarked by one who was not unfriendly:

"He seems to think his having done a thing today an unanswerable reason for doing it tomorrow," which fairly represents the character of his thirty-three-year reign.

George III had no respect for his predecessors, his grandfather and great-grandfather, who had been little more than royal pensioners residing abroad. The young King was resolved that he was not going to be, as they had been, "a cyfer." He would use the royal prerogative to steer another course, back to the days when a king was King. He tried hard enough to do this, but his equipment was not of the best.

George had an unfortunate upbringing. At thirteen, he had lost his father, Frederick, Prince of Wales, a wild and absurd creature who spent most of his time in ridiculous quarrels with his father. The youth was then taken closely in hand by his almost equally absurd mother, Augusta, a stupid German princess, "a demon of discord," whose vaulting ambitions for her son—and for herself—were matched only by her ignorance and her passion for petty intrigue.

The Dowager Princess of Wales so isolated her son, heir apparent to the throne, that he saw almost nobody of his own age, and few but the "ladies" who fluttered about in his mother's *salon* at Leicester House, and the preceptor-tutors she chose for him. A number of them George later recalled with disgust, declaring that one was wholly incompetent; another, "a depraved, worthless man"; and a third, "intriguing, unworthy." As succinctly put by a great historian, the late Sir Lewis Namier, the most profound student of this British period:

> So the boy spent joyless years in a well-regulated nursery, the nearest approach to a concentration camp; lonely but never alone, constantly watched and discussed, never safe from the wisdom and goodness of grown-ups; never with anyone on terms of equality . . .*

No wonder the young prince, under such confinement and continuous pushing, was inclined to be obstinate, sullen, and sulky. In his resistance to unremitting discipline and pressure, he fell into "incomprehensible indolence, inattention, and heedlessness" that he described as "my greatest enemy."

Conquering this, he went to the opposite extreme, directing his attention to everything, no matter how minute, becoming as fascinated as his grandfather George II had been with meticulous detail. His letters and dispatches as King bore not only the calendar date, but the hour and exact minute of writing.

In addition to providing young George with tutors, his mother kept a sharp eye on what he was being taught. On learning that he was being instructed in logic, she critically remarked that this was an "odd subject" for one in her son's position to be studying. What need had a King of logic? He should be taught to exercise his will and authority.

George, it appears, took to logic, though of his own kind. Once he got an idea, nothing could shake it. He followed it, logically, wherever it led. As he once informed the younger William Pitt, urging him as chief minister to do the same:

"I never assent till I am convinced what is proposed is right, and then . . . I never allow that to be destroyed by after-thoughts,

---

* For a fascinating insight into the King's character and the influences that shaped it, see two essays, "King George III" and "George III Speaks Out," in Namier's *Crossroads of Power* (1962). The whole book should be read for the light it reflects on the American crisis.

which on all subjects tend to weaken, never to strengthen, the original proposal."

George was never one to reconsider, to have another look at changing elements in any situation. He would plunge ahead, come what might.

> Egocentric and rigid, stunted in feelings, unable to adjust himself to events, flustered by sudden change, he could meet situations only in a negative manner, clinging to men and measures with disastrous obstinancy.
>
> But he mistook that defensive apparatus for courage, drive, and vigour, from which it was as far removed as anything could be.*

In addition to a wretched education and family background, George had other handicaps as man and monarch. The most serious was a physical disability—he was subject to spells of insanity. The first occurred in 1765 just as the Stamp Tax troubles boiled up. The next occurred in 1788 when he became so peevish, abusive, and violent that he had to be put in a strait jacket—or, as the royal physician preferred to call it, "a strait waiscoat."

Spells recurred in 1801, 1804, and 1810. At the inception of one of these, when he was under the hallucination that people were creatures of various kinds, he went to address the House of Lords, all of whom were resplendent in bright silks and satins, their chests glittering with Stars of the Garter, insignia of the Order of the Bath, and other shining badges.

"My Lords and Peacocks," he solemnly addressed them—and may not have been so far off at that.

Finally, in 1811, George's mind became completely deranged, and never recovered balance. For nine years, down to his death in 1820 at the age of eighty-two, the old King, now both blind and mad, lived secluded and under strict confinement in Buckingham Palace.

Seeing almost none but servants, he talked to himself incessantly, holding long imaginary conversations with old friends and former ministers long since in their graves—perhaps with the ghosts of prissy and boring Lord Grenville, "champagne" Charles Townshend, sleepy Lord North, and others with whom he had worked in pushing measures that led, step by step, to the great debacle in America. The King never ceased talking about that disaster. He

---

* These two parapraphs are quoted from Namier's *Crossroads of Power*.

could never really comprehend what had happened—how and where things had gone wrong. What happened was so illogical in his terms.

However tragic its end and rough in its middle passage, George's reign opened auspiciously, bright with promise. The young King was a welcome new kind of Hanoverian. He could speak English, without an accent—though in the affected clipped speech of the upper classes, scarcely understood down below, but still recognizably English. He was affable and approachable, liked to talk with people and, what was quite noteworthy in a monarch, occasionally listened when others spoke. Attending the coronation ceremonies, even the fastidious and often finicky Sir Horace Walpole was impressed:

> For the King himself, he seems all good nature and wishing to satisfy everybody . . . I was surprised to find the levee room had lost so entirely the air of the lion's den. This sovereign don't stand in one spot with his eyes fixed royally on the ground and dropping bits of German news; he walks about and speaks to everybody.
>
> I saw him afterwards on the Throne, where he is graceful and genteel, sits with dignity, and reads his answers to addresses well.

In conversation, George had a bluff but not unpleasant style. He was given to reiteration and to ending almost every statement in a personally distinctive way.

"Good morning," he would say in his heartiest manner. "Isn't it a splendid day? Splendid day! Splendid! What? What!" Or as he once told a large audience of courtiers gathered around him:

"Read Burke's *Reflections* [a blistering attack on the French Revolution and all of its works]. It will do you good! Will do you good! Do you good! What? What!"

George was welcomed as a new kind of Hanoverian in another respect. Not a philanderer, he was a good family man,* conventional in his habits, pious but tolerant in his religious views. He had promised himself that, once he were king, he would attempt "with vigour to restore religion and virtue," and set an example for correcting "the great depravity of the age, . . . the wickedest age that ever was seen."**

---

* Having married in 1761 a German princess, Charlotte of Mecklenburg Strelitz, who shared his taste for homely domesticity.

** Though scarcely the wickedest, it was an age of loose morals in both private and public life, as reflected in the pages of Fielding, Smollett, Goldsmith, Sterne, Dr. Johnson, and others, and in the prints of Hogarth and Gillray.

Though the King's simple domesticity, his lifelong conjugal fidelity, and his want of elegant and expensive tastes were scorned and openly laughed at in high-flying upper circles, especially among the great Whig nobles who found him "a dull dog," these were the traits that endeared him to the rising, solid, sobersided *bourgeoisie.*

Morally, spiritually, and culturally, he was one of them. His example pleased them by imparting a new luster to their rather humdrum penny-pinching virtues. The families of prosperous burghers and struggling small shopkeepers were flattered to have their values stamped, as it were, with the Great Seal.

The King was also known and well liked as "farmer George." When making a trip, or "royal progress," he frequently had the great State coach stopped and stepped out to chat with country people met along the roads, taking obvious pleasure—and giving it, too—in talking with them about crops, weather, market prices, livestock breeding, and how they and their families were getting along. He often inquired about their recipes for making apple dumplings, of which he was very fond. The royal chefs evidently left much to be desired in their apple dumpling department.*

Altogether, George impressed his subjects as a proper English gentleman, and all had been pleased when he exclaimed on mounting the throne:

"Born and bred in this country, I glory in the name of Briton!"

At first, he equally impressed his American subjects, even such skeptics as Benjamin Franklin who attended the coronation and came away thinking the young King was virtuous, generous, and able, "the very best in the world, and the most amiable."

While still Prince of Wales, George had had as his adviser and tutor the Earl of Bute, a thoroughgoing Tory, descended from the royal Stuart line. To forward the Prince's political education, the Earl obtained from his friend, William Blackstone, a manuscript copy of the latter's celebrated *Commentaries on the Laws of England.*** In

---

* Among his many fine satirical caricatures, Gillray put out prints entitled "Farmer George and His Wife" and "A Lesson in Apple Dumplings."

** Volume I of the *Commentaries* was published in 1764, the remaining three by 1769. For generations, down to this century, Blackstone remained the lawyers' Bible on English Common Law and greatly influenced early American jurisprudence. Henry doubtless agreed when Jefferson early took exception to Blackstone's "wily sophistries" which were, he said, making "Tories of all England" and of some naïve Americans lacking in "native feelings of independence."

this work, rather shallow and often quite misleading, George read such doctrine as:

> The King is not only the chief, but properly the sole, magistrate of the nation, all others acting by commission from and in due subordination to him . . . He governs the kingdom; statesmen, who administer affairs, are only his ministers.

This was heady doctrine, which George found delightfully intoxicating.* It gave added authority to his mother's constant exhortations:

"George, be King! Be King!"

With his "dear friend" Bute at his side, the young King felt prepared and was quite determined to play a strong hand from the start. Obviously, the first thing to do was to "reform" the government, put it back in its old form. George did not propose to govern beyond the law, at mere whim and caprice. It was too late for that. But he would break the power of the great Whig nobles who had so long ruled through their control of Parliament. He would free himself from the dictation of parties and ministers and become, in effect, the first minister of the State. The Crown was to be released from "leading strings."

As a step toward that, George decided to break up the Cabinet system under which the ministry as a whole acted as a unit under the leadership of a chief minister, who sat as chairman of the Cabinet, a small committee consisting of those ministers in charge of the most important departments.** Once the Cabinet took a decision, usually by majority vote, all ministers had to support it and were responsible to the chief minister and the Cabinet for carrying it out.

To break up this system of joint responsibility, Bute proposed that each minister should confine himself strictly to the affairs of his department, that he should not report to a Cabinet but directly to the King, and be responsible to him alone. Any minister could be dis-

---

* George did not forget Blackstone, rewarding him by making him King's Counsel in 1761 and Solicitor General to the Queen in 1763, both of which were largely honorific but very lucrative offices.

** The hard core of the Cabinet consisted of five members *ex officio*—the two Secretaries of State (one for foreign affairs, the other for home affairs), the Lord President of the Privy Council, the First Lord of the Treasury, and the Lord Chancellor, the chief legal officer. Except for the two State Secretaries, who might or might not be commoners, all others were necessarily lords.

missed at the royal pleasure. The King would appoint his ministers as he chose, and not have any "forced" on him by a Cabinet system.

Hastening to make changes, young George immediately made Bute a member of the Privy Council and first Lord of the Bedchamber. The Bedchamber Lords stood to the King as the Ladies-in-Waiting did to the Queen, helping to dress and undress their Majesties, and performing ceremonial chores. Bedchamber Lordships were highly prized and avidly sought. One could put a bug in the King's ear about one thing or another on occasion and, besides, the job paid £500 [$15,000] a year.

At this time, several Lords angrily quarreled one day about who was to put on the King's shirt. One withdrew in a huff and resigned. This would never do, and George made Bute first Lord of the Bedchamber to preserve peace and good order there, a matter of prime political importance. There were seventeen Bedchamber Lords, all rich and of the most exalted rank in the realm, each wielding enormous power. Besides, and quite as important, they "owned" or controlled, among them, some forty seats in the House of Commons, a sizable bloc, almost a tenth of the membership. Discretion demanded that Bedchamber aides be kept in good humor, for this had been found to be "a very cheap way of keeping them steady to support Government."

With the Bedchamber straightened out, the young King and aging Earl moved against William Pitt, "the Great Commoner," then at the height of his influence and popularity for his success in prosecuting the Seven Years' War. They so undermined his authority and so angered him by petty harassments that he resigned, as they had hoped, and Bute took over as prime minister.

Now rid of "the Great Commoner," who stood in their way, they then assaulted the very bastion, the keep, of Whig power—the Treasury, a prolific source of patronage and political plunder.

For some years, the Duke of Newcastle, a great Whig magnate, had been First Lord of the Treasury, and the first duty of the First Lord, according to Whig practice, was to "manage" the House of Commons and provide enough votes to pass any bill desired by Whig ministries. Though it took a bit of doing, such "managing" was not too difficult.

Representation in the Commons had a crazy quilt pattern. It had not changed in centuries, nor would it for another three-quarters of a century, not till 1832, when passage of the first Parliamentary Reform Bill averted almost certain violent revolution.

In the reign of George III, a member sat in the Commons for Dunwich, which had completely disappeared, having been slowly washed away by the North Sea. Yet the lord holding title to the submerged lands "elected" someone to sit for Dunwich in the House. So, too, with the abandoned coal pits at Appleby, the pigeon lofts at Richmond, and the moldering castle ruins at Old Sarum, which had neither a house nor an inhabitant. In six other constituencies, almost unpopulated, eligible voters numbered three or less.

Meantime, large commercial and manufacturing centers like Birmingham, Manchester, and Sheffield had grown up, but had no representation at all in the House.

In the old constituencies, property and other qualifications narrowly restricted the right to vote. Fewer than 11,000 voters in all elected 254 of the 513 members representing the English and Welsh constituencies. Representation of Scotland, which had some 2,000,000 people, was even more of a farce. Its 44 members were chosen by fewer than 1,500 electors.

The Duchy (county) of Cornwall, small and sparsely populated, was politically "owned" by the Treasury and returned forty-four members, as many as all of Scotland and five times more than the most populous county in the kingdom, Middlesex, which contained Westminster, Southwark, and the City of London. Seats in the House were regarded as property and notoriously bought and sold "like stock in Change Alley." The price of a good "safe" seat at this time averaged £3,000 [$90,000].

The mass of British people had no more representation in the House than the American colonists, and began to object to this. But the King and the Whig lords, whatever their differences, agreed on one thing—the structure of the House was not to be touched in any particular, but should remain as it had been for almost five centuries, notwithstanding major shifts in population and the growth of strong new economic interests. To the complaint that the House was not representative, the King, the King's Friends, and the Whig nobles answered with one voice that it was not meant to be so.

By far the largest single bloc of votes belonged to the Treasury. It "owned" scores of seats in what were known as Treasury boroughs, where its candidates always won because no one chose to face hopeless odds in running against them. The Treasury controlled even more seats through the influence and active electioneering of its 11,000 agents—tax collectors, excisemen, customs officers, and others. These agents, if they valued their jobs, saw to it that they mustered a majority of votes for Treasury candidates in the localities where they were stationed.

The Duke of Newcastle, a most powerful Whig politician, had headed the Treasury for some time. To Bute, it seemed to be "both absurd and impossible" that this elaborate apparatus for "managing" the House of Commons should remain in the hands of Newcastle. "Shall this feeble old man," exclaimed Bute, be tolerated by the King and suffered to continue his "attempts to fetter him in either House?" Obviously, not!

The Court now proceeded, as with Pitt, to harry the Duke out of office, and Bute, already prime minister and Privy Councillor, became First Lord of the Treasury. Bute had no intention of cleaning up "corruption" in the Treasury; he planned to use it against the Whigs.

The stage was now set to build a strong Court party, the King's Friends. If corruption by the Treasury had been lush before, it now became even more so, reaching heights—or depths—never known before. The Treasury bought more pocket and "rotten" boroughs, and had its agents stir themselves more energetically in corraling votes for King's Friends.

Also, under Bute's direction, the Treasury found more money to spend on what might be called special projects. Whenever the King wanted a particular measure passed, it was not uncommon for the pay office at the Treasury to hand out bribes of £200 [$6,000] or even more to buy votes in the Commons. Such bribes were not paid surreptitiously, but quite openly over the counter. To influence decision on a particularly important matter, the executive secretary of the Treasury Board, so he officially reported, paid out one morning more than £25,000 [$750,000] to see that House members voted "right."

Under the existing system, was it any wonder, asked an early advocate of parliamentary reform, that the House of Commons was "filled with idle schoolboys, insignificant coxcombs, led-captains and toad-eaters, profligates, gamblers, bankrupts, beggars, contractors, commissaries, public plunderers, ministerial dependents, hirelings, and wretches who would sell their country or deny their God for a guinea."

The King's popularity, so high at the time of his coronation, soon slipped into a rapid decline. At first, popular discontent was directed not so much against him as against his "dear friend" Lord Bute, who appeared to be ruling the kingdom as first minister. Among other reasons, Bute was unpopular because he was a Scot and, in English eyes, a "foreigner"—as much of a foreigner as George I and II had been. Also, he had long been a close friend of the King's absurd mother, always attending the court she held in Leicester House, and the rumor ran that there was something more than friendship between them. This may have been mere gossip, but it was widespread, and it hurt. Posters, handbills, and ill-natured squibs appeared: "No petticoat government! No Scotch Minister! . . ."

Not to burden the King with his own unpopularity, Bute decided to resign as prime minister, but he remained close to the throne as chief adviser, continuing as prime minister in fact, if not in name. His successor as chief of ministry was Lord Grenville, whose ingenious stamp plan to tax the colonies was welcomed by the King. Certainly, he agreed, the colonies should contribute directly to the support of Empire, and do something to pay for their own protection and keep.

When it became obvious that the Stamp Tax could not be collected except by armed force, the King agreed that some modification might be made. But he felt strongly that the Stamp Act should not be repealed, that its underlying principle should not be impaired; the colonies should be subject to direct taxation in one form or another.

For a king to intervene and try to influence votes on a question before the House of Commons had long been considered highly improper, even "unconstitutional." Nevertheless, George sent Bute and other leaders of the King's Friends into the House to let it be known that His Majesty's "private" opinion was that the Stamp Tax was fundamentally all right and should not be repealed, that its underlying principle should be maintained.

Americans apparently knew nothing about this. They assumed that the King, their "friend," had played a major role in lifting the "infamous" Stamp Tax off their backs. Not that this had been a burden, for they had chased out all the stamp masters and not bought a stamp.

Still, there was a victory to celebrate. In Virginia, a proposal had been made in the House of Burgesses that the occasion should be commemorated by putting up a stone obelisk and a statue of "good King George."

What Patrick Henry thought about this proposal is not known. He could not have objected to setting up a stone obelisk which would be, in a sense, an enduring memorial to him and his Stamp Tax

Resolutions. He may have had some reservations about erecting a statue to the King whom he had so recently and vehemently castigated as a tyrant. Still, Henry must have voted for the project. If he had opposed it, he would not have been named a member of the committee to carry it out.

But the Burgesses, while authorizing the project, failed to appropriate any funds for the purpose. This was just as well, for it saved the taxpayers some money. If a statue of the King had gone up in Williamsburg in front of the Palace or the Capitol, it would have come down fairly soon and been gleefully smashed to pieces.

At the time of repeal, New York erected a large equestrian statue of the King, made of lead. In 1776, it was toppled from its pediment in Bowling Green, broken into bits, and the lead in it melted down to provide musket balls for Continental soldiers, so that the costly statue was not a complete loss.

XIII
Another Tax Explosion

You will not see a shilling from America.

—Edmund Burke

Stamp Tax repeal, suddenly relaxing tensions all around, brought a year of relative quiet and content. Americans were pleased to be once more enjoying "salutary neglect," free of more bothersome interferences and impositions from London. It seemed as if this happy state might long continue.

Not content to let well enough alone, almost as if bent on baiting the colonists, British authorities decided to revive the tax question —and in a very dubious and highly objectionable form.

Having been recalled to office, William Pitt was head of the ministry, but after a short time only nominally so. He soon became wholly incapacitated. Suffering painfully from gout and the onset of a severe nervous disorder that impaired his faculties, even his mind at times, Pitt retired to the country and paid absolutely no attention to parliamentary and any other business, not answering letters, refusing to see any visitors, not even the King, who, much to his annoyance, was denied his request for a fifteen-minute talk.

At this time, too, Pitt seriously compromised himself as "the Great Commoner" by accepting from the King, who had more than once publicly wished him dead, a peerage as Earl of Chatham.

Pitt's Whig friends were shocked. Horace Walpole spoke for them in saying that, politically, Londoners "have brought in their verdict of *felo de se* [suicide] against William, Earl of Chatham."

Of Pitt, Edmund Burke once said, rather maliciously: "The least peep in that [the royal] closet intoxicates him, and will to the end of his life."* In any case, the remainder of Pitt's life was anti-climactic. His peerage removed him from the Commons to the House of Lords, where he had never had any influence, and never would have.

Late in 1766, with Pitt nominally in command but incapacitated, leadership in the administration passed by default into the eager hands of an ambitious, younger, and quite brilliant man, Charles Townshend, chancellor of the exchequer, who took over as first minister *de facto*. Second son of Lord (Charles, Third Viscount) Townshend, he was in his early forties, but already a veteran in public life. He had been in Parliament for almost two decades, ever since he was twenty-two, when his family had bought him a seat in the Commons. At the moment, he was sitting for the "safe" Treasury borough of Harwich. Down the years he had held many responsible positions—earlier, as a follower of Pitt; now, as one of the King's Friends.

By all accounts, Townshend had a fine mind, wit, charm, eloquence, and "a wonderful capacity for business of every kind." Many of his more discriminating contemporaries thought that, as an orator and debater in the House, he was the equal of such giants as Pitt and Edmund Burke—and in some respects, their superior—"the most delightful speaker I ever heard," said one who was a fine speaker himself.

In the annals of Parliament, Townshend's "champagne" speech on a question about India, delivered when he was so filled with "bubbly" that he had great difficulty standing upright and fairly steady, is a classic for its easy grace, its penetration, its solid information and weight, its brilliant flashes of wit, and a rollicking humor that had even the angriest members of the opposition rolling with laughter.

Townshend had enormous talents and might have been the greatest man of the age, "and probably inferior to no man in any age," as Horace Walpole said, had it not been that his faults were equally

---

* Burke, too, liked the sniff of the royal closet, though he was seldom there, and never as prime minister, or as a peer.

enormous. He lacked emotional and intellectual ballast, being impulsive, mercurial, and headstrong, notably deficient in patience and judgment.

Townshend had ardently championed Lord Grenville's stamp plan, and strongly opposed its repeal. Now that he was in command, he would find another way of taxing the colonies, letting it be known that he was concentrating on the matter.

While dreaming up his scheme, he kept even his Cabinet colleagues, as they complained, completely in the dark about what he had in mind.* It would come to them—and everybody—as a bright surprise, an easy way of upholding the "superintendency of the Mother Country" and the "independency of the Crown."

Americans had won their point about not paying a stamp tax or direct taxes in any form—what they called "internal" taxes. But they had long been paying "external" taxes in the form of customs duties imposed by Parliament on certain imports. Such duties constituted a form of tax, to be sure, but had been accepted without too much complaint, never having been challenged in principle. The duties had never been used to raise revenue, merely to regulate trade with the aim of assuring British business a virtual monopoly in the American market.

Very well then, thought Townshend, who "passed for the cleverest fellow in England," he would raise revenue in the colonies by extending customs duties to cover an additional list of items—specifically, tea, paper, window glass, pigments and other materials used in making paint. Thus he would confound the colonial "logicians" always talking about the distinction between "internal" and "external" taxes. All such talk was nonsense, Townshend told the Commons: "The distinction is ridiculous in the opinion of everybody, except the Americans."

Townshend had the united support of the Court party, which felt, according to Burke, that the King, since abandonment of the Stamp Tax, "stood in a sort of humiliated state" and would remain so until something were done to reassert Britain's authority, as set forth in the Declaratory Act, "to bind the colonies in all cases whatsoever."

Predicting strong resistance in the colonies, Edmund Burke, sitting in the Commons for the first time, warned Townshend and his

---

* Lord Shelburne, minister in charge of the colonies, wrote Pitt to complain that neither he nor any other member of the administration had the slightest notion of what Townshend was up to.

supporters of their folly, exclaiming: "You will not see a shilling from America!"

How right he was. But at the moment, few in the House agreed with him. The Commons, after brief debate, authorized Townshend's tax scheme. The House of Lords happily concurred and on June 29, 1767, the King had the Great Seal placed on the provocative Townshend Acts, expressing great satisfaction with what had been done to put the colonists in their place—which was at heel.

Along with new taxes, Townshend decided, and Parliament agreed, that the colonies stood in need of other "reforms." The trade laws should be very strictly enforced. There should be no more "accommodation" between customs officers and colonial shippers importing goods subject to duties.

An easy *modus vivendi* had been worked out between customs and importers. When a ship put in with dutiable cargo, a small part of the cargo would be declared and cleared on payment of the prescribed charges. Then customs officers would busy themselves with something else while the largest part of the cargo was unloaded and carted away duty-free. Thus, an almost open contraband trade flourished in all American seaports, particularly in New England, especially in Boston and Providence, but also at Norfolk in Virginia.

There was a friendly community spirit about all this. Customs officers had no desire to make themselves obnoxious to their neighbors, or to those with whom they dealt almost daily along the waterfront, by prying too closely into their affairs. In return for their calculated blindness on occasion, ill-paid customs officers were "taken care of" by shippers and merchants profiting handsomely from deliberate inattentions.

The Townshend Acts decreed that there were to be no more "cozy accommodations" in American seaports. When a ship put in, every dutiable article on board had to pass customhouse inspection and be paid for. There were to be no more merely token payments on cargo subject to the trade laws.

To break up the old permissive system, Britain established a new American Board of Commissioners of the Customs, with headquarters in Boston. Given extensive powers, the board proceeded to restaff the customhouses by discharging old employees and replacing them with men who had not yet been seduced by colonial merchants.

The merchants were very unhappy about this, crying out against this new face of British "tyranny," denouncing the commissioners as "so many bloodsuckers upon our trade." Handbills and posters soon appeared recommending that the commissioners receive the same kind of "warm" reception as had been given to "that set of miscreants under the name of Stamp Masters, in the year 1765."

Among other powers, the new board was specifically authorized to continue issuing writs of assistance—those much-hated general search warrants which gave customhouse officers the right to call on local constables and other colonial officials to assist them in search of contraband. Without specifying what goods or "smugglers" they were looking for, customs officers could decide to enter and search any place at all, day or night—a warehouse, a shop, an office, a private dwelling. As the colonists loudly complained, these searches were "fishing expeditions" leading to many grave and some very mean and spiteful abuses.

It was John Adams' opinion that the spark which fired the American Revolution was the impassioned speech delivered against the writs of assistance delivered in a Massachusetts high court by James Otis in 1761, four years before publication of Henry's Virginia Resolves. Adams' opinion must be respected, but seems untenable.

Writs of assistance affected only the seaport towns, and only a relatively small number of people there. On the other hand, the Stamp Tax directly or indirectly affected almost everybody, arousing general resentment and resistance, not only along the seaboard but in the back country from Maine to Georgia.

As a means of raising revenue, the Townshend tax plan was piddling business and peculiarly ill-advised. At the highest estimate, it would bring in about £40,000 [$1,200,000] a year. This would not do much to help defray the costs of Empire. And yet, because of its scornful and challenging nature, reflecting open contempt of American opinion, it was bound to arouse the colonists to the highest pitch of protest.

Because it was the first to meet after the bad news from London, the Massachusetts legislature took the lead in denouncing the Townshend Acts and organizing resistance against them. Meeting at Boston in January, 1768, the colony's House of Representatives sent protests to London, pointing out that the new Townshend duties, unlike other "external" taxes, were not for the regulation of trade but for raising revenue, as Townshend frankly acknowledged. They were therefore clearly "unconstitutional." Americans had never paid revenue-raising "external" taxes, and never would.

Of greater moment than argumentative pleas to Parliament and the Crown, the Representatives urged Sons of Liberty throughout

Massachusetts to revive the boycott associations that had been so effective in having the Stamp Tax removed. This time, these "voluntary" associations should "persuade" everybody to join—people of all ranks and conditions, rich and poor, large city merchants and small country storekeepers, artisans and farmers, lawyers and doctors, ministers and tavern keepers—all buyers and sellers and consumers without exception. The legislature then issued a circular letter urging the other colonies to do likewise.

The Massachusetts governor, Francis Bernard, a testy and double-dealing man disliked and distrusted even by those who shared his high Tory views, angrily dissolved the legislature, denounced its circular letter as "seditious," and began writing the most alarmist reports, almost hysterical in tone, to his superiors in London. The Bay Colony, if he was to be believed, was virtually in open rebellion.

About this time, Parliament created a new post of Cabinet rank. Previously, there had been a Secretary of State for Foreign Affairs and another for Home Affairs. Now, reflecting increased concern about imperial affairs, there was to be another principal secretary —a Secretary of State for Colonial Affairs. To this post was appointed one of the King's Friends, the Earl of Hillsborough, an Anglo-Irish peer, who knew little and cared less about the basic issues in the American dispute.

Among the many almost unbelievably incompetent and inept Cabinet ministers of the day, Hillsborough probably ranks first, though the distinction is hairline and difficult to draw. Yet the Earl retained his vital post through the next five critical and turbulent years.

Meantime, even before his acts went into force, Charles Townshend had suddenly died "of a putrid fever," making as much of a joke of death as he had of life.* His death necessitated a shift in the Cabinet.

Though Pitt was still nominally in command, the actual direction of affairs passed into the hands of the Marquis of Rockingham—"do-nothing Rockingham," as some critics called him. But his chronic aversion to action turned out to be not so bad at this juncture. Rather liberal in his views, Lord Rockingham had doubts about enforcing the Townshend duties, having no desire to have a head-on collision with the colonies.

* "Our comet is set," wrote Horace Walpole. "Charles Townshend is dead. All those parts and fire are extinguished; those volatile salts are evaporated; that first eloquence of the world is dumb! that duplicity is fixed . . . He joked on death as naturally as he used to do on the living."

But there was one in his Cabinet who held a very different view—the new Secretary of State for the Colonies. Lord Hillsborough had scarcely been sworn in and learned the run of his office when alarmist reports began coming in from Governor Bernard of Massachusetts and other royal governors. Without a word to his colleagues, without any Cabinet consultation whatever, the zealous new Secretary sat down and, in the name of the King, dashed off to the colonies two letters of imperious command.

If he had consulted with his more experienced Cabinet colleagues, there is no reason to believe that any very serious objections would have been taken to the substance or even to the officious tone of the letters. Still, if they had been subjected to some review and discussion, the letters might not have been quite so stupid and infuriating.

Hillsborough's first letter went to Massachusetts, to Governor Bernard, instructing him to take immediate action on the resolutions passed by the legislature against the Townshend Acts. His Majesty, said the Secretary, considered the resolutions "to be of the most dangerous and factious tendency, calculated to inflame the minds of his good subjects in the colonies, and promote an unwarrantable combination, and to exhibit an open opposition to and denial of the authority of Parliament, and to subvert the true principles of the Constitution."

The resolutions were "unfair," continued the Secretary, being "contrary to the real sense of the Assembly, and procured by surprise." This was quite false, the Secretary's ignorance here being based on Bernard's misrepresentations.

Hillsborough ordered the governor to call immediately for the election of a new House of Representatives. As soon as it met, it was to proceed at once to rescind all resolutions passed in regard to the Townshend Acts. If the House failed to respond, it was to be dissolved forthwith, and not to be called again until there was some assurance that it would perform as directed. The new House met and promptly reported to the governor:

> If the votes of this House are to be controlled by the direction of a Minister, we have left us but a vain semblance of liberty.
>
> We have now only to inform you that this House has voted not to rescind; and that, on division on the question, there were ninety-two nays, and seventeen yeas.

Bernard thereupon dissolved the House. Sam Adams and other

majority leaders took pains to see that the names of the "seventeen yeas" were widely publicized in the colony. When the House next met, it was noted with interest on both sides of the aisle that very few of the rescinders had been re-elected.

Hillsborough's second dispatch took the form of a circular letter to the governors of the other colonies. Each governor was told what to do about the Massachusetts circular letter:

> It is His Majesty's pleasure that you should, immediately upon the receipt hereof, exert your utmost influence to defeat this flagitious attempt to disturb the public peace by prevailing upon the Assembly of your province to take no notice of it—which will be treating it with the contempt it deserves.

Hillsborough's circular letter was treated with the contempt it deserved, being openly laughed at. The Secretary should have known that, with the slow passage of mail back and forth across the Atlantic, his letter would arrive far too late to have any effect. All of the colonies had taken note of the Massachusetts circular letter; some had already organized a general boycott of British goods.

At Williamsburg, with Patrick Henry absent most of the session, perhaps being off to the west on one of his land deals, the House of Burgesses roundly applauded the Massachusetts letter and seconded its proposals by sending out a circular letter of their own urging even stronger united action.

They also sent a petition to the King asking him to "redress their grievances." If the Townshend duties were allowed to stand, they declared, "the necessary result will be that the Colonies, reduced to extreme poverty, will be compelled to contract themselves within their little spheres and obliged to content themselves with their homespun Manufactures."

In raising the specter that the colonies would be forced to turn to "homespun Manufactures" the Burgesses made a telling point that would deeply concern major British mercantile interests. As for the colonists being "reduced to extreme poverty" by the Townshend duties, that was ridiculous, mere rhetoric and propaganda.

Indeed, the duties were surprisingly low, and would have caused little, if any, hardship. The colonists' main point was something else again. They did not intend, if they could possibly avoid it, to be taxed directly by Britain in the form of duties, or in any other way. Taxation in America should remain where it was, and always had been—in the hands of the colonial assemblies.

Aware of what the fundamental argument was all about, "good King George" rather roughly rebuffed Virginia's plea that he intervene in the dispute, telling the Burgesses that he very much disliked their petition:

> Our firm Resolution [is] to support and preserve entire Our antient, just, and constitutional Right to enact Laws by, and with the Advice & Consent of our Parliament, to bind all & every part of Our Empire in all Cases whatsoever, . . . and to reject as null and void every Act and Proceeding in Our Colonies inconsistent with and derogatory from Our said Right, and that We do therefore highly disapprove their said Petition to Us.

Virginia had one great advantage in continuing to promote agitation against the Townshend Acts. It did not at this time have a royal governor peering over the shoulders of the Burgesses and ready to dissolve the House at a moment's notice.

After being in office for ten years, Governor Francis Fauquier had recently died. A man of many accomplishments and of genuine distinction, unlike so many other royal governors, Fauquier was sincerely mourned throughout the colony. Though in a very difficult position, he had always managed to maintain a precarious fine balance between his official duties on the one hand and his personal and more liberal views on the other, winning the respect and even the affection of most Virginians—being the best royal governor Virginia ever had, said Jefferson, who knew him well and admired him highly.

While a new governor was being selected and sent over from London, the president of the Governor's Council, John Blair, served as acting governor. A native-born Virginian, identifying himself with the planters among whom his family had lived for several generations, Blair let the Burgesses take all the time they wanted as they went about their business of building up resistance to the Townshend Acts—for which "laxity" Blair was very sharply criticized in London.

Lord Hillsborough's directives were not only useless, but aroused even greater clamor. Shortly after the Massachusetts legislature had refused to rescind its resolutions urging resistance to the Townshend Acts, the Boston selectmen (aldermen) issued a call for representatives of all Massachusetts communities to meet in Boston to consider the "constitutional crisis." This meeting accepted a most inflammatory resolution previously adopted by a large popular meeting in Boston—that all men should forthwith provide themselves with arms, munitions, and other necessary supplies.

The reason? Because an invasion seemed imminent. By whom? The French!

As this was explained at the meeting, everybody in the audience must have laughed, for the reason given was obviously so specious and flaunting. Everybody knew from whom the "invasion" might come, and it soon did.

Apprehensive about the general situation as well as his personal safety, about which he was always nervous, Governor Bernard had been asking for troops, and some were now sent him. Two regiments of tough British regulars—some 700 men, soon increased to 4,000—were shipped down from Halifax on seven warships, which dropped anchor in Boston Harbor and remained there for some time, with their guns commanding the town.

The two regiments of Redcoats—the soon hated "Lobsterbacks"—landed and marched into Boston with fixed bayonets and muskets charged, meeting no opposition. This was the first large military move in the conflict, and its significance did not escape the leaders in any of the colonies. Boston was now a garrisoned town; the "turbulent" populace was to be overawed. The British did not endear themselves to Bostonians by taking over Faneuil Hall and part of the State House for military headquarters, or by taking over Boston Common as a camp and parade ground for the troops. Friction between the citizenry and the soldiery was constant.

Soon after learning of the provocative proceedings in Massachusetts, the House of Lords met and, in a particularly angry mood, adopted a series of drastic proposals. British authority as expressed in the Townshend Acts and others should be strictly enforced, no matter what the cost. The colonists' boycott Associations should be suppressed, by force if necessary. The boycott was illegal, plainly subversive of "British rights." The colonists should hold no more popularly elected and unauthorized "conventions" which flouted the authority of royal governors and were an insult to the King. Those guilty of such insults and other "outrages," thundered the Lords, should be instantly called to book and be dealt with, summarily.

The Cabinet agreed. To effect the purpose, the government dug up an ancient law passed more than two centuries before, in the reign of Henry VIII and never used since. It was proposed that this moldy old statute should be applied to the colonies for which it had not been intended; England had no colonies at the time the law was passed.

This desiccated statute was now to be resurrected and its interpretation stretched so that leaders of boycott Associations and other American "malcontents"—like Patrick Henry, or Sam Adams, or John Adams, or Richard Henry Lee, or George Washington, or Thomas Jefferson, or almost anyone at all—could be summarily seized and shipped to England to be tried there for sedition, even treason.

When this and other of the Lords' ill-natured proposals came before the House of Commons, the only opposition came from Colonel Barré and a few others. Addressing the ministers in charge of the bills, Barré spoke pointedly, and the ministers would have done well to listen:

> Away with these partial, resentful trifles calculated to irritate, not to quell or appease—inadequate to their purpose, unworthy of us!
>
> Why will you endeavor to deceive yourselves and us?
>
> You know that it is not Massachusetts only that disputes your right, but every part of America. From one end of the continent to the other, they tell you that you have no right to tax them . . . Consider well what you are doing.
>
> Act openly and honestly. Tell them you *will* tax, and that they *must* submit.
>
> Do not adopt this little, insidious, futile plan. They will despise you for it.

The "little, insidious, futile" plan passed the Commons by a large majority, and there was immediately a loud outcry from the colonies. In Virginia, however, it seemed for a time that things might quiet down.

After Governor Fauquier's death, the Crown made a good choice in naming as his successor Norborne Berkeley, Baron de Botetourt. The Berkeleys had long been interested in Virginia. An ancestor had been a principal stockholder in the First Virginia Company which founded Jamestown. Another had been a long-time governor, Sir William Berkeley—in Charles II's phrase, "that old fool" who provoked Bacon's Rebellion in 1676 and was dismissed in disgrace.

This younger Berkeley, Lord Botetourt, was not so old and certainly not a fool. In his early fifties, a bachelor, gay and personable, he had served for some years in Parliament—first, in the House of Commons; later, in the Lords—where he made something of a name for himself by his regular attendance and "close attention to Business," which could not be said for many of his colleagues. While the Virginia governorship was not one of the bigger political plums to be handed out of the King's basket, the office paid a salary of £2,000 [$60,000] a year, plus expenses and perquisites of perhaps equal value—certainly nothing to be sneezed at, even by a Lord, particularly one like Botetourt who, because of heavy gambling losses and a load of other debts, was being chased by his creditors.

The new governor arrived in grand style, putting in on the warship *Rippon,* seventy-four guns. Landing at Hampton Roads, he was met there by a large distinguished party on horseback and in coaches, and escorted with ceremony to Williamsburg. Botetourt had received from the King very minute instructions on just how to proceed—among others, this:

> . . . to make particular enquiry into the Characters, Views, and Connexions of, and to hold converse with, the Members of Our said [Governor's] Council, separately and personally, as also with the Principal Persons of Influence and Credit in Our said Colony, and endeavor to lead them . . . to disclaim the erroneous and dangerous Principles which they appear to have adopted . . . and desist from their unwarranted Claims and Pretensions and yield due submission to the supreme Authority of Parliament.

As the General Court was sitting, Williamsburg was filled with "the Principal Persons of Influence and Credit," and Botetourt soon met them all. As the Governor's Mansion, or Palace, having been unoccupied for almost a year, was found to be "totally unprovided with everything" (what a wonderful negative), his Lordship was wined and dined every day by his new friends, at their town houses or great plantation estates, or in the Apollo Room at the Raleigh, or at Wetherburn's to sample its renowned arrack punch.

Botetourt was pleased with his new friends, liking "their style exceedingly." In turn, Virginians liked him, being much impressed, even on the part of experienced men of the world not easily impressed.

"Our long expected Governor arrived at length. His Lordship's good sense, affability, and politeness give general pleasure," observed Richard Henry Lee, "but how far his political opinions may agree with those of Virginia remains yet to be known."

The question soon had an answer. Botetourt, as instructed, called for the election of a new House of Burgesses, which met in May, 1769. At the opening of every General Assembly session, there was a traditional and rather elaborate ceremony at which the governor greeted the legislature and addressed it in the Capitol. Botetourt took the occasion to impress rustic colonials with the trappings of imperial power, putting on a show of pomp and circumstance such as Williamsburg had never seen before. The town was impressed, even though it was rather blasé in such things, having long been used to the ducal splendors of richer Grandees.

With a crowd of the curious assembled, the lord governor emerged from the doors of the Palace, clad in a red coat lined with gold thread, plum-colored breeches, and silk stockings, looking every inch a Vice Regent from head to toe, from his well-powdered wig to the polished silver buckles on his slippers. With liveried servants lined up on each side, he slowly and majestically walked down the Palace steps and entered a great State coach brought from England, a gift of the royal family.

Gleaming with white enamel, having large red wheels, its elaborately carved trim bright with gilt, the coach had been built for King George and been given to Botetourt by the King's uncle, the Duke of Cumberland. Three spans of large, beautiful, cream-colored horses had also been imported—from Hanover, Germany—to draw the coach. The equipage was quite a sight as it moved away from the Palace and down the Duke of Gloucester Street.

Arriving at the Capitol, Botetourt was ceremoniously escorted upstairs to the Council Chamber, where he settled himself and his robes in the large ornamental governor's chair. Sitting his chair regally as if it had been a throne, he then sent word to the Burgesses that he was ready to receive them for an audience, greeting them graciously and announcing he had brought what he felt sure all Virginians would regard as very good news:

> It is a peculiar Felicity to me, and a great addition to the many Honours I have received from my Royal Master, that I have it in command from his Majesty to declare and communicate what will be so honourable to this Colony and must therefore be so agreeable to you, his gracious Intention that,

> for the future, his Chief Governours shall reside within their Government.*

Though happy enough with him so far, the Burgesses were not as impressed as they might have been with his Lordship's news. All royal governors, with their powers to dissolve legislatures at will and exercise other restraints, were becoming increasingly a nuisance, whatever their status. After the audience, the Burgesses returned to their chamber and went to work, finding much to do.

As in every election since 1765, Henry had been returned to the House. At this 1769 session, he and his friends welcomed another "Young, hot, and Giddy" member, an invaluable ally, who would soon rise high in councils of State—Thomas Jefferson, now twenty-six, who took a seat among the Burgesses for the first time, having been elected from a westerly county, Albemarle, where he was born, had lived, and would continue to live most of his life.

Working together, Henry and Jefferson now became close friends. "The exact conformity of our political views strengthened our friendship," said Jefferson, acknowledging Henry's unchallenged leadership in the House. "It was to him that we were indebted for the unanimity that prevailed among us." As the old leaders of the House stood "substantially firm" in support of the Patriot cause, "we had not, after this, any differences of opinion in the House of Burgesses on matters of principle, though sometimes on matters of form." Jefferson later described how this was brought about by a strategy that might well be pondered by leaders in all fields impatient to rush a cause forward:

> Subsequent events favored the bolder spirits of Henry, the Lees, Pages, Mason, etc., with whom I went on all points. Sensible, however, of the importance of unanimity among our

---

* Previously, ever since 1688, Virginia had not had a "Chief" governor residing in the colony. During that period Virginia had been administered by lieutenant governors under a long-established arrangement. The lord governors, as such, received a salary of £2,000 a year, never came near the colony, and had no responsibility whatever. From his salary, the lord governor paid a lieutenant governor £800 [$24,000] a year. The lieutenant governor did not report to or through the lord governor, but in earlier days, directly to the Board of Trade and Plantations, later to the Secretary of State for the Colonies.

During his thirty-two years as lord governor, the Earl of Orkney pocketed £38,400 [$1,150,000] for doing absolutely nothing. Lord Governor Botetourt, at least, had a desire to have a look at Virginia and perhaps do a little something to help pay his keep—an innovation.

> constituents, although we wished to have gone faster, we slackened our pace that our less ardent colleagues [Peyton Randolph, Richard Bland, George Wythe, Robert Carter Nicholas, Edmund Pendleton, Archibald Cary, *et al*] might keep up with us; and they on their part, differing nothing from us in principle, quickened their gait somewhat beyond that which their prudence might of itself advised, and thus consolidated the phalanx which breasted the power of Britain.
>
> By this harmony of the bold with the cautious, we advanced with our constituents in undivided mass, and with fewer examples of separation than, perhaps, existed in any other part of the Union.

Getting down to business, the Burgesses reiterated familiar arguments against the Townshend Acts, urged widening and strengthening of the boycott Associations, and took the strongest objection to the resurrection of the ancient long-dead statute to be used in justifying the seizure of American "malcontents" and shipping them to England to stand trial there. This was "highly derogatory of the rights of British subjects, as thereby the inestimable privilege of being tried by a jury from their vicinage, as well as the liberty of summoning and producing witnesses in such trial, will be taken away from the party accused."

Getting wind of what the Burgesses were doing, Botetourt decided that his duty required him to put an immediate stop to this "abominable business." Not waiting for the State coach to be brought around this time, he hastened to the Capitol and sent a messenger to the Burgesses to inform them that they should wait on him immediately in the Council Chamber.

The House had anticipated this. Consequently, it had ordered the doors locked and gone into closed session, leaving the governor's messenger to cool his heels outside for some time. The Burgesses took their time about finishing their business, which included a unanimous decision to send copies of their resolutions to all the colonies. That done, the doors were opened, the messenger delivered to Speaker Randolph the governor's peremptory order, and the Burgesses trooped upstairs to the Council Chamber, where Botetourt greeted them not unpleasantly, but curtly dismissed them:

"Gentlemen," he said, "I have heard of your Resolves, and augur ill of their effect. You have made it necessary for me to dissolve you, and you are accordingly dissolved."

If His Lordship hoped, as he doubtless did, that the Burgesses would disperse, go home, and get out of the way, he was quickly disappointed. As prearranged in the event of dissolution, many of the more influential members of the House, led by Henry and Lee, "repaired to the house of Mr. Anthony Hay"—the "house" being a euphemism for the Raleigh Tavern, owned and operated by Hay.

The Burgesses had invited some prominent townspeople and others to join them, including Andrew Sprowle, leader of the merchants as chairman of the trade, later a "virulent Tory." Assembling in the large beautiful Apollo Room, with Speaker Peyton Randolph in the chair as moderator, the meeting was conducted "with the greatest order and decorum," said young Jefferson, who was quite impressed, not having attended a meeting of the kind before.

At the gathering, which was really a rump session of the House, it was not Patrick Henry, Richard Henry Lee, or other "firebrands" who proposed the strongest measures, but a "cool" and somewhat older member, Colonel George Washington, a Burgess now for some ten years.

Washington never liked to speak from the floor of the House or in public meetings, and seldom did. But he now rose to read a series of resolutions drafted by his friend and neighbor, George Mason of Gunston Hall, a truly great American, later largely responsible for our Bill of Rights—too often, unhappily, more honored in the breach than the observance.

The Mason-Washington proposals, unanimously adopted, spelled out in greater detail the measures the House had officially adopted, but in one major point went far beyond them. Operations of boycott Associations were extended and more clearly defined. Unless the Townshend duties were repealed and other grievances redressed within three months, the boycott would be applied to the importation of slaves, a lucrative British trade, and to the importation of wines and liquors—something most Virginians would find hard to bear.

Under the revised boycott agreement, the Associators in every county elected a committee of five, "who, or any three of them, are hereby authorized to publish the names of such signers of the Association as shall violate their agreement," and thus make violators subject to the scorn and the social-political-economic pressures of their Patriot neighbors.

Also, "when there shall be an importation of goods into any county," the local committee should, "in a civil manner, apply to the merchant or importers concerned and desire to see the invoices and papers respecting such importation, and if they find any goods therein contrary to the Association, to let the importers know that it is the opinion and request of the country that such goods shall not be opened or stored, but reshipped to the place from which they came. And in case of refusal, without any manner of violence, inform them of the consequences, and proceed to publish an account of their conduct." One of the unstated "consequences" was that recalcitrants might be given, as many were, a coat of tar and feathers.

As Patrick Henry was invited to be the first to sign the revised Association agreements, that meant that he had stoutly and eloquently supported the Mason-Washington proposals. With their work completed, those gathered at the Raleigh decided to use its fine facilities for the purpose of drinking a round of rousing toasts to celebrate the occasion.

"To the King!" was first, as tradition and etiquette required. Then, to the Queen and royal family. Next, "To the lord governor!" There was no rancor here, no hardened enmity, no revolutionary spirit. It was a gay occasion, and many in the company may have been a bit tipsy when they came to the last of the eleven toasts, which expressed a desire to preserve the unity of Empire:

"May the Rose [of England] flourish, the Thistle [of Scotland] thrive, and the Harp [of Ireland] be tuned to the cause of American liberty."

A Grandee not disposed to rebellion, John Page of Rosewell, wrote to a friend in London to exclaim his amazement at the stupidity of British policy:

> I like the Association, because I think it will bring repeal of the disagreeable acts of Parliament. All North America will join this scheme. How must your manufacturers curse the Minister who has driven the colonies to this.
>
> I am astonished at Ld. Hillsborough. His method . . . of supporting the civil power in America, as he terms it, will render him eternally ridiculous & odious to the English and Americans. I am amazed at the influence he seems to have over both houses of Parliament . . .
>
> Is it not shocking to think that he not only executed that dangerous & impolitic scheme of sending troops to Boston, but was able to get the approbation of Lds. & Commons?
>
> Is not every honest Englishman alarmed?

Reporting to London on the state of affairs in Virginia and elsewhere, Governor Botetourt gave his superiors in London some good advice, which went unheeded. Echoing what Colonel Barré had told the Commons not long before, Botetourt wrote:

> Opinions of the Independency of the Legislatures of the Colonies are grown to such a Height in this country that it becomes Great Britain, if ever she intends it, immediately to assert her Supremacy in a manner which may be felt, and to lose no more time in Declarations which irritate but do not decide.

The British government was not prepared to advance. Nor was it yet prepared to retreat, though it soon would under mounting pressure on both sides of the Atlantic, particularly on the part of powerful British mercantile interests which had been pinched hard by the American boycott. The volume of British imports to the colonies had fallen alarmingly, as merchants, manufacturers, and others painfully discovered when they toted up their accounts for 1769.

In New York, their trade had declined from more than £490,000 [$15,000,000] for 1768 to less than £76,000 [$2,280,000] for 1769 —a decline of more than 80 per cent. The drop was not so sheer in other colonies, but everywhere appreciable. The large Massachusetts trade dropped more than half.

Things could not long continue this way, it was obvious. The British government had either to break the boycott by any and every possible means, or retreat. It decided to retreat.

On March 1, 1770, the House of Commons passed a bill repealing all of the Townshend duties except that on tea, which was retained not for revenue purposes but as a reassertion of Parliament's right to tax the colonies as it saw fit and to bind the colonies, as the Declaratory Act proclaimed, "in all cases whatsoever."

The colonists did not much mind the retention of the tax on tea. What mattered was that Parliament, for the second time in five years, had been forced by American resistance to reverse its position and give in. The colonists were fast learning the basic principle of practical politics—it pays to raise hell.

It is a sad commentary on human affairs, down to our day, that "sweet reasonableness" and sensible quiet argument never get very far as such—that nothing fundamental gets done until a sizable bloc of people gets organized and starts raising enough hell to persuade those in power that they had better start listening to what is being said.

XIV
Along the Way to Scotchtown

. . . a learned lawyer, a most accurate thinker, and a profound reasoner.

—JOHN MARSHALL

Late in 1767 or early the next year, in the midst of the Townshend troubles, Patrick and his family left their isolated Round Top house in Louisa County and returned to Hanover County. As a fire long ago destroyed many of the old Hanover Court records that might furnish information, it is not known just where the Henrys lived for the next few years.

A surmise may be made, however. In want of any evidence to the contrary, it seems probable that they moved back to the hamlet of Hanover Courthouse and into Shelton's tavern where they had previously lived so many years.

The tavern had obvious advantages. It stood just across the road from the Hanover Courthouse where Henry, from the first, had conducted a major part of his law business. He was spared the long solitary rides from Round Top on Court Days. Being centrally located, he was readily available almost every day to clients seeking legal counsel and advice in such matters as drawing wills, deeds, mortgage papers, and other out-of-court business.

For Henry's wife Sarah, the tavern owned by her father offered a welcome change from the lonesome life she had led at Round Top. Of necessity, her husband was away from home for days at a time as he made the round of courts in neighboring counties, and for weeks and even months while sitting as a Burgess in Williamsburg, leaving Sarah with almost no one to talk with except her children and a few Negro household servants, all slaves.

With people coming and going at the tavern, with a gay party now and again, the hamlet of Hanover Courthouse offered what must have seemed to be an almost metropolitan bustle of life, a relief from the lonely uneventful quiet at Round Top. Besides, Sarah would have been close to her family, who lived nearby at Rural Plains, and could visit and gossip with old friends in the neighborhood where she had been born and brought up.

Henceforth, down to 1776, Henry represented Hanover in the House of Burgesses. But after repeal of the Townshend duties early in 1770, nothing of any consequence came before the House for several years. During this period, Henry performed conscientiously his run-of-the-mill legislative duties, proposing a few minor bills, sitting on more important committees, lending a hand in drawing up recommendations and reports.

As had happened after repeal of the Stamp Tax, the boycott Associations broke up, and British trade quickly revived. But as the duty on tea had been retained as a matter of principle, many colonials continued an individual boycott by refusing to buy tea, also as a matter of principle. Arguments about "constitutional" rights died down and became little more than an echo.

General peace prevailed in the colonies, broken by a few such incidents as a clash one night in a Boston street between a crowd of rough waterfront townsmen and British soldiery who had been harassed all day by rather drunken gangs. A squad of soldiers, apparently misunderstanding an order from their commanding officer, fired into a menacing crowd, killing five and wounding more—an incident that Sam Adams, Paul Revere, and other Sons of Liberty took pains to blow up into the "Boston Massacre."*

The unfortunate incident had one important effect, giving local

---

* Ironically, the clash occurred on March 5, 1770, the day the Townshend duties were repealed, to the great relief of both the Mother Country and the colonies.

Patriots an additional sense of power. Speaking for the Sons of Liberty, Sam Adams demanded that the soldiers be withdrawn immediately from town. The governor complied and ordered the two regiments removed to islands in the harbor. The Twenty-ninth Worcesters and the Fourteenth West Yorks soon became known as "Sam Adams' regiments."

In spite of the Boston fracas and a few other incidents, the political lull continued and enabled Henry to concentrate on his personal affairs–on his law business, in particular. With his mounting fame as a Patriot leader and as a brilliant trial lawyer, his practice continued to grow, and his income accordingly.

In 1769, Henry was admitted to practice before the colony's highest tribunal, the General Court,* which sat in Williamsburg four times a year–in April and October, on civil suits; in June and December, on more serious criminal offenses where punishment could be loss of life or limb.

Becoming a General Court attorney added to Henry's prestige, but, in a sense, restricted his practice. General Court lawyers were not allowed to practice in the county courts. This rule had the salutary purpose of discouraging "frivolous & vexatious" litigation. If a person lost a weak suit in a county court, his lawyer was less apt to urge him to appeal to the General Court, for the lawyer would have no more financial interest in the case. He would have to turn it over to a General Court attorney. On the other hand, General Court attorneys were forbidden to work on cases in the county courts that might later be appealed to the higher court.

As a county lawyer, Henry had handled as many as 647 civil cases a year. As a General Court lawyer, his cases were far fewer, but the stakes were much larger. In 1771, he handled only 102 cases, but his collected fees for the year totaled about £1,300 [$39,000]–the highest income he had from his practice in pre-Revolutionary days.**

---

* As previously remarked, the General Court consisted of the twelve members of the Governor's Council, plus the governor, but the governor seldom sat. The Council members, appointed by the Crown, constituted the upper house of the General Assembly, and few of them were trained in the law.

** Each year, Henry also handled a large number of criminal cases, never undertaking such cases unless the full fee had been paid in advance. As he kept no account of such "cash" fees, his yearly income from that source is not known, but it must have been considerable. His services were eagerly sought as defense counsel in criminal cases, for he had a way with juries. He also had an income from the lands he owned.

Henry had a signal honor paid to him as a lawyer the next year. Treasurer Robert Carter Nicholas was still struggling, without much success, to obtain from his predecessor's estate something to fill the "chasm in the public coffers" left by Speaker-Treasurer Robinson. Getting on in years, always a conscientious public servant, Nicholas decided that, to concentrate on his duties as treasurer and a leader among the Burgesses, he would give up his lucrative law practice.

Nicholas first offered his practice to young Thomas Jefferson, not yet thirty. Jefferson had been doing well enough at the law, but he declined the offer, having already decided that he preferred public affairs to pursuit of the law. Nicholas then offered his practice to Patrick Henry, who accepted.

It will be recalled that Nicholas had been one of Henry's bar examiners, had found that the candidate's knowledge of the law left much to be desired, had finally agreed, "after much importunity," to sign Henry's application for a license on the latter's promise that on his return to Hanover Courthouse he would really dig in, do his homework, and learn some law. That he did his homework very well, in Nicholas' considered judgment, is attested by the fact that the treasurer now handed over to thirty-six-year-old Henry what was admired and envied as "the first [i.e., finest] practice at the bar" in Virginia.*

This is sufficient answer to Jefferson's later venomous jibe that Henry was "woefully deficient as a lawyer," unable to contend with others "on a mere question of law," and "so little acquainted with the fundamental principles of his profession, and so little skilled in that system of artificial reasoning on which the Common Law is built, as not to be able to see the remote bearings of reported cases; and hence . . . it happened with him not unfrequently, whenever he did attempt to argue a question of law, to furnish authorities destructive to his own cause."

To add a few comments on Jefferson's strictures: First, none of Henry's clients, so far as known, ever complained about his "woeful" deficiency as a lawyer or his want of skill "in that system of

---

* Nicholas had long handled the legal affairs of many of the oldest, richest, and more conservative families in the colony. That Nicholas, rather conservative himself, even thought of turning over his clients' affairs to such young firebrands as Jefferson or Henry reflects the changing social and political climate of the day. The holding of radical views had become, if not fashionable, at least socially acceptable, even in the highest circles.

artificial reasoning on which the Common Law is built." His reasoning was never "artificial," and he won an extraordinary percentage of cases.

Second, a later Chief Justice of the United States Supreme Court, the great John Marshall, knew Henry, had heard him in the courtroom, and once remarked to an old friend that Henry was "a learned lawyer, a most accurate thinker, and a profound reasoner." Marshall added:

> If I were called upon to say who of all men I have known had the greatest power to convince, I should perhaps say Mr. Madison, while Mr. Henry had without doubt the greatest power to persuade.

Certainly, Henry was not a deep-probing and far-ranging legal scholar like George Wythe, Thomas Jefferson, and others. He had little interest in the historical background and evolutionary development of the law. But, with his enormous power of concentration, he could master in a surprisingly short time what he needed to know about existing law for a particular purpose.

On one occasion, he undertook a case dealing with admiralty law, and amazed everybody, judges and all, with his knowledge and argument in that field. No one suspected that he knew anything about admiralty law. Nor did he know until occasion required him to dig into the subject.

By all accounts, Henry was best in criminal cases where argument about fine points of law was far less important than bringing out favorable facts, glossing over unfavorable facts, and evoking the sympathy of the jury for the accused.

As defense counsel for offenders being tried in the General Court, Henry had to contend against the attorney general, brilliant John Randolph, who was "among the most elegant gentlemen in the colony, . . . one of the splendid ornaments of the bar, . . . a polite scholar as well as a profound lawyer, and his eloquence also was of a high order. His voice, action, style were stately, and uncommonly impressive."

But "gigantic as he was in relation to other men," wrote Wirt with his usual extravagance, Randolph "was but a pigmy when opposed in a criminal trial to that arch magician Henry," who was "perfectly irresistable":

> Mr. Henry adapted himself, without effort, to the character of the cause; seized, with the quickness of intuition, its defensible

> point, and never permitted the jury to lose sight of it . . . He never wearied the jury by a dry and minute analysis of the evidence, . . . [but] produced all his high effects . . . by the resistless skill with which, in a very few words, he could mould and colour the prominent facts of a cause to his purpose.
>
> He had wonderful address, too, in leading off the minds of his hearers from contemplation of unfavourable points . . . in order to disguise or eclipse an obnoxious fact . . . Some feint, in an unexpected direction, threw [juries] off their guard, and they were gone. Some happy phrase, burning the soul, . . . struck them with delightful surprise and melted them into conciliation; and conciliation toward Mr. Henry was victory inevitable.
>
> In short, he understood the human character so perfectly, knew so well all its strength and all its weaknesses . . . that he never failed to take them, either by strategem or storm.
>
> Hence he was, beyond doubt, the ablest defender of criminals in Virginia, and will probably never be equalled again.

Unquestionably, as the records show, Henry had immense success as defense counsel in criminal cases. As Wirt had never heard Henry plead a case—in fact, had never met him or even seen him—a better and more particular account of Henry's demeanor in the courtroom was left by St. George Tucker, a distinguished lawyer, jurist, and author. In his younger years, while studying law in Williamsburg, Tucker used to frequent the General Court to follow the proceedings and arguments there, being greatly impressed by Henry and his manner of speaking and his good manners in general:

> He was emphatic, without vehemence or declamation; animated, but never boisterous; nervous, without recourse to intemperate language; and clear, though not always methodical.
>
> His manner was solemn and impressive; his voice neither remarkable for its pleasing tones or the variety of its cadence, nor for harshness. If it was never melodious (as I think); it was never, however, raised harsh. It was clear, distinct, and capable of that emphasis which I incline to believe constituted one of the greatest charms in Mr. Henry's manner. . . .
>
> When speaking in public, he never (even on occasions when he excited it in others) had anything like pleasantry in his countenance, his manner, or the tone of his voice. You would swear that he had never uttered or laughed at a joke.

> In short, in debate either at the bar or elsewhere, his manner was so earnest and impressive, united with a contraction or knitting of his brows which seemed habitual, as to give his countenance a severity bordering on the appearance of anger or contempt suppressed, while his language and gesture exhibited nothing but what was perfectly decorous.

Henry's manner and address to the court and the jury, said Tucker, "might be deemed the excess of humility, diffidence, and modesty" except for a slight smile when expressing "a modest dissent from some opinion on which he was commenting; he then had a half sort of smile in which *want of conviction* was, perhaps, more strongly expressed than that critical or satirical emotion which probably prompted it." When overruled by the Bench, Henry always submitted to the "*superior wisdom*" of the court "with a grace that would have done honour to the most polished courtier in Westminster Hall."

"In his reply to counsel, his remarks on the evidence and on the conduct of the parties, he preserved the same distinguished deference and politeness, still accompanied by the never-failing index of this sceptical smile when the occasion prompted."

Tucker left a graphic description of what Henry looked like in 1773, at the age of thirty-seven, a year after he had taken over Robert Carter Nicholas' practice in the General Court:

> His visage was long, thin, but not sharp; dark, without any appearance of blood in his cheeks, somewhat inclining to sallowness; his profile was of the Roman cast, though his nose was rather long than high; his forehead long and straight, but forming a considerable angle with the nose; his eyebrows dark, long, and full; his eyes a dark gray [actually, they were sky-blue], . . . penetrating, deep-set in his head; his eyelashes long and black, which, with the color of his eyebrows, made his eyes appear almost black; . . . his cheekbones rather high, . . . his chin long but well-formed, and rounded at the end, so as to form a proper counterpart to the upper part of the face.

As Henry rose from poverty and backwoods obscurity to some affluence as a barrister and widening fame as a political leader, he adjusted his scale of living and style of attire to the change. In his younger years he had been noticeably careless and even sloppy in his dress, except for his care always to wear clean linen. During Henry's first years as a country lawyer, his attire was an affront and a disgrace, according to Jefferson:

> Whenever the courts were closed for the winter session, he would make up a party of poor hunters* of his neighborhood, would go off with them to the piney woods of Fluvanna and pass weeks in hunting deer, of which he was passionately fond, wearing the same shirt the whole time, and covering all the dirt of his dress with a hunting shirt.

And worse, said Jefferson, he would often appear in such a costume to plead a case in court. It is very strange that Jefferson, alone among Henry's contemporaries, made any comment even slightly resembling this. What is more, Jefferson cannot himself have seen what he reported. He was recording hearsay, for during the first six years of Henry's practice Jefferson was in Williamsburg as a student at the College of William and Mary and later reading law with George Wythe.

At the end of the momentous Stamp Tax debate, Henry was seen clad in buckskin breeches as he led his "lean horse" up the Duke of Gloucester Street. It is quite certain that he did not wear buckskins during the debate in the House. He probably donned them to protect himself against the weather on his long ride home to Shelton's tavern.

In any case, Henry had discarded buckskins and rough linsey-woolsey country clothes. In 1769, when he appeared before the General Court to take up practice there, he was dressed "in a black suit of clothes and (as was the custom of the bar then) a tie-wig," tied behind, and "with a bag to it."

Henry affected a tie-wig not only because it was fashionable among better lawyers, but also for a very personal reason. The hairline on his high forehead early began to recede, and he became increasingly bald. He was very self-conscious about this. He never appeared in public without a wig and when at home, wore a skull cap.

When speaking in public, whether at a political meeting or in the courtroom, Henry found another use for his wig. When he became animated, he would now and again "twirl his wig several times in rapid succession." This twist always commanded attention, fascinating and amusing his audience.

Henry had another "twist" which he, always something of an actor, often employed in a dramatic way. Henry was about six feet tall,

---

* Meaning that they were "poor" in pocketbook, not "poor" as hunters. All of them were probably crack shots, as Henry was.

but as he habitually walked and stood with a stoop, he seemed to be much smaller and shorter than he was. Often, when he came to the peak of an oratorical flourish, he would slowly straighten up to his full height and suddenly acquire in the eyes of beholders a whole new physical dimension, the effect of which was startling.

Having become relatively affluent, Henry decided to set himself up in style as a country squire, buying a mansion and surrounding plantation of considerable size—Scotchtown, it was named. It lay in Hanover County, not far from Mount Brilliant where Henry had lived for a time in his teens and where his now elderly parents, John and Sarah, still lived.

The mansion, which was one of the better manor houses of the day, had been built before 1732, for in that year Colonel William Byrd II came to visit his friend Charles Chiswell, a native-born Scot, who had obtained, for next to nothing, a grant to some 7,000 acres of unclaimed public land in what was then virtual wilderness.

The always elegant Colonel Byrd found the Scotchtown house and its appointments quite to his liking. He was "very handsomely entertained," he confided to his diary, "finding everything very clean, and very good"—with one exception. A young housemaid rifled his baggage, found the bottle of brandy he always carried with him, and proceeded to drink all of it. The maid, said Byrd, was a baronet's daughter, "but her complexion, being red-haired, inclined her so much to lewdness that her father sent her . . . to seek her fortune on this side of the globe," and she was shipped to Virginia like another Moll Flanders.

Learning of Byrd's loss, Chiswell quickly made amends and restored his guest's happiness, Byrd noted, "by filling my bottle again with brandy"—and his host doubtless ordered a good lashing for the poor thirsty redhead.

A frame structure, one of the largest such structures of the day, the Scotchtown house stood on a high brick foundation. It had a large central hall entered through wide doors from stone porches in front and back. Laid out on the main floor were eight sizable rooms —not too many for a family that soon numbered eight.

Downstairs, in a sort of sub-basement having a floor only a few feet below ground level, there were also eight comfortable rooms, with windows set into the high brick foundation to let in light and air. Above the main floor, under the high peaked roof, was a long, unpartitioned attic running the length of the house—a good place for the children to romp and play when it was storming outside, or too cold, or too hot.

Behind the house were the usual outbuildings—storehouses, granaries, tobacco shed, stables for the horses, cow barns, a blacksmithy, a carriage shed, and such things. Farther back were small wooden shacks occupied by some thirty Negro slaves, most of whom—men, women, older and even younger children—toiled in the tobacco, corn, wheat, and other fields that sloped gently away from the house on all sides.

Scotchtown was not to be compared with Washington's Mount Vernon, the Byrds' Westover, Stratford Hall of the Lees,* John Page's Rosewell, or Robert Carter's fabulous Nomini Hall.

Still, Scotchtown, though not so large and splendid, provided ample space and had its elegancies. Dorothea Payne, better known as the celebrated Dolley Madison who charmed everybody visiting the White House while her husband was President, lived at Scotchtown for a time in her younger years. In her *Memoirs* she recalled that the central hall in the house and the two main living rooms had hardwood paneling—imported mahogany and native walnut—from floor to ceiling, and that the main rooms were warmed by corner fireplaces which had handsome, highly-polished black marble mantelpieces supported at the sides by carved figures in white marble.

Henry was able to buy Scotchtown "at a bargain" because of a curious chain of circumstances. On the death of his father, Colonel John Chiswell as oldest son inherited, among other things, the 7,000-acre Scotchtown property. Quite rich, related to the Randolphs and other Tidewater lords, the younger Chiswell appears to have been a dashing, spirited, and rather imperious Grandee—and, through cavalier exuberance, came to a violent end.

One day, in a Cumberland County tavern, where he was playing cards for high stakes, he became embroiled in a heated quarrel with another player at the table, one Routledge, a "commoner" who lived in the neighborhood. Losing his temper, the colonel drew his sword and ran it through Routledge, who died on the floor.

Loud general agitation resulted, with the slain man's friends and many others demanding that every step be taken to make sure that Chiswell remained in jail until tried for murder. Justice was going to be done in this case, they declared, for many felt strongly that in Virginia the laws were not equally applied, that there was one

---

* Where General Robert E. Lee was later born.

law for the rich and aristocratic, and another for the common folk. There was to be none of that here.

In view of widespread clamor, the Cumberland County authorities refused to release Chiswell on bail until three of his influential friends, all members of the Governor's Council and the General Court, came up from Williamsburg and went on his bond. Traveling to Williamsburg with them, the colonel retired to his town house on Francis Street and there soon killed himself, fearing that he would be convicted and hanged "in answer to popular demand."

Chiswell had expressed a wish to be buried at Scotchtown. This was arranged, but there were complications. Rumor ran, and it was widely credited, that the colonel's reported suicide was a hoax, that he had taken this means to flee the colony, disappear, and not have to face "the offended majesty of justice." When the coffin arrived at Scotchtown, a large crowd of grim and determined men was gathered there and refused to allow the funeral service to proceed until the coffin was opened up to see who or what was inside. The crowd quieted down and dispersed after the corpse was identified as Chiswell's by a respected leader in the neighborhood, William Dabney, Chiswell's cousin and a Henry relative. If not present at the grisly burial scene at Scotchtown, Patrick Henry certainly knew of it, for the whole Chiswell case was widely talked about not only in the back country but in Williamsburg.

On Chiswell's death, his Scotchtown and other properties passed into the hands of his daughter Susannah, third wife of the elderly Speaker-Treasurer John Robinson. On the latter's death not long after, the Chiswell properties formed part of his estate, which was being slowly liquidated to help fill up the "chasm in the public coffers" left by Robinson. The original Scotchtown plantation of 7,000 acres was broken up and sold in sections at auction prices. It was thus that Henry was able to pick up the manor house and the surrounding 1,000 acres "at a bargain," paying £600 [$18,000], later selling it at great profit.

The Henrys moved into Scotchtown in 1771, and the first years there must have been happy ones. Henry had a steadily increasing income, ample for all needs and for some frills. He had become a respected country squire with an imposing establishment. In the house, in the gardens, in the fields, in the woods, the children found many things to do and plenty of room to roam around in, and it appears they roamed around plenty, and almost at will.

Henry's ideas about bringing up youngsters were, to say the least, individual. He seems to have modeled his children's schooling somewhat along the lines of his own. His lifelong friend Samuel Meredith described the pattern:

> In the management of children, Mr. Henry seemed to think the most important thing is, in the first place, to give them good constitutions. They were six or seven years old before they were permitted to wear shoes, and thirteen or fourteen before they were confined to books or received any kind of literary instruction. In the meantime, they were as wild as young colts, and permitted to run quite at large. He seemed to think that nature ought to be permitted to give and show its own impulse, and that then it is our duty to pursue it. His children were on the most familiar footing with him, and he treated them as companions and friends.

This was somewhat qualified by a son-in-law, Spencer Roane, who said: "Mr. Meredith's statement is in a great measure true," but the children "were sent to school before thirteen or fourteen. I have thought Mr. Henry was not sufficiently attentive to the education of his children, which I ascribed to the great facility with which he acquired his own education."

Sadly, the happy days at Scotchtown soon became less sunny, clouded by a tragic development. In 1772, after the birth of her sixth child, Henry's wife began showing signs of mental disturbance. Her condition quickly got worse, and in a short time Sarah lost her sanity completely.

The colony's first insane asylum had recently been built in Williamsburg. Every such institution of the day—and down almost to our day—was a foul prison, a shrieking bedlam, a sheer horror. No one with any compassion at all could think of committing a person to such a hellhole if an alternative could possibly be managed.

Henry had the means to manage, and Sarah was kept at home, being placed under strict confinement in a downstairs room where she was tended day and night by Negro housemaids and visited occasionally by the family doctor, who did what he could for her, which was not much. Often violent, she had to be kept bound fast in a "strait-dress" and strapped to prevent her from destroying herself or harming those around her. The children, probably, were kept away and seldom, if ever, saw their distraught mother.

Under sad necessity, the oldest child and Henry's favorite, Martha (Patsy), now in her late teens, took over as mistress of the house and did very well, especially in watching over and caring for the younger children–John, William, Anne, Elizabeth, and Edward.

When not off on necessary business, Henry would go downstairs several times a day to comfort his distressed wife, feed her, and talk with her. Communication was difficult, for Sarah was usually off in some far-away fantasy world of her own, where she lived till she died some three years later.

Sarah's painful plight and suffering must have weighed heavily on Henry's heart and mind as he became deeply involved, playing a central role, in a new and more serious conflict between the colonies and the Mother Country.

XV
Correspondence

. . . struck a greater panic into the Ministers than anything that has happened since the Stamp Act.

—William Lee

The repeal of most of the Townshend duties early in 1770 produced in the colonies a period of general quiet that lasted till late in 1773. There were a few excursions and alarms, but only one was serious—a New England excursion into "piracy, or worse," in London's view.

That view had substance. If a similar act had been committed in home waters, those involved would have been arraigned for treason, certainly convicted, and carted forthwith to Tyburn Hill to be publicly hanged, drawn, and quartered before a howling mob as was the custom of the day. Londoners liked nothing better than a good hanging, particularly if it was multiple.

While all Townshend duties except that on tea had been removed, other highly unpopular Townshend acts remained on the books and were being ever more strictly enforced, to the great annoyance and financial loss of merchants and shipowners who had been carrying on a rich contraband trade in violation of the restrictive trade laws. This large contraband trade, centering in New England, had long been more or less winked at, and now powerful mercantile and shipping interests complained that the rules were being suddenly changed on them. This was not merely aggravating, but "unfair," they said.

Not long after the new regulations went into effect, the *Liberty* put in at Boston and tied up. The vessel, laden with Madeira wine, belonged to perhaps the richest of many rich Boston merchant-importers, John Hancock, first signer of the Declaration of Independence. Some pipes of Madeira were unloaded from the *Liberty* and passed through customs after the prescribed duty had been paid.

In the old winking days, this payment on a token part of the cargo would have sufficed, and customs officers would have looked the other way as the rest of the cargo was brought ashore duty-free. But a new chief officer at the Boston Customhouse demanded that all of the cargo on board the *Liberty* be landed and passed through customs after full payment of duties. In the eyes of Bostonians, this was unprecedented and preposterous.

Hancock's men gathered a waterfront gang, seized the customs men, and locked them in the cabin of the *Liberty* while all the remaining cargo was unloaded and carted away duty-free. Striking back, Crown officials seized the vessel and had it towed out into the harbor and anchored under the guns of a warship. They then took action in the Admiralty Court to have the vessel confiscated.

Nothing came of this trial. No witnesses except Crown officers could be found to testify against Hancock and his men. Americans were determined not to be "informers" on their fellow countrymen. The court action had to be dismissed, and the *Liberty* was soon returned to Hancock, with no fine or other penalty assessed against him. As British authorities increasingly complained, it was too easy for the colonists to break the "law" with impunity, and something drastic should promptly be done to correct this.

Under another of the "detestable" Townshend acts, the Royal Navy had been ordered to assist enforcement of the trade laws by assigning more vessels to patrol larger ports and their sea approaches. These vessels had authorization to stop and search and, if necessary, seize any ship suspected of being a "smuggler."

H.M.S. *Gaspée,* an armed schooner, took up patrol in Narragansett Bay and waters off Rhode Island. She was commanded by an arrogant and officious martinet, Lieutenant William Dudington, who, like so many Crown officers sent to the colonies, despised the "natives" and nursed the highest notions about his station, authority, and prerogatives. He insisted that his personal interpretations of royal orders be carried out to the letter.

Dudington arbitrarily interfered with all shipping, both licit and illicit, seizing and holding cargo plainly noncontraband. At his order, American vessels passing his schooner were to dip their colors in salute to the Royal Ensign flying on the *Gaspée*. If this were not done, he angrily chased the offending vessel, even to its dock and there forced compliance with his *diktat*. On more than one occasion he fired his cannon on small boats carrying market produce into Newport. All Rhode Islanders agreed that Dudington was a nuisance, to be removed at the first opportunity.

On June 9, 1772, late in the afternoon, the *Gaspée* challenged a small Providence packet, the *Hannah*, carrying both passengers and freight. Not wishing to be stopped, boarded, and searched, the skipper of the packet decided to make a run for it, heading for shallow waters along the shore, hoping that his smaller vessel might get through while the much heavier *Gaspée*, in hot pursuit, might hit a sand bar and get stuck there, which is what happened. And with the tide going out, it was evident that Dudington and his men would remain stuck there for twelve hours, until the next high tide came in to refloat their vessel.

In triumph, the *Hannah* sailed into Providence to report the good news, but with bitter complaints from both passengers and crew that they had been fired at repeatedly with small cannon, though no one had been hurt.

That night, eight long whale boats, manned by burly sailors and longshoremen, pushed off quietly from Providence docks and, with muffled oars, rowed some six miles down the Narragansett west shore to the stranded *Gaspée* which they managed to board, taking it completely by surprise. In a bit of a scuffle, Lieutenant Dudington was shot and slightly wounded, but the crew offered almost no resistance. Putting the still blustering lieutenant ashore, along with his men, the raiding party put a match to the *Gaspée* which went up—and down—in flames.

To destroy a vessel of the Royal Navy, to fire at its commanding officer, constituted a most serious offense, bordering on armed insurrection. Many American leaders disapproved of the action, feeling that the Rhode Islanders had gone too far, fearing that all the colonies might suffer as a consequence.

News about the *Gaspée* brought a sharp and angry reaction in London. The Crown appointed a five-member Commission of Inquiry to find out and run down those responsible for the affair, and bring them "to condign punishment." The commission consisted of the royal governor of Rhode Island, the chief justices of Massachusetts, New York, and New Jersey, and Admiral Montague, chief of the Vice Admiralty Court at Boston. To aid the investigation, the King issued a proclamation offering a reward of £500 [$15,000] for information leading to the arrest of the culprits, and promising a full pardon for any of those involved who would come forward to act as informer.

Suspects were not to be tried in Rhode Island or elsewhere in the colonies. Rather, they were to be shipped to London to be tried there for treason before the tough austere Admiralty Court where verdicts were handed down by the judges, without benefit of trial by jury. Any suspect with even the slightest evidence against him would be as good as hanged the moment he stepped on board the ship transporting him to England, for British authorities were in an angry mood, determined to stamp out "insubordination" once and for all. They would make an example of the *Gaspée* raiders.

The inquiry commission set to work trying to gather some information solid enough to stand up as evidence in court. It held its first open hearing at Newport in January, 1773, without accomplishing much. Information of any kind was very difficult to come by. Nobody in Rhode Island seemed to know anything about the burning of the *Gaspée,* except that it had happened in some mysterious way. Perhaps a powder magazine had blown up?

With the commission still investigating, the matter and manner of the *Gaspée* inquiry came up for consideration before the House of Burgesses at Williamsburg. The House had been summoned for quite another purpose by a new royal governor. After only two years in office, Lord Botetourt died late in 1770. However short his tenure, he had endeared himself to almost all Virginians, winning their respect, even their affection.

The Burgesses certainly spoke a general desire in deciding that a statue of him should be erected to commemorate the late lord governor's able and amiable qualities. This time, not following the pattern followed some five years earlier in authorizing a statue of "good King George," the Burgesses appropriated money for the purpose and ordered a life-size white marble figure of Lord Botetourt, "best of governors and best of men." Chiseled by Richard Hayward of London, the statue was placed on a pediment in the Capitol Yard. Later, it was removed to the campus of William and Mary and set up on a baroque pedestal in front of the college's semi-Wren building, where it still stands, showing his lordship in a high full wig, attired in long sweeping baronial robes, and carrying a fur muff—a rather curious detail.

The change in the governorship was much for the worse. Botetourt was succeeded by John Murray, Earl of Dunmore, a bar-sinister descendant of the royal Stuart line and as wrongheaded as any of that ill-starred breed. Before coming to Virginia, Lord Dunmore, one of Lord Bute's favorites, had served as governor of New York where his policies and personality had been found highly objectionable.

Young Edmund Randolph probably took Dunmore's measure rather well in saying that the new lord governor was "coarse and depraved," often very drunk—a man whose sentiments and manners "did not surpass substantial barbarism; a barbarism not palliated by a particle of native genius." Randolph's was an *ex post facto* view, plainly colored by memories of happenings leading up to the Revolution. Even so, it was generally agreed that Dunmore was no Botetourt.

Arriving in Williamsburg late in 1771, Lord Dunmore, always autocratic in his views, was pleased that he did not have to deal with a "restless" House of Burgesses. He delayed calling a session for more than a year, until the spring of 1773, when untoward developments forced his hand.

Tobacco prices kept falling; even the richer planters were getting deeper into debt, unable to meet bills of credit drawn on merchant-bankers in London, Bristol, Glasgow, and other large centers. Times were generally bad. They suddenly became worse with the discovery that someone was doing a large and profitable business in counterfeiting Virginia paper currency.

Obviously skilled in their craft, the counterfeiters worked in such "an ingenious and Masterly manner" that their spurious bills fooled not only the merchants, but even Treasury experts. Though "every prudent precaution was used," Treasurer Nicholas and his staff accepted the bills. As a consequence, with so much good and bad paper money circulating, the value of Virginia currency fell, which affected the credit not only of individuals, but of the colony itself.

This nefarious business had to be stopped. It came as a shock to the Burgesses when it was found that the chief counterfeiter was one of their own—Paschal Greenhill, representing Pittsylvania County. Summarily, without bringing them before a magistrate, Lord Dunmore threw all of the Pittsylvania ring into jail and asked the Burgesses to take appropriate action to end such dark-of-the-moon business. The House quickly passed an act making it a capital offense, subject to death without benefit of clergy, for anyone caught counterfeiting the paper currency "of any British colony or plantation in America."

But the House, led by Henry, took very strong objection to the lord governor's arbitrary manner of proceeding in the counterfeiting case. He should have followed "the usual Mode" in having the suspects brought before an examining magistrate to hear the charges against them before they were placed in jail. Dunmore's action greatly endangered "the safety of innocent Men," and was a "doubtful construction . . . of Criminal Law"—one that should certainly not serve as a precedent for any future such action.

The governor replied that he might consider the point but would continue "to exercise the Powers I am vested with, whensoever the exigencies of Government and the good of the Country require such exertion"—and he, and he alone, would be the judge of that.

Having dealt with counterfeiting, the Burgesses eagerly turned to a larger question, intercolonial in scope, and quickly came to a memorable decision.

They were alarmed, they said, by the nature of the *Gaspée* inquiry, "said to have been lately held in Rhode Island, with powers to transport persons accused of offences committed in America to places beyond the seas to be tried." Americans everywhere were "disturbed by various rumours and reports of proceedings tending to deprive them of their ancient, legal, and constitutional rights."

What to do? Under the circumstances, the younger Burgesses decided that if anything was going to be done, they would have to do it, as Jefferson noted.

> Not thinking our old and leading members up to the point of forwardness and zeal which the times required, Mr. Henry, R. H. Lee, Francis L. Lee, Mr. Carr, and myself agreed to meet in the evening in a private room of the Raleigh to consult on the state of things.

All agreed that the greatest need was to come "to an understanding with all the other colonies to consider the British claims as a common cause of all, and to produce a unity of action; and for this purpose, a Committee of Correspondence in each colony would be the best instrument for intercommunication."

This idea was probably proposed by Richard Henry Lee who five years before, during the Townshend duty troubles, had suggested something similar to John Dickinson of Pennsylvania. Those at the Raleigh were also no doubt aware that several months before, late in 1772, Sam Adams had started setting up an extensive chain of local corresponding committees in Massachusetts.

Such local committees were put to good use and exercised considerable influence. But the scope of their operations was limited. The local Patriot groups could speak only for themselves, having no official or semiofficial status. What Lee, Henry, Jefferson, and others desired was a larger official system for regular communication and consultation among the leaders in all the colonies. This could be accomplished if the lower legislative body in every colony appointed a permanent standing Committee of Correspondence and Inquiry charged with the task of keeping up a constant flow of information among the colonies about ideas, plans, and news of happenings.

After the Raleigh group had adopted a series of resolutions to be submitted for debate in the House, it was "proposed to me to move them," said Jefferson, no doubt because he had written the final draft of the proposals.

> But I urged that it be done by Mr. Carr, my friend and brother-in-law, then a new member, to whom I wished an opportunity should be given of making known to the House his great worth and talents.

It was so agreed, and in a brilliant speech young Dabney Carr, just thirty,* introduced the resolutions. Henry and Lee spoke strongly and at length on the necessity of their adoption. Then, a strange silence fell in the House. No one else rose to say a word for or against, as if members did not yet know their minds and were hesitant to commit themselves. This seemed to be ominous. But when Carr's motion was put to a vote, it passed unanimously, or at least with no one voting against it—or, as the record reads, *nomine contradicente*. It is certain that many Burgesses were not in favor, but decided to keep quiet, influenced by the political climate of the day.

The House decided that the new Committee of Correspondence and Inquiry should consist of eleven members, placing on the com-

---

* Unfortunately, this was Carr's first and last speech in the House, for several months later he suddenly died. Jefferson was not alone in lamenting the premature loss of this "powerful fellow-labourer." If Carr had lived, he might well have become another of the great Virginians of his generation.

mittee the most eminent of its members—the speaker of the House, Peyton Randolph, as chairman; the chairmen of the six long-established standing committees (Richard Henry Lee, Robert Carter Nicholas, Richard Bland, Edmund Pendleton, Benjamin Harrison, and Archibald Cary); plus such non-chairmen leaders as Patrick Henry, Thomas Jefferson, Dabney Carr, and Dudley Digges.

Any six of these constituted a quorum. The committee was to function the year round, and not just when the House was sitting. A subcommittee of three was chosen to conduct day-to-day routine business when the House was not in session. Those appointed to the subcommittee were Peyton Randolph, Robert Carter Nicholas, and Dudley Digges, chosen because they lived in or near Williamsburg and could readily meet together when occasion warranted.

The day after the House set up its Committee of Correspondence, Lord Dunmore dismissed the Burgesses on the ground that they had no more work to do. Whereupon, the members of the committee met and found plenty to do.

They drew up a circular letter to be sent to the speaker of the lower house in each of the colonies. The speakers were urged to bring the Virginia resolutions "before their respective assemblies, and request them to appoint some person or persons of their respective bodies to communicate from time to time with the said [Virginia] Committee."

Chairman Randolph had been instructed to forward copies of the circular letter "by expresses"—by special couriers—which he did. As the Massachusetts House of Representatives had almost simultaneously sent out a circular letter on the same subject, it may well be that the courier hurrying north to Boston and the one riding south to Williamsburg passed somewhere along the road without the one knowing the mission of the other.

Having sent out its circular letter, the Virginia Committee of Correspondence, as instructed by the Burgesses, began looking into the inquiry about the *Gaspée* affair to ascertain upon what "principles and authority" it was being conducted. It did not have to look very far, for the inquiry soon collapsed of itself.

The royal commission investigating the affair, faced with a wall of conspiratorial silence, had to throw up the job, reporting its inability to gather any information at all. All Rhode Islanders, it seems, had suffered a strange case of amnesia on the night the *Gaspée* burned. No one had seen or heard anything out of the way that night. Providence had gone to bed early and slept tight till morning when it woke up to hear—what a surprise!—about what had happened.

A number of people in Providence, though keeping most discreetly silent, knew very well what had happened and who was involved. The attack on the *Gaspée* had been planned and organized at a large meeting in the Sabine Tavern, where the leaders were two prominent citizens, a rich merchant and a rich shipowner, whose contraband operations had been seriously hampered by the ubiquitous presence of the *Gaspée*. In reporting to London the failure of their investigation, the members of the inquiry commission had the grace to say that Lieutenant Dudington, by his officious and arbitrary actions, had done much to provoke the incident, that he was a pain not only to Rhode Islanders but to his own men.

Patriot circles in all the colonies warmly welcomed Virginia's proposal for establishing official correspondence committees to exchange information on all matters of general or even particular concern that might come up. A most enthusiastic response came from Boston, in a letter to Richard Henry Lee from Sam Adams:

> The reception of the truly patriotic resolves of the House of Burgesses of Virginia gladdens the hearts of all who are friends of liberty . . .
>
> I hope you will have the hearty concurrence of every Assembly on the continent. It is a measure which will be attended with great and good consequences.

Within four months, four more colonies had standing Committees of Correspondence. Within a year, all colonies had such committees except Pennsylvania and North Carolina.

The "truly patriotic resolves" of the Virginia Burgesses drew an equally strong response, though of a quite different nature, from British authorities. One of Richard Henry Lee's brothers, William,* wrote from London that the proposal to establish an intercolonial correspondence network had "struck a greater panic into the Ministers than anything that has happened since the Stamp Tax."

The Lords of the Board of Trade and Plantations, having major

---

* William Lee had established himself in London as a prosperous merchant and was serving as an alderman of the populous, liberal, and powerful City of London, financial center of the British Empire. Lee was the only native-born American ever elected to that post. During the next few troubled years, Lee and his brother Arthur, also living in London, were invaluable sources of information on what was going on in the inner circles of the British government.

responsibilities in colonial policy and administration, were much perturbed by the Virginia resolutions. Lord Dunmore had hastily forwarded copies of these, together with the names of those most actively involved. Henry's name stood near the top of the list. All of these "malcontents" should be carefully watched and struck down immediately, so the Lords of Trade recommended in writing directly to the King:

> As these proceedings of the House of Burgesses of Virginia appear to us to be of an extraordinary nature, and we think that the inviting the other colonies to a communication and correspondence upon such matters as are stated in these proceedings is a measure of the most dangerous tendency and Effect, we humbly submit to Your Majesty to take such measures thereon as Your Majesty, with the advice of Your Privy Council, shall think most proper and expedient.

If the proposed intercolonial correspondence system struck panic in the British ministry, it threw American Royalists and Loyalists (dubbed "Tories," though many were not) into despair and impotent rage. They angrily denounced the system as the "foulest, subtlest, and most venomous serpent ever issued from the egg of sedition."

It must be said for American Loyalists that, more clearly than British ministers, or even American Patriots, they saw the correspondence system not only for what it was but for what it could readily become.

Here was the machinery of revolution. Here was a broad base on which to build national unity and expanding organization. Here was a training school in practical politics for those who would soon take command in affairs all along the seaboard, gearing the policies of one colony to those of others.

But, immediately, nothing much happened. It remained for Lord Frederick North, in one of his sleepier moments, to light the fuse that burned rapidly to set off the final great explosion.

XVI
Tea—and Hot Water

. . . a shock of Electricity
—THOMAS JEFFERSON

In 1770, shortly after the repeal of all Townshend duties except that on tea, a new prime minister had been named, Lord Frederick North, leader of the King's Friends since the death of Townshend. Not yet forty, being a few years older than Patrick Henry, North had been sitting in the House of Commons for more than fifteen years, since the age of twenty-two, when his father, the powerful Earl Guilford, had given him a seat under family control. During those years, North had also served in various high administrative posts as a Treasury Lord, Paymaster General, Chancellor of the Exchequer, and a member of the Privy Council.

It soon became fashionable for Americans to picture Lord North as an ogre, fiendishly bent on destroying every last one of the colonists' liberties. His policy gave that impression. But personally, North was an easygoing amiable man, conciliatory in temper, rather liberal in his private views. It was he who, over strong opposition in the Commons and the Lords, even by the King, had succeeded in lining up support for the repeal of the Townshend duties.

As a political leader, North liked to talk quietly and privately with individual members of Parliament. He had a strong distaste for windy oratory and protracted debate. One likes him best, perhaps, when he is seen dozing on the Front Bench in the Commons during long and boring discussions on the floor. Whenever debate came to an important and critical point, a colleague would nudge him; Lord North would wake up, get his bearings by asking a few questions about what had been said, and usually overpower the opposition with his wit and charm.

But as a prime minister, North had two grave faults. He had no serious interest in public business and, because of disinterest, applied himself to that business only spasmodically and with half a mind. North was the first to acknowledge quite frankly that he was incompetent in the high post he held. Time and again he asked the King to be allowed to resign. On one occasion, after eight years in command, he put the matter very bluntly in a letter to George III, giving the King fair warning of just what he could expect:

> Lord North cannot conceive what can induce His Majesty, after so many proofs of Lord North's unfitness for his situation, to determine at all events to keep him at the head of the Administration, though the almost certain consequences of His Majesty's resolution will be the ruin of His affairs.

One could scarcely be more forthright, and Lord North was certainly right. But the King would not hear of his resignation, describing it as "desertion"—with the result that North, against his conscience and better judgment, stayed at the helm through twelve tumultuous years, down to 1782, when he finally screwed up courage enough to resign after Lord Cornwallis' disaster at Yorktown.

North had been guiding affairs little more than two years when another American storm blew up—curiously, by way of far-off India, when the powerful East India Company, by far the largest commercial enterprise in Britain, ran into serious financial difficulties.

For some time it had been doing an average business of £2,000,000 [$60,000,000] a year, regularly paying dividends running as high as 10 and even 12.5 per cent a year. But late in 1772, with business falling off, the company skipped its semiannual dividend for the first time in memory—an event that aroused a "frenzy of indignation among shareholders, speculators, and the public at large." The value of company stock on the London Exchange sharply fell by almost half, from £280 [$8,400] to £160 a share. The only worse shock could have come if "the old lady of Threadneedle Street," the Bank of England, had been found in a faint.

Though privately owned and directed, the East India Company was a pillar of empire, virtually an arm of the government, holding most of the vast subcontinent of India in thrall, ruling it and exploiting it to its great profit. The great India House in London was, actually, a second Foreign Office, having a major voice in Far East affairs.

The British government had a direct financial interest in promoting the welfare of the company. The government had long been supplying a considerable part of the military forces and supplies used by the company in subjugating India. It seemed only fair that the company, out of its fabulous profits, should pay back something on the help it received and thus lighten the load on British taxpayers, most of whom had no financial or other interest in supporting operations on the far side of the globe.

As a consequence, an arrangement had been worked out under which the company paid the Treasury £400,000 [$12,000,000] a year. But there was this proviso—nothing would be paid if the company's annual dividend fell below 6 per cent. That a semiannual dividend had been skipped was of serious concern. The Treasury had been counting on that dividend, and needed it.

The company's present difficulties arose in part because it had on hand a huge surplus of tea—17,000,000 pounds of it. The financial gloom would lift if a market could be found for this. But where? In a controlled market, of course—in the American colonies.

The government took steps to assure the company a virtual monopoly in the colonial market. Parliament removed a law requiring the company to sell its tea in Britain at public auctions where it was bought by middlemen who sold it to retailers at home and abroad.

The company was now going to be allowed to ship its tea directly to America to be sold there by agents, or "consignees," appointed by the company. This was thought to be a very clever and simple scheme that would effectively serve several purposes at once, and without arousing any commotion.

First, it would put the company back on its feet and enable it to pay its annual tribute of £400,000 to the British Treasury. Second, without imposing any new tax, it would raise additional revenue in the colonies, for the company tea would pay the prescribed import duty of 3d. a pound. Third, the government would be at no trouble and expense in carrying out the scheme, for the company would manage everything through its agents. Fourth, the plan should greatly discourage the smuggling business in the colonies. Through tax remissions and other rebates authorized by the government, the company, even after paying import duties, could undersell colonial merchants who had bought tea through regular channels, and even those who had bought tea smuggled in duty-free from Holland and other places.

To Lord North and his colleagues it seemed that even the most grumpy and testy of Americans would be pleased to pay less for the enjoyment of "a good hot cup of tea." That was the feeling among many in the colonial rank and file, but not of their politically minded leaders.

It seemed to the latter that the East India Company, notorious for its rapacity and really vicious exploitation, was about to wrap its long tentacles around another victim. If it could establish a virtual tea monopoly in the colonies, what was to prevent it from establishing a monopoly in the sale of silk, spices, wine, chinaware, and other articles? This would ruin American merchants.

Besides, the Townshend tax on tea still stood, and the many Committees of Correspondence took up the cry that the tax should not be paid under any circumstances. Sons of Liberty were soon forcing the East India Company's "consignees," all of them Americans, to resign or take to their heels with all the desperate speed of the stamp masters before them.

The *Dartmouth,* the first of three tea ships Boston-bound, entered the harbor and tied up on November 27, 1773. The following day, and the next, there were large demonstrative public meetings called by Sam Adams and the Liberty Boys, who demanded that the tea should not be landed, but be shipped back to England untouched.

The public demand that the tea ships turn around and sail for home was rejected. Governor Hutchinson took the position that the tea should be landed and go through customs, paying the tax, before anything else was done. But in view of popular agitation, no immediate attempt was made to land the tea. Matters remained at an impasse for almost three weeks, with Boston in a state of high excitement.

Under trade law regulations, an incoming ship had to discharge its cargo and pass it through customs within twenty days of arrival. Otherwise the cargo could be seized and even confiscated for nonpayment of import duties.

On the evening of December 16, as the twenty-day grace period for unloading was about to expire, Sam Adams called a public meeting at a Boston landmark, the Old South Church. Thousands of people gathered to crowd into the church or stand packed around it.

Adams, Paul Revere, and other leaders knew what was going to happen and were prepared.

The master of the *Dartmouth,* a Captain Rotch, announced to the meeting Governor Hutchinson's final refusal to allow the tea ships to leave the harbor until their cargoes had been landed and duties paid on them. Rotch also announced that it was his resolve, and Governor Hutchinson's, to have the ships unloaded the next morning.

This was what Sam Adams, chairman of the meeting, had expected to hear, and he gave a signal. A few minutes later, while the meeting was still going on, a large band of ill-disguised "Mohawk Indians"* suddenly appeared and ran whooping down the streets to the waterfront, to Griffen's wharf, where they boarded the *Dartmouth* and sister ships, and happily spent the night tossing all their tea into the harbor—342 chests, valued at £18,000 [$540,000].

No one was hurt in the raid, for the crews on the ships offered no resistance. Indeed, some of the sailors amused themselves by helping the "Indians" throw the tea overboard. No other cargo on the vessels was touched.

The Boston Tea Party set a fashion. New York held one. Patriots in Charleston, South Carolina, forced the local consignees to place their tea in a warehouse where it was stored until sold in 1776 to raise money for the Revolution. Maryland Patriots set fire to a tea ship, the *Peggy Stewart,* which went down off Annapolis with all her cargo.

Dumfounded by all this, aware at last of the danger, declaring that it was no longer a question of taxes but whether Britain possessed any authority whatever over "haughty American Republicans," Parliament began considering severe retaliatory measures.

Lord North never acted unless he had to, but here something obviously had to be done. There could not be another retreat as on the Stamp Tax and the Townshend duties. Not wishing to stir up general resentment and resistance in the colonies, North decided to single out Boston for punishment. He would isolate the town, "a scene of riot and confusion" for too long, and make her pay for her latest "violent and outrageous proceeding." North and the Cabinet had convinced themselves that if the attack were made only on Boston, very few colonists elsewhere would respond to her cries for

---

* "Or were they Narragansetts?" laughed a proper Bostonian.

help, having enough concerns of their own. Boston might even be used as a divisive influence in the colonies.

Lord Chatham, Edmund Burke, Charles James Fox, and a few more urged caution, but their counsel for moderation and negotiation was impatiently brushed aside. A member of the Commons, one "Mr. Van," unquestionably spoke for most of his colleagues in declaiming:

> The town of Boston ought to be knocked about the ears and destroyed. *Delenda est Carthago* . . . I am of the opinion that you will never meet with that proper obedience to the Laws of this country until you have destroyed that nest of locusts.

Lord North was not prepared to go that far. But the measures he proposed were stringent enough, and these passed by overwhelming majorities. Until the tea was paid for, and Boston in particular and Massachusetts in general showed some signs of reform, the rule was to be this:

There was to be no shipping into the port of Boston except for the transport of military supplies, and food and fuel for the town. Rioters should be sent to England for trial. Massachusetts' libertarian charter was revoked, and it was ordered that no town meetings should be held except those approved by the governor, who was given new authoritarian powers. Appointing a new governor to replace native-born Thomas Hutchinson, a civilian, the Crown named English-born General Thomas Gage, British Army commander-in-chief in America, who moved up from his New York headquarters to Boston with four regiments, which, so Gage judged, "would be sufficient to prevent any disturbance."

Among other forward Americans, Benjamin Franklin advised Boston to pay for the tea and make obeisance. But Sam Adams and local Patriots were now in control and would have none of that, dispatching Paul Revere, "the horseman of the Revolution," to New York and Philadelphia to solicit aid, writing a circular letter to all the colonies to persuade them that the struggle at Boston was their own.

The replies to this letter brought surprising support, for, as George Washington observed, why should Americans "supinely sit and see one province after another fall a prey to despotism?"

The first clear and unequivocal response to the Boston letter came from Virginia. The House of Burgesses had not met in more than a year, not since being abruptly dissolved for advocating its Committee of Correspondence system. Now it was called into session again by Lord Dunmore—not because he wanted to, but because he had to, for he had blundered into trouble.

Without asking any counsel or advice, the lord governor had precipitated a boundary dispute with Pennsylvania and had called out troops. These troops, in their marauding, had killed a number of people in friendly Indian tribes, who went on the warpath and were now harassing the Virginia frontier. To extricate himself from his difficulties, Dunmore wanted the Burgesses to appropriate funds so that he could raise more troops and buy more supplies to hold back the angry Pennsylvanians and Indians.

The Burgesses were in no hurry to do anything about what they called "Lord Dunmore's War." They were still considering his request for money—which, incidentally, was never granted—when word came about the Boston Port Bill and the other "Intolerable Acts." Even the most conservative were much upset by the news. Younger and more radical members decided that the occasion should be seized on to arouse Virginians "from the lethargy into which they had fallen."

Jefferson had an idea his friends favored. He and Patrick Henry, Lee, and a few more went upstairs to the Council Chamber where there was a library, and there found just what they were looking for —a volume containing texts of religious proclamations issued by New England Pilgrims and Puritans. Using these texts as a model, though "somewhat modernizing the phrases, . . . we cooked up," in Jefferson's phrase, "a resolution . . . for appointing the 1st of June, on which the Boston Port Bill was to commence, for a day of fasting, humiliation, and prayer."

On that day all Virginians were "to implore Heaven to avert from us the evils of civil war, to inspire us with firmness in support of our rights, and to turn the hearts of the King & Parliament to moderation and justice."

As Jefferson was a freethinker and no one in the group was known as being particularly religious or addicted to prayer, it was decided that a more fitting person should be asked to introduce the resolution. They found their man in a devout churchman, Treasurer Robert Carter Nicholas, whose "grave and religious character was more in unison with the tone of our resolution." The Burgesses adopted the resolution unanimously, without any discussion or debate.

After all, who could object to prayer?

Lord Dunmore did. Always a bumbler and a dolthead, he had

been paying no attention to what was going on in the House. He did not learn of the proclamation till two days later when it was published in the *Virginia Gazette* for all to read. Instantly summoning the Burgesses to appear before him in the Council Chamber, he sent them packing:

> Mr. Speaker and Gentlemen of the House of Burgesses, I have in my hand a paper published by order of your House, conceived in such terms as reflect highly upon His Majesty and the Parliament of Great Britain, which makes it necessary to dissolve you, and you are dissolved accordingly.

Anticipating this, the Burgesses had "all agreed to go home and see that preachers were provided in our counties and notice given to our people, . . . who came together in great multitudes, wondering what it meant," having their curiosity satisfied and learning much more besides. The June 1 prayer meetings were a great success. "The effect of the day through the whole colony was like a shock of electricity," said Jefferson, "arousing every man and placing him erect and solidly on his centre."

No doubt many thousands of Virginians did as Washington did, who noted in his diary on June 1, 1774; ". . . went to church and fasted all day."

After dissolution of the House and before returning home to organize prayer meetings, a large number of Burgesses stayed on in Williamsburg for several days. With Speaker Randolph in the chair as moderator, almost ninety of them, more than two-thirds of the membership, gathered in the Apollo Room at the Raleigh Tavern "to consider the state of things."

All agreed that the Boston Port Bill and related measures constituted "a most dangerous attempt to destroy the constitutional liberty and rights of all North America." No colony could preserve its rights "unless the united wisdom of the whole be applied."

Unaware that New York had just adopted a similar proposal, those at the Raleigh Tavern meeting instructed the Virginia Committee of Correspondence to urge on all the colonies the necessity of soon calling together, at some convenient place, a general intercolonial conference, or congress—a suggestion immediately and enthusiastically seconded by New York, Massachusetts, Rhode Island, Pennsylvania, and Maryland.

A few days later, Peyton Randolph rounded up some twenty-five

Burgesses still in Williamsburg. The roundup included Henry, Washington, Jefferson, Lee, Nicholas, and Pendleton.

This group, while admitting that it was too small to speak for the "generality," expressed its conviction that it was speaking for all in calling on Virginians to choose delegates for a Convention of the People to be held in Williamsburg on August 1. This large popular convention would declare the colony's final authoritative views on the Boston Port Bill and other "Intolerable Acts," the holding of an intercolonial conference, and "other important questions," on which it would take appropriate action.

One of the towering Virginians of the day, a truly great American too little honored, Washington's friend and neighbor, George Mason of Gunston Hall, formerly a Burgess, happened to be in Williamsburg on business. A leader "of the first order of wisdom among those who acted on the theatre of the Revolution," as Jefferson described him, Mason was well acquainted among the older leaders, but he now met Patrick Henry for the first time, the beginning of a long friendship and close collaboration.

Affairs in Williamsburg, Mason wrote a friend shortly after, "are conducted and prepared with a great deal of secrecy, and by a very few members, of whom Patrick Henry is the principal." Mason added:

> He is by far the most powerful speaker I ever heard. Every word he says not only engages but commands the attention; and your passions are no longer your own when he addresses them.
>
> But his eloquence is the smallest part of his merit. He is, in my opinion, the first man upon this continent, as well in abilities as public virtue.

Had he lived in Rome while it was still a republic, Mason concluded, "Mr. Henry's talents must have placed him at the head of that glorious Commonwealth."

Virginia warmly welcomed the idea of holding a People's Convention, and counties began electing delegates—choosing, with few exceptions, their incumbent Burgesses. Albemarle chose Jefferson; Fairfax, George Washington; Westmoreland, Richard Henry Lee; Hanover, Patrick Henry and his half-brother, John Syme. So that the convention, when it met, was virtually the House of Burgesses.

Meeting at Hanover Courthouse on July 20, the county freeholders gave Henry and Syme their instructions in a series of resolutions.

As it is probable that Henry had wholly or largely drafted the resolutions, he cannot have been surprised by what he was instructed to do. Said the freeholders:

> We are free men; we have the right to be so, and to enjoy all the privileges and immunities of our fellow subjects in England . . . We shall never give up the right of taxation. Let it suffice to say, once for all, *we will never be taxed but by our own representatives.*

The freeholders then declared that, from a distance, they were in no position to know the "justice" of the Boston tea business.

> But this we know, that the Parliament, by their proceedings, have made us and all North America parties in the present dispute, and deeply interested in the event of it; insomuch, that if our sister colony of Massachusetts Bay is enslaved, we cannot long remain free.

Henry and Syme should make it their "great object to obtain a speedy repeal of those acts, and for this purpose we recommend the adoption of such measures as may produce the hearty union of all our countrymen and sister colonies . . ."

> We judge it conducive to the interests of America, that a general congress of deputies from all the colonies be held, in order to form a plan for guarding the claims of the colonists and their constitutional rights . . .
>
> UNITED WE STAND, DIVIDED WE FALL.*

The First Virginia Convention, meeting in Williamsburg on schedule, was very well attended. "We never before had so full a meeting of delegates at any one time," Washington was pleased to note.

Britain had further infuriated the colonies by two new acts. One authorized British military officers, if other space was wanting for quartering their troops, to commandeer rooms in any private house they pleased. This was regarded as an invasion of both property and privacy. Householders could not stomach the prospect that tipsy soldiers and sailors might be taking over the "settin' room," and

---

* This popular slogan was evolved from a phrase used six years before by John Dickinson:

"United we conquer, divided we die."

The "evolved" slogan was sharper and better, less extreme, having a good ring to it.

perhaps chasing their daughters—some of whom might have liked a bit of a chase. Colonial home life could be very dull and uneventful.

Parliament had also recently passed the Quebec Act, which, for one thing, granted religious toleration to the French Catholics in Canada. Toleration is always admirable in itself. But as many at the time pointed out, Britain might have applied the noble principle nearer home—to the harried Catholics in Ireland and to Roman communicants in England, Wales, and Scotland.

The Quebec Act was a politic and strategic move—and it worked. It detached Catholic Canada from the rebellious and intolerant Protestant colonies to the south, and thus retained it as a military base in the event of hostilities. Quite as bad, the act extended the boundaries of Quebec Province westward and downward to the Ohio River, thus arbitrarily stripping Virginia and other colonies of their claims to a vast expanse of western lands granted to them under early royal charters.

In view of the mounting crisis, already pointing toward a clash of arms, the Virginia Convention had many things to ponder as it reviewed the state of affairs and tried to anticipate what might come next.

Though elected to sit, Jefferson was not present. On his way to Williamsburg, he suffered a severe attack of dysentery, a frequent Virginia complaint, and had to return home. But, as usual, Jefferson had been at pains to prepare himself for the occasion, having written a long paper entitled "Bill of Rights," later published as *A Summary View of the Rights of British America,* a strong and closely reasoned statement of some very radical doctrine.

Unable to present it himself, Jefferson forwarded a copy of the paper to Patrick Henry, and another to his uncle Peyton Randolph, presiding at the Convention. It irked Jefferson considerably that Henry did not acknowledge receiving the document, "communicated it to nobody," and never spoke a word about it either at this time or later.

Henry may have judged Jefferson's views too controversial to be brought up for debate at a time when every effort was being made to get general agreement on the strongest possible action. Or it may be that he simply stuck the paper in his pocket, forgot it, or lost it. Henry was, said Jefferson, "the laziest man in reading I ever knew."

Nor did Chairman Randolph choose to have Jefferson's paper presented on the floor for formal debate. Rather, he ordered it laid on the table where it could be read by those who wished. This also annoyed Jefferson.

Later, however, Jefferson came to agree that neglect of his paper had been just as well, for the views it expressed were too advanced for the time.

"Tamer sentiments were preferred and, I believe, wisely preferred, the leap I proposed being too long as yet for the mass of our citizens." Jefferson was always inclined, as a friend observed, "to run before the times."

During its session, which lasted only a week, the Convention showed great political maturity and conducted its business with dispatch and remarkable unanimity.

Having denounced each and all of the coercive acts imposed on Massachusetts, the delegates took particular note of a proclamation recently issued by the Bay Colony's new governor, General Gage. The latter had pronounced it high treason for the people to assemble and petition for redress of grievances, or for them to form boycott Associations to further their interests. Associators and such were to be subject to immediate summary arrest.

This, said the Convention, "is the most alarming process that ever appeared in a British government." Not even the King could exercise "such unheard-of powers." Any attempt to carry out the proclamation would "justify resistance and reprisal." Here was a new term in the context–not merely resistance, but "reprisal!"

To strengthen the colony's boycott Associations and broaden their operations, the Convention agreed that all British imports, including slaves, should be cut off four months later, on November 1. In the meantime, of course, no one should buy tea, "that detestable Instrument of Tyranny." Those who had tea on their shelves should not drink it. As memoirs of the day reveal, many a Patriot wife and mother publicly took this total abstinence pledge, only to slip away into a closet several times a day to enjoy quietly a spot of tea by herself, so warm and comforting.

All export trade to Britain was also to be cut off for the first time, but Virginians allowed themselves some latitude here, setting the cutoff date a year later. With a large tobacco crop coming in, they felt that they could not afford to place an immediate ban on exports. If the tobacco could not be sold in Britain, by far its largest market, the income of planters would suffer severely. A year's grace would allow the planters time to shift to other crops.

The proposal for holding an intercolonial conference had advanced to the point where arrangements had been made for such a conference to meet at Philadelphia early in September, less than a month away. The Convention decided that Virginia should send a delegation of seven, and elected the members in this order:

Peyton Randolph, Speaker of the House, chairman of the Committee of Correspondence, chairman of the Convention (104 votes); Richard Henry Lee, George Washington, Patrick Henry (89 votes), Richard Bland, Benjamin Harrison, and Edmund Pendleton. On the delegation, it is evident, the more conservative greatly outnumbered the more radical—i.e., Lee and Henry, though Washington, on many issues, stood with them.

Jefferson's name had been placed in nomination, but he did not receive enough votes for election, only fifty-one. If Jefferson had been present, it is probable that he would have been chosen in place of one of the more conservative—Pendleton, or perhaps Harrison, a great big bear of a man who was the weakest in the delegation, but a powerful Grandee, father of a future United States President and grandfather of another.

The Convention next proceeded to instruct the delegates. They were "to express, in the first place, our faith in and true allegiance to his Majesty, King George the Third, our lawful and rightful sovereign."

Also, Virginia's sincere approval "of a constitutional connexion with Great Britain."

Also, its ardent desire "for a return of that intercourse of affection and commercial connexion that formerly united both countries."

After this formal bow to the King and the British Constitution, the Convention went into a familiar complaint about "unconstitutional" measures, especially the "late oppressive acts respecting the town of Boston and the province of Massachusetts."

Also, while awaiting developments, Virginians should bestir themselves to see what they could do individually to help beleaguered Boston, a recommendation that brought forth a few interesting ideas. In a letter published in the *Virginia Gazette,* a Patriot suggested that planters give up horse racing and send their savings to Sam Adams and his men. This would have entailed heavy sacrifice, for next to women (often their wives), and cards, dice, and toddy, Virginians loved horses and racing them on every possible occasion, either on the track or down village streets. Consequently, nothing was done about giving up horses.

It was a more practical idea to suggest, as was done, that owners of "ponies" and racing fans donate a percentage of their winnings to "blue-nosed" Boston. Entailing no hardship, this would have been a happy combination of sport, virtue, charity, and gaming. Nothing came of this either.

Of more substance as an individual contribution to the cause was Washington's pledge to the cheering members of the Convention:

> I will raise one thousand men, subsist them at at my own expense, and march myself at their head to the relief of Boston.

Though it was not too far off, the time for that was not yet.

XVII
To Philadelphia

I hope you will stand firm.
I know George will.
—MARTHA WASHINGTON

Returning to Scotchtown after the Convention, Henry had a few weeks to make preparations for his long journey to Philadelphia. He had worries about his sick and distraught wife whose condition grew progressively worse. He had to make sure that the house and plantation were in good working order, for he might be away for some time.

Above all, he had to take thought on what should be done—and, quite as important, the limitations on what could be done—at the first large intercolonial conference. There would doubtless be many different views to reconcile, many different arguments to support or refute, much work to be done in bucking up the fainthearted.

To help pay their expenses, the Virginia Convention had recommended that the delegates to Philadelphia should each receive £100 [$3,000], the money to be raised by voluntary contributions in the various counties, each county to be responsible for £15 [$450]. When a planter in Caroline County was approached for a small contribution, he refused to part with a penny, angrily exclaiming: "Can't the poor Dogs pay their own Expenses!"

He was immediately waited on by Sons of Liberty in the neighborhood, perhaps with a bag of feathers and a bucket of tar in hand. In any case, this non-Patriot got off easier than most by making a large contribution and agreeing to make a public apology in the columns of the *Virginia Gazette* for his remarks.

On August 29, 1774, Henry saddled up and rode into the adjoining county of Caroline, heading toward Edmundsbury, built by Edmund Pendleton on his large plantation. The two men had arranged to meet there and then proceed to Mount Vernon, where Washington was to join them. What the two talked about as they jogged along the hot dusty road is not known. But they could have found plenty to talk and argue about, for they did not see eye to eye on many matters, and would often clash sharply in later years.

Though differing in views and temperament, Henry and Pendleton had several things in common; both were respected leaders in the House of Burgesses; both were distinguished lawyers; both were self-made men—Henry rather more than Pendleton, though the latter's beginnings had been humble enough.

A somewhat older man, being fifteen years Henry's senior, Pendleton had been born the last of seven children in a rather poor family; his father died just before his birth. As Pendleton once said of his youth, he grew up "without any classical education, without patrimony, without the influence of what is called family connection." When about fourteen, he was apprenticed to the clerk of the Caroline County Court, Major Benjamin Robinson, for a period of six years and six months.

During his long apprenticeship, he studied law, much on his own as Henry had done. In 1741, when only twenty, he passed his bar examinations and began practicing in the county courts. Seven years later, he was admitted to practice before the General Court.

Pendleton was elected as a Burgess from Caroline County in 1752 and continued to serve down to the Revolution. Though a very able man—"the ablest man in debate I ever met," said Jefferson—Pendleton owed his early rapid rise largely to the fact that he happened to have served his apprenticeship under Major Benjamin Robinson. The major called Pendleton and his abilities to the attention of his nephew, Speaker-Treasurer John Robinson, then the most powerful political figure and one of the richest men in the colony. The speaker showed Pendleton many favors, placing him on important committees, pushing him ahead, and the two became fast friends.

It will be recalled that, after the great financial scandal in 1766, eight years before, Pendleton had been implored by the family and its friends to take over the heavy responsibility of being chief executor of the Robinson estate. Perhaps Henry and Pendleton, as they rode along, talked a bit about the legal and other problems involved in liquidating that estate which still owed a huge debt to the Treasury.

Henry may have asked, as many Burgesses were doing, why it was taking so long to liquidate the estate, especially since the colony badly needed money to meet the present crisis—a question that Pendleton would not have liked, for he was bent on preserving as much of the estate as possible for the Robinsons. This he managed to do by procrastination, finally paying off the debt to the Treasury in 1781 in depreciated paper currency.

Though both were Patriots, Henry and Pendleton differed markedly in their political views and general attitudes. While opposed to the Stamp Tax, as most Virginians were, Pendleton had voted against Henry's resolutions as being far too strong. He was always, throughout his life, a middle-of-the-roader, advising caution and restraint, being "cool, smooth, and persuasive." Henry was often very impatient with him in these days—and he with Henry.

It may be, though it is most unlikely, that they tacitly agreed not to bring up controversial issues as they rode along—that they passed the time of day in exchanging pleasantries. Both were very charming and sociable, fond of lively conversation, full of good stories and ribald jokes. Whatever their political differences, Henry probably found Pendleton to be, as Jefferson did, "the most amiable and pleasant of companions."

On August 30, after two days in the saddle, the two weary travelers arrived at Mount Vernon late in the day to be welcomed by Washington and his wife Martha. No doubt Henry brought a warm personal greeting, perhaps even a letter, from his old friend Colonel Nathaniel West Dandridge to his niece Martha, born a Dandridge. Washington's neighbor, George Mason, rode up from Gunston Hall to join the company and spend the night. One wishes that Washington had recorded in his diary what these four leaders talked about that evening, but all he noted in his typically laconic way was that Henry and Pendleton arrived "after sunset."*

* Washington's diary is amazingly free of any significant information, any good gossip, any personal comments or judgments, any wit or humor—and consequently, very dull, leaving the reader annoyed with the author for not having said what he might on many fascinating occasions.

The next morning the household was up early, at least by sunrise, as was the custom of the day. Washington liked to go out before breakfast and ride around sections of his 5,000-acre estate and, as he usually did, probably invited his guests to accompany him so that they might see and admire what he was doing, and make comments and suggestions.

Washington prided himself, perhaps most of all, on being a master of what he called "the arts of husbandry." By study, experience, and experiment, he had made himself an expert in new ways of tillage, in the rotation of crops, in the careful selection of seed, and in the breeding of horses, cattle, and other livestock. It pleased him much when the Agriculture Society of South Carolina awarded him "a premium for raising the largest Jackass."

Whether or not Henry and Pendleton rode out to have a look at the Mount Vernon plantation, they soon sat down to breakfast, which in big Virginia houses was always quite a meal, especially if guests were present. This was noted with disapproval by a brilliant young Englishman who settled in Virginia at this time, Dr. John Mitchell, whose invaluable research contributed greatly to the detection of the cause of yellow fever, and its prevention. Dr. Mitchell ascribed much of the sickness in the colony to an excessive meat diet:

> . . . the ancient custom of eating meat at breakfast still continues. At the top of the table, where the lady of the house presides, there is constantly tea [?] and coffee. But the rest of the table is garnished with roasted fowl, ham, venison, game, and other dainties. Even at Williamsburg it is the custom to have a plate of cold ham upon the table, and there is scarcely a Virginia lady who breakfasts without it.

After breakfast, Henry and Pendleton stayed on for a time and enjoyed a midday dinner before Negro slaves were ordered to bring the horses—all well groomed overnight, with saddles and bridles highly polished. As the party mounted and prepared to depart, Martha Washington stood on the porch and wished her guests a happy journey.

"God bless you, gentlemen," she said. "I hope you will stand firm. I know George will." She could have had no doubts about Henry, but she may have had some about "harmonious" Pendleton.

Riding down the high slope to the Potomac, the three horsemen were ferried across to the Maryland shore and headed for Annapolis, where they were ferried across the broad Chesapeake and then struck northward through Maryland and northern Delaware toward Pennsylvania. They knew they were going to be late for the opening of the Philadelphia meeting, scheduled for September 1, and it was already the first. But they were in no hurry, riding along at a leisurely pace. In the blasting summer heat, they did most of their riding before noon, then seeking out a pleasant tavern where they idled away the afternoon and evening and spent the night.

On the afternoon of September 4, a Sunday, the Henry-Pendleton-Washington party was approaching Philadelphia. News of their coming had somehow been announced, for they were met on the outskirts of the city by hundreds of prominent Philadelphians on horseback, several militia companies in full regalia, and a large band.

With pipes playing, trumpets sounding, and drums rolling, they were escorted into town and down Walnut Street to the recently completed City Tavern, already renowned as one of the finest hostelries in the country, rivaling the Raleigh in Williamsburg, Fraunces in New York, and the Green Dragon in Boston. The new arrivals, after supper at the new City Tavern, went to spend the night in the handsome brick house of young Dr. William Shippen,* who had married a sister of Richard Henry Lee, who was also staying at the Shippens'.

Meantime, a week before, the Massachusetts delegation of five had arrived—James Bowdoin, Thomas Cushing, Robert Treat Payne, and "a brace of Adams," Sam and his younger cousin John. A dynamo in things that interested him, Sam Adams was improvident, impoverished, and impractical in everything but practical politics, in which he had a genius for effective and imaginative organization. It was he who conceived the idea of establishing a chain of committees of correspondence, an invaluable instrument in forwarding the Patriot cause. As clothes did not interest him at all, he went around very shabbily dressed, a characteristic readily accepted by his many friends and devoted supporters, but the latter now had a question.

What kind of an impression would shabby Sam make on elegant gentlemen from all the colonies about to assemble in Philadelphia?

To make Sam more presentable, his friends clubbed together and bought him for the occasion a whole new set of bright apparel—a scarlet coat, a new cape, new shoes, new silk hose, and a wig to replace the familiar old one that looked so raggedy and moth-eaten.

---

* Dr. Shippen, in 1762, taught the first courses in anatomy in the country and, in 1777, when the need was greatest, was appointed director general of all military hospitals serving the Revolutionary armies.

Besides, they gave him twenty johannes—a Portuguese gold coin worth more than 36s.—so that "incendiary"* Sam had some £36 [$1,000] in his pocket for spending money.

Traveling rather handsomely "in a coach and four, preceded by two white servants well mounted and armed, with four blacks behind in livery, two on horseback and two footmen," the Massachusetts delegates took three weeks coming down from Boston, stopping along the way at Hartford, New Haven, New York, and elsewhere to sound out the leaders in these communities on their opinions about what should be done. They were pleased, in general, with the sentiments expressed.

As with Henry, so it was with John Adams—this was his first journey out of his native colony, and Adams found much to admire and much to question, too. In New York, the delegation put up at Hull's, "at the sign of the Bunch of Grapes." Adams, like so many before him and since, was of a divided mind about New York, being unable to decide whether he liked it or not, saying that it would be "a subject of much speculation to me." With his friends, Adams was wined and dined in the highest society by Livingstons, Platts, McDougalls, Duanes, and others, but was not much impressed with the company he met.

> With all the opulence and splendor of this city, there is very little good breeding . . . I have not seen one real gentleman, one well-bred man, since I came to town.
>
> At their entertainments, there is no conversation that is agreeable; there is no modesty, no attention to one another. They talk very loud, very fast, and all together.
>
> If they ask you a question, before you can utter three words of your answer, they will break out upon you again, and talk away.

Like Henry and other leaders, Adams was well aware that he was treading on dangerous ground, had taken his life in his hands, and during his journey he wrote to his friend James Warren, another revolutionary, to express a doleful thought:

> There is one ugly reflection. Brutus and Cassius were slain. Hampton died in the field, Sidney on the scaffold, Harrington in jail, &c. This is cold comfort.

* The greatest "incendiary in the King's dominion," said Massachusetts' royal governor. But the latter had never dealt with Patrick Henry.

Nearing Philadelphia, the Massachusetts delegates were greeted by a large company that rode out to greet them. The company included "Dr. Benjamin Rush and several others of the most active Sons of Liberty in Philadelphia, who desired a conference with us," said Adams. "We invited them to take tea [!] with us in a private apartment. They asked leave to give us some information and advice, which we thankfully granted."

The information given to them was a bit shocking. They were told that people in general, or at least in Pennsylvania, regarded all of the Massachusetts delegates as "desperate adventurers," dependent for their livelihood on "courting popularity" by stirring up violent anti-British agitation. They were even suspected of harboring the idea of independence. Adams made notes on what happened at the meeting outside Philadelphia:

> Now, said they, you must not utter the word Independence, nor give the least hint or insinuation of the idea, neither in the Congress or any private conversation; if you do, you are undone, for Independence is as unpopular in Pennsylvania and in all of the Middle and Southern colonies as the Stamp Act itself. No man dares to speak of it . . .
>
> You are thought to be too warm, too zealous, too sanguine; you must therefore be very cautious. You must not come forward with any bold measures; you must not pretend to take the lead.
>
> You know Virginia is the most populous . . . They are very proud of their "antient Dominion," as they call it; they think they have the right to lead the Southern colonies; and the Middle colonies, too, are much disposed to yield to them.

All of this made a deep impression on Adams and his colleagues, and Adams made a further enlightening comment:

> This conversation, and the principles, facts, and motives suggested in it have given a color, a complexion, and character to the whole policy of the United States from that day to this.*
>
> Without it, . . . Mr. Jefferson [would not] have been the Author of the Declaration of Independence, nor Richard Henry Lee the mover of it.**

* Adams was writing in 1822, almost forty years after the conversation.

** This suggests that Adams would have been happy to write the Declaration himself, no doubt with cousin Sam assisting, if they had not decided to let Virginians take the initiative.

Pondering the warning they had received about not proceeding too fast, the Massachusetts delegates rode into town and, though "dirty, dusty, and fatigued, . . . could not resist the importunity to go to the tavern [Smith's new City Tavern], the most genteel one in America," which now became the political headquarters of the convention.

At Smith's, after some conversation, "a supper appeared, as elegant as any ever laid upon the table," said Adams. Used to the Puritan ways of Boston, he was greatly impressed, as all delegates were, by the warm hospitality and lavish entertaining that prevailed in predominantly Quaker Philadelphia.

In its physical and other aspects, the city itself greatly impressed all delegates who had not visited it before. A widely traveled British officer, Lord Adam Gordon, had recently described it "as perhaps one of the Wonders of the World, if you consider its Size, the number of its Inhabitants, the regularity of its Streets, their crossing one another all at right angles, their spacious publick and private buildings, the quays and docks, the magnificense and diversity of places of worship (for here all Religions that profess the Name of Christ are tolerated equally), the plenty of provisions brought to Market, and the Industry of all its Inhabitants" . . .

It was indeed, said Lord Gordon, "the first Town in America, and one that bids fair to rival almost any in Europe. It is not a hundred years since the first tree was cut where the City now stands"—a pleasant peaceful community already containing more than 3,000 houses.

The Massachusetts delegates had to admit, however reluctantly, that Philadelphia was at least equal to Boston, perhaps even superior. As John Adams observed, "The streets of this town are vastly more regular and elegant than those in Boston, and the houses are more grand, as well as neat. They are almost all painted, brick buildings and all." And what a "hospitable and polite" city!

September 1 came and went without a meeting of the conference as scheduled. Too few delegates had arrived—less than half of those expected, and none as yet from Virginia, New York, Maryland, North Carolina, or Georgia. In want of a formal meeting the delegates on hand met in the City Tavern and "spent the evening together," getting acquainted and sounding out one another's views. In general, members of the various delegations had not met before and only knew one another by name, if by that.

While waiting for the main business to begin, John and Sam Adams went bustling around talking to everyone about what should be brought before the conference and what effective action might be taken there. They were very pleased to learn of the arrival of the first contingent of the Virginia delegation—Peyton Randolph, Richard Henry Lee, Richard Bland, and Benjamin Harrison—and hastened to the City Tavern to be introduced to them.

Randolph was, John Adams noted, "a large, well-looking man," impressive in appearance and engaging in manner; Lee, "tall, spare, . . . a masterful man;" Bland, "a learned, bookish man." Though not much impressed with Benjamin Harrison,* Adams liked what he had seen of the Old Dominion delegation.

"These gentlemen from Virginia appear to be the most spirited and consistent of any," he said. They represented "fortunes, abilities, learning, eloquence, acuteness equal to any I ever met with in my life"—and he had yet to meet Henry, Washington, and Pendleton.

Next evening, Adams was again in the company of two of the "spirited" Virginians, Lee and Harrison, meeting them at a gay evening party given by a Pennsylvania delegate, Thomas Mifflin, later a major general under Washington.

At Mifflin's, the guests enjoyed "an elegant supper, . . . and drank sentiments till eleven o'clock." Lee and Harrison "were very high," Adams noted, using that term in a modern sense. It appears that Lee had been invited to have midday dinner at the spacious house of an old friend, now a Pennsylvania delegate, rich and conservative John Dickinson, and the company had sat around "drinking Burgundy the whole afternoon."

In a day of rather heavy tippling generally, Lee and Harrison must have been "very high" indeed to have their tipsy state remarked by Adams, who liked to imbibe himself, but with Puritan restraint, though the bounds of that restraint were often very elastic.

Adams' enthusiasm about the character of the Virginia delegates was shared by many others, including Caesar Rodney of Delaware, who said of them, "more sensible fine fellows you'd never wish to see." Another delegate remarked that, compared to the spirited Virginians, the men from Boston were milksops. But the Bostonians were not as soppy as they seemed. They were playing it "cool," as they had been advised.

By Monday, September 5, forty-four of fifty-six delegates were on

---

* Adams later characterized Harrison as "an indolent, luxurious, heavy gentleman, of no use in Congress or committee, but a great embarrassment to both."

hand—Washington, Henry, and Pendleton had arrived the evening before—and this number was deemed sufficient to open the session and get down to business.

The delegates had been offered the use of the assembly chamber in the State House, but they declined this invitation, having been offered the use of Carpenters' Hall, recently erected as its headquarters by the Carpenters' Company of Philadelphia, a craft guild organized a half century before. The delegates assembled at the City Tavern on Monday morning, September 5, and marched a few blocks to have a look at the Hall.

Though it was not yet completed in all details, the main construction had been done, and the delegates were much impressed with the Hall after taking "a view of the room, and of the chamber where is an excellent library. There is also a long entry where gentlemen may walk, and a convenient chamber opposite the library. The general cry was that this was a good room."*

With that decided, the delegates sat down in comfortable Windsor chairs with which the room was furnished. Delegations did not necessarily sit together as a bloc. Rather, most delegates sat where they pleased.

The first order of business, of course, was to organize the meeting, and here it is obvious that proceedings had been prearranged, probably by John and Sam Adams, who had persuaded various delegations that Virginia and the southern colonies should be encouraged to take the lead.

A South Carolina delegate, Thomas Lynch, a very wealthy planter of very liberal views, rose to nominate Peyton Randolph as chairman or speaker of the meeting, praising him for having "presided with great dignity over a respectable society and to the great advantage of America." It was no doubt also by prearrangement that no one else was nominated, that there was no contest, and Randolph was declared elected unanimously.

The next order of business was to choose a secretary to keep the minutes of the meetings. Having met and talked with him a few days earlier, John Adams had picked his candidate, a young Pennsyl-

---

* Not the least of the Hall's attractions was the "long entry" where gentlemen might walk and talk. Almost all of the delegates were experienced legislators, having served in their colonial assemblies, and they knew, as their modern counterparts do, that many important matters are actually decided not in floor debate, but by compromises made and understandings reached in private conversations held in entryways, corridors, and cloakrooms.

vanian, a brilliant scholar in Greek and the Scriptures, Charles Thomson, known as "the Sam Adams of Philadelphia, the life of the cause of Liberty" in the town. He had not been elected as a delegate because his views were too radical for the prevailing Pennsylvania conservatism led by Joseph Galloway, a rich lawyer, later an active Tory.

With the southern colonies again taking the lead, Thomas Lynch of South Carolina, who had nominated Peyton Randolph as chairman, now placed Thomson's name in nomination for the post of secretary, a motion that was carried.* A doorkeeper was sent to find Thomson, who had just been married and was off on his honeymoon.

But on that day he happened to be in town, having come in to pay his respects to some of his wife's family. Just as he was dismounting in Chestnut Street, the doorkeeper found him and told him that the meeting in Carpenters' Hall requested his presence.

Bidding his servant put up the horses, Thomson went immediately to the Hall where there "was indeed an august assembly," he said, "and deep thought and solemn anxiety were observable on their countenances." He walked up the aisle, bowed to Peyton Randolph who was in the chair, and asked his pleasure.

"Congress desire the favor of you, Sir, to take their minutes."

Thomson bowed "in acquiescence" and took his "seat at the desk," little realizing at the moment that he would occupy that desk for fifteen years, down to 1789 when the new Federal Constitution went into effect. A tall, thin, and distinguished-looking man, faithful and efficient in his duties, always very courteous and obliging, "reticent as the Sphinx," Thomson was, as his epitaph aptly reads, "The Confidential Secretary of the Continental Congress."

In later years he began writing a history of the Congress and of the events that swirled around it before, during, and after the Revolution. His would have been an invaluable work, for he enjoyed the enviable position of having known all great American leaders of the time. He knew not only what had gone on in public, but also what had been going on behind the scenes. In the end, however, he decided to burn his manuscript and the voluminous notes he had taken through the years because he feared that what he had to say about

---

* To the shock and chagrin of Joseph Galloway, who attributed Thomson's election to the machinations of the "Bostonians"–of Sam Adams, in particular.

some of his contemporaries and their acts might greatly embarrass their descendants.

Among the Indians, whom he had warmly befriended and helped, Thomson was known as Wegh-wu-law-mo-end, or the Man Who Tells the Truth. Rather than tone down his history by omitting or evading unpleasant truths about some Patriots, he chose to destroy his manuscript. For posterity, this was a great loss.

The delegates in Carpenters' Hall made three decisions early. The assembly was to be known as the Continental Congress. The chairman was to have the title of and was to be addressed as Mr. President. All meetings were to be held behind closed doors. Nothing about the proceedings was to be made public unless specifically authorized by majority vote.

XVIII
Continental Action

I am . . . an American.

—Patrick Henry

With all organizational preliminaries out of the way, Congress turned to its main business, and the floor was opened for debate. A vital question first came up:

How were the colonial delegations to vote?

Should each colony have an equal voice? Or should the larger and richer colonies have more votes than the smaller? If so, how was the respective "weight" of the colonies to be judged—by population, or area, or value of property, or what?

After a silence, Patrick Henry rose in a far corner of the chamber to make the first speech—and this, too, was probably by prearrangement. Secretary Thomson, having just taken his seat, has left us his impression of the occasion and of Henry:

> I did not then know him. He was dressed in a suit of parson's gray, and from his appearance I took him for a Presbyterian clergyman, used to haranguing the people.
>
> He observed that we were met in a time and on an occasion of great difficulty and distress; that our public circumstances were like those of a man in deep embarrassment and trouble,

> who had called his friends together to devise what was best to be done for his relief—one would propose one thing, and another a different thing, whilst a third would think of something better suited to his unhappy circumstances, which he would embrace and think no more of the rejected schemes, with which he would have nothing to do.
>
> I thought that this was very good instruction to me with respect to the taking of the minutes. What Congress adopted, I committed to writing; with what they rejected I had nothing further to do; and even this method led to some squabbles with the members who were desirous of having their speeches and resolutions, however put to rest by the majority, still preserved upon the minutes.

Henry may have started by making general remarks along the lines recalled by Thomson, but he quickly came to the point at issue, as John Adams noted in his diary:

> Mr. Henry . . . said that this was the first general congress which had ever happened; that no former congress could be a precedent; that we should have occasion for more General Congresses, and therefore that a precedent ought to be established now; that it would be a great injustice if a little colony should have the same weight in the councils of America as a great one.

To Henry's last statement, a New Hampshire delegate, John Sullivan, later a major general under Washington, took exception and rejoined: "A little colony has its all at stake as well as a great one."

Debate on the crucial and potentially divisive voting issue continued for two days. Rhode Island and other smaller colonies supported Sullivan's position. John Adams, John Jay of New York, the Pennsylvanians, and others favored the thesis of Henry, who said at one point:

"Will not the people complain that ten thousand Virginians have not outweighed one thousand others?"

To this, Samuel Ward of Rhode Island made the telling reply that Virginia had a great number of counties "very unequal in point of wealth and numbers," and yet each county had equal representation and an equal voice in the House of Burgesses.

Eager to prevent what might develop into a disastrous split in Congress at the very outset, Richard Henry Lee, supported by Richard

Bland and Christopher Gadsden of South Carolina, took a diversionary course and raised a practical question: whether Congress was "provided with proper materials to ascertain the importance of each colony." On what facts and figures was judgment to be based? Lee said he was afraid there were none. John Adams came around to this view, as did Henry, who said:

> I agree that authentic accounts cannot be had if, by authenticity, is meant attestations of officers of the Crown.
>
> I go upon the supposition that government* is at an end. All distinctions are thrown down. All America is thrown into one mass. We must aim at the minutiae of rectitude . . . It is one of the great duties of the democratical part of the constitution to keep itself pure . . .
>
> I did propose that a scale should be laid down; that part of North America which was once Massachusetts Bay, and that part which was once Virginia, ought to be considered as having a weight . . .
>
> I will submit, however; I am determined to submit if I am overruled . . . I am for giving all the satisfaction in my power.
>
> The distinctions between Virginians, Pennsylvanians, New Yorkers, and New Englanders are no more. I am not a Virginian, but an American.

After not much more debate, Congress decided on voting procedure—one colony, one vote. But this decision, it was stipulated, was not to be regarded as a precedent for future meetings at which the rule might be changed. The decision, however, did establish a precedent followed for some years.**

From the start of the Congress, Patrick Henry and Richard Henry Lee had been most effective on the floor on points of order and in their longer speeches and pleas. Wrote a Connecticut delegate, later a prominent Revolutionary leader, Silas Deane:

---

* Henry obviously meant "the rule of the British government"—not that all government was at an end, as some carping and rather stupid critics have tried to make out. Government was going to be taken over by the colonial assemblies and the Continental Congress, as was soon done.

** The principle of equal "unweighted" representation is incorporated in the Federal Constitution under the provision that each State as such, whether large or small, rich or poor, has equal representation—two members—in the United States Senate.

> Mr. Henry . . . is the completest speaker I ever heard. If his future speeches are equal to the small samples he has hitherto given us, they will be worth preserving . . . I can give you no idea of the music of his voice, or the high-wrought yet natural elegance of his style and manner.
>
> Col. Lee is said to be his rival in eloquence, and in Virginia and to the Southward they are styled the Demosthenes and Cicero of America. God grant that they may not, like them, plead in vain for the liberties of their country.
>
> These last named gentlemen are now in full life, perhaps near fifty,* and have made the constitution of Great Britain and America their capital study ever since the late troubles between them have arisen.

As debate on the delicate voting question was nearing an end, a rumor came from the north that Boston had been bombarded, and a number of people killed. This gave all the delegates pause. "I cannot say that all faces gather paleness," wrote one, "but they all gather indignation, and every tongue pronounces revenge." Muffled bells throughout Philadelphia were set to tolling, and people began "to run as in a case of extremity, not knowing where or why." The cry went up, "War! war! war!"

This entirely changed the complexion of things. After two anxious days, word came that the rumor was false, and Congress relaxed a bit. Still, bombardment of Boston and an open clash of arms could not be ruled out. If the report "had proved true," John Adams wrote his wife, "you would have heard the thunder of an American Congress"—as it did thunder less than a year later, after Lexington and Concord.

Having settled the question about voting procedure, Congress named committees to look into various important matters and report as quickly as possible. One was a Grand Committee consisting of two delegates from each of the twelve colonies represented in Carpenters' Hall.** Richard Henry Lee and Edmund Pendleton—with Patrick Henry added later—represented Virginia on this committee that was to consider the rights of the colonies and to recommend the best means of protecting and conserving them.

Another main committee was appointed "to examine and report

---

* Henry was not yet forty; Lee, forty-two.

** Georgia was not represented at this Congress because the royal governor had prevented the choosing of delegates.

the several statutes which affect the trade and manufactures of the colonies." This committee consisted of twelve members, one each from the delegations present, with Patrick Henry representing Virginia.

Congress early decided, as Virginia suggested, that the Grand Committee, rather than reciting all of the colonists' grievances against Britain from the first days of settlement, should restrict itself to "consideration of such rights only as have been infringed by acts of the British parliament since the year 1763," at the end of the French and Indian-Seven Years' War—at which time Britain took a new tack in colonial policy by adopting the Sugar Act, Stamp Act, Townshend Acts, new customs regulations, quartering of more British troops, Quebec Act, the East India tea business, the Port of Boston Bill, and related coercive measures.

In the Grand Committee, Richard Henry Lee argued that the colonists' rights were "built on a fourfold foundation: on nature, on the British Constitution, on charters, and on immemorial usage." Against this, Galloway of Pennsylvania, Duane of New York, and other conservatives, chiefly centered in the middle colonies, contended that American claims were "well founded on the British Constitution, and not on the law of nature." These conservatives wished to avoid any talk about natural rights, which might be extended and prove to be dangerous and upsetting to the social and economic *status quo*. Keep to tradition and what was written in the book.

"I have looked for our rights in the law of nature, but could not find them . . . ," said Galloway. "I have looked for them in the constitution of the English government, and there found them. We may draw them from this source securely." Galloway went so far as to echo Charles Townshend's charge of "nonsense" about the distinctions Americans drew between internal and external taxes—a point of view undercutting much colonial argument.

One day while the committees were still deliberating and Congress was impatiently awaiting their reports, Paul Revere came riding in with news and a most important document from Boston. Sam Adams, in Philadelphia, had been writing to his friends at home urging that Patriots in and around Boston, and elsewhere in Massachusetts, should take some strong positive stand, which might encourage Congress to do likewise.

Sam Adams and his cousin John, among others, were distressed by the slow proceedings and ambivalent attitudes of Congress members. John Adams found the delegates dilatory and "jealous of each other—fearful, timid, skittish." In a moment of exasperation, he termed them "one third Tory, one third Whig, one third mongrel." Congress obviously needed a prod or two, a shot in the arm, a kick from behind—and Sam Adams' friend Joseph Warren supplied these.

As urged by Adams,* Warren called a large meeting of the Patriots in Suffolk County, which included Boston, and persuaded the meeting, without much urging, to adopt a series of resolutions that he had drafted, incorporating suggestions made by the two Adamses. Paul Revere had undertaken to set out immediately, and with all speed, to carry a copy of the Suffolk Resolves to Philadelphia.

Stronger in tone and substance than any proposals yet adopted by any large representative American assemblage, the Suffolk Resolves, after reciting familiar grievances, stated flatly "that no obedience is due from this province to . . . the recent acts of Parliament, but that they should be rejected as the attempts of a wicked administration to enslave America." All collectors of taxes should hold all monies in their hands until Massachusetts was restored to a "constitutional" basis; nothing should be paid that might go to the Crown account until grievances were redressed. Americans should avoid riot and disorder, and act in such a way "as to merit the approbation of the wise, and the admiration of the brave and free, of every age and country."

Nevertheless, just in case, each town should see to it that all of its commissioned militia officers were staunch Patriots prepared to "use their utmost diligence" in having the people "acquaint themselves with the art of war as soon as possible, and . . . appear under arms at least once a week." This was open defiance of British power, and not far short of an act of concerted shooting rebellion.

The Suffolk Resolves came before Congress on September 18 and were unanimously adopted, with the delegates recommending "a perseverance in the same firm and temperate conduct" as shown by those attending the Suffolk County meeting, "trusting that the effect of the united efforts of North America in their behalf will carry such conviction to the British nation of the unwise, unjust, and ruinous policy of the present administration as quickly to introduce better men and wiser measures. . . ."

---

* Sam Adams, wrote Joseph Galloway at this time, "eats little, drinks little, sleeps little, thinks much, and is most indefatigible in the pursuit of his object. It was this man who, by his superior application, managed at once the factions in Congress at Philadelphia and the factions of New England."

Congress ordered the publication both of the Suffolk Resolves and their endorsement of them *in toto*. John Adams was elated, entering in his diary:

> This was one of the happiest days in my life. In Congress we had generous noble sentiments and manly eloquence. This day convinced me that America will support Massachusetts, or perish with her.

Conservatives were becoming increasingly uneasy about the general trend of the proceedings. It seemed to them that Congress was bent on sharpening the conflict with Britain, whereas it should be seeking, as all delegations had been instructed, to find some formula for lessening the conflict and restoring peace and harmony. Joseph Galloway thought he had such a formula, one well-designed to thwart what he called "the violent party." His proposal, a sort of flank attack, certainly took that party by surprise and almost prevailed.

On September 28, ten days after Congress had acted on the Suffolk Resolves, Galloway presented "A Plan of the proposed Union between Great Britain and the Colonies." The plan provided for a governor general of the colonies to be appointed by the Crown; for a Grand Council to consist of members elected by the colonial legislatures for a term of three years, with decisions of the Council subject to veto by the governor general. The Council was to serve as an inferior but distinct branch of the British legislature, having considerable jurisdiction in general colonial matters. The assembly in each colony was to continue to sit and legislate in provincial and local affairs.

The plan promised the colonies a much larger degree of self-government, of home rule, especially in view of the provision that general bills affecting the colonies could originate either in the Grand Council or in Parliament, but that no such bill would be valid without the consent of both. Each had a veto on the other.

In debate, Galloway's plan had strong support, not only on the part of Pennsylvanians, but of John Jay and James Duane of New York, who spoke for the dominant commercial and landed interests of that colony. To Edward Rutledge of South Carolina, Galloway's was an "almost perfect plan." But the radicals, led by Virginia and Massachusetts men, would have nothing to do with it. They contended that Congress had no authority to adopt such a plan that would so radically change the colonial pattern.

Richard Henry Lee, the first to speak in opposition, strenuously argued that the adoption of Galloway's proposal "would make such changes in the legislatures of the colonies" that he could not even consider the plan until he had further instructions from Virginia. In the course of his remarks strongly attacking the proposal, Patrick Henry said, according to notes taken by John Adams:

> The original constitution of the colonies was founded on the broadest and most generous base. The regulation of our trade was compensation enough for all the protection we ever experienced from her [England].
>
> And what would result if the Galloway plan were adopted?
>
> We shall liberate our constituents from a corrupt House of Commons, and throw them into the arms of an American legislature that may be bribed by that nation which avows, in the face of the world, that bribery is a part of her system of government.
>
> Before we are obliged to pay taxes as they do, let us be as free as they; let us have our trade with all the world. We are not to consent by representatives of representatives.
>
> I am inclined to think the present [British] measures lead to war.

Henry, so John Adams recorded at the time, "has a horrid opinion of Galloway, Jay, and the Rutledges. Their system, he says, would ruin the cause of America. He is very impatient to see such fellows and not be at liberty to describe them in their true colors."

When the Galloway plan was put to a vote, it lost by a very narrow margin—by a vote of six to five.* The plan was not killed outright—rather, on a motion that it should be laid on the table for future consideration. But the plan was as good as dead, for no attempt was made to revive it.

While it is not recorded how the several delegations voted, several things are quite certain. Pennsylvania, New York, and South Carolina favored Galloway's scheme, and probably had the support of New Jersey and Maryland. Virginia, Massachusetts, and "democratical" Rhode Island were certainly opposed, and probably were supported by Connecticut, New Hampshire, and Delaware.

But for the Congress' unanimous endorsement of the Suffolk Re-

---

* As there were twelve votes in Congress, one colony must have abstained—North Carolina, perhaps?

solves committing it to a very forward position, the Galloway plan of union might well have passed. If it had, so some have argued, the Revolution might have been averted, or at least postponed.

This supposition, largely academic, entirely overlooks a basic fact —the Galloway scheme, if approved by Congress, would still have had to be accepted by the King, the Lord North ministry, and a majority in Parliament. None of these was in the least disposed at the moment to entertain an idea of a major shift in colonial policy and administrative structure—least of all a plan to give an elective Grand Council in America the right to veto acts of Parliament dealing with colonial affairs. If the Galloway plan was too conservative for Congress, it was far too radical for those in command at London, who were resolved to maintain the authority of the British Empire as it was. They saw no reason for reform, and certainly not for a change forced by rebellious and defiant Liberty Boys.

While there were some spirited moments in Carpenters' Hall, as in debates on how the colonies should vote and on Galloway's scheme, the proceedings of Congress were usually tiresome, dull, and "slow as snails," wrote John Adams to his wife Abigail: "We go to Congress at nine, and there we stay, most earnestly engaged in debates upon the most abstruse mysteries of State, until three in the afternoon." Every proposal, no matter how absurd or irrelevant, was minutely examined and "entertained with logic and rhetoric, law, history, politics, and mathematics." Adams added that he was "wearied to death" with the life he led:*

> The business of the Congress is tedious beyond expression. This assembly is like no other that ever existed. Every man in it is a great man, an orator, a critic, a statesman; and, therefore, every man upon every question must show his oratory, his criticism, and his political abilities.
>
> The consequence of this is that business is drawn and spun out to an immeasurable length.

But tedium was relieved by gay dinner parties almost every day, "a perpetual round of feasting." At four in the afternoon, after Congress had adjourned for the day, delegates went to dine "with some

---

* For significant and illuminating detail about what went on at Philadelphia, both in and out of Congress, one has to lean heavily on the lively and often witty diary and letters of John Adams. But for him and his tireless pen, our insight into the "innards" of the First Continental Congress would be very dim indeed.

of the nobles of Pennsylvania . . . and feast upon ten thousand delicacies, and sit drinking Madeira, Claret, and Burgundy till six or seven, and then go home fatigued to death with business, company, and care."

On one occasion, Patrick Henry and John Adams were among scores of distinguished guests at an elaborate dinner party in the great mansion of Chief Justice Benjamin Chew. Adams, as usual, noted the sumptuous fare:

> Turtle, and every other thing, flummery, jellies, sweetmeats of twenty sorts, trifles, whipped sillabubs, floating islands, fools, &c., and then a dessert of fruit, raisins, almonds, pears, peaches. Wines, most excellent and admirable.

Quakerism stressed modesty and simplicity as a way of life, but the entertainment offered by the "simple" Quakers of the City of Brotherly Love was anything but simple, as many in Congress remarked.* John Adams frequently complained in letters to his wife that he was "being killed by kindness in this place," and how happy he would be when he got home. But he was protesting too much in a familiar husbandly way.

Adams was obviously enjoying himself immensely, apparently never turning down an invitation to dinner, or to a banquet, or to a convivial evening at the City Tavern, unofficial headquarters of Patriots in the city.

"Yet I hold up surprisingly well," bouncy John assured Abigail, sitting quietly at home.

In spite of "slow as snails" proceedings in Carpenters' Hall and the gay exhausting social life of Philadelphia, work in Congress inched along. After several weeks of wandering debate, the Grand Committee appointed to consider the best grounds on which the colonies might base their asserted rights made a report—or rather, two reports, neither of which wholly satisfied anybody.

It was generally agreed, however, that American rights rested upon the foundation of the British Constitution, colonial charters and grants, and "immemorial usage," but an appeal to natural rights, or the "law of nature," should be reserved in case it were needed to answer Britain's "constitutional" arguments—and it was so used.

The other main committee, of which Henry was a leading member,

---

* A Quaker host at one dinner offered his guests "a bowl of fine Lemon [rum] Punch big enough to have Swimm'd half a dozen of young geese."

handed in its report on the British trade laws affecting the colonies. Out of this report grew a new, strengthened, and extended boycott aimed at all British trade under a policy of "non-importation, non-consumption, and non-exportation."

But when this policy should go into effect was another question. A Pennsylvania delegate proposed November 1, little more than a month off, as the deadline for imports. Patrick Henry argued that this was too soon, that merchants should be given a bit more time to get their affairs and shelves in order. In proposing that the deadline be set back a month to December 1, a motion that was carried, Henry remarked, somewhat sardonically:

"We don't mean to hurt even our own rascals, if we have any."

While still debating the deadline for imports, Congress unanimously passed a resolution, published and distributed in all colonies through newspapers, handbills, and other means:

> That the Congress request Merchants and others in the several colonies not to send to Great Britain any order for goods, and to direct the execution of all orders already sent to be delayed or suspended until the sense of the Congress, on the means to be taken for the preservation of the liberties of America, is made public.

The ban on imports precluded any more importation of slaves by the Royal African Company or any other British entrepreneurs engaged in the highly profitable and wholly nauseating African slave trade. The colonies, particularly those in the South, had made a number of attempts to stop this nefarious trade. It was not that they were opposed to slavery as such, but they did oppose the further importation of slaves for two reasons.

First, they feared slave insurrections by those who had been recently shanghaied, or sold by tribal chiefs, to toil their lives away in captivity on American soil. There had been a number of such insurrections rather alarming in scope, and slaves constituted almost half of the population in the southern colonies. Virginians preferred native-born slaves who could speak some English and knew better how to grow tobacco than newcomers, "the outlandish."*

Second, southern planters found that the continuing inflow of

---

* Wrote Colonel William Byrd II: "The poor Negroes are a kind of Adamites, very scantily supplied with clothes and other necessaries . . . However, they are even with their master, and make him but indifferent crops, so that he gets nothing by his injustice but the scandal of it."

"shoals of slaves" depreciated the market value of the trained slaves they already owned, and such slaves were the most valuable "livestock." In the inventory and appraisement of Patrick Henry's estate after his death, the first items listed were:

1 negro man Jessee	£200
1 ditto ditto John	100
1 ditto woman, Pegg & her children, Shadrack, Nancy, Pleasant, Jessee, Reuben, and Letty	300
Dafney & her children	165
. . . Alce, a young wench	100

Altogether, Henry's 67 slaves—men, women, and children—were valued at £3,968 [almost $120,000]. His other livestock—22 horses and colts, 11 "work steers," 156 head of cattle, 155 hogs, 60 of sheep —were appraised at £1,040.5, only a quarter of the value of his slaves.

Henry's attitude toward slavery, if not wholly admirable, was at least frank and forthright, without any cant or hypocrisy. To him, slavery was "an abominable practice, . . . totally repugnant to the first impressions of right and wrong, . . . a species of violence and tyranny . . . inconsistent with the Bible and destructive to liberty." And yet, said Henry, "I am a master of slaves of my own purchase!" Why? Because of the "general inconvenience" of living in Virginia without them.

> I will not, I cannot justify it. However culpable my conduct, I will so far pay my devoir to virtue as to own the excellence and rectitude of her precepts, and lament my want of conformity to them. . . . I could say many things on the subject, a serious view of which gives a gloomy perspective to future times.*

While the nonimportation and nonconsumption items were readily accepted, the proposed ban on exports to Britain stirred considerable debate in Congress. The Virginia delegates had been expressly instructed to use their utmost influence to prevent tobacco exports from being cut off for another year, until the next crop was in and sold. South Carolina wanted to exempt her profitable export trade in

* For the full text of Henry's longest statement on slavery, see Appendix D (pp. 485–86).

indigo and rice. Other colonies wanted to hold their export markets as long as possible. It seemed at one time that the nonexportation scheme might be rejected.

In the end, however, it was agreed that there should be a total ban on exports to Great Britain, Ireland, and the British West Indies. But the ban was not to go into effect for almost a year—on September 1, 1775, if by then the British had not satisfactorily redressed the colonies' many grievances. Months before that deadline arrived, open armed hostilities had broken out and all trade relations with Britain, the "enemy," were cut off abruptly.

As its session drew toward adjournment and major decisions had been taken, Congress decided that several important reports and documents about its proceedings should be prepared for publication. It appointed committees to draft (1) an Address to the King asking him to throw out Lord North's ministry and reverse its "obnoxious" policies, (2) a Declaration of Rights and Grievances addressed to the British people, (3) a Memorial (more or less a report) to the colonial assemblies on what had happened in Philadelphia, and (4) a public letter to the inhabitants of Canada and other British possessions in North America urging them to support the Continental Congress and its cause.

The letter, drafted by Richard Henry Lee, was directed particularly to the Canadians whose support could have been of great help. Lee's letter fell on deaf ears. The Canadians, predominantly French Roman Catholic, had just been granted religious toleration by Protestant Britain under the Quebec Act. Not that Anglican Britain was particularly tolerant in principle or practice about religious matters; merely that it saw the Quebec Act as a smart move in political expediency, which it certainly was, for it detached Canada from the increasingly revolutionary colonial cause.

From publication of the Suffolk Resolves and the endorsement of them by Congress, French Canadians knew that one of the "grievances" complained of in the Resolves was this:

> That the late act of Parliament for establishing the Roman Catholic religion and the French laws in that extensive country now called Canada, is dangerous in an extreme degree to the Protestant religion and to the civil rights and liberties of all America; and, therefore, as men and Protestant Christians, we are indispensably obliged to take all proper measures for our security.

In view of this, French Catholic Canadians were not at all disposed to throw in their lot with the Protestant English colonies to the south, a majority of which were quite intolerant, being strongly and actively anti-Catholic, particularly the four Puritan colonies in New England. French Canada found no grievance at all in being granted a large measure of religious toleration and being allowed to keep traditional French laws in force.

The other letters and documents adopted by Congress for publication broke no new ground in argument. They were propaganda pieces, giving a familiar recital of American "rights" and British "wrongs." But in the Declaration of Rights and Grievances there was a significant, sharp, and very relevant item, proposed by John Adams:

> That the keeping of a standing army in these colonies, in time of peace, without the consent of the legislature of that colony in which such army is kept, is against law.

In short, General Gage and his Lobsterbacks should get out of Boston and environs, or they might get pushed out.

The committee named to draw up the Address to the King included Richard Henry Lee (chairman), Patrick Henry, John Adams, Sam Adams, and such conservatives as John Dickinson of Pennsylvania and John Rutledge of South Carolina. One evening John Adams went to Henry's lodgings to discuss what should go into the document.

On this occasion, wrote Adams, Henry told him that "he had no public education; at fifteen he read Virgil and Livy, and had not looked into a Latin book since. His father left him* at that age, and he has been struggling through life ever since. He has high notions, talks about exalted minds, &c."

The first draft of the Address to His Majesty was found to be unsatisfactory by the majority in Congress. In his biography of Henry, William Wirt stated, using information supplied to him by Jefferson, then in his seventies, that Henry was the author of the unsatisfactory draft.

---

* Adams seems to have inadvertently omitted a phrase here. Henry's father never "left him." The two remained in a close relationship until John Henry died, with his son Patrick often coming to his father's support in his various financial and other difficulties in later years. What Adams probably intended to write was something like this: that when Patrick was fifteen, his father left him "to his own devices," or "to make his way on his own," or some such phrase. That would have been true.

Using this as a peg, Wirt went into some of his usual sermonizing about how chagrined Henry was to have flunked his first major test in English composition. This would not have happened except for "his early neglect of literture," a neglect that impaired "the wonderful gifts which he had derived from nature." Unfortunately, "the years of his youth had been wasted in idleness."

The author of the "unsuccessful" draft of the Address was not Henry, but Richard Henry Lee, chairman of the committee. What, if anything, Patrick Henry contributed to the draft is not known. But certainly he and two of his committee colleagues, John and Sam Adams, offered ideas and perhaps some phrases, for all were good sharp phrasemakers.

Nor was the draft unsatisfactory in the sense of that term intended by Jefferson and echoed by Wirt; i.e., that it was ill-conceived and badly written. As might have been expected from a Lee-Henry-Adams collaboration, the draft was deemed by many delegates to be too clear and strong in statement and tone, and the leader of the conciliators, John Dickinson, was given the task of toning it down.

Wirt also used other misinformation given to him by Jefferson, who was not even present at the 1774 Congress and in later years had become, under circumstances to be discussed, quite malicious in regard to Henry. In a passage, the substance of which still recurs in serious historical works, Wirt wrote that Henry, while supreme in "declamation," was no good in committee work among "cool-headed, reflecting, and most able men," and was "completely thrown into the shade" when put to the "severer test of intellectual excellence, *the details of business*" . . . There is no evidence for this but Jefferson's say-so as transmitted by Wirt.

In this case, as in others when he was severely criticizing friend and foe, Jefferson worked in a curious and revealing fashion. Using the data supplied him on Henry's part in the First Continental Congress, Wirt wrote a draft and sent it to Jefferson for his comment and review. In the draft, Wirt had liberally quoted Jefferson and identified him as the source of his information. Jefferson did not correct any of the "facts" he had given, but he protested to Wirt that he wished to remain anonymous, that he was not to be quoted on the 1774 Congress—no doubt for the good reason that he knew nothing about it firsthand, not being present. To Jefferson, Wirt replied:

> Your repose shall never be endangered by any act of mine, if I can help it. Immediately on the receipt of your last letter,

> and before the manuscript had met any other eye, I wrote over again the whole passage relative to the first Congress, omitting the marks of quotation, and removing altogether your name from the communication.

This took Jefferson off the hook until many years later when the letter telling him not to worry about his "repose" came to light in Wirt's papers. Wirt evidently destroyed all copies of his unsatisfactory first draft on the First Congress, for none was found in his voluminous papers. One cannot help regretting that we do not know exactly what Jefferson was quoted as saying in that draft from which his name was later removed "altogether."*

After sitting for almost two months, having accomplished a good deal, especially in laying the foundation for a unity of policy among the colonies, Congress prepared to adjourn. Just before their departure from "the happy, the peaceful, the elegant, the hospitable, and polite city of Philadelphia," as John Adams admiringly described it, he and Henry spent an evening together in "familiar conversation," reviewing what Congress had done and what might be expected as a result.

Adams "expressed a full conviction that our resolves, declarations of rights, enumeration of wrongs, petitions, remonstrances and addresses, association and non-importation agreements, however they might be expected by the people in America, and however necessary to cement the union of the colonies, would be but waste paper in England."

To this Henry replied that "they might make some impression among the people of England, but agreed with me," said Adams, "that they would be totally lost upon the government."

How right they were. When the Congress resolutions were received in London, Chatham highly praised them in the House of Lords as very statesmanlike and urged a course of understanding and moderation. His counsel, though backed by others, was ignored. In the House of Commons, Lord North tossed the American documents on the table with the remark that he had not even bothered to read them, and proceeded to send more troops and warships to General Gage in Boston.

On their leave-taking evening, Adams drew out of his pocket and

---

* For a pedestrian but nevertheless rather interesting account of Wirt and the curious twists of his career, literary and political and otherwise, see *Memoirs of the Life of William Wirt* (1850), by John P. Kennedy.

read to Henry a "short and hasty" letter he had just received from a Massachusetts friend, Major Joseph Hawley of Northampton. The letter contained "a few broken hints" on what Hawley "thought was proper to be done, and concluding with these words: 'After all, we must fight.' "

Henry listened "with great attention," said Adams, "and as soon as I had pronounced the words, 'After all, we must fight,' he raised his head and with an energy and vehemence that I can never forget, broke out with:

" 'By God, I am of that man's mind!' "

Adams was of that mind, too, though not revealing it at the moment. Henry was the only man in Congress, wrote Adams later, "who appeared . . . sensible of the precipice, or rather the pinnacle on which we stood, and had candor and courage enough to acknowledge it."

Unknown to Major Hawley, Adams, and Henry, "good King George" shared their views about the developing crisis. While the rather mild Congress petitions were on their way to London, the King wrote to Lord North to praise him for chalking out a hard policy line at last and to exhort him to walk that line straight to the end, no matter what:

> The New England governments are in a state of rebellion; blows must decide whether they are to be subject or independent.

It was evident to an increasing number that blows would soon be struck unless one side or the other was prepared to veer off the collision course or back away, which neither was disposed to do.

XIX
Posture of Defense

Give me liberty or give me death.

—PATRICK HENRY

Not long after his two months' stay in Philadelphia, Henry was the guest of a Virginia friend, Colonel John Overton. There were other guests, and one of them asked Henry:

"Do you suppose that Great Britain will drive her colonies to extremities? And if so, what will be the issue of the war?"

Henry glanced around at the company, wondering how discreet he should be, and then replied:

"She will drive us to extremities—no accommodation will take place—hostilities will soon commence—and a desperate and bloody touch it will be."

"But do you think, Mr. Henry, that an infant nation as we are, without discipline, or ammunition, or ships of war, or money to procure them—do you think it's possible, thus circumstanced, to oppose successfully the fleets and armies of Great Britain?"

"I will be candid with you. I doubt whether we shall be able, alone, to cope with so powerful a nation." Then rising from his chair and speaking quietly but with intense force:

> But where is France? Where is Spain? Where is Holland? The natural enemies of Great Britain—where will they be all

> this while? Do you suppose they will stand by, idle and indifferent spectators to the contest?
>
> Will Louis XVI be asleep all this time?* Believe me, no! When Louis XVI shall be satisfied by our serious opposition, and our Declaration of Independence, that all prospect of conciliation is gone, then—and not till then—will he furnish us with arms, ammunition, and clothing; and not with these only, but he will send his fleet and arms to fight our battles for us; he will form with us a treaty offensive and defensive . . .
>
> Spain and Holland will join the confederation. Our independence will be established, and we shall take our stand among the nations of the earth.

At mention of the word "independence," all at Colonel Overton's table are said to have been startled, never having heard any such bold proposal for the solution of current problems.

This account of the table talk at Overton's, first recorded many years later, after Henry's death, need not be taken too literally. It seems to be more than a bit aprocryphal. It is obviously colored by remembrance of later developments, as if Henry long before had clearly and accurately anticipated them, which is doubtful.

Still, in view of his conversation with John Adams on "We must fight," Henry may at this time have been flirting with the idea of independence, as was Adams, though the latter noted that down to 1776 the slightest mention of independence was taboo. It was a "Hobgoblin of so frightful a Mien that it would throw a delicate Person into Fits to look it in the Face."

Henry was once asked "whom he thought the greatest man in Congress." He did not name John Adams, as he well might, considering their close association at Philadelphia and their agreement in radical views. Rather, he said:

"If you speak of eloquence, Mr. [Edward or his younger brother John?] Rutledge, of South Carolina, is by far the greatest orator.** But if you speak of solid information and sound judgment, Colonel Washington is, unquestionably, the greatest man on that floor." As another said of him, Washington was always "cool, like a bishop at his prayers."

---

* France was still smarting from its disastrous defeat by Britain in the Seven Years' War, which had ended little more than a decade before.

** Henry was being rather self-consciously modest here, for he had been praised on every hand for being the most moving and persuasive speaker at Congress.

As Henry was usually anything but "cool" himself, it is revealing that he singled out Washington for his highest praise. But he had long admired Washington for his integrity, his monolithic character, his abilities and zeal. The two established a lifelong friendship, though there was a short estrangement between them in their last years, arising from a misunderstanding caused by malicious gossip. But they were reconciled before their deaths in 1799. One of Henry's last letters was a warm message to Washington.

As recommended at Philadelphia for all the colonies, Virginia set up a provincial Committee of Safety, with subcommittees in counties, towns, and smaller communities. These committees had two chief functions—first, to enforce the boycott agreement; second, to see that Patriots should extend their view to the possibility of "mournful events and be in all respects prepared for every emergency."

Sons of Liberty everywhere became more active than ever before. In Connecticut, the General Assembly ordered all towns to double their supply of "powder, balls, and flints," and decreed that the militia in each county be mustered once a week. Some Rhode Islanders made away with forty-four cannon at Newport and transported them to Providence, rather saucily informing the Royal Navy commandant that they, as "loyal subjects of the Crown," would be happy to use the guns "against any power that might offer to molest the colony." In all the colonies, men were arming and drilling, even in "Quakerish" Pennsylvania where religious opposition to war was strong. From Williamsburg, Lord Dunmore reported disturbing news to London:

> Every county is now arming a company of men, whom they call an independent company, for the avowed purpose of protecting their committees, and to be employed against government if occasion requires.

Following Virginia's lead in this, a Maryland convention urged all men aged sixteen to fifty to form themselves into military companies, and in another resolution added the wry comment:

> . . . that such militia will relieve our Mother Country from any expense in our protection and defence, will obviate the pretense of a necessity for taxing us on that account, and render it unnecessary to keep any standing army—ever dangerous to liberty—in this province.

This was regarded as such a sharp amusing jibe at British policy that it was incorporated almost verbatim in resolutions adopted by many town, city, county, and provincial conventions, including that held in Fairfax County with Washington presiding.

As scheduled, the Second Virginia Convention met on March 20, 1775, five months after the Continental Congress adjourned. But the meeting was not held in Williamsburg this time. Lord Dunmore was there, in a surly mood, and had at his command a force of sailors and marines on board several warships anchored in the James River only a few miles away.

It seemed prudent, therefore, to hold the Convention elsewhere. The choice went to the young and still scraggly town of Richmond, at the head of navigation on the James, more than fifty miles inland from Williamsburg. If the irascible lord governor decided to move against the Convention and seize its leaders, they would have some warning and a chance to escape—certainly preferable to the possibility of being trapped in Williamsburg and shipped to England to be tried as "traitors," with the likelihood of ending up by being hanged, drawn, and quartered on Tyburn Hill.

In want of other space, the Convention met in St. John's Church, a simple white frame structure with a three-tiered square tower.* Peyton Randolph, as usual, was chosen unanimously to be chairman, or moderator. After three days of rather rambling debate and discussion, Patrick Henry rose to offer three resolutions:

> That a well-regulated militia, composed of gentlemen and yeomen, is the natural strength and only security of a free government, . . . [and] would forever render it unnecessary for the Mother Country to keep among us for the purpose of our defense any standing army of mercenary forces . . .
>
> That the establishment of such a militia at this time is peculiarly necessary . . . to secure our inestimable rights and liberties from those further violations with which they are threatened.
>
> *Resolved, therefore,* That this colony be immediately put into a posture of defence; and that [there] be a committee to prepare a plan for the embodying, arming, and disciplining such a number of men as may be sufficient for that purpose.

---

* Built in 1741, St. John's still stands, a center of historical and architectural interest in the modern city.

Though there was nothing essentially new in these resolutions—other colonies had already passed similar ones—Henry's proposals met with considerable and rather heated objections on the floor. All Convention members had been chosen because they supported the Patriot cause, but there were sharp differences among them on how far, and how fast, that cause should proceed.

Unfortunately, there is not a word in the Convention journal about who spoke or who said what during the course of the "animated debate." But many years later, a prominent Virginian, St. George Tucker, who had been present on the occasion, though not as a delegate, recalled that the strong opposition to Henry's resolutions had come from the middle-of-the-roaders led by Edmund Pendleton, Richard Bland, Benjamin Harrison, and Henry's old friend, Treasurer Robert Carter Nicholas. These men did not object to the resolutions as such, but regarded action on them as "premature," wanting to wait and see what happened next. Urging the necessity of action now, Henry rose to make the speech for which he is best remembered. Addressing Peyton Randolph in the chair, as if speaking to him personally, Henry said in a "calm and collected" way:

> No man, Mr. President, thinks more highly than I do of the patriotism, as well as the abilities, of the very honorable gentlemen who have just addressed the House. But different men often see the same subject in different lights; and therefore, I hope it will not be thought disrespectful to those gentlemen if, entertaining as I do, opinions of a character very opposite to theirs, I should speak forth my sentiments freely and without reserve.
>
> This is no time for ceremony. The question before the House is one of awful moment to this country. For my own part, I consider it nothing less than a question of freedom or slavery.

On this, there should be freedom of debate, the only way to arrive at the truth, Henry continued. If he held back his opinions at such a time, he would consider himself guilty of treason.

> Mr. President, it is natural for man to indulge in the illusions of hope. We are apt to shut our eyes against a painful truth . . . Is this the part of wise men engaged in a great and arduous struggle for liberty? Are we disposed to be of the number of those, who having eyes, see not, and having ears, hear not?

> . . . For my part, whatever anguish of spirit it may cost, I am willing to know the whole truth; to know the worst, and to provide for it.

Why had Britain been building up her armies and fleets in America? Did she have a threatening foreign foe in this part of the globe? No! The increasing military forces had only one objective–to subjugate the colonies and "rivet" them in chains.

> Let us not . . . deceive ourselves longer. Sir, we have done everything that could be done to avert the storm now coming on. We have petitioned; we have remonstrated; we have supplicated; we have prostrated ourselves before the Throne . . .
>
> Our petitions have been slighted; our remonstrances have produced additional violence and insult; our supplications have been disregarded; and we have been spurned with contempt from the foot of the Throne . . .
>
> There is no longer any room for hope. If we wish to be free, if we mean to preserve inviolate those inestimable privileges for which we have been contending, . . . we must fight.
>
> I repeat it, Sir, we must fight! An appeal to arms, and to the God of hosts, is all that is left to us.

Up to this point, Henry had been speaking rather softly and calmly, establishing the base of his argument, but he now rose to impassioned heights as he came to his main point:

> They tell us, Sir, that we are weak, unable to cope with so formidable an adversary.
>
> But when shall we be stronger? Will it be the next week, or the next year? Will it be when we are totally disarmed, and when a British guard shall be stationed in every house? Shall we gather strength by irresolution and inaction? . . .
>
> It is in vain, Sir, to extenuate the matter. Gentlemen may cry peace, peace; but there is no peace. The war is actually begun. The next gale that sweeps from the north will bring to our ears the clash of resounding arms. Our brethren are already in the field.
>
> Why stand we here idle? What is it the gentlemen wish? What would they have?
>
> Is life so dear, or peace so sweet, as to be purchased at the price of chains and slavery?
>
> Forbid it, Almighty God!

> I know not what other course others may take. But as for me—give me liberty, or give me death!

One who heard this speech, John Roane, recalled many years later the deep impression made on him by Henry's style and dramatic manner of delivery, saying that his "voice, countenance, and gestures gave an irresistible force to his words." Said Roane in the best view we have of Henry in the act of speaking:

> When he said, "Is life so dear, or peace so sweet, as to be purchased at the price of chains and slavery?" he stood in the attitude of a condemned galley slave, loaded with fetters, awaiting his doom. His form was bowed, his wrists were crossed, his manacles almost visible . . .
>
> After a solemn pause, he raised his eyes and chained hands toward heaven and prayed in words and tones which thrilled every heart, "Forbid it, Almighty God!" He turned toward the timid Loyalists in the house, who were quaking with terror at the idea of the consequences of participating in proceedings which would be visited with the penalties of treason by the British crown, and he slowly bent his form yet nearer to the earth and said, "I know not what course others may take," and he accompanied the words with his hands still crossed, while he seemed to be weighed down with additional chains . . .
>
> After remaining in this posture of humiliation long enough to impress the imagination . . . he arose proudly and exclaimed, "But as for me"—and the words hissed through his clenched teeth, while his body was thrown back, and every muscle and tendon was strained against the fetters that bound him . . . then the loud, clear, triumphant note, "Give me liberty," electrified the assembly.
>
> It was not a prayer, but a stern demand which would submit to no refusal or delay . . . and as each syllable of the word "liberty" echoed through the building, his fetters were shivered, his arms were hurled apart, . . . his hands were open, and his arms elevated and extended; his countenance was radiant; he stood erect and defiant, while the sound of his voice and the sublimity of his attitude made him appear a magnificent incarnation of Freedom . . .
>
> After a momentary pause, only long enough to permit the echo of the word "liberty" to cease, he let his left hand fall powerless to his side, and clenched his right hand firmly, as if

> holding a dagger with the point aimed at his breast. He stood like a Roman senator defying Caesar . . .
>
> He closed the grand appeal with the solemn words, "or give me death," which sounded with the awful cadence of a hero's dirge, fearless of death and victorious in death.
>
> And he suited the action to the word by a blow upon the left breast with his right hand, which seemed to drive the dagger to the patriot's heart.

As earlier remarked, Henry when speaking publicly was often something of an actor—and at times, more than a bit of a ham actor, as here.* Even so, his words and his posturing carried the day, and the Convention enthusiastically adopted his arming resolutions.

To recommend the best means of implementing them, a committee was appointed, with Henry as chairman and with Richard Henry Lee, Washington, Jefferson, Pendleton, Benjamin Harrison, and Robert Carter Nicholas among its members. Next day, this committee brought in a report that was quickly adopted with only a few minor amendments.

Virginians, as they were already doing, should form "one or more volunteer companies of infantry and troops of horse in each county, and be in constant training and readiness to act on any emergency." Tidewater counties should organize troops of horse, while counties to the west and north should "pay a more particular attention to the forming a good infantry."

Most important and significant, these volunteer companies were to be responsible only to the Committee of Safety in their respective counties, and not to Lord Governor Dunmore who was commander-in-chief of the regular militia. In large part, the volunteers were trained militiamen, but now wearing another cap.

Henry was also appointed to serve on several other important committees—among them, one "to prepare a plan for the encouragement of arts and manufactures in this colony." Taking only a week

---

* Henry's speech, with gestures, has undoubtedly been declaimed many more times than any other by Americans in what used to be called "elocution contests" in high school and college. This writer, when much younger, won a few prizes himself by thumping his upheld right fist, holding an imaginary dagger against his left breast and piercing himself to the heart. But he did not tumble to the floor, turn over, and expire there, as might have been expected, for that was not one of his instructions. He stood upright with his heart still bleeding, and with the audience hoping that the show—the whole show-off—would soon end.

for its deliberations, the Convention at Richmond adjourned, having meantime named seven delegates to represent Virginia at the Second Continental Congress to meet at Philadelphia early in May, little more than a month off. The delegates were the same as those sent to the first Congress, but with a different order of election: Peyton Randolph (107 votes), Washington (106), Henry (105), Lee (103), Pendleton (100), Benjamin Harrison (94), and Richard Bland (90).

Reflecting the continued strength of the moderates, Pendleton moved up from last to fifth place. Young Thomas Jefferson was placed in nomination, but received only eighteen votes—and this but a year before he was assigned at Philadelphia the task of drafting the Declaration of Independence. His rise, in its own way, was as spectacular as Henry's.

With the colonists drilling regularly in volunteer companies and collecting arms, gunpowder, and other supplies, some of them smuggled in from England, Scotland, and the French and Spanish West Indies, British authorities were rightly apprehensive. Orders came from London that Crown officials in the colonies, the royal governors and top military officers—in particular, General Gage in Boston, the Army commander-in-chief—should put a stop to all this. They were to seize the military stores that the colonists were secretly and "illegally" building up. They were also to seize the chief "malcontents" and stop their mischief, and take every precaution to see that no more arms and ammunition fell into their hands.

On Lord Dunmore's orders, late on the night of April 20, 1775, a detachment from the marine forces on board the *Magdalen,* a Royal Navy vessel anchored in the James, came ashore and marched quietly into Williamsburg. There they "raped" the Powder Horn, or the Magazine, an octagonal small brick structure on the Duke of Gloucester Street, a storage place for arms and ammunition. Taking out fifteen kegs of gunpowder, the marines loaded them on carts supplied by Dunmore and carried them to the *Magdalen* where they would be out of reach of any enterprising Patriots looking for badly needed supplies.

Next morning, when it was learned what had happened, all in Williamsburg were greatly concerned and excited. News about the "rape" of the Powder Horn quickly spread throughout the colony, causing widespread alarm. Was this a step toward disarming the Patriots?

In view of his responsibilities, the lord governor had certainly acted rightly, fully within his rights as commander-in-chief of the Virginia military forces, in taking a precautionary step to see that munitions did not fall into the hands of rebels who might "rape" the Powder Horn themselves.

Dunmore might have been wiser if he had removed the gunpowder with an open show of force, instead of by a sneaky midnight raid. But he evidently did not think himself strong enough to face what might be a violent frontal clash. In any case, his clandestine operation was very ill-advised, arousing the gravest apprehensions. If he could seize and carry off gunpowder in a stealthy midnight raid, so he might seize and carry off the persons of the chief "rebels," which was not a happy prospect for Henry, Lee, Washington, Jefferson, Mason, and others.

As news of the Powder Horn incident spread to the back counties, the already organized volunteer military companies began to assemble, many of them at Fredericksburg, some forty miles north of Hanover Courthouse. These chose Washington as their commander-in-chief and informed him that, if he approved, fourteen companies of light horse would be ready in four days to move against Dunmore in Williamsburg and hoped to be joined along the way by "other bodies of armed men willing to appear in support of the honor of Virginia."*

Meantime, while preparations for the march were being made, a messenger was hurriedly dispatched to Williamsburg to learn "whether the gunpowder had been replaced in the public magazine." Word quickly came back from Peyton Randolph that the gunpowder affair was well on the way to being satisfactorily settled. Assured by this, and having received letters from Washington, Richard Henry Lee, and Pendleton cautioning against any hasty action, the officers at Fredericksburg, more than a hundred of them in command of a dozen or more companies of light horse, agreed reluctantly after some argument to do nothing more at the moment except to publish a strong statement:

---

* Unknown as yet to Virginians, the war against Britain had begun a day before the gunpowder incident. It began on April 19 when General Gage, governor of Massachusetts, sent out from Boston a British force to seize and destroy military supplies at Lexington and Concord, and to seize the persons of Sam Adams and John Hancock reported to be in the neighborhood. Alerted by the midnight ride of Paul Revere and William Dawes, Adams and Hancock scrambled away and escaped. News of the armed clash at Lexington and Concord brought Minutemen streaming toward Boston from all parts of New England.

> We do now pledge ourselves to each other to be in readiness, at a moment's warning, to reassemble and by force of arms to defend the law, the liberty, and rights of this or any other sister colony from unjust and wicked invasion.

Henry, not holding a commission in any volunteer company, had not been present at Fredericksburg. The decision taken there so highly displeased him that he immediately issued from Scotchtown a call to Hanover County volunteers to come under arms to meet him on May 2 at the small river port of New Castle, on the upper York, there to discuss "business of the highest importance to American liberty."

About 150 armed men appeared, most of them on foot. In an impassioned plea Henry told them that, regardless of the decision taken at Fredericksburg, something had to be done immediately to make absolutely sure that the powder removed from the Magazine was restored, or payment made for it. They should march on the Palace in Williamsburg and force Governor Dunmore to meet their demands. With loud shouts, the company readily agreed and by acclamation elected Henry to lead them, making him Captain Patrick Henry, his first and next to last military command.

Though old enough, Henry had not served in the French and Indian War, perhaps because he and his young bride were in such dire financial straits after fire had burned them out of their Piney Slash farm. Yet, even if never in the field on active service, young Henry must have had, down the years, some training in the rudiments of being a soldier, perhaps as a private in the rear rank, for his father John had been for a time colonel of the Hanover County militia and would not have neglected his son's education in the field of bearing arms and obeying orders. But Patrick, both when young and older, was not much given to obeying orders.

Colonel John Henry had died more than two years before his son called the meeting of volunteers at New Castle. What the colonel had thought of Patrick's mounting opposition to Crown policy is not known. But there are reasons to believe that he had not been too pleased.

In Virginia, as in England, the King's birthday was celebrated each year as a holiday, with demonstrations, parades, and much merry-making. Friends recalled seeing Colonel Henry on such occasions:

> There are those yet alive who have seen him at the head of his regiment, celebrating the birthday of George III with as

> much enthusiasm as his son Patrick afterward displayed in resisting the encroachments of that monarch.*

Henry's column of 150 Hanoverians set out from New Castle to assault the Palace in Williamsburg, if necessary, and were joined along the way by hundreds more from other counties.** News of the march aroused grave concern in Williamsburg, and in conservative and Royalist circles everywhere.

Lord Dunmore sent his wife and family to a warship, the *Fowey*, anchored in the York River about ten miles away. He ordered in from the *Fowey* a marine detachment, set cannon around the Palace, and collected arms and munitions inside to resist any attack.

The commander of the *Fowey* notified Williamsburg authorities that if his marines or the Palace were attacked, he would be "under the necessity to fire upon the town." This threat to bombard their "defenceless town" horrified Williamsburgers, both Patriots and others. They were not responsible, they said, for any attack that might come. They had not had anything to say or do about the matter.

Patriots elsewhere were severely critical of Henry. Who had authorized his action? Not a single Committee of Safety! Was every Patriot leader, without consulting other leaders, to take off on his own in undertaking missions that seemed good to him? That way lay confusion and chaos. This was not a time for private enterprise in the cause of common defense. Instead of marching on Williamsburg, why wasn't Henry doing what he was supposed to do—be on his way to Philadelphia to sit as a delegate in the Second Continental Congress opening at just this time?

Besides, Henry's action was a direct affront—almost a challenge—to the venerable Peyton Randolph who, writing from Williamsburg, had assured Washington and other leaders that the gunpowder business was well on the way to being settled satisfactorily. Randolph was probably in the very center of negotiations and, as Speaker of the House and President of the Continental Congress, he could be trusted.

Many messages, brought by special couriers riding posthaste, came

---

* After the colonel's death early in 1773, his Mount Brilliant house and plantation were sold, and Henry's mother Sarah went to live with her daughter Jane, who had married Samuel Meredith, Henry's friend from childhood and an ardent Patriot.

** With his usual extravagance, Wirt says "5,000 men at least," which is preposterous on the face of it. In view of the hasty call and decision, word of the march could not have spread that fast.

to Henry from Patriot friends urging him to reconsider his rash and headstrong course. Henry did not deign to reply, retaining the couriers. He was resolved not to be diverted, delayed, or deterred.

At the end of the second day of the march, his forces reached Doncaster's Ordinary (tavern), about fifteen miles above Williamsburg. Here they halted to await, as Henry had arranged, a report on other business.

Along the way, Henry had sent off a small party under the command of his friend, Ensign Parke Goodall, a man of some military experience. This party of seventeen, all mounted and well armed, rode into adjacent King William County to Laneville, a large and elegant manor house built and owned by Richard Corbin, receiver-general in the colony.*

Goodall and his men were to demand that Corbin pay them out of Crown revenues a sum of £330 for the gunpowder Dunmore had removed from the Magazine in Williamsburg. If the receiver-general refused, he was to be seized and, with all proper respect and courtesy, brought back to talk with Patrick Henry. The excursion was fruitless. Goodall rode to Doncaster's Ordinary to report that he had not found Corbin, that he was not at home, but presumably in Williamsburg.

Thereupon, Henry sent an emissary into Williamsburg to find him. A deal was arranged, largely through the efforts of Carter Braxton, a Burgess of moderate views and also the receiver-general's son-in-law. The emissary came back with £330 [about $10,000], payable in bills of exchange drawn on London.

This sum represented twice what the powder was worth because most of the kegs removed from the Magazine were only half filled. But Dunmore got the better of the "bargain" in a substantial way. He still had the powder kegs in his hands, and as Washington and the Continental Army soon learned, powder in any quantity was hard to find at any price.

Henry wrote a receipt for the money, saying that he would hold it until he had instructions from the Continental Congress or the next Virginia Convention, "unless it shall be necessary, in the meantime, to use the same in defence of this colony."

Henry also immediately sent to Williamsburg a note to his friend, Treasurer Nicholas, whose large law practice he had taken over several years before, saying that the "affair of the powder is now settled

---

* For Corbin and the office of receiver-general, see Appendix E (pp. 486–87).

so as to produce satisfaction to me, and I earnestly wish to the colony in general." If Nicholas had any apprehensions about what might happen, wrote Henry, he and his men were ready to escort "the public treasury to any place in this colony where the money would be judged to be more safe than in the city of Williamsburg." If Nicholas feared "the least danger, a sufficient guard" was at his service.

"I beg the return of the bearer may be instantly because the men wish to know their destination. With great regard, I am, Sir, your most humble servant."

Nicholas, who thoroughly disapproved of what Henry had been doing, sent back a very cool and almost curt reply, saying that he could very well perform his duties as treasurer without Henry's help, that he had "no apprehension of the necessity or propriety of the proffered service."

With that, Henry and his forces turned around and started for home. As soon as they were well out of the way, Lord Governor Dunmore screwed up his courage and issued, in the form of a proclamation, a blast against "a certain Patrick Henry, . . . and a number of his deluded followers," who had "taken up arms and styling themselves an Independent Company, have marched out of their County, encamped, and put themselves in a posture of war, and have written and dispatched letters to divers parts of the Country, exciting the people to join in these outrageous and rebellious practices to the great terror of all His Majesty's faithful subjects, and in open defiance of law and government; and have committed other acts of violence, particularly in extorting from His Majesty's Receiver-General the sum of Three Hundred and Thirty Pounds under pretence of replacing the Powder I thought proper to order from the Magazine . . ."

Henry was, so Dunmore told London, "a man of desperate circumstances,* who has been very active in encouraging disobedience and exciting a spirit of revolt among the people for many years past."

Therefore, said Dunmore, he had thought it proper, "with the advice of His Majesty's Council and in His Majesty's name, to issue this my proclamation, strictly charging all persons, upon their allegiance, not to aid, abet, or give countenance to the said *Patrick Henry,* or

* The British made a grave error in attributing all of the discontent in the colonies to men in "desperate circumstances" who made a career of stirring up strife as a means of livelihood.

any other persons concerned in such unwarrantable combinations, but on the contrary to oppose them and their designs by every means; which designs must otherwise inevitably involve the whole Country in a most direful calamity . . ."

> Given under my hand and the seal of the Colony, at Williamsburg, this 6th day of May, 1775, and in the fifteenth year of His Majesty's reign.
>
> Dunmore
>
> God save the King.

Henry was always somewhat defensive about his gunpowder exploit, wishing to silence the widespread criticism coming chiefly from Williamsburg and the Tidewater. He defended himself by saying that the "rape" of the Powder Horn was very fortunate, for news of it and his action in response had aroused the people.

> You may in vain talk to them about the duties on tea, etc. These things do not affect them. They depend on principles too abstract for their apprehension and feeling.
>
> But tell them of the robbery of the Magazine and that the next step will be to disarm them, you bring the subject home to their bosoms, and they will be ready to fly to arms to defend themselves.

While it was granted that this might be so, it was argued against Henry that the decision to strike a sudden blow in the Old Dominion should have been taken not by just one man, but jointly by a council of leaders.

If Henry had his critics, he also had numerous warm supporters. A week after the march on Williamsburg began, the Hanover Committee of Safety assumed responsibility for the action, praising the Hanover men and "the many volunteers of the different counties" who had joined the march. Congratulations on the dash and success of his venture came to Henry from Safety Committees and volunteer companies in most parts of the colony—but none came from Washington, Lee, Jefferson, George Mason, Peyton Randolph, Nicholas, Pendleton, or other Patriot leaders.

On May 11, having been delayed by his Williamsburg excursion, Henry left Scotchtown for Philadelphia where the Second Continental Congress was already in session. Fearing that an attempt might be made to seize him as an outlaw under the Lord Governor's proclamation, an armed escort accompanied Henry to the Potomac and saw him safely ferried across into Maryland, where he was beyond Dunmore's reach.

On May 18, Henry took his seat in the Second Continental Congress which had convened a week before. Peyton Randolph had again been elected unanimously to be President of Congress. Members on the floor were, almost wholly, those who had attended the previous session, but there were a few new members of prominence—notably, many-talented Benjamin Franklin, now almost seventy, who had returned home to Philadelphia after living more than ten years in London as resident agent of Pennsylvania, and later of Massachusetts and Georgia as well. Because of his Patriot activities, the British had recently fired him as postmaster general in the colonies, but Franklin soon became our first U.S. postmaster general.

Another notable who first appeared in Congress at this session was a Massachusetts delegate, John Hancock, the rich Boston shipowner-importer-merchant. Aged thirty-eight, a year younger than Henry, Hancock was something of a dandy in his dress and manner, but very libertarian in his political views and extraordinarily generous in making financial contributions to the Patriot cause. One day some years before, when John and Sam Adams were walking and talking along a Boston street, said Sam, always a practical political man, pointing to Hancock's handsome house: "The good people of Boston did a good thing for themselves this day by enlisting that young man's fortune." Another newcomer was Lyman Hall, who came from Georgia to give that colony representation in Congress for the first time.

Several prominent spokesmen of the conservatives in the previous Congress were absent either because of their desire or because they had failed of re-election as delegates—among others, Joseph Galloway of Pennsylvania and John Low of New York. John Dickinson of Pennsylvania took over leadership of the reconciliationists who were still trying to avert a war that had already begun on the village green at Lexington.

On May 24, shortly after Henry took his seat, President Peyton Randolph withdrew from office and departed for Williamsburg because Governor Dunmore had summoned the House of Burgesses to discuss a last-minute conciliation plan offered by the British—a plan that led to "the Olive Branch Petition," which will be considered later. As Lord North's peace plan might be a trap, it was judged highly prudent to have Randolph presiding in the House of Burgesses when the plan came up for examination. Virginia Patriots did not wish to buy a Trojan Horse.

On Randolph's withdrawal, John Hancock was chosen as president of Congress, a post he continued to hold for two years.* Anticipating what might happen, the Virginia Convention had named Jefferson as Randolph's alternate at Philadelphia, and that young man soon arrived to make his first appearance on the national stage where he would rise to fame so quickly.

From the outset, the Second Continental Congress concerned itself almost exclusively with the outbreak of hostilities and the military and political measures that should be taken in consequence. Congress early decided "that for the purpose of securing and defending these colonies, and preserving them in safety . . . , these colonies be immediately put into a state of defence." It recommended to the several colonies what strategic military positions in their jurisdiction should be immediately secured. One site was in the Highlands on the Hudson, at West Point, where a strong fort was soon erected.

The records of this Congress are so laconic and spare, so lacking in detail on floor or committee debate on any measures, that it is not known who said what on what. But it is certain that Henry, after his "We must fight" oration a few months before, actively supported Congress actions on military preparations. It is equally certain he was not pleased when Congress, at the same time, decided to send another "humble and dutiful petition imploring his Majesty to redress American grievances and restore the former harmony between Great Britain and these colonies, so ardently wished for by the latter."

On the day Henry joined Congress, word came that Fort Ticonderoga, the British bastion on Lake Champlain in upper New York, had been taken by surprise by a force, mostly Green Mountain Boys, led by Ethan Allen who demanded the surrender of the fort, so it was said, "in the name of the great Jehovah and the Continental Congress." Ticonderoga surrendered with scarcely a shot. Capturing a number of cannon and a considerable supply of small arms and ammunition, Allen and his men laboriously carted and dragged these over the Green Mountains to place them in the hands of the 10,000 or more Minute Men encamped around Boston where General Gage and his men were holed up.

A plea came from Massachusetts leaders that the Continental

---

* Had Randolph lived to attend the 1776 Congress, there can be little doubt that he would have again been elected, perhaps unanimously as before, to serve as president. But Randolph, in his middle fifties, died suddenly of apoplexy late in 1775.

Congress should take over the direction and charge of the New England forces surrounding Boston, all of them eager for action against Governor General Gage and his Redcoats, who had been recently reinforced. This plea posed a new problem. Up to this time Congress had acted only in an advisory capacity, making recommendations to the several colonies on what should be done. Should it now become something of a central government with requisite authority to carry out its directives and functions?

Many delegates were in doubt about this, being very apprehensive, regarding such a step as rash and exceedingly dangerous. It would pit the colonies, relatively weak and ill-organized, against the mightiest power in the western world, having a long-established government, great resources, a large well-trained experienced army, and a navy that ruled the Seven Seas. That prospect was enough to give pause to even the most stouthearted.

But they screwed up their courage and persevered. After weeks of lengthy debate, sometimes eleven hours at a sitting without any recess to snatch a bite to eat,* Congress decided to assume command and pay the charges of all forces raised for Continental defense.

But this raised another problem, a very ticklish and touchy one. Who was to be made commander-in-chief of the Continental Army?

The forces ringing Boston were led by General Artemus Ward of Massachusetts, who was an experienced officer. There had been no criticism of him and his operations. Should he be chosen? A number of delegates thought so. It might create serious discontent in the New England forces, as yet the only ones in the field facing the "enemy," if Ward were relieved of his command.

On the other hand it was argued, in effect, that the war should not be just a Massachusetts show. The colonies still remained very jealous of one another, each quick to assert its own prerogatives and prejudices. Would the troops of one colony willingly obey a

---

* At this Congress, unlike the first one, there was almost no elaborate entertaining of delegates by hospitable Philadelphians. Delegates were too busy to dine out. When they did, their hosts offered them "simple beef and pudding," as Benjamin Franklin remarked.

Washington appears to have been one of the few delegates who managed to eat at regular hours, meeting or no meeting. As his diary records, he usually found time to dine with his Philadelphia friends at their houses, or with other friends at the new City Tavern, or Peg Mullen's Beefsteak House on Water Street, a choice spot.

commander who came from another? It seemed doubtful if the commander-in-chief came from Massachusetts.

John Adams and other New England delegates held this view. To remove "all jealousies" and "more firmly cement" intercolonial unity, they felt that the chief command should go to someone from the southern colonies. Adams had already picked his man—George Washington—and in conversations both in and out of Congress began urging his selection. He had the support of a Connecticut delegate who found Washington to be "discreet and Virtuous, no harum scarum ranting Swearing fellow, but Sober, steady, and Calm."

Strangely, the strongest opposition to Washington's candidacy came from a member of the Virginia delegation, Edmund Pendleton, one of Washington's close friends. Pendleton argued that as Artemus Ward, a New England general, was in command of the New England army, and as no fault had been found with him, he should remain in command.

But the real reason for Pendleton's action probably was, as suggested by his brilliant biographer, David John Mays, "that Washington's appointment would commit Virginia irrevocably to the defence of Boston and a radical course." A moderate all his life, Pendleton never favored such a course, and often tried to block anything of the kind, though never getting too far to the right, being anxious always to keep one foot in the middle.

On June 15, 1775, Thomas Johnson of Maryland rose and nominated Washington for the post of commander-in-chief. Then followed John Adams who spoke at some length in detailing the character, qualities, abilities, and experience that should be possessed by the man chosen to head the Continental Army.

As Adams went on, President John Hancock sat beaming in the chair. Though with little or no military experience, Hancock thought for some reason that Adams was talking about him. When Adams, in the manner of political conventions, ended his encomium about "the man who" and strongly seconded the nomination of Colonel Washington, President Hancock almost dropped from his chair. Wrote Adams:

> Mr. Hancock . . . heard me with visible pleasure; but when I came to describe Washington for the commander, I never remarked a more sudden and striking change of countenance. Mortification and resentment were expressed as forcibly as his

> face could exhibit them. Mr. Samuel Adams [also] seconded the motion, and that did not soften the President's physiognomy at all.

Washington was elected unanimously to be "Commander-in-chief of the forces raised, or to be raised, in defence of American liberty." Washington waited overnight to make up his mind about this, and next day informed Congress that he would accept the post, though he felt "great distress from a consciousness that my abilities and military experience may not be equal to the extensive and important trust."

That same day he remarked in conversation with Henry: "This day will be the commencement of the decline of my reputation." Always modest, Washington little realized that he was on the rise to world fame.

As John Adams said at this time: "The liberties of America depend upon him, in a great degree." If Washington had been so minded, American liberties could have been easily subverted by him during the Revolution and after, and attempts were made to persuade him to do so.

About a week after his election, General Washington asked Henry to submit to Congress "sundry queries to which he desired the Congress would give an answer." Henry was named chairman of a committee of five to draft a reply to the queries. Their reply evidently satisfied Washington, for he departed shortly to take command of the New England forces besieging Boston. On July 3, he arrived in Cambridge, and there in Brattle Square, under a huge elm soon named Liberty Tree and, in sight of cheering troops, drew his sword and took command of the Continental Army that he would lead through discouraging and often terrible years to final victory.

Congress, in adopting an organizational plan for the army, had selected four to serve as major generals under Washington—Artemus Ward of Massachusetts, who had been in command of the troops around Boston; Israel Putnam of Connecticut, who had led troops from that colony to join the forces around Boston; Philip Schuyler of New York, who was assigned to strengthen Fort Ticonderoga and Crown Point in northern New York, and make preparations for an invasion of Canada; and a former British Army officer of some distinction, British-born Charles Lee,* a brilliant but erratic man who had switched allegiance and become an ardent Patriot, living in west-

---

* This Lee was not related to the numerous Lee family of Virginia.

ern Virginia. As adjutant general, Congress chose another former British officer of distinction, British-born Horatio Gates, who had also settled in western Virginia. To serve under the top command, Congress named fifteen brigadier generals.

Some two weeks before Washington arrived in Cambridge, the first frontal clash between American and British forces had occurred across the river from Boston, on Breed's Hill, in what became known as the Battle of Bunker Hill, though it was not fought there. Bunker Hill was not an American victory. Nor was it a defeat either, though the colonials had to retreat in the end when they ran out of gunpowder, but only after inflicting heavy losses on the British. While they had powder, they stood their ground resolutely, repulsing repeated charges by seasoned British regulars.

Up to this time, most British authorities and top military commanders had only contempt for the colonists in general, and for their "raw" militia companies in particular. There was nothing to be feared from them. No matter how loud Americans talked, they did not have the courage of their convictions. They would not stand and fight. They were, almost without exception, "poltroons."

On the basis of reports received from the British military in the colonies, the Earl of Sandwich assured the House of Lords, before a shot had been fired, that there would be no resistance by Americans, who were "raw, undisciplined, cowardly men . . . If they did not run away, they would starve themselves into compliance with our measures . . . Are these the men to fright us? . . . Believe me, my Lords, the very sound of a cannon would carry them off . . . as fast as their feet would carry them."

General Lord Jeffrey Amherst declared that, if given 5,000 men, he could march from one end of the colonies to the other without opposition. Benjamin Franklin heard another British general, one Clarke, swear a mighty oath that with only a thousand Grenadiers, he could march from Maine to Georgia and geld all the males, except those he "persuaded" to castrate themselves.

In his report to Lord Barrington, Secretary of War, General Gage dismissed the Lexington-Concord clash as "an affair that happened here on the 19th instant," and was nothing to worry about, though his troops had been considerably annoyed on their retreat to Boston, "receiving fire from every hill, fence, house, barn, etc." But Americans would not come out in the open, stand up in regular military order, and fight.

Another British officer denounced them as "impudent rascals," adding that if he had orders, he would "seize them all and send them to England . . . What a sad misfortune it was to this country, the repealing the Stamp Act; every friend of Government here asserts in the strongest terms that this has been the cause of all their misfortunes. . . ."

With an intercolonial army on its hands under the command of General Washington, Congress took steps to provide men and supplies by authorizing the issue of $2,000,000 in bills of credit, to be redeemed later by funds raised in the several colonies in proportion to population. As more and more of such bills were issued, Continental paper currency rapidly depreciated in value until, by the end of the Revolution, a Continental bill was worth only 1/250th of its face value. This resulted in a fantastic inflation of prices that caused great hardship to many and brought into the language a phrase that is still used—"not worth a Continental," meaning "not worth oak leaves," in Jefferson's phrase.

As it had virtually declared a state of war against Britain, Congress rejected the conciliatory plan for accommodation of rival claims that had been proposed by Lord North. With the grudging assent of the King, North had persuaded Parliament to adopt a plan that might provide a base for negotiation, its essentials being: (1) Parliament, if the King approved, would "forbear" from levying all but regulatory (Trade Law) taxes on any of the colonies, provided (2) each such colony taxed itself, through its own assembly, to provide adequate financial support for common defense and royal authority within its jurisdiction.

Many Americans were disposed to consider this, for it granted the two chief arguments with which the conflict had started. The British, at last, were recognizing the distinctions Americans made between "internal" and "external" taxes, and were prepared to let the colonies tax themselves for internal revenues.

But North's plan, it was argued, was divisive, as it was rather obviously intended to be. What Britain wanted to do was to go back to the days when she dealt with each of the colonies separately, and not through a unifying Continental Congress. In the House of Lords, William Pitt, Earl of Chatham, had proposed that the Continental Congress be recognized as the spokesman and bargaining agent of all the colonies, but his motion was overwhelmingly defeated.

Official Britain wanted to have nothing to do with a continental union. Every step should be taken to break it up, principally by the political and military strategy of trying to isolate New England, with the hope and the firm conviction that colonies to the south would drag their feet in furnishing men and money for its support. Intercolonial jealousy was indeed a fact.

Even after rejecting Lord North's conciliation plan, there were many in Congress who felt that one last try should be made to see if the differences at issue could not be compromised or somehow patched up before things got worse. Led by John Dickinson, the last-ditch reconciliationists carried the day, and Congress entrusted Dickinson with drawing up what became known as "the Olive Branch Petition."

This petition was a plea to the King to restore the "harmony" that had formerly reigned between the Mother Country and the colonies for so long. His Majesty should prevent any more hostile measures against the colonies until a base for accommodation and conciliation had been found. Americans had the most earnest desire to remain, as they always had been, very loyal and obedient subjects of his "Sacred Majesty," though they would fight to the death against "enslavement" by Parliament. But they had "no inclination . . . to set up for independency, which we utterly disavow . . ."

Though his opinion about the Olive Branch Petition is not known, Henry must have felt as John Adams did that it might "find many admirers among the Ladies and fine Gentlemen, but it is not to my taste. Pettyness, Juvenilities, and much less Puerilities become not a great assembly like this, the Representative of a great People." Always the diplomat, Benjamim Franklin favored the petition, saying that he was willing to give Britain "one more chance, one opportunity more, of recovering the colonies." But he added his fear that it was an opportunity Britain would not have "sense enough to embrace, and so I conclude she has lost them forever."

Franklin was quite right. The King angrily rejected the Olive Branch Petition, denouncing it as "an insult, . . . a mockery." And it was a mockery in view of other actions taken by Congress to arm the colonies.

In any case, this was the last of "humble" petitions, addresses, memorials, and remonstrances sent to "good King George," the Lords, or the Commons. The conflict had moved beyond paper exchanges and verbal logistics.

An era had ended. Though few on either side of the Atlantic glimpsed it clearly at the moment, American independence was just rounding into sight, but it would take six years of grievous battle to seal it at Yorktown, and by the Treaty of Paris two years later.

XX
Colonel, First Regiment

I leave the service, but leave my heart with you.

—PATRICK HENRY

Early in August, 1775, when Congress recessed for six weeks, Henry and his colleagues from the Old Dominion hastened home to attend the Third Virginia Convention, which was already in session at Richmond, with Peyton Randolph in the chair.

The Convention had many urgent matters to consider, principally the most effective way of quickly placing the colony in a better "posture of defense." Always extremely anxious about his personal safety, Lord Governor Dunmore had removed himself and his family from the Palace in Williamsburg and again gone aboard H.M.S. *Fowey* anchored not far away in the York River.

In spite of repeated assurances that he was not in any personal danger, nothing could persuade Dunmore to come ashore. Under the protection of British soldiers, sailors, and marines, he would govern the colony from the *Fowey,* flagship of the flotilla of warships in Virginia waters. Beside the *Fowey* and the *Magdalen,* which still had safely on board the gunpowder removed from Williamsburg, the flotilla consisted of the *Mercury* (twenty-four guns), the *Kingfisher* (sixteen guns), the sloop *Otter* (fourteen), and some other vessels, mostly smaller. While this was not a powerful force, it was strong enough to threaten trouble and considerable harassment.

With the lord governor's flight from Williamsburg, virtually abdicating his office, the Virginia Convention assumed the responsibility of establishing a *de facto* government to direct the colony's affairs. It elected a standing Committee of Safety to act as its executive arm and carry out the Convention's policies and directives. This powerful central committee, with Edmund Pendleton as chairman, had eleven members—among others, such of Henry's friends and supporters as George Mason, Richard Bland, Paul Carrington, Dudley Digges, John Page, and Thomas Ludwell ("Colonel Tom") Lee, brother of Richard Henry Lee.

The Convention decided that, as a start, two colonial regiments should be recruited and organized as the first line of defense—or offense.* The first regiment was to consist of three field officers, thirty-two line officers, and eight companies with seventy-three enlisted men each, including three sergeants, a drummer, and a fifer—about 600 men. The second regiment was to have one less company.

Behind these regiments there was to be organized, as a second line of defense, companies of Minutemen—some 8,000 in all—to be recruited from the county militias. For the purpose of recruiting, the colony was divided into twelve military districts, and it was ordered that recruited militia men were to be better and more frequently trained than "hitherto customary." The Convention also decided that six special companies should be raised and posted on the western frontier against possible Indian attacks. The decision to raise two regiments as the first line of defense raised debate: Who was to command the regiments?

This question came up before Henry's return from Philadelphia. There was much animated talk, and electioneering, both on and off the Convention floor about possible candidates. There were several: Captain Hugh Mercer, an experienced officer who had served with high distinction under Washington in the French and Indian War; Captain William Woodford, another experienced field officer, a neighbor, close friend, and more or less a protegé of Pendleton, head of the Committee of Safety; and Thomas Nelson, a man of no outstanding military experience, but an ardent Patriot, son of a very rich merchant and Tidewater planter.

* The Convention first decided to raise three regiments. But because of practical difficulties—a serious want of arms, ammunition, money, and supplies—the number was reduced to two for the moment.

From Philadelphia, Henry let it be known that he would like to be considered for top command. Those opposed to this argued that, except for leading a motley force toward Williamsburg in the gunpowder affair, Henry was "totally unacquainted with the art of war, and that such a person was very unfit to be at the head of troops who were likely to be engaged against a well-disciplined army, commanded by experienced and able generals." To this, Henry's friends replied that he had "solicited the appointment," which he would not have done unless he thought "himself qualified to command."

Henry may well have felt that since he had been preaching the doctrine of "We must fight," the least he could do was to go into the field himself, and preferably on horseback leading troops to the battlefront.

In the Convention, four names were placed in nomination for the post of commanding the First Regiment. After the balloting, the tally sheet revealed forty-one votes for Captain Hugh Mercer, forty for Henry, eight for Nelson, and one for Captain William Woodford. As no candidate had received a plurality, as required, a second vote had to be taken. Before this balloting began, Nelson and Woodford withdrew their names and urged the selection of Captain Mercer who was, as all agreed, "a fine soldier." But Henry won by a narrow margin and became colonel of the First Regiment and, *ex officio,* commander-in-chief "of all forces raised, or to be raised, in the colony." Captain Woodford was chosen as colonel of the Second Regiment.

The choice of the Convention created complications and gave rise to deep resentments that were not soon forgotten. The first complication arose immediately when Captain Mercer and a half dozen experienced officers declined to serve under Henry as commander-in-chief. This deprived Virginia of practical and proved military abilities that the colony could ill afford to lose.

The always touchy question of military rank was involved here. These reluctant officers* felt that they had been unfairly passed over in favor of a political appointee, which was the case. Also, they may sincerely have had serious misgivings about Henry's military capacities and judgment, and had no desire to be involved in any

* All of them later served in the Continental Army. Mercer rose to become a general, one of Washington's most trusted commanders, and fell mortally wounded in the Battle of Princeton early in 1777. He was honored as a hero throughout the colonies; in Philadelphia, 30,000 attended his burial service.

disastrous mistakes he might make. As his friend Washington soon remarked, writing from Boston:

> I think my countrymen made a capital mistake when they took Henry out of the senate to place him in the field; and pity it is that he does not see this and remove every difficulty by a voluntary resignation.

After a visit to Scotchtown, where his demented wife was desperately ill, Colonel Henry set out for Williamsburg which had been chosen as the mobilization point for the two regiments and some select volunteer companies. News of Henry's appointment to chief command had greatly stimulated recruiting, particularly among the rank and file and the junior officers.

As he approached Williamsburg, Henry was met and "escorted to town by the whole body of volunteers, who paid him every mark of respect and distinction in their power, in testimony of their approbation of so worthy a gentleman to the appointment of that important trust which the Convention had been pleased to repose in him."

For a camp site, Henry chose cleared level ground behind the three small buildings of the College of William and Mary at the head of the Duke of Gloucester Street. Here, officers began training their men in squad, platoon, company, battalion, and regiment maneuvers and operations. Some of the men were in uniform, but most were not, wearing hunting shirts and farm clothes. The force soon became known as "the Shirtmen."

The authorities had promised to provide tents—one for each officer, one for every two noncommissioned officers, and one for every six privates. But few tents could be found anywhere, and it was now late in September, with winter coming on. Food from the surrounding countryside was adequate for the moment, but almost everything else was in short supply—firearms, gunpowder, bullets, shoes, leggings, clothes, and blankets, among other essentials. The commissary began buying old rugs to serve as blankets. Some smoothbore muskets had been bought for distribution among the soldiers, but the more effective rifle—"squirrel gun"—was scarcely to be had at any price. Consequently, each member of a rifle company was asked to bring along his "squirrel gun," for which he would receive a rental of 20s. [$30] a year. For a time, some soldiers had no firearms at all, not so much as a pistol.

One of the select rifle companies to join the camp at Williamsburg came from Culpeper County to the west. These men were dressed in a uniform of a kind. They wore green hunting shirts with "Liberty or Death" appearing in large letters across their chests. They carried a flag showing, in the center, a coiled rattlesnake about to strike and underneath "Don't Tread on Me." They wore buck-tails in their hats and had tomahawks and scalping knives tucked in their belts. As the "Culpeper Minute Men," looking rather savage, came swinging down the dusty road toward Williamsburg, they frightened a number of people along the way. Among the Culpeper "savages" was young Lieutenant John Marshall, later Chief Justice of the United States Supreme Court.

Before camp was made at Williamsburg, Lord Dunmore was using his fleet and enjoying himself in keeping Virginia "in continual hot water." The small British fleet, while not really a menace, was decidedly a nuisance–bombarding smaller coastal towns to terrorize the populace, capturing American fishing boats and other small vessels to arm them and convert them to war use, sending parties ashore to raid the countryside for fresh food and other supplies.

Gathering his forces, Dunmore occupied Norfolk, the colony's largest town and main seaport. From this as a base, the British could strictly control all shipping in and out of Chesapeake Bay. Norfolk had another advantage–it was the colony's chief center of Tories, many of whom were English and Scottish merchants and agents who had established themselves there and prospered. These men had close personal and business ties with their homelands, and had no use at all for the revolutionary activities that had so seriously impaired their business operations and cut their profits.

From Norfolk, on November 7, Lord Dunmore issued a proclamation placing Virginia under martial law. He commanded that "every person capable of bearing arms resort to His Majesty's standard, or be looked upon as a traitor to His Majesty's crown and Government, and thereby become liable to the penalty the law inflicts upon such offences–such as forfeiture of life, confiscation of lands, &c., &c."

Virginians might quietly scoff at the governor's bluster and his "&c., &c." But they were very gravely concerned when they read the next paragraph of the proclamation by "Wronghead," as Pendleton called him:

> . . . and I do hereby declare all indented servants, Negroes, and others (appertaining to Rebels) free, that are able and willing to bear arms, they joining His Majesty's troops as

> soon as may be, for the more speedily reducing this Colony to a proper sense of their duty to His Majesty's crown and dignity.

Dunmore's offer to free and arm able-bodied male Negro slaves and white indentured servants ("bond slaves") entirely alienated the planters, even the most conservative among them. But his offer had its appeal to those slaves and servants, most of them illiterate, who happened somehow to hear about it. Hundreds of these managed to run away from their masters and join the British—only to be later deserted and left to their fate by Dunmore when he had no further use for them.

Prodded by General Washington and the Continental Congress, both asking why so little was being done in Virginia, the Committee of Safety decided that something had to be done about Dunmore; he should be driven from his strategic base at Norfolk. It was Washington's opinion that "the fate of America a good deal depends on his being obliged to evacuate Norfolk this winter or not." This should be accomplished, he said, "even if it takes the force of the whole colony to do it."

If not accomplished, Washington and others feared that Dunmore's forces would grow "like a snowball" from the "formidable numbers" of slaves who, wishing to be free, might join the British. With the British and Americans at each other's throats, all the southern colonies lived in dread that the slaves, at least half of their populations, might take the opportunity to rise in a broad insurrection.

Early one evening a boat was passing along close to the shore of the wide York River. Two fugitive slaves hailed it, thinking it British. The boat put in, and out jumped some armed Americans, who captured the Negroes and summarily shot them. There were many other similar incidents in the colony.

Liberty Boys were quite ruthless in dealing with "black boys" running away in the hope of securing and enjoying a bit of liberty themselves. The question of slavery, "that peculiar institution," shadowed all of the proceedings and libertarian talk of the day, and continued to do so for almost another century, when the conflict about it finally erupted in our shattering Civil War—and the social, political, and economic consequences of slavery have been felt and suffered for another century, seldom more acutely than in our day.

Learning of the Safety Committee's decision to move against Dunmore's forces at Norfolk, Colonel Henry was very anxious, as commander-in-chief, to lead and direct the attack. But he was passed over, on the ground—merely a pretext—that he and his First Regiment were needed in Williamsburg to guard it against surprise attack. Undoubtedly at the urging of the chairman and executive head of the Committee of Safety, Edmund Pendleton, who distrusted Henry's military judgment—and often his radical political judgments as well —the assignment for conducting the Norfolk expedition went to Pendleton's friend and crony, Colonel William Woodford of the Second Regiment.

All Henry was to do, so he was informed, was to help in seeing to it that Woodford's force was dispatched in good time and as well equipped as possible. Henry did this, but was nettled by being bypassed for command.

Woodford's "Shirtmen," about 500 in all, were ferried across the James and marched to the Norfolk area to set up camp there. Then, for several weeks, nothing happened. Taking his duties as commander-in-chief seriously, Colonel Henry was worried, wondering what was going on, having had no reports. He sent an aide from Williamsburg with a letter to Colonel Woodford:

> Not hearing of any dispatch from you for a long time, I can no longer forbear sending to know your situation, and what has occurred. Every one, as well as myself, is vastly anxious to hear how all stands with you. In case you think anything could be done to aid and forward the enterprise you have in hand, please to write it. But I wish to know your situation, particularly with that of the enemy, that the whole may be laid before the Convention here . . . The bearer has orders to lose no time, and to return with all possible haste.

Henry was evidently not yet aware of an arrangement made between Pendleton and Woodford that the latter should deal in all matters directly with the Committee of Safety, and not through the titular commander-in-chief, Colonel Henry. Woodford's reply to Henry's letter of inquiry was curt, almost insulting, certainly displeasing:

> I have received yours per express, in answer to which must inform you that, understanding you were out of town,* I have not written you before . . . I wrote them [the Committee of Safety and members of the Virginia Convention] yesterday and

* Henry was not out of town.

> this morning, which they no doubt will communicate to you, as commanding officer of the troops at Williamsburg.
>
> When joined, I shall always esteem myself immediately under your command and will obey accordingly; but when sent to command a separate and distinct body of troops under the immediate instruction of the Committee of Safety, . . . I look upon it as my indispensable duty to address my intelligence to them as the supreme power in this colony. If I judge wrong, I hope that honourable body will set me right.
>
> I would wish to keep up the greatest harmony between us for the good of the cause we are engaged in, but cannot bear to be supposed to have neglected my duty when I have done everything I conceive to be so.

To clear up the matter of the chain of command, Henry placed the question before the Committee of Safety. Was he commander-in-chief, or not? The answer was yes—and no. When the two provincial regiments and other forces were in the field together, he was the commander-in-chief. But when a force was detached on a special assignment, the commander of that force—such as Colonel Woodford—was to get his orders directly from the Committee of Safety and make his reports and requests to it. Of course, Woodford should correspond with Colonel Henry as titular commander-in-chief and keep him informed.

With the arrival of an American force in the vicinity, Lord Dunmore sent a force down some twelve miles from Norfolk to fortify a position on one side of Great Bridge, which spanned a branch of the sluggish Elizabeth River. On the other side, Woodford's Shirtmen moved up to prevent the British from advancing further.

The British force had some 600 men—such regular troops as marines, sailors, and soldiers, plus some Virginia Tories and a few companies of escaped slaves. The Americans outnumbered this force about two to one. But the British had several advantages. Among others, they had shorter and better supply lines; they had built their fortifications on higher ground; they had brought in cannon, while the Virginians had only small arms—muskets and rifles—which could not reach the British position.

Learning that a force from North Carolina was on the march to join Woodford's Shirtmen, Dunmore ordered an attack to rout the Virginians before reinforcements arrived. Because of the bridge and connecting causeways over swampy ground, the British had to advance in a column, six abreast. The Americans let the column approach quite close before opening a withering fire from the front and from both sides, inflicting many casualties. The column reeled, turned about, retreated across Great Bridge, and that same night, under cover of dark, drew back to Norfolk to get under the protection of cannon on British men-of-war in the harbor.

Turning runaway slaves loose to fend for themselves,* Dunmore had his regular troops board the ships and moved out into Chesapeake Bay, taking along some of the richer and more active local Tories. A few days later, the combined Virginia-North Carolina force entered the town and began plundering and burning the houses, shops, and warehouses of more prominent Tories. The American force could do nothing about Dunmore's fleet which was cruising unmolested well beyond the range of any guns the Americans had on hand.

Dunmore soon returned to Norfolk—on New Year's Day, 1776—and from his fleet and with landing parties reduced much of the town to rubble. When the British ships withdrew, the Americans proceeded to plunder, burn, and destroy the rest of the town so that it could no longer be "a nest of Tories," entirely overlooking the fact that most of the townspeople were not Tories. Here was another glaring example of the ruthless and witless application of the doctrine of "military necessity," as a member of the Committee of Safety protested, pointing out that Norfolk and its port facilities, if preserved, could have been an invaluable asset to the Patriot cause.

While the battle at Great Bridge was a relatively small engagement, the victory there was encouraging and achieved its ultimate objective. It deprived Dunmore of a commanding land base, forcing him and his ships to make use of a small island in Chesapeake Bay. Some months later, Dunmore and his men were forced to evacuate this island, and sailed away. Virginians had seen the last of their last lord governor. Thus, Virginia's inland waters were cleared of prowling royal forces, and remained so for several years, though British men-of-war continued to patrol the ocean coast, effectively blocking sea traffic into the Chesapeake.

Henry continued to press for clarification of his military status and

---

* Later, some of the runaways were hanged. Others were shipped away and sold to sugar planters in the West Indies. Those who had not borne arms were pardoned, though no doubt they were brutally lashed and otherwise severely punished on being returned to their irate masters.

authority. Was he, as colonel of the First Regiment, *ex officio* commander-in-chief of Virginia forces? Or was he not? Moderates and conservatives who disliked and distrusted Henry declared that he was merely trying to assert and maintain his authority which had been eroded by detaching the Second Regiment from his command and sending it against Dunmore under Colonel Woodford. On the other hand, and this is more likely, Henry may have felt that if he was going to be held responsible for whatever happened, then he should have clear responsibility and authority as commander-in-chief.

This question placed the Committee of Safety—in particular, its president, Edmund Pendleton—in a painful quandary. Certainly, Henry was the most popular Patriot leader in the colony and had a large and devoted following, especially among the rank and file. It would not do to affront him and his many supporters, who had already taken Pendleton down a peg or two,* holding him responsible—as, indeed, he was—for bypassing Henry and giving Colonel Woodford command of the troops sent against Dunmore. Besides, as Pendleton admitted, there seemed to be no way of relieving Henry of command. He had "done nothing worthy of degradation"—in fact, he had been kept from doing anything but the most routine duties—"and must keep his rank."

On the other hand, Colonel Woodford should not be offended either. He had just won a victory at Great Bridge and driven the British out of Norfolk. The Committee of Safety therefore felt obliged to adopt a resolution designed to straddle the issue in the hope that everybody would be pleased—or be at least placated—thus avoiding any open rupture. A member of the Safety Committee wrote to Colonel Woodford:

> Whether you are obliged to make your returns to Colonel H——y, and to send your dispatches through him to the Convention and Committee of Safety, and also from those bodies

* Four pegs, in fact. When the next Virginia Convention came to elect members of a new Committee of Safety, Henry's supporters were so strong and so angry about Henry's treatment that Pendleton was dropped from first to fourth place on the balloting for candidates. Dudley Digges received the most votes, and ordinarily would have been chairman. But as its most experienced and active member, eager to retain control of affairs, Pendleton continued as president and chief executive of the Safety Committee, being virtually governor of Virginia for an interim period of about seven months.

through him to you, must depend upon ordinance and the commission he bears. You will observe his commission is strongly worded, beyond what I believe was the intention of the person who drew it . . .

The dispute between you must be occasioned, I suppose, . . . by disregard of him as commander . . . I am apt to think, though I am not a military man enough to determine, your correspondence should have been with him as commanding officer.

I have talked with Colonel Henry about this matter; he thinks he has been ill-treated and insists the officers under his command shall submit to his orders. I recommend it to him to treat the business with caution and temper, as a difference at this critical moment between our troops would be attended with the most fatal consequences, and took the liberty to assure him you would, I was certain, submit to whatever was thought just and reasonable.

This snarl about rank and authority was soon unraveled a bit, but with no great satisfaction to any but certain members of the Committee of Safety. As committee chief, Pendleton was resolved to find one way or another of forcing Colonel Henry out of his post as commander-in-chief.

At this time, a new Virginia Convention authorized the raising of seven more regiments. In writing his friend Colonel Woodford about this, Pendleton reported:

The Field Officers of each Regiment will be named here & recommended to Congress; in case our Army is taken into Continental pay, they will send Commissions—a General Officer will be chosen there I doubt not & sent us; with that matter I hope we shall not intermeddle lest it should be thought propriety requires our calling or rather recommending our present First Officer [Henry] to that station . . .

Believe me, Sir, the unlucky step of calling that gentleman from our councils, where he was useful, into the field in an important station, the duties of which he must, in the nature of things, be an entire stranger to, has given me many an anxious and uneasy moment . . .

In the course of these reflections, my greatest concern is on your account. The pleasure I have enjoyed in finding your

> Army conducted with wisdom & success . . . makes me more uneasy at a thought that the Countrey should be deprived of your Services, or you made uneasy in it by any untoward circumstances, . . . for the Colony cannot part with you . . .

The Virginia regiments, most of them as yet existing largely on paper, were soon "taken into Continental pay." The Committee of Safety had recommended to the Virginia Convention that the original regiments, the First and the Second, should not be included. These were to continue as provincial forces, which meant that Henry, as colonel of a provincial regiment, would be outranked and be subordinate to every colonel with a Continental command. He would no longer be even titular commander-in-chief of Virginia forces.

This maneuver by Pendleton and his friends was so transparently designed to humiliate Henry by demoting him and placing subordinate officers over him that the Convention rejected the scheme. It recommended, and Congress agreed, that the First and Second Regiments should be put on Continental pay, and that Henry be named colonel of the First.

When Henry appeared before the Committee of Safety at its request, Pendleton handed him his revised commission to sign. Henry sat down to read the document carefully. Rising, he handed the commission back to Pendleton unsigned and, with scarcely a word, left the room. Without giving his reasons, Colonel Henry had, in effect, resigned, and this ended his brief military career of less than seven months.

Pendleton must have smiled inwardly at his triumph. He would no longer have to deal with Henry in military matters. He had neatly spiked Henry's hope of being given higher command as a brigadier general.

But Henry, in a personal way, had his triumphs, too. When news of his resignation got out, as it immediately did, his troops in Williamsburg "went into mourning and, under arms, waited on him at his lodgings." There, his officers presented to him a simple and very moving address that warmed Henry's heart:

> Deeply impressed with a grateful sense of the obligation we lie under to you for the polite, humane, and tender treatment manifested to us throughout the whole of your conduct, . . . permit us to offer you our sincere thanks as the only tribute we have in our power to pay to your real merits . . .

> Your withdrawing yourself from service fills us with the most poignant sorrow as it at once deprives us of our father and general; yet, as gentlemen, we are compelled to applaud your spirited resentment to the most glaring indignity.
>
> May your merit shine as conspicuous to the world as it hath done to us . . .

It is not often that a commanding officer gets such an obviously sincere salute. In answer, Henry thanked his officers and their men for their approbation of his conduct, saying that it did him "the highest honor," adding:

> I return you, and each of you, . . . my best acknowledgements for the spirit, alacrity, and zeal you have constantly shown in your several stations. I am unhappy to part with you. I leave the service, but I leave my heart with you.
>
> May God bless you, and give you success and safety . . .

After receiving Henry's "kind" answer to their address, the officers insisted that Henry, before departing, dine with them at the Raleigh Tavern. After dinner, they proposed to honor him by escorting him out of town, but this was not done because of an ominous development in camp. There was great "uneasiness" among the soldiers, who were meeting in large noisy groups and demanding their immediate discharge, declaring that they would serve only under Henry.

In this situation, Henry decided to delay his departure and stay over another night, which he spent in visiting the barracks where he used every possible argument and all of his eloquence to persuade "the soldiery to lay aside their imprudent resolution, and to continue in the service." The Patriot cause was all-important, and nothing should be done to impede its success. Henry's usual persuasiveness prevailed, the soldiers were "pretty well reconciled," and the mutinous spirit subsided.

Henry was honored and praised not only by the officers of the First Regiment, but by those of the Second under Colonel Woodford. Some thirty of these drew up and later had published in the *Gazette* an address of high tribute to Henry as both a statesman and a soldier:

> Deeply concerned for the good of our country, we sincerely lament the unhappy necessity of your resignation, and with all the warmth of affection assure you that whatever may have given rise to the indignity lately offered to you, we join with

> the general voice of the people* and think it our duty to make this publick declaration of our high respect for your distinguished merit. To your vigilance and judgment as a senator, this United Continent bears ample testimony . . .
>
> To your extensive popularity, the service is also greatly indebted for the expedition with which the troops were raised; and while they were continued under your command, the firmness, candour, and politeness that formed the complexion of your conduct toward them, obtained the signal approbation of the wise and virtuous, and will leave upon our minds the most grateful impression . . .
>
> We have the fullest confidence in your abilities and in the rectitude of your views, and however willing the envious may be to undermine an established reputation, we trust the day will come when justice shall prevail and thereby secure you an honourable and happy return to the glorious employment of conducting our councils and hazarding your life in the defence of Your country.

Years later it was reported on good authority** that the Committee of Safety chiefly found fault with Henry because he was lax in enforcing military discipline. This may have been so, but only in a minor way. Henry was never much of a disciplinarian either with himself or with others. He was always free and easy with men of all ranks and conditions. No one on the committee doubted Henry's "courage or his alacrity to hasten to the field," according to the Carrington report, "but it was plain that he did not seem to be conscious of the importance of strict discipline in the army," such as observance of rank.

Rather, he "regarded his soldiers as so many gentlemen who had met to defend the country and exacted from them little more than the courtesy that was proper among equals." It was felt by some that to lead a regiment of such men against the British would "insure their destruction," which is questionable, "and it was a thorough conviction of this truth that prompted the decision of the Committee" that, in one way or another, Henry should be removed

---

* A member of the Committee of Safety, John Page, friendly to Henry, noted with concern that there was considerable agitation and anger among people throughout the colony about the Henry affair.

** By Clement Carrington, son of Paul Carrington, a member of the Safety Committee and usually a Henry supporter.

from command. If that was the base of the committee's decision, it was pretty feeble.* Politicking by Pendletonite moderates offers a more sensible explanation of what happened.

Whether Henry, if given a chance, would have made a great commander is idle conjecture. On entering service, he was technically deficient as a soldier from want of experience and study, but he might have mastered the *mystique* of command with his usual speed and concentration.

This much, at least, is certain—as commander, he would have had the utmost loyalty and respect of his men and that, in battle, is often the decisive factor, overcoming whatever tactical mistakes may have been made in bringing up troops and placing them in position.

In all things, Henry had an *élan* that had to be acknowledged and admired, even by his enemies.

---

* Henry may not have recognized the "importance of strict discipline in the army," but certainly his troops were never anywhere near so out of hand as Colonel Woodford's in the sacking and destruction of Norfolk. Woodford's "Shirtmen," as soldiers will, first proceeded to "liberate" the wine cellars and taverns in the town. Their drunken looting for several days was so bad and disgraceful that Woodford did everything possible to suppress the news, for which he was praised by Pendleton, who commended him for using his usual good judgment and discretion.

XXI
Independence

Resolved, that these United Colonies are, and of right ought to be, free and independent states . . .

—RICHARD HENRY LEE

Doffing his military trappings, Henry returned home to Scotchtown early in March, 1776. Several months previously, his wife Sarah (Shelton) had died, mercifully relieved at last of her cruel sufferings in body and mind. As had been so since the start of her mother's incapacitating illness, management of the household was in the competent hands of Henry's oldest and favorite child, Martha (Patsy), now in her early twenties and married to John Fontaine.*

After two months of quiet life at Scotchtown, Henry returned to Williamsburg as one of Hanover County's delegates to the Fourth Virginia Convention. This was the last of such revolutionary conventions in the Old Dominion, for the march of events had brought all of the colonies to a high divide, a point of critical decision.

Either the colonies had to move forward to new positions, or they

* Of Huguenot descent, Fontaine was closely related to the Reverend James Fontaine Maury whose plea in the Parsons' Cause had been so surprisingly and completely demolished by Henry in the first big case he argued. It should be said here about "good little Mr. Maury" that he was one of the relatively few Anglican parsons in Virginia who warmly embraced the Patriot cause. Most of his colleagues abandoned their pulpits, fled the colony, or remained behind to become active British partisans. This gave American Anglicism a black eye which was not soon cleared up, as later lamented by Bishop Meade and others.

had to turn around and pull back. There was no thought of retreating in the minds of Henry, Washington, Jefferson, Richard Henry Lee, George Mason, and other Patriot leaders in Virginia. They would press forward, come what might.

1. Fourth Virginia Convention

Meeting on the first Monday in May, 1776, the Convention sat for less than two months. That was long enough, however, for it to come to some momentous decisions and accomplish an astonishing amount of work to give body to those decisions.

Recent military news had been heartening. Taking the British completely by surprise, General Washington had occupied Dorchester Heights, from which his cannon and mortars commanded Boston and its harbor. This placed General Sir William Howe in such a perilous position that he decided he had to evacuate Boston, sailing away to Halifax with his troops and a thousand or more Massachusetts Loyalists, many of whom came from the colony's oldest and richest families. A Loyalist army in North Carolina had been smashed, thus delaying a planned British attack in the South. Lord Dunmore and his men were still on their island refuge in Chesapeake Bay, making a nuisance of themselves. But it seemed clear that they could not stay much longer, for they were being starved out, wanting supplies of all kinds. The British had abandoned Dunmore ("Wronghead") as a fool.

The political scene had been suddenly and unexpectedly lighted up as brightly as it had been almost eleven years before by Henry's Stamp Tax Resolutions, and all Patriots looked up. On January 10, 1776, just before the meeting of the Third Continental Congress, there had appeared a pamphlet entitled *Common Sense,* written in Philadelphia and signed "by an Englishman." It soon became known that the author was Thomas (Tom) Paine, who had arrived in the country about two years before.

Not yet forty, being about Henry's age, Tom Paine had been brought up as a Dissenter, a Quaker, and for a time followed his father's trade as a staymaker (corsetmaker). Leaving his birthplace at Thetford, Norfolkshire, he went to London and then to Sandwich where he became an exciseman. Returning to London for a spell of teaching, he rejoined the excise service and remained there for some years. He preached occasionally to Quaker and other dissenting congregations and, when not drinking, spent his leisure in writing poetry and prose.

One of his published pieces, critical of the British administration, caught the eye of Benjamin Franklin, then still in London as resident agent of Pennsylvania and several other colonies. Recognizing the power of his pen and sympathetic with his then radical democratic views, Franklin suggested to Paine that he might find America more congenial and more receptive to his line of thought, offering him a broader and more fertile field for the use of his marked talents.

Carrying letters of introduction from Franklin and with a bit of "Poor Richard's" gold in his pocket, Paine arrived in Quaker Philadelphia in 1774 and within a year made a name for himself, becoming editor of the *Pennsylvania Magazine* and contributing to the *Pennsylvania Journal*–one of his contributions being a slashing attack on slavery.

But his main interests lay elsewhere. From the day he arrived, he had been thinking of the developing revolutionary crisis, and he sat down to set forth his ideas about it, hoping to write something that would clarify the situation and thus forward the Patriot cause which he had passionately embraced.

Appearing early in 1776, *Common Sense* caused a sensation. Brushing aside the long and tiresomely repeated legalistic arguments about the constitutional rights of the Crown, the Parliament, and the colonies, Paine declared that it was idle for Americans to continue talking as if their sole desire was to restore things as they had been before 1763, in the days of the "Old Empire." In Paine's pages, "good King George" became a "royal brute," deserving of no allegiance. The colonies had to move forward, not backward. And they would if they had a clear aim and shining goal. What could fire them and unite them? Only one thing. The colonists had to have something worth fighting for–independence!

"Sound doctrine and unanswerable reasons!" declared General Washington, to whom Jefferson had sent a copy of *Common Sense*.

Independence, though previously talked about quite privately by Henry, John Adams, Sam Adams, and a few others, suddenly ceased to be the "hobgoblin" word it had been less than two years before at the time of the First Continental Congress. Few works ever published had the astounding success and the powerful immediate impact of what Paine called his "little book." It was perfectly tuned to the times. It sent forth a clarion call that men wanted to hear; it crystallized thought, sent the blood racing, and fired desire for decisive action. A pox on any more halfway measures! Paine's *Common*

Sense was the tocsin of 1776 as Henry's Stamp Tax Resolutions had been eleven years earlier.

Published in a small edition early in January, 1776, *Common Sense* was almost instantly in such great demand that 300,000 copies were printed and sold within three months, according to contemporary accounts. And the total soon rose to half a million copies*—and this at a time when a printing of 1,500 copies of any book at all was a large edition. Widely distributed, *Common Sense* was avidly read and earnestly discussed in Patriot circles everywhere from Maine to Georgia.

Common Sense owed its enormous success and wide popular appeal to the clarity of its views and to the clarity of its plain, simple, and often very eloquent prose. Paine was writing not only for lawyers, veteran legislators, rich landed proprietors, and other sophisticates, but more especially for the plowman, the shoemaker, the blacksmith, the small country storekeeper, the frontiersman carving out for himself a homestead in the wilderness. With clear imagery and many graphic phrases, he spoke a language that all of these could readily understand. Paine gave Americans not only a goal—independence—but also a vision of what the land might become—a haven for the suppressed:

> O! Ye that love mankind! Ye that dare oppose not only the tyranny but the tyrant, stand forth! Every spot of the old world is overrun with oppression. Freedom hath been hunted around the globe . . . Europe regards her like a stranger, and England hath given her warning to depart. O! receive the fugitive, and prepare in time an asylum for mankind.

In their styles of expression, Patrick Henry and Tom Paine were much alike. Both were inclined to be hortatory. Though both commanded good solid English idiom, neither bothered himself to encumber his prose with literary affectations and embroideries,

---

* This was as if today, with our present population, a political polemic sold 30,000,000 copies within six months—what a gold mine for publisher and author. Though poor, Paine did not pocket his earnings. Rather, he donated them to the Patriot cause and soon enlisted in the Continental Army.

For his book, Paine was later given £500 by the Pennsylvania legislature, awarded an honorary M.A. degree by what became the University of Pennsylvania, and was invited to become a member of the exclusive and most distinguished American Philosophical Society, founded by Franklin and still meeting periodically to discuss serious matters in all fields of human culture.

avoiding the Latin and Greek tags and the classical allusions that were so fashionable at the time. Both spoke directly to the question in hand, and directly to the heart of the reader or listener, in terms of his immediate interests and sympathies. Both spoke with a deep passion that deeply affected others. They aimed at making men think, feel, and move—above all, to make them move. And move them they did, in great numbers.

If Henry was the Demosthenes of his age, Paine was one of the master pamphleteers of all time. His later *Crisis* papers, *Rights of Man,* and *Age of Reason* brought him world-wide acclaim in democratic circles—and heaps of abuse from privileged aristocrats and smug ecclesiastics who scarcely knew what he was talking about, though they vaguely sensed that his doctrine was "subversive," as it was. More than Henry, Paine had no use for the old order, hoping it would be scrapped as soon as possible—by force, if necessary. Wishing a basic change in society, Paine was a true revolutionary, as Henry was not. As will be seen, American independence was enough for Henry.

It was in the wake of the enormous popular appeal of *Common Sense* and of General Sir William Howe's evacuation of Boston that the Fourth Virginia Convention met in Williamsburg early in May, 1776. On the death of Peyton Randolph, Pendleton had been elected to preside at the previous Convention. As he had performed his duties to general satisfaction, it would have been usual practice for the new Convention to choose him unanimously, by acclamation, to serve again as president.

But Henry, his close friends, and his many followers would not go along with this. They were still angry with Pendleton, being more than ever convinced that he was responsible for spiking Henry's military career. To balk Pendleton in his desire to preside at the new Convention, these men nominated Colonel Thomas Ludwell Lee, one of Richard Henry Lee's many distinguished brothers, a man in his middle forties, six years older than Henry and long a forward Patriot.

If Henry had wished to run for the presidency himself, he undoubtedly could have had the nomination—and probably would have been elected. But he declined to run, perhaps fearing that a more or less personal conflict with Pendleton would arouse animosities and create a deep division at a time when unity of action was imperative. It is plain, on the other hand, that Henry did nothing to discourage his followers in their drive to unseat Pendleton. He may have felt that, himself out of the race, the challenge to Pendleton would be more clearly a contest on matters of principle and procedure between moderates and the more radical.

The leader of the strong opposition to Pendleton was Henry's old friend, Thomas Johnson, who as a Burgess had supported Henry in the Stamp Tax debate and had ever since been on Henry's side. It was Johnson who nominated Colonel Thomas Ludwell Lee to oppose Pendleton, a nomination that was seconded by Bartholomew Dandridge, who was Martha Washington's brother. The Dandridges and the Washingtons were not Pendletonites.

The choice of Colonel "Tom" Lee to oppose Pendleton has another significance. As a member of the powerful Committee of Safety, Lee was displeased with a number of things the committee had done under Pendleton as chairman and executive director. To have been defeated by a dissident colleague would have been a major rebuke to Pendleton, and to all the moderates who were inclined to go slow and drag their feet on many pressing issues. Though the vote is not recorded, Pendleton succeeded in being elected as president of the Fourth Virginia Convention, presumably by a narrow margin. Whatever the margin, Pendleton took his victory to be a vote of confidence and in thanking the Convention for the honor done him, said:

"I esteem [it] the more, as it affords a publick testimony that my former endeavors for the proper discharge of that trust have not been unacceptable to my country." Recommending "calmness, unanimity, and diligence," Pendleton discoursed on various matters, but was very careful to keep "out of sight the subject of independence, which he well knew the party of Henry intended to bring forward."

With officers elected and organizational matters settled, the Convention began deliberating on "the state of the colony" and things in general. The prospect at the moment seemed rather encouraging though everybody knew that a long, hard, bitter struggle lay ahead, one entailing great sacrifice and suffering, and perhaps a final shattering defeat, with any number of rebel leaders going to the gallows. But these leaders were ready to take their chances.

After more than a week of rather heated debate, during which various proposals were advanced, the Convention decided unanimously* that the Virginia delegation sitting in Philadelphia at the Third Continental Congress should be instructed to offer a motion that the United Colonies declare themselves "free and independent states, absolved from allegiance to, or dependency upon, the Crown and Parliament of Great Britain."

Though Henry felt that the colonies should move forward "in the strongest and most positive manner" toward declaring their independence, he had serious doubts about doing this immediately. Before that were done, he thought some other things should be done, and he favored delay until they were done, or at least until there was some fair prospect of their accomplishment. Writing to John Adams, at the Continental Congress in Philadelphia, Henry explained his position and his views:

> Before this reaches you, the resolution for finally separating from Britain will be handed to Congress . . . I put up with it in the present form for the sake of unanimity. 'Tis not quite so pointed as I could wish.

Henry had submitted a sharp draft resolution, which was not adopted. Two other draft resolutions were put forward; neither was adopted. Taking the three drafts, Pendleton, as president of the Convention, put together a composite resolution designed to please everybody. But it did not please Henry or Colonel Thomas Ludwell Lee, who wrote his brother Richard Henry Lee in Philadelphia:

"The preamble is not to be admired in point of composition, nor has the resolve of independency that peremptory and decided air which I could wish." Henry shared this view, but he was more concerned about other major considerations, as he told John Adams:

> Excuse me for telling you of what I think of immense importance: 'tis to anticipate the enemy at the French court. The half of our continent offered to France may induce her to aid our

* While the decision was unanimous in the sense that no one spoke against it, a very distinguished member abstained from voting—Treasurer Robert Carter Nicholas, "who demonstrated his title to popularity by despising it when it demanded a sacrifice of his judgment." Not favoring a declaration of independence because he was "dubious of the competency of America in so arduous a contest," according to young Edmund Randolph, a member of the Convention, Nicholas "alone had fortitude enough to yield to his fears on this awful occasion, although there was reason to believe that he was not singular in the conviction. But immediately after he had absolved his obligation of duty, he declared that he would rise or fall with his country, and proposed a plan for drawing forth all its energies in support of that very independence."

> destruction, which she certainly has the power to accomplish. I know the free trade with all the States would be more beneficial to her than any territorial possessions she might acquire. But pressed, allured, as she will be—but, above all, ignorant of the great thing we mean to offer—may we not lose her? The consequence is dreadful.

Though not known to Henry, and only to relatively few, secret communications had already been opened with the French Court, which expressed some interest in the American situation, hoping to exploit it to France's imperial advantage by using it to reduce the power of the British Lion that had snatched away Canada and inflicted other great humiliations upon France little more than a decade before in the settlement of the French and Indian-Seven Years' War.

Having opened his mind to what he regarded as the transcendent importance of obtaining French support for the Patriot cause, Henry raised another major point in his letter to John Adams:

> Excuse me again. The confederacy—that must precede an open declaration of independency and foreign alliances.
>
> Would it not be sufficient to confine it, for the present, to the objects of offensive and defensive nature, and a guaranty of the respective colonial rights?
>
> If a minute arrangement of things is attempted, such as equal representation, etc., etc., you may split and divide; certainly will delay the French alliance, which with me is everything.

Others did not share the doubts of Nicholas, the hesitations of Pendleton, or Henry's desire to delay in the matter of moving forward to the final break. News of the Virginia Convention's decision about independence set off celebrations throughout the colony. In Williamsburg, the Union Jack waving over the Capitol was hauled down and a Continental flag run up in its stead, to salvos of cannon and small arms, using up scarce gunpowder. Troops marched through the streets and wheeled in open areas to the sounding of horns, the beating of drums, and the shrilling of fifes. More than a century and a half of British rule had ended, and Williamsburg rejoiced, as the *Virginia Gazette* reported:

> . . . some gentlemen made a handsome collection for the purpose of treating the soldiery, who next day were paraded in Waller's Grove, . . . attended by the gentlemen of the Committee of Safety, the members of the General Convention, the

inhabitants of the city, etc. The resolutions being read aloud to the army, the following toasts were given, each of them accompanied by a discharge of artillery and small arms, and the acclamations of all present:

1. The American Independent States;
2. The Grand Congress of the United States and their respective legislatures;
3. General Washington, and victory to the American arms.

The Union flag of the American states* waved upon the Capitol during the whole of this ceremony; which being ended, the soldiers partook of the refreshments [no doubt largely liquid] prepared for them by the affection of their countrymen, and the evening concluded with illuminations and other demonstrations of joy. . . .

The Convention had also decided that, regardless of what other colonies did, Virginia was going to declare her independence. But this required some preparations. If anarchy were to be avoided, the framework of a new form of government had to be designed and hammered together with all speed.

Unanimously, the Convention resolved that a committee be appointed "to prepare a Declaration of Rights and such a plan of government as will be most likely to maintain peace and order in this colony, and secure substantial and equal liberty to the people."

The committee named to undertake these vital and most difficult tasks was a large and very distinguished one. Its more than thirty members included leaders of both the radical and moderate groups—for the radicals, Patrick Henry, George Mason, Thomas Ludwell Lee, Bartholomew Dandridge, Mann Page, Edmund Randolph, and young James Madison, sitting in a council of state for the first time; for the conservatives, Robert Carter Nicholas, Richard Bland, and Archibald Cary, among others. To make sure that some check was held on the radicals, President Pendleton appointed a moderate as chairman of the committee, his spirited friend Colonel Archibald Cary, known to some as "the bruiser."

A few days later, Henry wrote to John Adams in Philadelphia, thanking him for a letter and for a pamphlet enclosed. This pamphlet entitled *Thoughts on Government, Applicable to the Present State of the American Colonies* urged immediate separation from Britain and establishment by the individual colonies of new governments

---

* What appeared on the flag is not known. It was some sort of improvisation for obvious reasons. It was not an official flag, for the union of the colonies as independent states had yet to be effected.

based entirely on popular elections—governments without any British monarchical or aristocratical trappings. The pamphlet was unsigned, but Henry rightly surmised who was its author, telling Adams that he was "exceedingly obliged" to him for sending the pamphlet:

> . . . I am not without hopes it may produce good here where there is among our most opulent families a strong bias to aristocracy. I tell my friends you are the author. Upon that supposition, I have two reasons for liking the book. The sentiments are precisely the same I have long since taken up, and they come recommended by you. Go on, my dear friend, to assail the strongholds of tyranny. . . .
>
> Our Convention is now employed in the great work of forming a Constitution. My most esteemed republican form [of government] has many and powerful enemies. A silly thing, published in Philadelphia by a native of Virginia, has just made its appearance here, strongly recommended, 'tis said, by one of our delegates now with you—[Carter] Braxton.* His reasonings upon and distinction between private and public virtue are weak, shallow, and evasive, and the whole performance an affront and disgrace to this country; and, by one expression, I suspect his Whiggery.
>
> Our session will be very long, during which I cannot count upon one coadjutor of talents equal to the task.** Would to God you and Sam Adams were here! It shall be my incessant study so to form a portrait of government that a kindred with New England may be discerned in it . . . I shall think perfection is obtained if we have your approbation.

---

* No wonder Braxton strongly recommended the "silly thing." Though he did not sign it, he had written it, as soon became known. Braxton's *Address to the Convention of Virginia on the Subject of Government* will be considered shortly.

** Biographers of George Mason and James Madison have been unduly exercised by Henry's remark that, in framing a republican constitution and a declaration of rights, he did not have one "coadjutor" of talent. Henry always had the highest admiration for Mason, and the two worked closely together for many years, usually seeing eye to eye. Mason had been elected a delegate to the Convention. But he had been delayed at home, and did not arrive in Williamsburg till a day or two before Henry wrote his letter. As Mason arrived on a weekend, when the Convention was not in session, Henry may not have known that he was in town to take his place on the Grand Committee.

As for young James Madison, just a few years out of college at Princeton, entering public life for the first time, it is unlikely that veterans like Henry often asked him for counsel and advice at this time.

> I am forced to conclude; but first, let me beg to be presented to my ever-esteemed S. Adams. Adieu, my dear sir . . .
> P.S. Will you and S.A. now and then write?

In a similar vein, revealing his thoughts and anxieties, Henry wrote to Richard Henry Lee. Should not ambassadors be sent to France "instantly" in the hope of obtaining aid and perhaps an alliance? "Delay may bring on us total ruin."

But before approaching the French, was not a "confederacy of our states necessary?" If that could be formed, and its objectives for the present "be only offensive and defensive, and a guaranty respecting Colonial Rights, perhaps dispatch might be had, and the adjustment of Representation and other lesser matters be postponed without injury."

Henry told Lee that he wished he could divide him in two, so that Lee could at once continue serving in Congress as "the ornament of your native Country and the vigilant foe of Tyranny," and also be in Williamsburg to take a hand in "the grand work of forming a constitution for Virginia . . . now before the Convention where your love of equal liberty and your skill in public counsel might so eminently serve the cause of our country," and animate by "manly eloquence the sometimes drooping spirit" of the Convention. Henry frankly did not like some of the things he was hearing, telling Lee:

> Perhaps I am mistaken, but I fear too great bias to Aristocracy prevails among the opulent.* I own myself a democrat on the plan of our admired friend, J. Adams, whose pamphlet I read with great pleasure.
>
> A performance from Philadelphia is just come here, ushered in, I'm told, by a colleague of yours, B——, and greatly recommended by him. I don't like it. Is the author a Whig? One or two expressions in the Book make me ask. . . .
>
> Vigor, animation, and all the powers of mind and body must now be summoned and collected together into one grand effort. Moderation, falsely so called, hath nearly brought on us final ruin. And to see those who have so fatally advised us still guiding, or at least sharing in our counsels, alarms me.**

---

* Though a rich Grandee himself, Lee had repeatedly said, and proved by deed, that he did not believe in the rule of "aristocratical" men or in domination by the "opulent."

** Henry was here obviously and particularly referring to Pendleton, known to some as "Mr. Moderation," a play on the phrase "Mr. Moderator," a title sometimes given to the presiding officer at a meeting. Pendleton was presiding at the Convention, and on the powerful Committee of Safety as well.

Adieu, my dear Sir . . .
P.S. Pray drop me a line now and then.

Writing from Congress in Philadelphia, Jefferson broke in to raise a disturbing question. Supported by George Wythe, also a delegate in Congress, Jefferson contended that the Virginia Convention had no authority to write and adopt a "*permanent* constitution," that it had been elected solely for the purpose of taking war measures, that another convention should be called specifically for the purpose of writing a constitution. Henry, Mason, Pendleton, and other Convention leaders united in rejecting this view. To call another convention at this time would only cause confusion and result in costly delays.

As the Grand Committee got down to work on its difficult tasks, Pendleton wrote to inform Jefferson about the progress being made in framing a constitution, telling him:

> Our Political Cooks are busy preparing this dish, and as Col. Mason seems to have the ascendancy in the great work, I have sanguine hopes it will be framed so as to Answer its end, Prosperity to the Community & Security to Individuals, but I am yet a stranger to the Plan. I find the importance of our business requires it & we must sweat it out with Fortitude.

With enormous problems to be solved, and with the weather hot and oppressive, it was indeed a sweat, but the difficult tasks were brilliantly accomplished in a remarkably short time—in less than two months—an enduring monument to the political maturity of Virginia and her leaders.

Though arriving late at the Convention to take a seat on the Grand Committee, Mason had come to Williamsburg with his pockets stuffed with drafts of proposals on all more important matters. Various resolutions had been offered, but Mason's proposals soon "swallowed up all the rest." He fixed the "grounds and plan of action" that, in the main, were finally followed "after great discussion and debate."

The first of the Grand Committee's chief documents came to the floor of the Convention on May 27. It was a Declaration of Rights, largely from the pen of George Mason, with Patrick Henry assisting. The authors of the declaration had drawn on many sources—particularly English sources, from Magna Carta to the Bill of Rights adopted in 1689, after James II had been dethroned for his absolutism and his tyrannies. But the declaration also reflected the influence of the new revolutionary doctrine of "natural rights" as set forth by Voltaire, Rousseau, Diderot, Condorcet, and other French *philisophes,* and by Tom Paine.

In his *Common Sense,* Paine had put forward ideas that he would later elaborate in his *Rights of Man,* published in England shortly after the outbreak of the French Revolution in 1789. A savage attack on monarchy and the privileged orders, translated into many languages, *Rights of Man* quickly became the political Bible of common people throughout Western Europe, which was everywhere seething with discontent about the restricting and discriminatory semifeudal *status quo.* There was almost a violent revolutionary upheaval in Britain during the middle 1790s. On one occasion, George III was shot at as he drove to Parliament to deliver a speech from the Throne and, on his way back to the palace, was dragged out of the royal coach and barely escaped under the massive protection of his uniformed guards. The kingdom's troubles stemmed, in considerable part, from the disaster Britain suffered in the successful revolt of her American colonies.

An historic document in the annals not only of America but of the world, the Virginia Declaration of Rights, as drafted largely by Mason and approved by the Grand Committee, consisted of sixteen articles. It specified any number of particular rights: freedom of assembly, thought, and speech; freedom of the press; freedom of elections on a popular basis; "speedy and impartial" trial by jury in all criminal cases, and with no excessive bail or fines, or cruel and unusual punishments; the right of all citizens to own and bear arms, for a well-trained civilian militia was the proper arm of defense in a free state, because a standing army, in times of peace, was "dangerous to liberty"; the right of civil authorities to control and command the military at all times. The final two articles dealt with religion. Article 16, as originally drafted, read:

> That religion, or the duty we owe to our Creator, and the manner of discharging it, can be directed only by reason and conviction, and not by force or violence; and, therefore, that all men should enjoy the fullest toleration in the exercise of religion, according to the dictates of conscience, unpunished and unrestrained by the magistrates, unless under the color of religion any man disturb the peace, the happiness, or the safety of

society; and that it is the mutual duty of all to practice Christian forbearance, love, and charity towards each other.

The two last articles as originally drafted did not, it should be noted, allow free "exercise of religion" by Jews and other non-Christians. These articles had been drafted by Patrick Henry, according to Edmund Randolph, a member of the Grand Committee. In her *George Mason* (1892), Kate Mason Rowland credited Mason with being the author of the religious articles, as he admittedly was of all the rest. The matter of authorship here is of no importance. The articles on the "exercise of religion" expressed the considered views of both Henry and Mason.

While never much of a church-goer, though he became deeply religious in later life, Henry always professed himself to be an Anglican, perhaps under the influence of his uncle and godfather, the Reverend Patrick Henry, rector of St. Paul's. But he had early defended the cause of Baptists, Quakers, Methodists, and other Dissenters—influenced in this, perhaps, from the days when his mother, ignoring the staid and stuffy services of her brother-in-law, the Reverend Patrick Henry, took young Henry every Sunday morning to hear the exciting and eloquent sermons preached by an inspired young divine, a Presbyterian, the Reverend Samuel Davies. As remarked before, Henry always thought Davies to be the most eloquent and thought-provoking speaker he ever heard, using much of Davies' oratory and manner as a model on which to fashion his own.

One of Henry's disagreements with Pendleton was that the latter, when sitting as presiding judge at the neighboring Caroline County Courthouse, had been particularly harsh in handing down sentences against Baptists and other Dissenter preachers who, as a matter of principle and conscience, deliberately violated the law requiring them to obtain in Williamsburg a license to preach. They did not require a license, they contended, to preach the word of God. They had as much right to preach their views and conduct services as Anglican parsons, who were part of the official State apparatus.

When Baptists and other "itinerant" preachers were offered their freedom if they would post a sizable bond to be forfeited if they did not cease and desist, these preachers declined to post bond and were thrown into jail, where, so the magistrates complained, they went on preaching through the bars on their prison windows to crowds gathered outside. Constables had to be called frequently to chase the crowds away, only to have a crowd soon assemble again.

In Bowling Green, seat of Caroline County, and in other county seats, there still stand memorials to the "heroism" of Baptist and other ministers who were imprisoned for long periods of time for "teaching and preaching the Gospel without having episcopal ordination, or a license from the General Court." Many times, at considerable sacrifice of time and money, Henry had hastened to Bowling Green and other county seats to do what he could, gratis, to aid the "wicked" ministers jailed by Pendleton and others.

None of the articles in the Declaration of Rights occasioned much debate and opposition except the first and most important, the original draft of which read:

> That all men are by nature equally free and independent, and have certain inherent rights, of which they cannot by any compact deprive or divest their posterity: namely, the enjoyment of life and liberty, with the means of acquiring and possessing property, and pursuing and obtaining happiness and safety.

It was immediately objected that this right might be construed to include Negro and Indian slaves, as well as white indentured servants, and that would never do. A long debate ensued, as Thomas Ludwell Lee informed his brother Richard Henry in Philadelphia:

> I will tell you plainly that a certain set of Aristocrats—for we have such monsters here—finding that their execrable system cannot be reared on such foundations, have to this time kept us at bay on the first line, which declares all men to be born equally free and independent. A number of absurd or unmeaning alterations have been proposed. The words as they stand are approved by a very great majority; yet by a thousand masterly fetches and stratagems the business has been so delayed that the first clause stands yet unassented to by the Convention.

After many days of inconclusive debate, Pendleton took the various amendments that had been proposed and molded an acceptable compromise. After the phrase about all men being "equally free and independent," he inserted the qualifying phrase, "when they enter into a state of society." That seemed to take care of the slavery question. Slaves obviously had not entered, nor could they enter, "into a state of society." They were chattels, pieces of property, like horses or other livestock.

With that question resolved—for the time being, at least—the Convention adopted the Declaration of Rights as amended and made it the base on which to frame a constitution. John Adams wrote to tell Henry how happy he was that Henry would have such a guiding hand in shaping Virginia's new constitution:

> The subject is of infinite moment, and perhaps more than adequate to the abilities of any man in America. I know of no one so competent to the task as the author of the first Virginia resolutions against the Stamp Act, who will have the glory with posterity of beginning and concluding this great revolution. Happy Virginia, whose constitution is to be framed by so masterly a builder!

Referring to Henry's expressed fear of too great a bias toward aristocracy among the opulent, Adams went on:

> The dons, the bashaws, the grandees, the patricians, the sachems, the nabobs, call them by what name you please, sigh and groan, and fret, and sometimes stamp and foam, and curse, but all in vain. The decree has gone forth, and it cannot be recalled, that a more equal liberty than has prevailed in other parts of the earth must be established in America.
>
> That exuberance of pride which has produced an insolent domination in a few, a very few, opulent monopolizing families will be brought down nearer to the confines of reason and moderation than they have been used to . . . It will do them good in this world, and in every other. For pride was not made for man, only as a tormentor.
>
> I shall ever be happy in receiving your advice by letter until I can be more completely so in seeing you here in person [at Congress in Philadelphia], which I hope will be soon.

George Mason had prepared a detailed plan designed to establish a constitution for a democratic republic. Carter Braxton, a member of the powerful "King" Carter clan, submitted another in what Henry called a "silly little thing"—an "Address to the Virginia Convention," published in Philadelphia and circulated widely in Virginia, bearing no signature but that of "A Native of the Colony."*

The plan proposed by Braxton, soon to become a signer of the

---

* Adams agreed with Henry about this "silly" thing, saying that it was "too absurd to be considered twice; it is contrived to involve a colony in eternal war."

Declaration of Independence, reflected the "bashaw" point of view that Henry and Adams so detested. Braxton held that democratic governments menaced elegance and refinement, the accumulation of wealth, and the development of manufactures, sciences, and the arts. He proposed a House of Representatives elected every three years. That body would choose twenty-four men to constitute a Council of State, or Senate, who were to hold office for life. The governor would be chosen by the House and Senate, and continue in office "during good behavior"—which, practically speaking, meant for life.

This plan had its ardent supporters, but it was brushed aside. Mason's plan, in the main, was adopted. It provided for a House of Delegates, its members to be elected annually, two from each county, as had been the case with the House of Burgesses. Virginia was divided into twenty-four senatorial districts, with each electing one senator to serve for four years. But to assure continuity and stability of membership, the terms of office for senators were so staggered that only six came up for election each year. The right of freeholders to vote remained as it was, with a property qualification attached.

There was to be another body, not legislative, but executive. It consisted of eight members elected by the House and Senate by joint ballot. These men constituted the Privy Council to advise and work with the governor.

Like the Privy Council, the governor was to be elected by joint ballot of the House and Senate. Mistrusting executive power as exercised by royal governors, the Convention drastically curtailed the authority of the governorship. The governor was specifically denied the power to prorogue or adjourn a scheduled meeting of the House and Senate. Nor could he, for any reason at all, dissolve the legislature when in session.

Even more drastic, the constitution denied the governor the right to veto any action taken by the legislature. When this article was under discussion, Henry, always a foe of executive power, now somewhat shifted position. To deny the executive the right to veto, he argued, would make the governor "a mere phantom, unable to defend his office from the usurpations of the legislature unless he could interpose on a vehement impulse or ferment in that body; and that otherwise he would be ultimately a dependent, instead of a coordinate, branch of power."

The constitution also laid it down that the governor, elected annually, could serve only three times in succession. After that, he had to be out of the office for four years before again becoming eligible for the governorship. Also, proceedings in his Privy Council were to be fully and carefully recorded, with the minutes of meetings signed by every individual present. The legislature could call at any time for the minutes of such meetings for the purpose of reviewing what had been discussed and decided. Virginians were obviously not in a mood to put much trust in the exercise of any executive power, having had too much of it before.

Just as the long and acrid debate on the constitution was nearing an end, a letter came from Jefferson in Philadelphia, offering a paper on what the Virginia constitution should contain, "on the mere possibility that it might suggest something worth incorporation into that before the Convention."*

Jefferson's proposals, raising new questions and reopening old ones, made everybody very unhappy. Not that anyone particularly objected to them. Merely, that his letter had come late, after Mason's constitutional draft as amended had been recommended by the Committee of the Whole and was now on the floor of the Convention for final decision. The summer heat was oppressive, and the members of the Convention were deadly tired of argument and debate.

They had no slightest desire, as Jefferson was later informed, to plunge once again into matters that "had been so long in hand, so disputed inch by inch, and the subject of so much altercation and debate; that they were worried with the contentions it had produced and could not, from mere lassitude, have been induced to open the instrument again."

But the Convention, liking the preamble that Jefferson had written for his constitutional plan, adopted it "by way of amendment to the Report of the Committee."

And so it was, said Jefferson, a bit acidly, that "my Preamble became tacked to the work of George Mason." Except for vanity, he had no reason to complain about that association.

On June 29, after five days of laborious final debate, a constitution was adopted and the Convention, transmuting itself into an interim House of Delegates, proceeded to the election of officers—

* At this very time, Jefferson was in seclusion in Philadelphia, busily drafting the Declaration of Independence. Yet he somehow found time to draft the essentials of a Virginia constitution.

first, a speaker of the house. As Pendleton had presided at the Convention, he was chosen to continue presiding as speaker. As all measures had to originate in the House, and as the governor was without power to veto any legislative act, the most powerful office under the new regime was that of speaker.

Patrick Henry was nominated as governor, as was Colonel William Nelson, an immensely rich Tidewater Grandee, who had been president of the Governor's Council under Lord Dunmore. John Page, one of Jefferson's young friends, was also nominated. Continuing his feud with Henry, Speaker Pendleton did some quiet and discreet electioneering for Nelson, rallying the moderates.

Years later, in talking with his close friend, Spencer Roane, a Henry son-in-law, Pendleton explained his position, saying that he had felt it "unbecoming for those who pushed on the revolution to get into the first offices," and therefore supported Nelson, who certainly met his specifications, for Nelson had done practically nothing in the Patriot cause. To Pendleton's remarks, Roane replied:

> We should have cut a pretty figure if that office had been given to a man who was no Whig, as Mr. Nelson was said to have been.

Henry won the election—with sixty votes, to forty-five for Nelson and one for Page. George Mason, apparently, had nominated Henry, for it was he who headed the committee sent to wait on Henry and notify him officially of his election. Henry immediately wrote to thank the members of the Convention for having paid him such a high honor and, after the usual political blarney about how insufficient he felt for the great task and its onerous duties, declared himself ready to "enter upon the duties of my office whenever you, gentlemen, shall be pleased to direct, relying upon the known wisdom and virtue of your honourable House to supply my defects. . . ."

Both candidates defeated by Henry were immediately placed on the Privy Council to work closely with the new governor. Nelson declined, asking to be excused because of his age and infirmities. His decrepitude must have come upon him very suddenly, for only a few days before he had been campaigning to become chief executive. It is evident that Nelson, like some other conservatives, did not wish to serve in the Henry administration or be identified with it in any way.

2. Third Continental Congress

While all of this was going on in Williamsburg, the Virginia delegation to Congress had done as instructed by the Convention. On June 7, the chief of the delegation, Richard Henry Lee, rose and made his historic motion:

> *Resolved,* That these United Colonies are, and of right ought to be, free and independent States, that they are absolved from all allegiance to the British Crown, and that all political connection between them and the State of Great Britain is, and ought to be, totally dissolved;
>
> That it is expedient forthwith to take the most effectual measures for forming foreign Alliances;
>
> That a plan of confederation be prepared and transmitted to the respective Colonies for their consideration and approbation.

This resolution stirred up great debate. Many opposed declaring independence at this time, wishing to await developments—particularly, steps toward forming a confederacy before any final break with Britain was made.

As Edward Rutledge of South Carolina remarked in a letter to John Jay of New York, it was ridiculous to think of proclaiming independence and seeking an alliance with any foreign power before the colonies were "united with each other, for daily experience evinces that the inhabitants of every colony consider themselves at liberty to do as they please upon almost every occasion. And a man must have the impudence of a New Englander to propose in our present disjointed state" any attempt at a foreign alliance. "No reason could be assigned for pressing into this measure but the reason of every madman, a show of our spirit. . . .

"I wish you had been here," continued the letter to Jay, who shared Rutledge's views. "The whole argument was sustained on one side by Robert Livingston [of New York], James Wilson [of Pennsylvania], John Dickinson and myself, and by the power of all New England, Virginia, and Georgia on the other."

After several days of clashing debate that sent sparks flying, it became quite evident, said Jefferson, "that the colonies of New York, New Jersey, Pennsylvania, Delaware, Maryland & South Carolina were not yet matured for falling from the parent stem, but that they were fast advancing to that state." It was therefore "thought most prudent to wait a while for them, and to postpone the final decisions to July 1," some three weeks off.

So that there might be no delay if a declaration of independence were found to be needed–which at the moment was far from certain–Congress elected a small committee to prepare such a declaration. At the same time, it named a committee to make recommendations on how to solve the problems of confederation, and another committee to explore the best approach to foreign powers.

The committee for drafting an independence declaration consisted of only five members–John Adams, Benjamin Franklin, Roger Sherman of Connecticut, Robert Livingston of New York, and young Thomas Jefferson, who, though only thirty-three, was an old hand at drafting documents.

Jefferson, sitting for the second time in Congress, had made a great impression on Adams. He had brought to Congress, said Adams, "a reputation for literature, science, and a happy talent for composition. Writings of his were handed about, remarkable for the peculiar felicity of expression. Though a silent member in Congress, he was so prompt, frank, explicit, and decisive upon committees and in conversation–not even Samuel Adams was more so–that he soon seized upon my heart."

When election of members of the committee came up, Adams went about drumming up votes for Jefferson, who won enough to top the list, thereby becoming chairman of the committee. Adams was second on the list, one vote behind. When the committee met to discuss the assignment, it asked Adams and Jefferson to draw up a draft of the declaration. Jefferson then suggested to Adams that he do the draft.

"I will not," answered Adams.*

"You should do it."

"Oh! no."

"Why will you not? You ought to do it."

"I will not."

"Why?"

"Reason enough."

"What can be your reasons?"

"Reason first–you are a Virginian, and a Virginian ought to ap-

---

* This was the conversation as it was recalled and quoted many years later by Adams.

pear at the head of the business.* Reason second–I am obnoxious, suspected, and unpopular. You are very much otherwise. Reason third–you can write ten times better than I."

"Well, if you are decided, I will do as well as I can."

"Very well," said Adams. "When you have drawn it up, we will have a meeting."

Jefferson went into seclusion, more or less, at his lodgings on Market Street, in the house of a bricklayer of German descent. There he spent days writing, revising, and polishing, and then recasting the whole again, for he wished to make the document, he said, "an expression of the American mind"–and express that mind he did in one of the great pronouncements of the ages.

He wrote the document out of his head, so to speak–out of his wide reading and study, out of deep reflection, out of his sensitive ear to what Americans were saying about their needs and interests, their ideas and desires.

"I only know," said Jefferson in later years, "that I turned to neither book nor pamphlet while writing it. I did not consider it as any part of my charge to invent new ideas altogether, and to offer any sentiment which had never been expressed before."

As Jefferson worked along, he showed preliminary drafts to Adams and to Franklin, "requesting their corrections, because they were the two members of whose judgments and amendments I wished most to have the benefit of before presenting it to the committee. . . . Their alterations were two or three only, and merely verbal. I then wrote a fair copy, reported it to the committee, and from them, unaltered, to Congress."

Richard Henry Lee's motion for independence came up in Congress on July 1, as scheduled. Sitting as Committee of the Whole, delegates stridently debated the issue. When a vote was taken, only nine colonies were in favor of the resolution.

South Carolina voted no, as did Pennsylvania. The Delaware delegation was split, one to one, and did not vote. The New York delegates asked leave to abstain, "to withdraw from the vote," a request that was granted. Though personally in favor of independence, the New York delegates were acting under instructions issued a year before when reconciliation, not independence, was the goal. The New York delegation therefore thought it not authorized to act until it received new instructions from home.

---

* Adams was here following the Massachusetts strategy, formulated two years earlier, that Virginians should be pushed to the forefront in all intercolonial matters.

The vote in committee was profoundly disturbing. Unanimity of action was absolutely imperative. Otherwise, the whole plan of a continental union would fall apart. Jefferson, John Adams, Sam Adams, Richard Henry Lee, John Hancock, and other radicals bestirred themselves. Alerted to the crisis, Caesar Rodney rode all night to Philadelphia from Dover, Delaware, a distance of some eighty miles, so that he might be on hand the next day to break the deadlock in the Delaware delegation and shift its vote to independence.

The radicals did their work swiftly and well. Overnight, the South Carolina delegates were persuaded to change their minds. The Pennsylvania delegation, with John Dickinson and Robert Morris deliberately absenting themselves, changed its vote from "nay" to "aye," and on July 2, Congress adopted the independence motion unanimously, but with New York again not voting.

Debate then shifted to Jefferson's draft of a declaration, which was sharply attacked from many sides. It contained a strong denunciation of the slave trade from Africa and the West Indies.*

This displeased South Carolina and Georgia, neither of which "had ever attempted to restrain the importation of slaves," said Jefferson, but, "on the contrary, still wished to continue it." The question was also "a little tender" with the New England colonies, especially Massachusetts and Rhode Island, "for though their people have very few slaves themselves, yet they have been pretty considerable carriers of them to others." Congress struck out Jefferson's passages on the slave trade, and other passages were deleted or amended.

Through two days of raging argument, John Adams was "the main pillar of debate." From whatever quarter attacks came, he rose and hurled them back, as Jefferson gratefully acknowledged. Adams "supported the Declaration with zeal and ability, fighting fearlessly for every word of it. As for myself," said Jefferson, "I thought it a duty to be, on that occasion, a passive auditor of the opinion of others, more impartial judges than I could be of its merits or demerits.**

---

* Jefferson was opposed not only to the slave trade, but to the institution of slavery in its entirety. But he did not raise that point at this time, for it would have been a hopelessly divisive issue.

** There may have been another reason, too. As Jefferson was not a good public speaker—indeed, a very dull and uninspiring one—he may have felt that quiet on his part would help rather than injure the cause. Jefferson has the distinction of being perhaps the only great statesman of history who was not entranced by the sound of his own voice.

During the debate I was sitting by Dr. Franklin, and he observed that I was writhing a bit under the criticism of some of its parts; and it was on this occasion that, by way of comfort, he told me the story of John Thompson, the hatter, and his new sign."

It was an amusing story about Franklin's young friend Thompson, who, having served his apprenticeship, was setting up a business of his own. Designing a handsome sign for his new hat shop, Thompson submitted it to friends for their comments and criticisms. When they had finished making amendments and deletions, there was practically nothing left of the original design except "hats." Pointing a moral, Franklin said to nervous and "writhing" young Jefferson: "I have made it a rule, whenever in my power, to avoid becoming the draftsman of papers to be reviewed by a public body." Jefferson disregarded the advice and went on drafting papers for review by public bodies almost all of his life, being none the worse for it.

Finally, on the evening of July 4, Congress adopted Jefferson's Declaration as amended. The vote was unanimous, though New York was again not voting. On that memorable Fourth of July, '76, only two men signed the document–John Hancock, as President of Congress; and Charles Thomson, as Secretary. The other delegates signed later–New York's not till July 15, after receiving new instructions from home.

Steps were immediately taken to dispatch copies of the Declaration throughout the country, and particularly to General Washington's army to be read before every unit of his troops. But the Declaration was first publicly proclaimed in Philadelphia, on July 8, before a large crowd gathered in the State House Yard.

"When in the Course of human events it becomes necessary for one people to dissolve the political bands which have connected them with another," the Declaration began, and went on:

> We hold these truths to be self-evident, that all men are created equal, that they are endowed by their Creator with certain unalienable Rights, that among these are Life, Liberty, and the pursuit of Happiness. That to secure these rights, Governments are instituted among Men, deriving their just powers from the consent of the governed, That, whenever any Form of Government becomes destructive of these ends, it is the Right of the People to alter or abolish it, and to institute new Government, laying its foundation on such principles, and

> organizing its powers in such form, as to them shall seem most likely to effect their Safety and Happiness. . . .

This was not merely independence. This was revolution—"all men are created equal," having "unalienable rights," one of which was "to alter or abolish" any government not based upon "the consent of the governed." Out of the early miseries and long travail of all the colonies, not only a new nation but a new political and social order had been born.

There was great rejoicing throughout the land. But Americans had good reason to be seriously worried, too. On July 3, it was reported that Admiral Lord Richard Howe, commanding a powerful fleet and 150 transports, had put 10,000 men ashore on Staten Island at the mouth of the Hudson, thus bottling up New York, the strategic center of the new nation. This was a very sobering consideration, not to be solved by ringing of bells, street parades, barbecues, drinking of toasts, and ceremonial salvos of musketry and cannon.

When John Hancock was signing the Declaraton of Independence, he remarked to Benjamin Franklin: "We must be unanimous; there must be no pulling different ways; we must all hang together." To this, Franklin is said to have replied:

"Yes, we must indeed all hang together or, most assuredly, we shall all hang separately."

A real and dismal prospect.

XXII
First Governor of the Commonwealth

. . . always reserve something for the hand of charity, and never let your door be closed to the voice of suffering humanity.

—PATRICK HENRY

On becoming the first governor of the new Commonwealth of Virginia, Henry received many congratulatory letters and messages. One particularly warmed him. It was "A Humble Address" from the officers and men of the First and Second Regiments whom he had commanded for so brief a time:

> May it please your Excellency:
> Permit us, with sincerest sentiments of respect and joy, to congratulate your Excellency upon your unsolicited promotion to the highest hônours a grateful people can bestow.
>
> Uninfluenced by private ambition, regardless of sordid interest, you have uniformly pursued the general good of your country; and have taught the world that an ingenuous love of the rights of mankind, an inflexible resolution, and a steady perseverance in the practice of every private and public virtue

> lead directly to preferment and give the best title to the honours of our uncorrupted and vigorous state.
>
> Once happy under your military command, we hope for more extensive blessings from your civil administration. . . .

In cordially thanking them, Henry wrote: "The remembrance of my former connexion with you shall ever be dear to me. I honour your profession, I revere that patriot virtue which, in your conduct, hath produced cheerful obedience, exemplary courage, and contempt of hardship and danger. Be assured, gentlemen, I shall feel the highest pleasure in embracing every opportunity to contribute to your happiness and welfare. . . ."

Colonel William Woodford of the Second Regiment, continuing his and his friend Pendleton's feud with Henry, took this occasion to exhibit his spite and enmity by inserting in the *Gazette* a public notice that he had not signed the "Humble Address," that it did not reflect "the sentiments of the Colonel," but only those "of the officers and their men." Henry could not have cared less and, it is hoped, had a good laugh at seeing everybody in the Second Regiment out of step but the blustering colonel.

Another letter that Henry highly prized came from the Baptist ministers and laymen who were meeting in Louisa County at the first general conference of Dissenters ever tolerated in Virginia. Previous attempts at such religious meetings had been broken up by the constables, who jailed the leaders. Times were changing in the Old Dominion. While laws against Dissenters were still on the books, they were no longer being enforced, so that there was now religious freedom *de facto,* if not *de jure.*

Henry's elevation to the governorship afforded them "unspeakable pleasure," wrote the Baptists. "Your public virtues are such that we are under no temptation to flatter you. . . . As a religious community, we have nothing to request of you. Your constant attachment to the glorious cause of liberty and to the rights of conscience leaves us no room to doubt of your Excellency's favorable regards while we worthily demean ourselves."

To set forth his views on the whole question of religious liberty, "freedom of conscience," Henry took time to write a long letter to the Baptists, parts of which read:

> I am happy to find a catholic* spirit prevailing in our

* Not Roman Catholic, but "catholic" in the original sense of the word, meaning broad-minded, tolerant, embracing all views. No Roman Catholic country

> country, and that those religious distinctions which formerly produced some heats are now forgotten. Happy must every friend to virtue and America feel himself to perceive that the only contest among us, at this critical and important period, is who shall be foremost to preserve our religious and civil liberties.
>
> My earnest wish is that Christian charity, forbearance, and love may unite all different persuasions as brethren who must perish or triumph together; and I trust that the time is not far distant when we shall greet each other as peaceable possessors of that just and equal system of liberty adopted by the last Convention. . . .

On July 5, Henry took his oath of office, arrayed in a scarlet cloak, black smallclothes, silk stockings, silver-buckled shoes, and a new dressed wig. He would show those who had long criticized him for being an "uncouth" rustic that he could dress as elegantly as any of them if he so desired and the occasion warranted.

But no sooner had he moved into the handsome Governor's Mansion, no longer known as the Palace, than he had to take an extended leave of absence because of serious illness. He was suffering from what, it appears, was the first of a series of malarial fevers that incapacitated him periodically the rest of his life.

Malarial and other fevers had plagued low-lying Tidewater Virginia since the first days of English settlement at Jamestown in 1607. These fevers and other ills—lumped together as "the summer sickness," as it was still known in Henry's day—had carried off half the population of Jamestown every year for twenty years. The "summer sickness" in the early days was as deadly as the devastating Black Plague that had swept through Europe some time before.

Leaving Williamsburg, Henry went home to Scotchtown, which stood on higher ground and away from malarial swamps. His "severe indisposition" forced him to take to his bed for almost a month. On August 2, the *Gazette* reported that the "worthy Governor" had so far recovered that he was up and around, taking a daily walk, and expressed the hope that he would soon be able "to attend to the duties of his high and important office."

But it was not until September 17, a month and a half later, that Henry was again in Williamsburg, to remain little more than

---

of that day was at all "catholic" in that sense of the term, demanding strict conformity in belief and ritual, prosecuting and persecuting "heretics."

a month, when he again informed the legislature that his "low state of health" made it impossible for him to attend to his duties. His doctors had recommended, he said, that he retire into the country until he was fully recovered. Henry returned to Scotchtown, where he remained for another month. Acutely aware of how much had to be done immediately, the governor must have been very ill indeed to absent himself for so long a time at such a critical period.

With Henry ailing and doing nothing but nurse his health, this is as good a time as any to interject a speculative thought. In view of what happened, which decisively shaped his later career, did Henry make a wrong turn in seeking the governorship? Instead of taking an office that was a "phantom," as he himself had described it, would he not have been happier and more effectual if he had remained on the floor of the House? There, he was in his element, with his voice resounding and sweeping others to accept his point of view on questions of high policy and important matters.

If he had remained in the House, he undoubtedly would have been chosen, as he had been before, as a leading Virginia delegate to the Continental Congress. By removing himself from the House, Henry would never again, as things turned out, participate in national councils of State or speak from a national platform to the people of the whole country.

The governor's job was a rather silent and cloistered one. The governor did not engage in debate about policy, and had no hand in making it. His job was to carry out what the House, under Speaker Pendleton, directed. Henry had had little experience as an executive and administrator, and never particularly distinguished himself as such. Besides, the paper work involved in being governor must have bored him and tried his patience to the limit. Henry always intensely disliked paper work, preferring to lay out broad lines of policy and let others fill in the details. In any case, whether he had made a wrong turn or not, he was now set on a new course as unfamiliar to him as when he became commander-in-chief of Virginia's military forces.

While Henry was still ill, he had one day an unexpected visitor—a tall strapping young Virginian of twenty-four, George Rogers Clark, soon to make a name for himself. After some schooling under an able Scot, Donald Robertson, with whom James Madison also studied, Clark took up surveying and went off in the western wilds to practice his profession, settling in Kentucky where new farms and settlements were being laid out.

In the western lands claimed by Virginia, the British had a number of military-trading posts taken over from the French in 1763—Vincennes, Kaskaskia, Kankakee, Detroit, and others. After the outbreak of hostilities at Lexington and Concord, the British commanders at these posts sent out agents to work among the Indians and persuade them to go on the warpath against the scattered American frontier settlements.

The Indians were ready to listen and often to act, for they hated the frontiersmen who were increasingly encroaching on their homelands, brazenly violating treaties and agreements, cheating them outrageously at every opportunity, shooting them on the slightest pretext, or none at all. Just a few years before, the great Cornstalk, chief of the Mingo, a most eloquent and friendly man, had been brutally murdered under a flag of truce, along with his wife and all their children, including a babe in arms.

The frontiersman has become a hero in American folklore. He was brave, tough, and hard. He had to be tough if he was to survive the hazards and traps of the wilderness. But he also was, all too often, violent and brutal, doing as he willed, being a law unto himself. Daniel Boone, the great pathfinder, became so disgusted with the company and ways of savage frontiersmen that he pulled up stakes in western North Carolina in 1767 and moved into the wilds of Kentucky to live among the Indians, much preferring their company. When Kentucky began to fill up with frontiersmen, trailed by land speculators and other sharpers, Boone pulled up stakes again and moved into the wilds of Missouri.

To combat British designs in Virginia's western lands, a militia had been formed, with George Rogers Clark in command as a major. Clark was also named to attend the Virginia Convention to present there the needs of the western settlements. Clark set out alone to walk, through hostile territory, some 500 miles to Williamsburg. Arriving in the Piedmont, Clark learned that the Convention had ended. He also learned that Governor Henry was at Scotchtown, not far away, and went there to introduce himself.

Dressed in buckskins, as Henry had once been, Clark greatly impressed the ailing governor as he explained his mission. The Kentucky and other western settlements, he said, needed far more than just verbal support in resisting the British and the restless Indians. Their most pressing need was for arms and gunpowder. Also, Kentucky wanted a county government of its own. At the moment, it was part of huge Fincastle County which had its seat hundreds of miles to the east. Being so far away, Fincastle authorities did not know much about Kentucky affairs and were not particularly concerned about them.

Henry entirely agreed with Clark about the importance of holding the west and about the best means of doing so. Making suggestions, the governor wrote a letter to his Privy Council, or his Executive Council, as it was soon renamed—"Privy Council" smacked too much of the British institution under the King's thumb. Carrying the letter with Henry's recommendations, Clark proceeded to Williamsburg and presented himself before the Executive Council. Things would have proceeded better if Henry had been present to raise his strong voice in support of immediate action.

Council members hesitated. They feared that if they gave the powder to Clark, they might be censured by the new House of Delegates when it met, and might even be held personally responsible for restitution. But they decided to supply the powder on two conditions. First, it was to be a loan, and Clark was to be responsible for restitution if the House objected to the transaction. Second, Clark would have to manage the transport of the powder himself.

In a sharp letter Clark replied that it was beyond his power to convey the powder at his own expense such a long distance through enemy territory and that he was "sorry to find that the Kentuckians would have to seek protection elsewhere," adding that he had no doubt they would get it. Clark was here alluding to the possibility, which he had thought about, of appealing for help to the Spanish, who held the territory west of the Mississippi and would no doubt welcome an invitation to expand eastward.

"If a country is not worth protecting," observed Clark tartly, "it is not worth claiming."

The veiled threat of calling on the Spanish for help was not lost on the Executive Council, which quickly reversed itself and removed all conditions. It issued an order that the requested gunpowder be delivered to Clark "by the keeper of the publick magazine . . . [and] be forthwith sent to Pittsburg and delivered to the commanding officer at that station, to be safely kept and delivered to Mr. Clark for the use of the inhabitants of Kentucky."*

The question of Kentucky's continued allegiance was resolved, and relations were strengthened when, early in its first session, the

* From what is now Pittsburgh, the powder was later floated down the Ohio and placed in Clark's hands.

House of Delegates passed a bill to cut Kentucky off Fincastle County and establish it as a huge new frontier county with officers and a courthouse of its own—a bill Henry was happy to sign.*

Having been absent at Scotchtown for almost four months, the governor returned to Williamsburg in mid-November to resume his heavy and complex duties, which he proceeded to carry out with wisdom, skill, and zeal. While a new government was being shaped and put into gear, a major problem in itself, there were so many things to be done, and with all possible speed—most important, meeting military needs that placed a severe strain on limited resources.

Henry had his critics in these trying years, but as chief executive he did as well as any governor in the other new states, and did better than most. His passionate dedication to building the Commonwealth and the confederated United States into going concerns was beyond challenge.

Henry and Virginians no longer had to worry about Lord Dunmore and his men, who had sailed away. The governor and his Executive Council were most concerned about the pressing problem of recruiting and equipping troops for the Continental Army as well as for the state's militia and volunteer units. Almost everything was in short supply: clothing, boots, blankets, muskets and rifles, pistols, powder, lead for bullets, and other necessaries. Horses had to be provided for the cavalry; horses and oxen, wagons and carts, had to be bought for hauling supplies. Money had to be raised to meet these needs and many others.

Virginia improvised a small navy by arming six sloops, which were renamed *Congress, Liberty, Defiance, Revenge, Scorpion,* and *Hornet.* These small vessels spent much of their time on guard at the mouth of Chesapeake Bay so that they could give the alarm if any British warships prowling the outer waters turned and headed for Virginia. They were also used to slip through the rather loose British blockade, carrying tobacco and other negotiable commodities to the Spanish and French West Indies. Returning, they brought back articles that were in critically short supply—in particular, salt, medicines, and textiles.

During Henry's three years in office, the Virginia Navy, controlled by him through a Navy Board, steadily expanded until it had seven-

---

* The county embraced all of what became, in 1792, the State of Kentucky, the fifteenth state in the Union—Vermont having become the fourteenth in 1791. The next state to be created was Tennessee, in 1796, followed by Ohio in 1803.

teen ships (the largest carrying thirty-two guns), fifteen brigs (the largest carrying fourteen guns), nineteen schooners, fifteen galleys, and several armed pilot boats and barges.

It was noted at the time "that by the export of tobacco from the Chesapeake, the credit of the colonies was chiefly, if not wholly, supported," and that by the inland navigation of the Chesapeake, "large quantities of provisions were conveyed to the middle colonies for the subsistence of the American army."

Anxious to get the earliest possible news of what was going on elsewhere so that he might take steps accordingly, Henry was in frequent correspondence with General Washington, and with Richard Henry Lee, head of the Virginia delegation at the national Congress. Finding that he was spending too much time writing such letters, Henry proposed, and the Council adopted, his suggestion that, to assure early and authentic reports on the movements of the British military, an official correspondent should be appointed and assigned to Washington's headquarters. John Walker of Albemarle County, one of Jefferson's neighbors and friends, was named to the post. Washington did not like this arrangement, writing Henry from Morristown, New Jersey:

> It will naturally occur to you, Sir, that there are some secrets on the keeping of which depends often times the salvation of an army; secrets which cannot, or at least ought not, be intrusted to paper; nay, which none but the Commander-in-Chief at the time should be acquainted with.
>
> If Mr. Walker's commission, therefore, from the Commonwealth of Virginia should be known, it would, I am persuaded, be followed by others of a like nature from other states, which would be no better than so many marplots.

To avoid setting a precedent by accepting Walker as a corresponding agent, said Washington, "I have taken him into my family as an extra aide-de-camp and shall be happy if, in this character, he can answer your expectations. . . .

> Let me earnestly entreat that the troops raised in Virginia for this army be forwarded on by companies, or otherwise, without delay, and as well equipped as possible, or we shall be in no condition to open the campaign.

Things had not been going very well—indeed, rather ill—for American arms. Anticipating that the British would move to seize New

York City which had great strategic value as a base for both army and navy operations, Washington withdrew his forces from Boston and marched them southwestward toward the Hudson, taking up a strong position on Long Island, on Brooklyn Heights which commanded the harbor. The British soon arrived in large force under the command of General Sir William Howe and occupied Staten Island unopposed. More troops arrived until Howe had on the island about 32,000 men—tough British regulars, for the most part, plus some German mercenaries, chiefly Hessians.

With the bulk of this force, General Howe crossed from Staten Island to Long Island to dislodge the Americans from Brooklyn Heights, which he did. Then, closely pursued by the British under Lord Cornwallis, one of the ablest of their generals, Washington's army began a long retreat—to the island of Manhattan, to White Plains, up the Hudson and across it, all the way through New Jersey, across the Delaware, and into Pennsylvania, stopping to fight now and again along the way.

Meantime, the American flotilla on strategic Lake Champlain had been defeated and completely smashed as a fighting unit. Fearing the British might attack and take the city, as they did not long after, Congress withdrew from Philadelphia and retreated to Baltimore to hold its sessions there. During 1776, worried Americans had only one really good piece of news from the field—the repulse of a sizable seaborne British attack on Charleston, South Carolina.

Virginians were very disturbed. It was under these depressing circumstances that "in December, 1776, . . . it was proposed in the House of Delegates to create a Dictator," according to an account written by Jefferson not long after. The dictator, again according to Jefferson, was to be "invested with every power, legislative, executive and judiciary, civil and military, of life and of death, over our persons and over our properties."

Jefferson's statement first appeared in his *Notes on the State of Virginia,* written in 1781–82 and published in 1784. It is curious, to say the least, that no other Virginia leader—in particular, such friends of liberty and ardent democrats as Richard Henry Lee and George Mason—made any mention of this diabolical scheme to establish a dictatorship.

It should be remarked here that if there was some talk along this line in the House, Jefferson did not hear it himself, for he was not present, as the House Journal shows. Because his wife was ill, he had left Williamsburg for Monticello.

In his *Notes,* Jefferson, cautious as always in his slurs, did not mention who was aspiring to be dictator. But many years later, in 1816, after Henry had been in the grave for almost twenty years and could not contradict him, Jefferson identified the culprit—by indirection, as usual. The circumstances surrounding this astonishing revelation are interesting.

A Frenchman, Louis Girardin, one of Jefferson's neighbors and friends, undertook to complete a four-volume history of Virginia begun by John Burk, who had died before finishing the final volume. The volume included events of 1776. Knowing nothing about such events firsthand, Girardin consulted with Jefferson frequently and was given free use of his library and papers. Jefferson reviewed the manuscript as it went along and endorsed the book when published. Having quoted Jefferson's *Notes* on the dictatorship business, Girardin added a sentence, which must have had Jefferson's approval and probably was inspired by him:

"That Mr. Henry was the person in view for the dictatorship is well ascertained."

The intimation here is that Henry aspired to become a Sulla or Caesar on the Roman model, or that he at least favored such an idea. Many otherwise balanced historians and biographers have taken Jefferson's anonymous charge seriously, and put it down to Henry's discredit. There is, however, no slightest evidence to support Jefferson's insinuations.

Certainly, as events showed, there was much talk both in and out of the Virginia legislature about the necessity of granting the "phantom" governorship some additional powers to meet a grave emergency. Things had not been going well in Virginia or elsewhere. Late in December, 1776, came very distressing and disturbing news from the north. Washington's army had been forced to retreat across the Delaware into Pennsylvania, with British forces in pursuit. If the British followed him across the Delaware, Washington might have to retreat again and move south into Virginia to make the Old Dominion the chief center of battle, an alarming prospect.

Receiving these discouraging and disheartening dispatches, the House of Delegates immediately decided "to take into their consideration the state of America." After two days of debate, the House adopted strong measures to meet the "present imminent" danger:

> *Resolved,* . . . [that] it is become necessary for the preservation of the State that the usual forms of government should

> be suspended during a limited time for the more speedy execution of the most vigorous and effectual measures to repel the invasion of the enemy:
>
> *Resolved,* therefore, That the Governor be and is hereby fully authorized and empowered, by and with the advice and consent of the Privy Council, from hence forward until ten days next after the first meeting of the General Assembly, to carry into execution. . . .

Then followed a list of what things the governor could do, dealing entirely with military operations and drawing money from the Treasury to pay for them. This paragraph of the resolution concluded:

> But this departure from the constitution of government, being in this instance founded only on the most evident and urgent necessity, ought not hereafter to be drawn into a precedent.

Also, the House decided to incorporate into its long resolution an instruction to the Virginia delegates to Congress that they should "recommend to the consideration of Congress whether it may not be necessary and expedient in the present dangerous and critical situation in America, in order to give vigour, expedition, and secrecy to our military measures, to invest the commander-in-chief of the American forces with more ample and extensive powers for conducting the operations of the war."

When the House of Delegates resolution was sent to the Senate, the upper body accepted all of it. But it proposed a small but important revision that was, in a way, an improvement. Verbally, it was better, but its intent was the same. In place of the phrase "the usual forms of government should be suspended," the Senate substituted a less sweeping clause, suggesting: "additional powers be given the Governor and Council."

The House readily accepted the revision, the resolution was quickly passed, and Governor Henry was asked to send copies of it by express to Congress, and to the governors of the neighboring states of Maryland and North Carolina, "to satisfy them that we are exerting ourselves in defending the liberties of America."

Six months after passage of the resolution, Henry's term as governor expired. Richard Henry Lee, it would seem, nominated him for re-election. One would surmise that if Jefferson's allegations about

Henry's aspirations to dictatorship had any substance, there would have been some opposition. There was none at all. As no other candidate was put forward, Henry was re-elected by acclamation in a joint session of the House and Senate. Thanking the General Assembly for the honor paid him, the governor said:

> The good of the Commonwealth shall be the only objects of my pursuits, and I shall measure my happiness according to the success which shall attend my endeavours to establish the public liberty.

Shortly after his re-election, Henry took leave of Williamsburg and returned to Scotchtown for a few weeks. He had a romance in hand. While at home, he no doubt spent much of his time in working out arrangements for a wedding that was solemnized four months later in Williamsburg, in the Governor's Mansion.

The wedding was a fashionable affair, with many friends and important personages attending. Henry had certainly climbed high on the social ladder since the day seventeen years before when he had first come to Williamsburg, dressed in buckskins, a somewhat uncouth but charming and brilliant young man hoping to pass his bar examinations.

The marriage ceremony, almost certainly, was performed under the Anglican rite. And no doubt the ceremony would have been performed by Henry's uncle for whom he was named, the Reverend Patrick Henry, if the latter had not died earlier in the year, having served as rector of St. Paul's Parish in Hanover County for some forty years. Until his uncle's death, Henry deferentially signed himself "Patrick Henry, Jr."

The bride, Dorothea Spotswood Dandridge, was a daughter of Colonel Nathaniel West Dandridge, one of Henry's old friends and first patrons. Henry was some twenty years older than his young bride whom he had known ever since he was a young man in his twenties and she was a toddler of three or four. In spite of the difference in their ages, the marriage appears to have been a happy one, and very fruitful, too. In time, Patrick and Dorothea had eleven children.

Henry had very positive ideas about the wife's place in what is called the holy bond of matrimony, and one wonders what vivacious and handsome young Dorothea thought about them, and what success, if any, Henry had in imposing his patriarchal and almost antediluvian views on her.* In considerable detail, mainly stressing "prudence" (not a usual Henry quality), he spelled out his views on how matrimony should be conducted. In a letter to a daughter by his first wife, Anne, on her marriage to Spencer Roane, Henry wrote:

> My dear Daughter:
>
> You have just entered into that state which is replete with happiness or misery [no one could take exception to that]. The issue depends upon that prudent, amiable, uniform conduct which virtue and wisdom so strongly recommend on the one hand, or on that imprudence which a want of reflection or passion may prompt on the other.
>
> You are allied to a man of honor, of talents, and an open generous disposition. You have, therefore, in your power all the essential ingredients of happiness; it cannot be marred if you now reflect upon that system of conduct which you ought invariably to pursue. . . .
>
> The first maxim which you should impress upon your mind is never attempt to control your husband by opposition, by displeasure, or any other mark of anger. A man of sense, of prudence, of warm feelings cannot and will not bear an opposition of any kind which is attended with an angry look or expression.
>
> The current of his affections is suddenly stopped; his attachment is weakened; he begins to feel a mortification the most pungent; he is belittled in his own eyes; and be assured that the wife who once excites those sentiments in the breast of a husband will never regain the high ground which she might and ought to have retained.
>
> When he marries her, if he be a good man, he expects from her smiles, not frowns; he expects to find her one who is not to control him–not to take from him the freedom of acting as his own judgment shall direct, but one who will place such confidence in him as to believe that his prudence is the best guide.

---

* Temperamentally, Dorothea seems to have been as little disposed to obey orders as Henry himself. In his will, her husband left her most of his estate, with the provision that if she remarried, she should get no more of the estate "than she can recover by Law." Dorothea married a Henry cousin, Judge Edmund Winston. In the end, however, she came back to Patrick and was buried beside him at Red Hill, as a Henry and not as a Winston.

> Little things, that in reality are mere trifles in themselves, often produce bickerings and even quarrels. Never permit them to be a subject of dispute; yield them with pleasure, with a smile of affection . . . A difference with your husband ought to be considered as the greatest calamity . . .
>
> Besides, what can a woman gain by her opposition or indifference? Nothing. But she loses everything . . . She creates her own misery, and then utters idle and silly complaints, but utters them in vain. . . .
>
> Cultivate your mind by the perusal of those books which instruct while they amuse. Do not devote much of your time to novels . . .* History, geography, poetry, moral essays, biography, travels, sermons, and other well-written religious productions** will not fail to enlarge your understanding, to render you a more agreeable companion and to exalt your virtue . . .
>
> I will add that matrimonial happiness does not depend upon wealth; no, it is not to be found in wealth, but in minds properly tempered and united to our respective situations. Competency is necessary. All beyond that is ideal. . . .
>
> In the management of your domestic concerns, let prudence and wise economy prevail. Let neatness, order, and judgment be seen in all your departments. Unite liberality with a just frugality; always reserve something for the hand of charity; and never let your door be closed to the voice of suffering humanity.
>
> Your servants [slaves] will have the strongest claim upon your charity; let them be well fed, well clothed, nursed in sickness, and let them never be unjustly treated.

Whether Dorothea had to listen to some masculine sermons along these lines is not clear. It appears, however, that she asserted herself and gained her husband's respect for her good judgment and shrewd common sense. According to family tradition, Henry never made a final decision in either his public or personal life without sounding out his wife's opinions.

---

* In his younger days, Henry had been found lying in bed and hugely enjoying Sterne's *Tristram Shandy,* considered in its day a rather bawdy novel on the practices of "marital bliss." He would scarcely have recommended this to his newly married daughter.

** What a regime for a lively young woman wanting at least to daydream a bit about something more adventurous and exciting than being neat, orderly, and prudent.

For Dorothea, coming to live in the Governor's Mansion was something of a homecoming. Her grandfather, Alexander Spotswood, had personally directed the building of the Mansion, and her mother had been born there. Taking over with ease her social and other obligations as the governor's wife, young Dorothea Spotswood Dandridge Henry played her role as the first First Lady of the Commonwealth of Virginia with tact and grace. Also, she had to take over the care of five children by Henry's first marriage, some of whom were almost as old as she. Young Dorothea appears to have been accepted and well-liked as a stepmother.

About the time of the marriage, Virginians had a sudden great fright. Coming down from New York under General Sir William Howe, British commander-in-chief on the continent, a large fleet of warships and transports carrying 15,000 men sailed into Chesapeake Bay and dropped anchor in Hampton Roads, about twenty miles from Williamsburg. Governor Henry immediately called up troops to meet the British if they attempted to land.

General Howe, it turned out, was not interested in Virginia at the moment. The fleet soon sailed up Chesapeake Bay to the head of navigation, where the troops disembarked and headed north toward Philadelphia. To block this advance, Washington drew up his forces along the north bank of Brandywine Creek.*

Outnumbered, outgunned, and outmaneuvered, the Americans had to give way and withdrew toward Philadelphia. Washington soon placed his small and dwindling army, hungry and ragged, in winter quarters at Valley Forge. Lord Howe's occupation of Philadelphia forced members of Congress to flee. Retreating westward, they first stopped at Lancaster and then moved on to York (Pennsylvania), which for almost a year was the struggling new nation's temporary capital.

Not long after this, when that awful winter at Valley Forge was at its worst, there came a letter from York addressed to "His Excellency P. Henry." The letter was not signed, and it was plain the author of it had been at pains to disguise his handwriting. It was also plain that the writer was a person of prominence close to the center of national affairs. It was a mystifying and most disturbing letter:

---

* It was near here along the banks of the Brandywine that twenty-five years later, in 1802, Eleuthère Irénée Du Pont built his first gunpowder mill, the foundation of a financial dynasty that has grown to become one of the greatest of our day.

Dear Sir:

The common danger of our country first brought you and me together. I recollect with pleasure the influence of your conversation and eloquence upon the opinions of this country in the beginning of the present controversy. You first taught us to shake off our idolatrous attachment to royalty and to oppose its encroachments upon our liberties, with our very lives. By these means you saved us from ruin. The independence of America is the offspring of that liberal spirit of thinking & acting . . .

But, Sir, we have only passed the Red Sea. A dreary wilderness is still before us, and unless a Moses or a Joshua are raised up in our behalf, we must perish before we reach the promised land.

We have nothing to fear from our enemies . . . America can only be undone by herself. She looks up to her councils and arms for protection; but alas! what are they?

Her representation in Congress dwindled to only twenty-one members—her Adams—her Wilson—her Henry—are no more among them. Her councils weak, and partial remedies applied constantly for universal diseases.

Her army, what is it? A major general belonging to it called it a few days ago, in my hearing, a mob. Discipline unknown or wholly neglected. The quartermaster's and commissary's departments filled with idleness, ignorance, and peculation;* our hospitals crowded with six thousand sick, but half provided with necessaries or accommodations, and more dying in a month than perished in the field during the whole of the last campaign.

The money depreciating, without any effectual measures being taken to raise it . . .

But is our case desperate? By no means. We have wisdom, virtue, and strength enough to save us if they could be called into action. The northern army has shown us what Americans are capable of doing, with a general at their head.

The writer was referring to the great victory the "northern army" had won a few months before at Saratoga in upstate New York—a victory that wrecked a well-conceived British plan to drive a

* As governor, Henry had been very critical of the operations of the quartermaster and commissary departments in Virginia.

wedge between the New England states and those to the south, thus making communication and transportation between them all but impossible.

General Burgoyne, author of the brilliant plan, was to march down from Canada by way of Lake Champlain and the upper Hudson Valley at the head of British, Hessian, Canadian, and Indian forces. Colonel Barry St. Leger, with a smaller force composed largely of Loyalists and Indians, was to come in from the west along the Mohawk Valley. General Sir Henry Clinton, in command at New York City, was to sail his ships loaded with troops up the Hudson, and the three columns would make a rendezvous somewhere near Albany and establish a strong base there. This could have been done if executed with any coordination and dispatch.

Coming down from Canada, easily capturing Crown Point, Fort Ticonderoga, and Fort Anne, Burgoyne then proceeded slowly, finding that he had to chop much of his way through wilderness and build roads to accommodate not only his cannon but also the fine carriages bearing the wives and mistresses of British and Hessian officers. Burgoyne's leisurely advance gave the Americans time to marshal their forces and call for reinforcements. St. Leger's column was stopped at Fort Stanwix and retreated. General Clinton started up the Hudson but, feeling that his rear was not sufficiently secure, turned his ships about and took his troops back to Manhattan.

Left alone in the wilderness, General ("Gentleman Johnny") Burgoyne, a gallant officer and a man of wit and charm, met the main American force at Bemis Heights, on the high sloping western bank of the upper Hudson in the township of Old Saratoga, about thirty miles north of Albany. After a series of thrusts and counterthrusts, bravely and skillfully executed on both sides, the Americans stormed and captured the strong British position on Bemis Heights, the fierce assault being led by Brigadier General Benedict Arnold, who lost a foot and lower leg in the engagement when hit by a cannon ball.*

---

* Much of the Saratoga battlefield has become a National Park. Before that happened, the D.A.R. and other patriotic groups began erecting monuments and markers to commemorate events and American heroes in the battle. By his initiative, spirit, and bravery, Brigadier Benedict Arnold had been mainly responsible for victory there. What to do about him?

The problem was solved in a rather wry and sardonic way. The interesting Arnold monument is a stone tablet standing about five feet high on a broad stone base. On the front of the tablet, in bas relief, there is nothing but a high army boot, memorializing the foot Arnold lost in the battle, the only part of him that remained "patriotic."

Retreating northward, with his supplies almost gone, Burgoyne soon found his army surrounded near Old Saratoga by a force that now outnumbered his, three to one. Further resistance was futile and on October 17, 1777—an important day in our annals—General Burgoyne capitulated under the "Convention of Saratoga," a very humane military document for that day or any other. Under its terms, Burgoyne's officers and men were disarmed, marched to Boston, and shipped back to England, having taken a pledge not to serve again in the American war.

As things turned out, but could only be appreciated later, the battle at Saratoga wrecking the British "wedge" plan was the turning point of the war. But it certainly did not seem so at the moment. At almost every other point, the tide of battle was running strongly against the Americans. Returning to talk about the success of the "northern army," the letter to Henry continued:

> The spirit of the southern army is in no way inferior to the spirit of the northern. A Gates, a [Charles] Lee, or a Conway would in a few weeks render them an irresistible body of men. The last of the above officers has accepted the office of inspector general of our army to reform abuses. . . .

Here was a scarcely veiled suggestion that General Washington be relieved of top command and be succeeded by one of the three officers mentioned, and that Henry's support of such a move would be welcomed. All three officers were British-born and British-trained professional soldiers with long experience. Major General Horatio Gates had commanded the victorious American forces at Saratoga and had recently been named head of the War Board. Major General Charles Lee was commander-in-chief of the Southern Department. A roving soldier of fortune, Major General Thomas Conway had served with the armies of France. Though all three had a European background and a former allegiance to Britain, their loyalty to the Patriot cause could not be challenged. The anonymous letter to Henry concluded:

> You may rest assured of *each* of the facts related in this

The back of the tablet has this inscription: "In Memory of the most brilliant soldier of the Continental Army, who was desperately wounded on this spot, . . . winning for his countrymen the Decisive Battle of the American Revolution, and for himself the rank of Major General."

But the Continental Army's "most brilliant soldier" is nowhere mentioned by name on the monument—which is fame of a sort.

> letter. The author of it is one of your Philadelphia friends. A hint of his name, if found out by the handwriting, must not be mentioned to your most intimate friend. Even the letter *must* be thrown in the fire.
>
> But some of its contents ought to be made public in order to awaken, enlighten, and alarm our country.
>
> I rely upon your prudence and am, dear Sir, with my usual attachment to *you* and to our beloved Independence, yours sincerely.

Henry pondered this puzzling letter for several weeks. What to do about it? Should he burn the letter, as requested, but make some of its contents public "in order to awaken, enlighten, and alarm our country?" Why all this secrecy? In the end, after almost a month, Henry decided that, instead of burning the letter, he would enclose it in a letter sent by express to Washington at Valley Forge;

> Dear Sir:
>
> You will no doubt be surprised at the enclosed letter, in which the encomiums bestowed on me are as undeserved as the censures aimed at you are unjust. I am sorry there should be one man who counts himself my friend who is not yours.
>
> Perhaps I give you needless trouble in handling this paper. The writer of it may be too insignificant to deserve any notice . . . But there may possibly be some scheme or party forming to your prejudice. The enclosed leads to such a suspicion. Believe me, Sir, I have too high a sense of the obligations America has to you to abet or countenance so unworthy a proceeding . . .
>
> I really cannot tell who is the writer of this letter, which not a little perplexes me. The hand-writing is altogether strange to me.
>
> To give you the trouble of this gives me pain. It would suit my inclination better to give you some assistance in the great business of the war, . . . for I really think your personal welfare and the happiness of America are intimately connected. . . .

Two weeks passed, and as no word had come from Washington about what seemed to be a pressing business, Henry wrote again to ask if his first letter had been received:

> I am anxious to hear something that will serve to explain

> the strange affair, which I am informed is taken up respecting you . . .
>
> I wish not to flatter; but when arts . . . are used to defame and traduce you, I think it not amiss, but a duty, to assure you of that estimation in which the public hold you. Not that I think any testimony I can bear is necessary for your support or private satisfaction . . . It will give me sincerest pleasure to manifest my regards, and render my best services to you and yours.
>
> I do not like to make a parade of these things, and I know that you are not fond of it; however, I hope the occasion will plead my excuse . . .
>
> Your very affectionate friend,
> and very humble servant,
> P. Henry

Harassed by many problems, including acute hunger in the camp at Valley Forge, Washington was not as prompt as he might have been in answering Henry's first letter, but finally found time to acknowledge it, saying that he was "under the most grateful obligations" to Henry for sending along the anonymous letter, and adding:

> I have ever been happy in supposing that I had a place in your esteem, and the proof of it you have afforded on this occasion makes me peculiarly so.
>
> The favorable light in which you hold me is truly flattering; but I should feel much regret if I thought the happiness of America so intimately connected with my personal welfare, as you so obligingly seem to consider it.
>
> All I can say is, that she has ever had, and I trust she shall ever have, my honest exertions to promote her interest.
>
> I cannot hope that my services have been the best; but my heart tells me they have been the best I could render.

Washington went on to remark that, undoubtedly, he had sometimes "erred in using the means in my power for accomplishing the objects of the arduous exalted station with which I am honored . . . Error is the portion of humanity, and to censure it, whether committed by this or that public character, is the prerogative of freemen." But criticism should be forthright and candid, and not made by anonymous letters.

> This is not the only secret insidious attempt to wound my

> reputation. There have been others equally base, cruel, and ungenerous because conducted with as little frankness. . . .

Washington was just about to sign and seal his reply when Henry's second letter arrived, and he immediately took up his pen to extend his remarks in another letter to Henry:

> . . . The anonymous letter, with which you were pleased to favor me, was written by Dr. Rush so far as I can judge from the similitude of hands.* This man has been elaborate and studied in his profession of regard for me, and long since his letter to you.
>
> My caution to avoid anything which could injure the service prevented me from communicating but to a very few friends the intrigues of a faction which I know was formed against me, since it might serve to publish our internal dissensions; but their own restless zeal to advance their views has too clearly betrayed them, and made concealment on my part fruitless.
>
> I cannot precisely mark the extent of their views, but it appeared, in general, that General Gates was to be exalted on the ruin of my reputation and influence.
>
> This I am authorized to say from undeniable facts in my own possession, from publications the evident scope of which could not be mistaken, and from private detractions industriously circulated.
>
> General Mifflin,** it is commonly supposed, bore the second part in the cabal; and General Conway, I know, was a very active and malignant partisan; but I have good reasons to believe that their machinations have recoiled most sensibly upon themselves.

---

* An early and ardent Patriot, Dr. Benjamin Rush of Philadelphia, one of Benjamin Franklin's close friends, had been a signer of the Declaration of Independence. Now in his early thirties, he had already won high distinction as a physician and for medical research, being a pioneer in determining the cause of deadly yellow fever. He was presently serving as Physician General of the Continental Army and finding grave fault with the want of accommodations and medical supplies provided for sick and wounded soldiers. Opposed to slavery, a prolific writer on health, education, and other subjects, Rush was a member of many medical, literary, and benevolent societies in this country and abroad. His teaching and lectures at the Medical College in Philadelphia made that city our first great center of medical science.

** Thomas Mifflin of Philadelphia was quartermaster general, later a member of the convention that framed the Federal Constitution, and a three-time governor of Pennsylvania.

Washington's surmise about the "machinations" recoiling were right, and he took steps to see that they did. Major General Gates and Quartermaster General Mifflin were removed from the War Board. Inspector General Conway and Physician General Rush "resigned." The "Conway Cabal," as it came to be called, withered away—if, indeed, there was any such cabal. Students of the affair have grave doubts that there was any organized "plot" to displace Washington.

Still, there was a disposition in many responsible quarters to get rid of Washington. Except at Saratoga, there had been nothing but retreat after retreat after retreat, in line with Washington's Fabian policy of withdrawing in face of superior forces. Americans should stand and fight! This was the view of Richard Henry Lee, Sam Adams, Dr. Rush, and others in and out of the Conway Cabal. Snapped John Adams, "I am sick of Fabian systems in all quarters!" Washington was also severely criticized for putting the army into winter quarters at Valley Forge. Wrote a brigadier general from there:

> The situation of the camp is such that in all probability the army must soon dissolve. Many of the troops are destitute of meat . . . The horses are dying for want of forage. The country in the vicinity of the camp is exhausted. There cannot be a moral certainty of bettering our circumstances while we continue here. What consequences have we rationally to expect. Our desertions are astonishingly great . . .
>
> I have from the beginning viewed this situation with horror! It is unparalelled in the history of mankind to establish winter quarters in a country wasted, and without a single magazine . . . There is no alternative but immediately to remove the army to places where they can be supplied unless effectual remedies can be supplied upon the spot, which I believe every gentleman of the army thinks unpracticable.

Washington had to agree about the general situation as winter deepened, but was not prepared to move. Rather, he appealed for help to all the governors, writing to Henry: "For several days we have experienced little less than famine in camp, and have had much cause to dread a general mutiny and dispersion." Unless vigorous measures were taken at once, another campaign would be impossible.

> I address myself to you, convinced that our alarming distresses will engage your most serious consideration, and that

> full force of that zeal and vigour you have manifested upon every other occasion will now operate for our relief in a matter that so nearly affects the very existence of our contest.

Promising to do everything he could, Henry issued new orders for gathering supplies and getting them to Valley Forge as quickly as possible. Henry also persuaded the Executive Council that Washington should be sent a special personal present for his pleasure and the "preservation of his health." The Virginia commissary was directed "to procure a stock of good rum, wines, sugar, and such other articles as His Excellency [Governor Henry] may think needful, and send them on to Headquarters."

Whatever doubts Washington may have had about the warmth of Henry's friendship were dispelled now. This time, Washington answered Henry's letter promptly, saying that the "agreeable present" had not yet arrived, but was reported to be on its way up the Chesapeake, and when it came, there could be no doubt that it would "find us in a humor to do it all manner of justice." The future might seem brighter when seen over a mug of hot buttered rum or a bottle or two of good Madeira.

In June, 1778, with the skies still dark, Henry's second term as governor expired. As no other candidate was placed in nomination, Henry was re-elected unanimously by the House and Senate. And who nominated "dictator" Henry on this occasion? It must certainly have been Jefferson, for he was named to head the committee sent to wait on Henry and inform him officially of his re-election. So much for Jefferson's later disquisition about the "dictatorship" plot of 1776. If Jefferson really believed what he subsequently wrote about Henry, it would have been his duty and desire to organize some kind of opposition to prevent Henry's unanimous re-election to both his second and his third terms. As it was, when something might have been done, Jefferson remained strangely silent and even, apparently, nominated Henry to continue in office for a third year.

An alliance with the French, which Henry had been so concerned about for so long, was finally cemented. Early in 1778, France decided to recognize the independence of the American colonies and soon, after a naval clash between the two powers, declared war on Britain. But still no desperately needed aid from abroad had been received. Even so, the French alliance offered hope and promise, and concerned Britain enough to cause a shift in her military and political maneuvers.

For one thing, war with France was not to be taken lightly and seemed to necessitate a redeployment of British arms in America. British forces should be regrouped and concentrated. To effect this, it was recommended by General Sir William Howe, British commander-in-chief on the continent, that Philadelphia should be abandoned.

The general, his officers, and their men had been having a merry time in Philadelphia during the winter of 1777–78 while the American forces at Valley Forge, not far away, were suffering such miseries and losses from hunger, thirst, frost, and disease. Why General Howe did not make a move toward Valley Forge, only twenty miles away, is a mystery. Even a strong feint in that direction would have sent Washington and his troops scattering in all directions, and that might well have been the end of the war. With organized resistance ended, the British could have proceeded rather easily to overpower local centers of resistance, one by one.

But General Howe made no slightest move toward Valley Forge. Perhaps he did not wish to interrupt the endless round of dinners, theatricals, and elaborate costume balls that he and his officers were enjoying in "hospitable" Philadelphia—certainly a more pleasant life than taking to the field in freezing weather.

Or perhaps he thought it would be wise not to stir up Washington and force him to take his men to greener pastures. Why not let them stay where they were and starve, as they seemed to be doing? Perhaps there might be a general mutiny, as Washington said he had cause to fear. That would be militarily an easy solution, and Britain might then gather up the pieces and fit them together again into her colonial empire.

Whatever his reason or reasons, General Howe did nothing, and for his inactivity he was relieved as commander-in-chief by General Sir Henry Clinton, who had left Burgoyne in the lurch at Saratoga. British evacuation of Philadelphia let Washington out of his "hole" at Valley Forge, and he followed the British in not too hot pursuit as they marched northward to regroup around New York City.

Prompted by the British defeat at Saratoga, and with the hope of breaking up the French alliance, Lord North won the King's grudging assent to a new plan for conciliating the American rebels. The plan proposed that the tax on tea, the Boston Port Bill, and other coercive acts should be repealed; that Parliament would pledge itself not to impose any more revenue-raising measures on the colonies; that a peace commission should be appointed and empowered to negotiate with Congress and agree, if absolutely necessary, to the suspension of all American acts passed by Parliament since 1763.

The peace commission, headed by the Earl of Carlisle, consisted of five members, two of whom were easygoing General Sir William Howe and his equally easygoing brother, Admiral Lord Howe. Arriving in Philadelphia, the commission found that Congress, getting wind of the mission, had already passed a resolution that any groups coming to terms with the commission should be branded as traitors. There was only one base for negotiations—withdrawal of British troops and formal recognition of American independence.

With the British evacuation of Philadelphia, the Lord North peace commission had to move north to New York. There, going over the head of Congress, it issued a Manifesto and Proclamation addressed to the American governors, legislatures, and rank and file, declaring that a general pardon would be granted to all who ceased opposing British rule. If that offer were not accepted, Britain would have to desolate a country which was "not only estranging herself from us, but mortgaging herself and her resources to our enemies . . . The question is how far Great Britain may, by every means in her power, destroy or render useless a connection contrived for her ruin, and for the aggrandizement of France."

To promote its purpose, the peace commission sent agents into the several colonies to enlist support for its aims. An agent came into Virginia with dispatches "directed to the Speaker of the Assembly, to the several officers of Government in the State, and to the ministers of the Gospel [Anglican]." The agent was seized and Governor Henry was pleased "to order the officer charged with the dispatches to depart this state with the same, and to inform him that, in future, any person making a like attempt shall be secured as an enemy of America."

Having accomplished nothing in the way of conciliation, the British peace mission returned to London. It was at this time that Lord North again offered his resignation to King George, pleading his incompetence as chief minister. North was already of the private opinion that the American war was lost, and wished to have nothing more to do with it. But if North thought the war was lost, Americans saw no reasons to believe the war was won, and it would not be won until three years later, after a succession of severe reverses.

After the British evacuation of Philadelphia, which was an American victory in a sense, the tide of battle continued to run strongly against the Americans. The British occupied Savannah and Augusta in Georgia, and all but took Charleston, South Carolina, soon returning to capture it. A French-American attempt to capture the British naval base at Newport failed. Forces under the command of the royal governor of New York were making raids along the Connecticut coast with impunity. Loyalists and Indians were successfully attacking settlements along the western frontiers of New York, Pennsylvania, Virginia, and the Carolinas.

In the summer of 1778, not long after being re-elected as governor, Henry had a bit of good news to report. Some months before, George Rogers Clark had returned to Williamsburg from Kentucky, hoping to get support for a plan he had in mind to eliminate or at least reduce British influence and power in the interior. Clark first talked with leaders in the legislature—in particular, with Jefferson, George Mason, and George Wythe. Liking his plan, these men sent Clark to discuss it with Governor Henry, who highly approved and took immediate steps to have it executed. The nature and goal of Clark's expedition were not publicly disclosed, being known to only a few, for the success of the military operation depended largely upon the element of surprise.

Having been named lieutenant colonel and commander of the enterprise, Clark proceeded to raise as speedily as possible what he called his "little army," to consist of 350 men, seven companies of fifty each. For the transportation of troops and supplies down the Ohio River, he was to apply to the commander at Pittsburgh "for Boats, & during the whole transaction you are to take especial care to keep the true destination of your force secret. Its success depends upon this."

Clark was ordered to "show humanity to such British Subjects and other persons" as fell in his hands. If such gave "undoubted evidence of their attachment to this State (for it is certain they live within its limits)," they should be treated as fellow citizens, and their persons and property duly secured. Clark's orders, signed by Henry, continued:

> But if these people will not accede to these reasonable demands, they must feel the miseries of war, under the direction of that Humanity that has hitherto distinguished Americans & which it is expected you will ever consider as the Rule of your Conduct & from which you are in no instance to depart . . .
>
> It is in contemplation to establish a post near the mouth of the Ohio. Cannon will be wanted to fortify it. Part of those at

> Kaskasky will be easily brought thither or otherwise secured, as circumstances will make necessary.

The Clark expedition had several purposes. First and primarily, it was to stop attacks along the frontier by the Indians, incited by the British. It was not only to drive the British out—but to keep the Spanish out. Spain claimed all of the vast country west of the Mississippi, and might be tempted to take advantage of the present turmoil to move eastward across the river and establish control in lands granted to Virginia by old royal charters. In all this, there was a long-range strategic view. Henry, Jefferson, Mason, Wythe, and others saw that effective American control along the frontier would have a very important bearing "in establishing our northwestern boundary" when, and if, America won the war and terms of peace were negotiated.

With skill and great daring, Colonel Clark and his "little army" of frontiersmen succeeded brilliantly in surprising and taking one British outpost after another—Kaskaskia, Vincennes, Cahokia, and others. Clark never had enough men and supplies to carry out his aim of capturing Detroit, Britain's strongest base in the region. Even so, he won more or less effective control of Kentucky and a vast expanse north of the Ohio River, later set off as the Northwest Territory which embraced the present states of Ohio, Indiana, Illinois, Michigan, Wisconsin, and a large part of Minnesota. Governor Henry wrote to the Virginia delegates in Congress that he was happy to report that Colonel Clark's "success has equalled the most sanguine expectations."*

Not long after this, Governor Henry and all Virginians had good cause to be alarmed. There had been no military clashes in Virginia since Lord Dunmore and his small force had been driven out some three years before. In the spring of 1779, a British fleet, escorting

---

* Clark, "the Hannibal of the West," was treated very shabbily by his countrymen. Years later, when he was living in great poverty near Louisville, Kentucky, Virginia got around to honoring him by sending a delegation to present him with a ceremonial sword. Clark listened as patiently as he could to the usual blah on such occasions. Taking the ceremonial sword, Clark plunged the blade deep into the ground and broke it in half with his crutch, saying:

"When Virginia needed a sword, I gave her one. She sends me now a toy. I want bread!"

Clark was an older brother of William Clark of the Lewis and Clark Expedition sent out in 1804 by President Jefferson to explore the recently acquired Louisiana Purchase from the Missouri River to the Pacific Northwest.

troop transports, suddenly put into Chesapeake Bay and anchored in Hampton Roads. Next day, this force took Portsmouth when the garrison there, too weak to resist, had to flee, having first destroyed "one capital ship of the State, and one or two private ones loaded with tobacco" to prevent these from falling into the hands of the British.

Henry immediately sent to Congress by express rider a dispatch urging that action be taken to "procure a fleet superior to the enemy's force to enter the Chesapeake at this critical period." Congress had no "superior" fleet to send to the Chesapeake, or anywhere, though it had a few marauders at sea under the command of dashing Captain John Paul Jones, who was preying on British shipping in European waters.

To contain the British in Chesapeake Bay, Governor Henry issued a proclamation "requiring the county lieutenants and other military officers of the Commonwealth, and especially those on the navigable waters, to hold their respective militias in readiness to oppose the attempts of the enemy wherever they might be made."

The militia companies could not be effectively mustered in time, and those companies that appeared in the field were found to be woefully short of arms. Consequently, the British met little or no opposition as they moved about in the Chesapeake and in the lower waters of the York River and the James, making raids ashore to pillage the countryside. They easily occupied not only Portsmouth, but Gosport and Norfolk, and then the town of Suffolk, which they put to the torch after capturing a large store of supplies destined for the Continental Army. The loot included 1,200 barrels of pork that the men at Valley Forge could well have used and been elated to see.

The British attack, it turned out, was not really an invasion, but only an "incursion" to terrify the inhabitants, cause confusion, and make it more difficult for Virginia to supply the Continental forces, as it had generously been doing somewhat to the neglect of its local forces. After two weeks of marauding, having destroyed almost all of the few small vessels that constituted what was styled "the Virginia Navy," the British sailed away, very pleased with themselves, having caused damage later estimated at £1,000,000 [$30,000,000], a heavy blow to Virginia's strained resources.

In the midst of these troubles, Henry's third term as governor expired. The state constitution had stipulated that a governor could serve only three successive annual terms and could not again be eligible for four years. Henry's friends and supporters brought up the argument that his first term really did not count, that it had been "merely provisory," that he had been elected by the Virginia Convention and not by joint ballot of the House of Delegates and the Senate as the constitution stipulated.

Henry would have nothing to do with this dubious maneuver, no doubt seeing very clearly that to raise a constitutional issue at this critical time would be highly dangerous and could only result in bitter dissensions. On May 28, 1779, Henry announced his intentions in a note to the Speaker of the House:

> Sir:
>
> The term for which I had the honor to be elected governor by the late Assembly being just about to expire, and the Constitution, as I think, making me ineligible to that office, I take the liberty to communicate to the Assembly through you, Sir, my intention to retire in four or five days.
>
> I have thought it necessary to give this notification of my design in order that the Assembly may have the earliest opportunity of deliberating upon the choice of a successor to me in office.
>
> With great regard, I have the honor to be, Sir, your most obedient servant.
>
> P. Henry

To succeed Henry, three men were placed in nomination–Jefferson, General Nelson, and John Page, who had been an unsuccessful candidate against Henry in 1776 and had since worked closely with Henry as president of the Governor's Council. On the first ballot, Jefferson had fifty-five votes; Page, thirty-eight; and Nelson, thirty-two. As a plurality was required, a second ballot was held to determine the choice between the two top runners. Jefferson won, but by a narrow margin–sixty-seven votes to sixty-one for Page.

Jefferson's years as governor were as trying as those of Henry, who appears to have been rather happy to leave office.

XXIII
Return to the Assembly

. . . I even doubt whether I can remain down below long enough to serve in the Assembly. I will, however, make the trial . . .

—PATRICK HENRY

Leaving the Governor's Mansion, Henry retired to the country—but not to Scotchtown, which had been his home for six or seven years. He had sold his estate there about the time of his marriage to his second wife Dorothea, who apparently never stayed at Scotchtown where Henry's first wife Sarah had so tragically died.

Having bought Scotchtown at a bargain, Henry realized a considerable profit on its sale. Much of his profit* he invested in buying another larger estate, with a house and almost 10,000 acres, in the wilder country to the west. Situated some 200 miles southwest of Richmond, the plantation lay in hilly country along Leatherwood Creek, a tributary of the River Dan which comes tumbling down

---

* In 1776, the governor had been granted a salary of £1,000 a year, raised to £2,000 the next year, and to £3,000 the third year, paid in paper currency. But as that currency was rapidly depreciating, the salary scarcely paid expenses. Henry had no income from his law practice which he had suspended in 1774, devoting his full time to public affairs as the political crisis deepened.

from the Blue Ridge and courses across southern Virginia before curving down into North Carolina.

Henry had several reasons for moving to the lonesome Leatherwood country. For one thing, he always preferred the rustic ways of the Piedmont to the elegance of Tidewater Virginia dominated by the Grandees with their aristocratic airs. Second, he may have wished to remove himself and his family as far away as possible from the danger of a British invasion from the coast. Third, he may have hoped that in the hilly higher Leatherwood country he would be free of the fevers he had suffered in low-lying Tidewater. If he had any such hope, it was soon dashed. No sooner had he arrived at Leatherwood than he was laid low with a severe malarial attack.

Ill and tired, treasuring his solitude, Henry for a time did not concern himself at all about what was going on in the outside world. He apparently did not even bother to read the *Virginia Gazette* to learn what was happening in Williamsburg and elsewhere. If he had, he would have learned much sooner than he did the fact that the legislature, shortly after his departure from Williamsburg, had elected him to be a Virginia representative in Congress.

An official letter informing him of this evidently went astray. When nothing had been heard from Henry in almost four months, another letter was sent. This one was received, and Henry replied in a brief note to the Speaker of the House:

> Sir:
>
> The vote of the Assembly appointing me a member of Congress never reached my hands until several months after it passed. However, a tedious illness has prevented me from all attentions to business until lately; and now I am circumstanced* so as to make my attendance in Congress impossible.
>
> I beg you will please inform the General Assembly of this in order that another member may be chosen in my stead. . . .

A little later, in February 1780, Henry received a long and very friendly letter from Governor Thomas Jefferson, who was shouldering the same heavy problems that Henry had borne. Both men were in a gloomy mood, as they had reason to be.

The British, strengthening their forces in the South, controlled Georgia and most of South Carolina, and were evidently planning to move up the seaboard to Virginia. Military aid from the French

* He was "circumstanced" by the fact that his wife Dorothea was about to have her second child, Henry's eighth.

had so far been very disappointing. If the situation was alarming in the South, it was desperate in the North.

In the winter of 1779–80, Washington put his troops into quarters near Morristown, New Jersey. There, conditions were even worse than at Valley Forge two winters before. Supplies were so short that the soldiers' rations were cut sharply, and then again and again, until the troops were receiving only an eighth of their normal minimum ration. Their pay, pitifully small, was five months in arrears. Mutiny was brewing, and soon broke out.

In his letter to Henry, Governor Jefferson implored him to return to public life to give counsel and inspiration in the dangerous and disheartening situation. Thanking Jefferson, Henry wrote:

> The kind notice you were pleased to take of me was particularly obliging as I have scarcely heard a word of public matters since I moved up in the retirement where I live.

A number of developments, especially war profiteering and corruption, had sickened him, Henry added, "and made me sometimes wish to be in retirement for the rest of my life." However, he gave Jefferson a promise:

> I will . . . be down to the next Assembly, if I am chosen. My health, I am satisfied, will never again permit a close application to sedentary business, and I even doubt whether I can remain down below long enough to serve in the Assembly. I will, however, make the trial . . .
>
> I have had many anxieties for our Commonwealth, principally occasioned by the depreciation of our money. To judge by this, which somebody has called the pulse of the State, I have feared that our body politic was dangerously sick. God forbid it may not be unto death.
>
> But I cannot forbear thinking the present increase of prices is in great part owing to a kind of habit which is now of four or five years growth, which is fostered by a mistaken avarice, and like other habits hard to part with—for there is really very little [hard] money hereabouts.
>
> What you say of the practices of our disguised Tories perfectly agrees with my own observation, and the attempts to raise prejudices against the French, I know, were begun when I lived below.
>
> What gave me the utmost pain was to see some men, indeed very many, who were thought good Whigs, keep company with

> the miscreants, wretches, who, I am satisfied, were labouring for our destruction. This countenance shewn them is of fatal tendency. They should be shunned and execrated . . .
>
> But this is an effort of virtue, small as it seems, of which our countrymen are not capable . . .
>
> I most sincerely wish you health and prosperity. If you can spare time to drop me a line now and then, it will be highly obliging to, Dear Sir, your affectionate friend and obt. Servt. . . .

Henry was living in Henry County, a recently created frontier county named for him. Standing as one of two county representatives to the House of Delegates, Henry was triumphantly elected, as usual. Though the House met on May 1, 1780, Henry did not take his seat in Richmond* till eighteen days later, perhaps delayed by illness or because of the birth of his latest child.

Back on the floor of the legislature, after four years' absence while governor and on his retirement to Leatherwood, Henry quickly regained the leadership he had enjoyed in the late House of Burgesses. He was one of nine Delegates placed on the all-important Committee of Ways and Means that was wrestling with the problems of carrying on the war and trying to keep the new Commonwealth of Virginia on an even keel, more or less, in very stormy seas. The work of this committee was judged to be so vital that the naming of its members was not left to the Speaker. Rather, they were nominated on the floor and elected by the House as a whole.

As Henry remarked to Jefferson, Virginia's chief concern at the moment should be the monetary problem, which was seriously impairing all commerce, particularly in the vital field of procuring food, clothing, and other necessaries for the armies. Farmers and manufacturing shops were reluctant to sell their products for paper money that was rapidly depreciating from month to month. There was ruthless profiteering by jobbers and speculators.

"The Spirit of Avarice seems to have pervaded every breast al-

---

* Williamsburg had ceased to be the capital of Virginia after being so for almost two centuries. For reasons of safety during the war, the capital was moved inland to Richmond, a scraggly town of perhaps 700 people and with few facilities or amenities, having nothing like the Raleigh Tavern. Williamsburg went into a long period of decline and decay until the late 1920s when John D. Rockefeller, Jr., inspired by the Reverend W. A. R. Goodwin, rector of the local Bruton Parish Church, founded Colonial Williamsburg, Inc., which has since renovated and restored the old town, making it somewhat of a museum, a showplace of what upper-class Virginia life was like about 1776.

most," wrote Pendleton to Washington at this time, "and expel'd all the many sentiments so that paper money is as eagerly sought after as if it contained in itself the essence of meat, drink, and cloathing, or even all the virtues, tho' the graspers at the same time effect to decry it as of no more value than Oak leaves. . . ."

Congress had already issued some $260,000,000 in paper bills, and individual states had issued an equal amount. It was promised that these bills would later be redeemed at full value in cash, but almost no provision for their redemption had been made. Such bills continued coming from the printing presses until, in terms of coin, or "hard" money, they were worth only a fortieth of their face value.

Early in 1780, seeing that something had to be done to check ruinous inflation, Congress pledged itself to issue not more than $40,000,000 in new bills. Old Continental bills were to be retired and burned to reduce the quantity of paper money in circulation. The new bills were to be redeemable in specie within six years, plus accumulated interest at 5 per cent a year. Congress proposed to the states that they individually issue such bills, with redemption guaranteed by the national government. But that government had not yet taken any steps to provide funds to assure redemption, so that the "guarantee" was regarded as another paper promise, as it turned out to be.

When the proposal for general refinancing came before the Virginia Assembly, it was favored by Richard Henry Lee, George Mason, and others "as being the only expedient remaining for the restoration of public credit." Henry here strongly disagreed with his liberal friends, and "poured forth all his eloquence in opposition," offering a resolution with three main points:

> 1. That ample and certain funds ought to be established for sinking the quota of the Continental debt due from this State in fifteen years;
> 2. That certain funds ought to be established for furnishing to the Continental Congress the quota of this State for the current year;
> 3. That a specific tax ought to be laid [in Virginia] for the use of the Continental Congress in full proportion to the abilities of the people.

This was a sounder scheme than that proposed by Congress and advocated by Lee and Mason. A tax levied specifically for funding purposes would immediately strengthen public credit and, in the long run, enable the U. S. Government to meet its promise of redeeming its paper bills at face value in hard money. By able and eloquent argument Henry carried the House with him, and his resolution was adopted by fifty-nine votes to twenty-five—which was a triumph, but it was his only one at this session.

The day after the vote, Henry asked to be excused for the rest of the session. Again quite ill, he returned to Leatherwood, where he stayed more or less in seclusion for five months. Not long after he took leave of absence, the House returned to the monetary problem. Changing its mind about the Henry plan, mainly because it involved new taxation—which was at the heart of the fiscal problem—the House reluctantly adopted the Congress proposal, and the value of paper currency continued to fall swiftly until, in terms of specie, it was officially rated at 500 to 1 within a year. Soon, both new and old bills ceased circulating altogether; no one would accept them. Whether Henry's plan would have worked any better in the long run is a question. At least it would have acted as a brake on the precipitous slide over the precipice.

General military activities during the summer and fall of 1780, while Henry was at home, added up to little but frustrations and defeats. There had been a serious mutiny in Washington's camp at Morristown, New Jersey, where two veteran Connecticut regiments paraded under arms demanding full rations and their back pay, in arrears for months. The mutineers were curbed by Pennsylvania troops. But there was soon a mutiny also in the Pennsylvania Line, and another in the New Jersey Line, which was put down with great force, two of the ringleaders being executed.

Smarting under what he regarded as slights by the War Board, particularly incensed by a sharp reprimand by Washington, Major General Benedict Arnold, hero of Saratoga, tried to betray to the British the key fortress of West Point where he was in command. If he had succeeded, the American position in the North would have been very seriously weakened. Fortunately, quite by chance, the plot was discovered; Arnold managed to escape to the *Vulture,* a British warship in the Hudson. For his treachery, the British paid Arnold more than £6,000 sterling [$190,000], commissioned him as a brigadier general, and granted his wife and their five small children sizable pensions for life.

Arnold's plot, though smashed, raised a serious concern. Who might be the next high commander to defect? On his capture by the British, Major General Charles Lee initiated a secret correspondence with General Howe, though this was not known at the time.

In July, a large French fleet escorting transports carrying 5,000 soldiers and marines put in at Newport under the command of Comte de Rochambeau. This seemed to promise much. Washington immediately made plans to join this force with his for an attack on New York. But the plan had to be abandoned because a powerful British fleet soon appeared, established a blockade, and bottled up the French ships at Newport, thus denying Washington the naval support he needed for success in his move against New York. Still, in spite of this disappointment, it was encouraging to see some significant French aid at last, even though it were temporarily immobilized.

Spain had declared war on Britain, but hard-pressed Americans received little direct benefit from this—only a small loan of $174,000 after long dickering. Spain was not interested in the American cause except as a club to beat the British Lion. Her aim in the war was to use present troubles to recover Gibraltar, seized and held by the British since 1704, and to regain East and West Florida, which she had been forced to cede to Britain in 1763 after the Seven Years' War.

It seemed to the ruling autocratic Spanish Bourbons that to give any slightest countenance to colonial revolt might give ideas to millions of people in Spain's vast New World empire, which stretched from the Mississippi through Louisiana, Texas, New Mexico, Arizona, and California, south through Mexico, across the Isthmus of Panama, and down South America to Cape Horn—an empire Spain had plundered, and was still plundering, to her great enrichment. She wanted no independence movements there.

Of greater benefit to Americans, though still indirect, was the armed neutrality policy proclaimed by Catherine the Great of Russia early in 1780. She gave notice that her navy would be used to protect neutral Russian shipping against all belligerents, and that Russia would not accept Britain's sweeping definition of what was contraband.

Proposed by Russia, a League of Armed Neutrality was formed, being joined by Sweden, Denmark, Prussia, Holland, Portugal, and Austria, which then held major Italian ports in her empire.

Britain declared war on Holland, attacking and capturing the Dutch island of St. Eustatius in the West Indies. This was a blow to the Americans who had been slipping small fast vessels through the British sea patrols to bring back valuable supplies from the island, a chief center of contraband trade.

The League of Armed Neutrality greatly impeded British efforts to establish a total blockade of French ports. Wars with Spain and Holland forced Britain to scatter her forces, so that she could not bring her full might to bear on Americans and their French allies. Britain was having troubles in India, too.

On the American war front, the British high command had decided to center operations in the South under Lord Cornwallis, one of their abler generals, who had some 8,000 men in his command. After a series of American defeats, Major General Horatio Gates was sent down to take charge of the Southern Department, bringing along as the core of his army several thousand seasoned troops detached by Washington. To the army, Virginia and North Carolina contributed a number of regiments of state militia, composed largely of new recruits, raw and almost untrained.

Gates decided to move south against the large British base and supply depot at Camden, South Carolina, near the North Carolina line. Lord Cornwallis and his forces met the advancing Americans just north of the town on August 16, and the battle that occurred there was an American disaster. Making a wide and undetected sweep around behind, Colonel Banastre Tarleton's spirited and well-mounted dragoons came thundering down on the American rear, effecting a complete surprise. Experiencing their first taste of battle, and not liking it, almost all of the poorly trained and undisciplined Virginia and North Carolina militia units broke and ran, exposing more of the rear.

At Camden, Americans had almost 1,000 men killed, two or three times as many wounded, and more than 1,000 captured. Gates hastily retreated northward about 150 miles to regroup what remained of his army. As a result of this shattering American defeat, the worst of the war, Gates was relieved of command four months after being named to the post, and was replaced by Major General Nathanael Greene, a Rhode Islander.

With Gates' army disposed of, Cornwallis moved into North Carolina but halted his advance when a small American force of frontiersmen decisively defeated and captured a British force, composed largely of Carolina Tories, at the battle of King's Mountain. Feeling that his western flank was thus exposed, Cornwallis drew back and went into winter quarters in South Carolina, spending his time in laying plans to strike through North Carolina and into Virginia the next year, which he did. The British high command had decided that the American "rascals" could not be subdued, either in the South or the North, so long as Virginia was left untouched and free to go on being a chief supplier of the Continental armies. The war was now to be centered in Virginia, and some very rough hard times lay just ahead.

Such, then, was the general situation late in 1780 when Henry took his seat at the opening of the next Assembly session. He was named to serve on important standing committees—as chairman of the Committee of Privileges and Elections, and as a member of the Committee of Propositions and Grievances and of the Committee of Courts of Justice. He also served, often as chairman, on any number of special committees named to look into pressing problems and make recommendations—"for the better defense of the Southern frontier," for enlisting more troops, for better regulation and discipline of the militia, for better procurement of clothing and provisions for those under arms, for organizing and maintaining a navy, for the protection of shipping in Virginia waters, for settling the state's account with the national government, for redemption of the state's paper money in circulation, for issuing new bills, for other emergency matters.

In the midst of all this urgency, Henry took time to do a very thoughtful and gracious thing, which was characteristic of him. Upon being relieved of command in the Southern Department, General Gates had been ordered to come to Philadelphia to face a court of inquiry into what had gone wrong at Camden. On his way there, Gates made a short stop in Richmond. Learning of this, Henry proposed a resolution which the House of Delegates adopted:

> December 28, 1780
>
> *Resolved,* That a committee of four be appointed to wait upon Major General Gates, and to assure him of the high regard and esteem of this House;
>
> That the remembrance of his former glorious services cannot be obliterated by any reverse of fortune; and that this House, ever mindful of his great merit, will omit no opportunity of testifying to the world the gratitude which, as a member of the American Union, this country owes to him in his military character.

As he had been receiving nothing but brickbats from all sides, General Gates was very touched, replying that he would "ever remember with the utmost gratitude the high honor this day done me by the honorable House of Delegates of Virginia . . . That I have been once unfortunate is my great mortification," and that whatever his future services might be, his efforts would be animated, as they always had been, "by the truest zeal for the honor and interest of the United States."*

On the last day of the session—January 2, 1781—Henry offered a resolution, adopted by the House, authorizing Governor Jefferson to have the next legislature convene at any place he chose in the event that a meeting in Richmond was "rendered inconvenient by the operations of an invading enemy."

The resolution was timely. A British fleet of twenty-seven sail had just put into Chesapeake Bay, and on the very day the resolution was passed, the ships started up the James River toward Richmond, having on board about 900 Redcoats—under the command of General Benedict Arnold, eager to justify his pay as a turncoat and show his former fellow countrymen what he could do to help crush their cause. Three days later, this force reached Richmond, having ravaged the countryside along the way and encountering only feeble local resistance; most of Virginia's better troops had been sent to serve elsewhere.

In and around Richmond, Arnold's men seized or destroyed military stores, smashed a foundry for casting cannon, burned some public buildings, and then returned to the Chesapeake where they established themselves at Portsmouth while awaiting reinforcements. Several thousand militiamen took up positions around Portsmouth but did not dare to attack, being too disorganized and unsupplied to face the fire of Arnold's seasoned troops and the cannon on his ships.

Little realizing that the roof was about to fall in, the British government was in a confident mood. The War Minister wrote to General Sir Henry Clinton, commander-in-chief in America:

> The success of General Arnold's enterprise up James River, which the rebel newspapers confirm, must greatly facilitate His Lordship's [Cornwallis] operations by cutting off Greene's supplies and obliging the [Virginia] militia to take care of their own property.
>
> Indeed, so very contemptible is the Rebel force in all parts, and so vast is our superiority everywhere, that no resistance on their part is to be apprehended that can materially obstruct the progress of the King's arms in the speedy suppression of the Rebellion.

---

* Gates was never again called to command and soon retired to his estate in western Virginia, where in later years he emancipated his slaves, making ample provision for those unable to care for themselves. Gates was a kindly and generous man, unfortunately given to overestimating his abilities.

Early in March, 1781, the Assembly met in Richmond and sat for three weeks, being ready to move elsewhere at the first sign of danger. On a motion by Henry, the legislature sent to Congress an urgent plea for help; Virginia stood in a desperate state, and even greater danger threatened. When New England and the Middle States had been in danger, Virginia had generously come to their aid. Now let those states reciprocate with more alacrity than they seemed to be showing. To meet acute financial needs, and again on Henry's motion, Governor Jefferson was authorized to issue another £5,000,000 in paper bills, even though such bills were fast approaching the point of worthlessness. Under the circumstances, however, there was no help for that if current needs were to be met—at least, on paper.

Virginia's plea to Congress for men and money met with a favorable response in several important respects. It was ordered that all regular troops in Pennsylvania and neighboring states should be sent to the South. At the same time, Washington detached 1,200 seasoned veterans from his command headquarters, then in lower New York, and dispatched them to Virginia under the young Marquis de Lafayette, who had arrived as a volunteer four years before and was soon made a major general on Washington's staff.

These soldiers of the North did not want to march south. Many deserted; there were ominous mutterings among them as they passed through Philadelphia. Anticipating some discontent, Washington had ordered that these troops be given a month's pay "in hard money." This quieted their complaints, except for the constant gripes and grumblings that every soldier, in every army, thinks himself entitled to—and he is right. The weary man slogging along in the ranks has little to enjoy but his "bitching."

Shortly after the Assembly recessed, Arnold's forces at Portsmouth received a reinforcement of 2,000 Redcoats from New York, and soon began moving up the James again, marching inland on either bank to capture a number of towns, carrying off or destroying precious stores, sinking what remained of the Virginia navy, and offering a threat to Richmond where Lafayette was on guard with some militia units and his small body of regulars.

Reports came in that Lord Cornwallis was marching up from North Carolina to join up with Arnold's force for a grand assault on Virginia, to knock her out of the war. It was his firm conviction, Cornwallis reported to London, "that until Virginia is reduced, we cannot hold the more southern provinces; and that after its reduction, they will fall without much resistance, and be retained without much difficulty."

A call had gone out for the Assembly to meet at Richmond on May 7. In view of the circumstances, it is not surprising that relatively few members appeared on that day, not enough to constitute a quorum. Henry was one of those present. By the tenth a few more members had arrived and it was decided, quorum or no quorum, that because of "the approach of an hostile army," the Assembly should adjourn forthwith to Charlottesville, 100 miles to the northwest in the hills of Albemarle County, seemingly beyond the immediate reach of the British.

On May 20, ten days after the Assembly left Richmond, Lord Cornwallis joined forces with General Arnold along the James, crossed the river, and encamped in Hanover County. For a time, Cornwallis established his headquarters in Shelton's Tavern where Henry had so long lived. Deciding that he should first dispose of Lafayette and his men near Richmond, Cornwallis moved against them. Faced with a superior force that far outnumbered his, Lafayette retreated northward, with the British in pursuit. "The boy cannot escape me," Cornwallis confidently predicted, but the boy did. He continued his retreat until he met some Pennsylvania troops coming down under Major General Anthony Wayne, then faced about and started back to harass the British.

Failing in his pursuit of Lafayette, Cornwallis turned to plundering the country, capturing a valuable arsenal, which was in charge of Frederick William Augustus Henry Ferdinand von Steuben. An experienced Prussian officer, von Steuben had volunteered for service and become "the drill-master of the Revolutionary Army," establishing some much needed discipline in all ranks. As inspector general, initiating and effectively carrying out better measures to provide the tattered soldiers with food and clothing and on-time pay, a mighty morale-booster, Baron von Steuben contributed as much as any field officer to the victory of the Patriot cause.

While plundering the country around him, Cornwallis sent out two strong columns—one to reoccupy Portsmouth and keep the Tidewater under control; the other, consisting of Colonel Tarleton and his hard-riding dragoons, to gallop toward Charlottesville and surprise it, seize all of the legislature and Governor Jefferson, who lived nearby—a bold raid that all but succeeded. If it had, the immediate course of events would certainly have been changed.

Starting out, Colonel Tarleton, "a hunting leopard," stopped at Scotchtown and, according to tradition, rode his horse up the front steps and into the wide central hall, demanding the surrender of Patrick Henry, presumably thinking he still lived there.

Along the way, Tarleton surprised and raided other houses, capturing a number of prominent Patriots, taking some of them in their beds—among others, John Syme, Henry's half brother. Syme was a very homely man, notably ugly in his features, and when he was brought in his nightgown before Tarleton, it is said that the colonel, a scholarly man, remembering his Shakespeare, struck the attitude of Hamlet upon seeing his father's ghost and addressed Syme:

> Angels and ministers of grace defend us!
> Be thou a spirit of health, or goblin damned?

Riding through Louisa County, the dragoon column passed the Cuckoo Tavern. Watching behind a curtained window was Captain John Jouette. Suspecting the column's destination, Jouette jumped on a fast horse and sped away by back roads to alert Charlottesville —and just in time.*

On that same day, Jefferson rode from his home at Monticello to a high point on Carter's Mountain from where he could look down on Charlottesville and, with his spyglass, see what was going on there. Everything was quiet, nothing unusual. On his way home, he discovered that his walking stick, sheathing a thin sword, was missing and returned to the height to retrieve it—and it was well for him that he did.

Taking out his spyglass again, he saw Charlottesville swarming with Tarleton's dragoons in their bright distinctive white and green uniforms. Suspecting that dragoons might be waiting for him at Monticello, as they were, Jefferson did not return there but rode away with all speed along back roads to another of his estates, Poplar Forest, about sixty miles to the south. There he remained in virtual seclusion for some time, as Henry had done at Leatherwood after his last term as governor, for which both were criticized: They should not have withdrawn at a time of great crisis.

Jouette's alarm sent Assembly members to packing their papers and belongings, and they scurried away as fast as they could. Traveling in small parties, they made their way over the Blue Ridge Mountains into the Shenandoah Valley, to the frontier village of Staunton, where they had agreed to reassemble as quickly as possible. They were prepared to move farther west, to Warm Springs, if Tarleton's dragoons pursued them.

---

* On a motion by Henry, the Assembly soon voted to present Captain Jouette with "an elegant sword and a pair of pistols" for his dangerous dash to give a timely warning.

The report of the Assembly and the governor in full flight delighted Lord Cornwallis, and gave him new confidence about winning an early victory. All he had to do now was to catch that boy Lafayette.

The interruptions in legislative proceedings occasioned by the move from Richmond to Charlottesville, and then on to Staunton, left Jefferson in a rather anomalous position. His second term as governor had expired on June 2, while the Assembly was still in Charlottesville. Pressed with other problems, the House and Senate agreed to postpone electing a new governor for a few days. Before they got around to that, they had to flee to Staunton.

For various reasons, having been roundly criticized both for his actions and for his want of action in certain particulars, Jefferson was not eager to stand for re-election, it appears, writing Washington just before his second term expired:

> A few days will bring me that relief which the Constitution has prepared for those oppressed with the labors of my office, and a long-declared resolution of relinquishing it to abler hands has prepared my way for retirement to a private station.

At Staunton, the Assembly finally got around to electing a governor, after several weeks' delay. Three men were nominated–John Page, head of the Executive Council; Thomas Nelson, Jr., commander-in-chief of the Virginia militia; and Jefferson, who was not present, but more or less in hiding far away at Poplar Forest.

Jefferson had not formally withdrawn his candidacy, perhaps hoping that, without any effort on his part, he would be re-elected for a third term. That would be a vote of confidence, a vindication of his two administrations. He needed some mark of approval. Many assemblymen were severely criticizing him for not having joined them at Staunton. Some even accused him of cowardice, a charge that Jefferson deeply resented all his life, though he never offered any explanation of why he failed to join all the other leaders at Staunton when, at a moment of grave crisis, it was the seat of government and power in the state.

On the first ballot, the House and Senate chose General Nelson as Governor. Immediately, young Colonel George Nicholas, son of Treasurer Robert Carter Nicholas who had recently died, was on his feet to offer a motion, which was adopted:

> *Resolved,* That at the next session of Assembly an inquiry be made into the conduct of the Executive of this State for the last twelve months.

Colonel Nicholas submitted a bill of particulars on what the board of inquiry should look into, naming two delinquents "with acrimony" —General von Steuben, for not doing enough to protect the arsenal and other supply depots in his charge; and Governor Jefferson, for "not having made some exertions which he might have made for the defense of the country" at the time of General Benedict Arnold's expedition up the James to raid Richmond.

Nicholas' motion, virtually a motion of censure, was seconded by Patrick Henry. From this time dates the personal and political estrangement of Jefferson and Henry. Always very thin-skinned about criticism, Jefferson held Henry chiefly responsible. Certainly, Nicholas' motion would not have been offered, and the Assembly would not have passed it, if Henry had objected, for at that time he was master of the House.

In any case, Jefferson never forgave Henry and, down the years, began to belittle him and slur him on every occasion, denouncing him publicly and privately as almost a fraud as a lawyer, a sharper in business dealings, an irresponsible statesman with vaulting dangerous ambitions, and "mean and rotten-hearted" as a person. Henry never descended to such stupid ill-natured personal remarks about Jefferson, or any other, so far as is known.

When offering his board of inquiry resolution,* Colonel Nicholas "gave notice that he would . . . move to have a Dictator appointed" for the country as a whole. "General Washington and General Greene are talked of," one of Jefferson's friends informed him. Another wrote:

> When Mr. Nicholas sat down, Mr. Henry addressed the chair; he observed it was immaterial with him whether the officer proposed was called a Dictator, or Governor with enlarged powers, or by any other name; but surely an officer armed with such powers was necessary to restrain the unbridled fury of a licentious enemy, and concluded by seconding the motion. . . .
>
> After a lengthy discussion, the proposition was negatived.

Though Nicholas' dictatorship motion was lost, Henry and those at Staunton agreed that the powers of Governor Nelson and his Executive Council should be strengthened and greatly enlarged. They were to have absolute command and direction of all state forces and resources. They should take any steps necessary to make the militia more effective. They could suspend writs of *habeas corpus* in the

* The inquiry into Jefferson's administration did not come up till the war was over, and the matter was quietly dropped.

case of those trying to impede military operations by discouraging men to enlist, or by encouraging the enlisted to desert. Those suspected of doing this could be summarily hanged. The last issue of paper money was to be accepted as legal tender—without any questions, evasions, or complaints.

At the same time, the Assembly adopted an appeal to the national Congress for "instant effectual aid" to help Virginia in her "distressed situation." Drafted by Henry, the plea was a wail from the heart:

"We want men, money, arms, and military stores. We call for these in the utmost amount that the ability of Congress can possibly furnish." The sufferings of Virginians "compel us to make the demand, and justice ensures a compliance with it on the part of Congress."

If national affairs were in such bad shape that sufficient Continental forces could not be sent by land or sea, then, said the appeal, with the sentence underlined, *"we think it high time to call upon our European Allies and Friends for their most strenuous exertion."* Congress should immediately ask them for "those aids which are so essential to our preservation, and which it is their true interest to afford."*

Unknown to worried Virginians and most Americans, substantial aid from abroad was on the way. A large fleet of warships and troop transports had sailed from France under the command of the Comte de Grasse. Putting in at Santo Domingo in the French West Indies, de Grasse wrote from there to inform Washington that late in August he would sail north to engage the British in and around Chesapeake Bay.

Still confident of early success, Lord Cornwallis had the ground cut from under him by an order from his commander-in-chief, the latest in a series of stupendous blunders by the British high command. Watching activities in Washington's camp just north of the city of New York, General Sir Henry Clinton decided that the Americans were about to attack Manhattan, and ordered Cornwallis to detach a number of his troops and ship them to New York for its defense.

Cornwallis was advised that, for the interim, he should march down from the Piedmont to Tidewater and there establish himself at some port where he could maintain communications by sea with New York and receive supplies from there. Moving down, Corn-

---

* For a proposal that Henry allegedly made at the Staunton Session, see Appendix F (p. 487).

wallis shipped from Portsmouth the troops demanded of him and then moved up the York River to Yorktown, which he began to fortify.

Informed of this by Lafayette, having received de Grasse's message that a large fleet bearing 3,000 soldiers was heading for the Chesapeake, Washington decided on a bold plan. It turned out to be a stroke of genius. Making a feint toward Staten Island, to keep General Clinton worried and his forces pinned down, Washington sheered off and marched his American-French army toward the south as rapidly as possible, arriving in Williamsburg in mid-September. De Grasse had arrived, landed his troops, and gained command of Chesapeake Bay, bottling up Cornwallis' few ships in the York River.

Now having about 17,000 troops, almost half of whom were French, Washington soon advanced some ten miles to lay siege to Yorktown. With his force outnumbered two to one, Cornwallis had to abandon his outer line of fortifications, which enabled the Americans to bring up cannon and mortars to batter the inner lines. They soon assaulted and captured two strong redoubts on the British left flank; counterattacks failed to displace them. In desperation, Cornwallis prepared to ferry his troops across the York to the northern bank, but very rough weather prevented that venture. Next day, recognizing that he was hopelessly caught in a trap of his own devising, wishing to avoid futile bloodshed, Cornwallis began negotiations under a flag of truce, and on October 19, 1781, he and his 8,000 men laid down their arms.

It is a commentary on British ineptitude during the whole Revolution that, a week later, General Sir Henry Clinton, finding that he had been duped by Washington, arrived off the mouth of Chesapeake Bay with a large fleet bringing strong reinforcements. Learning of Cornwallis' surrender, he turned about and sailed back to New York, soon being replaced as commander-in-chief—and about time. It was Clinton who had let Burgoyne down at Saratoga.

Suddenly, to everybody's surprise, the war was over, with Americans triumphant. Just four months before, in the latest and worst of many crises, Virginia leaders had been fleeing pell-mell for their lives. The British War Minister had thought the rebellion as good as suppressed. American victory, won against apparently hopeless odds, seemed to be a miracle at the time—and it still does.

The debacle at Yorktown brought down the tottering ministry of Lord North, who finally resigned as he had long wanted to do, having become very dubious about the chance of winning the American war after Burgoyne's defeat at Saratoga four years before. In resigning, Lord North offered George III some good advice, perhaps the best advice he ever gave him.

The King had been telling Lord North time and again: "I can never suppose this country so far lost to all ideas of self-importance as to be willing to grant American independence; . . . giving up the game would be total ruin." Britain would fall "into a very low class among the European states." Lord North's parting advice to the King was that he had better give up the "game" or there would be "total ruin."

Late in February, 1782, the House of Commons drew up an Address to the Crown, urging His Majesty to agree "that the war might no longer be pursued for the impracticable purpose of reducing the American people by force." The majority in the House regarded the Address as so urgent and important that it should not be delivered through usual channels. Rather, they should go to St. James' Palace, as a body, and present the Address in person.

At the Palace, they were ushered with elaborate ceremony into the Royal Presence—and there standing next to the King on his right hand, arrayed in all the splendid trappings of a British major general, was Benedict Arnold! Lord Surrey and many others who had come to make the presentation regarded Arnold's presence as "an insult to the House," being so incensed that they talked of offering a motion of censure.

Having read the Address, the King hemmed and hawed. He finally said, speaking in generalities, that he would take such measures as seemed good to him. Quite dissatisfied with his evasive response, the Commons immediately adopted, with little opposition, another motion stating "that the House would consider as enemies to His Majesty, and to the country, all those who should advise the further prosecution of offensive war on the continent of North America."

As chief minister, Lord North was succeeded by Lord Rockingham, who had led the movement in Parliament to repeal the Stamp Tax some sixteen years before. Rockingham opened negotiations with the American commission in Paris consisting of Benjamin Franklin, John Adams, John Jay, and Henry Laurens. Jefferson had been offered a place on the commission, but declined it.* Articles of peace were drafted and, after much devious maneuvering on all sides, the Treaty of Paris was signed on September 3, 1783.**

* For Jefferson's reasons for declining, see Appendix G (p. 488).

** For a most interesting account of the involved diplomatic chess game that went on at Paris, where the Americans were all but rooked, see *The Peacemakers* (1966), by Richard B. Morris.

Under the treaty, Britain recognized the independence of the United States and ceded to it all British claims to a vast territory—extending, roughly, from Maine through Georgia and westward to the Mississippi River; the upper St. Lawrence and the Great Lakes formed the northern boundary. In the south, Spain regained East Florida (the peninsula) and West Florida, a wide swath of territory that extended westward along the Gulf Coast to Louisiana; this strip of territory included the southern parts of what became the states of Alabama and Mississippi.

Americans were conceded the "right," which they had previously enjoyed, of fishing off Nova Scotia and Newfoundland, and of drying and curing their catch along any unsettled shore in Labrador and Nova Scotia. All private debts between Britons and Americans were "validated"; i.e., made legally collectible. It was agreed that Congress should "earnestly recommend" to the states that they restore the invalidated rights.

Though hostilities had ended, that brought no rest. Peace posed its own problems, as acute as those of the war. If independence were to have significance, something had to be done immediately to shore up the still shaky American republic, which was still experimental in form. It was still far from certain that the new nation, as loosely organized under the Articles of Confederation, could long survive. It was staggering under an enormous burden of debt, both domestic and foreign. Congress, the central authority, lacked power. People throughout the country were complaining that little or nothing was being done to ease hardships caused by the long and grueling war. The young confederated republic, it seemed to many, was on the point of falling apart. Symptomatic of the general discontent was an alarming agitation among the soldiers of the Revolution, a development that aroused serious concern in all quarters.

In the spring of 1783, before the peace treaty had been signed, a delegation representing a large number of officers complained to Congress about arrears in pay, failure to provide for pensions that had been promised, and unpaid food and clothing accounts. When Congress failed to do anything about these complaints, an anonymous protest addressed to all army officers began circulating in Washington's main camp at Newburgh, New York.

The address found grave fault with Congress because of its "coldness and severity," advised officers everywhere to take a strong stand and to suspect anyone counseling "more moderation and longer forbearance," and called upon the officers at Newburgh to meet the next day for the purpose of drawing up and adopting a "last remonstrance."

If that remonstrance was ignored, that would justify the army in openly defying Congress, which pointed to the alarming prospect of civil war. Certainly, under the circumstances, there was every reason to believe that masses of discontented Americans would support the army in its demands for immediate reform.

Many civilian as well as military leaders approved of the Newburgh proceedings. But General Washington did not. He forbade the special meeting called to draw up the "last remonstrance," proposing that the officers at Newburgh hold a regular meeting for the consideration of grievances a few days later. Appearing at this meeting, Washington condemned the violent tone of the Newburgh Address and counseled patience, expressing his confidence that Congress, given time, would redress all grievances.

Washington's plea carried the meeting, and the officers adopted resolutions affirming their patriotism and their confidence in Congress, and repudiating the "infamous propositions" set forth "in a late anonymous Address." This, however, did nothing to change the basic conditions out of which the officers' complaints had grown.

There were other problems, too. Even before the peace treaty had been signed, Henry rose in the House of Delegates to make several extraordinary proposals. One dealt with the policy to be adopted toward American Loyalists, or Tories, who had constituted at least a third of the population along the seaboard up to and even during the war.

These people, braving social ostracism, threats, and brutal physical violence, had stuck to their principles. Wishing to remain united with Britain, they had openly or covertly opposed the "heresy" of American independence.

Some of these had put themselves under the protection of British forces in the country, or fled abroad, and had their properties confiscated. Should these refugees be invited to return?

Other Loyalists had remained in the country and not been much molested—at least, not in Virginia—so long as they remained quietly at home and did not attempt to stir up opposition to the Patriot cause. Among such quiescent Tories were Washington's close friend and first patron, Lord Fairfax, and the former royal receiver-general, Richard Corbin, who had paid Henry for the powder Lord Dunmore had stealthily removed from the Magazine at Williamsburg. Were these quiescent Tories now to be banished?

No questions aroused more heat and animosity among people in all ranks. Yet Henry, breasting the tide of popular passion and prejudice, introduced measures to deal with these problems in a remarkably magnanimous and statesmanlike way, saying that as the war was over, let bygones be bygones.

To effect that, Henry introduced a bill to repeal a law passed during the Revolution that prohibited any contact with British sympathizers in Virginia, and forbade the admission of any avowed British subjects into the state. During the war, no one had been more strenuous and effective in combating Tories and their views than Henry. Now, to everybody's surprise, he was pleading that political antagonisms and personal animosities be quietly and decently buried so that the country could unitedly get on with its main business, which was to grow and prosper.

Henry's proposal about dealing leniently with the Tories aroused vehement protests, being received in the House "with a repugnance apparently insuperable." One of the strongest protesters was Henry's close friend, John Tyler, now Speaker of the House, who in committee turned to Henry and asked, "How he, above all other men, could think of inviting into his family an enemy from whose insults and injuries he had suffered so severely."

It was not a question of personal feelings and concerns, Henry replied. Rather, it was a matter of state and national interest. What the country most needed was men, he said in explaining his position. "People form the strength and constitute the wealth of a nation." He hoped to see the new republic, so extensive and so potentially rich, settled "by some process a little more speedy than the ordinary course of nature." And how could this be done? Addressing Speaker Tyler, he said:

> Open your doors, Sir, and they will come in . . . Encourage the husbandmen, the mechanics, the merchants of the Old World to come and settle in this land of promise. Make it the home of the skillful, the industrious, the fortunate, the happy, as well as the asylum of the distressed . . .
>
> The population of the Old World is full to over-flowing. That population is ground, too, by the oppressions of the governments under which they live.
>
> Sir, they are standing on tiptoe upon their native shores and looking to your shores with a wistful and longing eye . . . Tell them to come, and bid them welcome . . .

> But gentlemen object to any accession from Great Britain, and particularly to the return of the British refugees.
>
> Sir, I feel no objection to the return of these deluded people. They have, to be sure, mistaken their own interests most woefully, and most woefully have they suffered the punishment due to their offenses.
>
> But the relations which we bear to them and to their native country are now changed . . . Peace has returned and found us a free people. Let us have the magnanimity, Sir, to lay aside our antipathies and prejudices, and consider the subject in a political light.
>
> Those are an enterprising moneyed people. They will be serviceable in taking off the surplus produce of our lands, and in supplying us with necessaries during the infant state of our manufactures. Even if they are inimical to us in point of feeling and principle, I can see no objection, from a political view, in making them a tributary to our advantage. . . .

Henry concluded his argument by saying: "As I have no prejudices to prevent my making this use of them, so I have no fear of any mischief that they can do us."

"Afraid of them!" he exclaimed, straightening himself up to his full height and speaking slowly, quietly, but with great intensity of tone. "Shall we who have laid the proud British Lion at our feet now be afraid of his whelps?"*

Henry carried his resolution and then introduced another one quite as controversial and unpopular. He proposed the repeal of all laws prohibiting trade with Britain in articles of any kind. Henry's arguments on this were "beyond all expression eloquent and sublime," as admitted even by those who initially were most strongly opposed to the measure. Said Henry:

> Why should we fetter commerce? . . . Let her be free as air. She will range the whole creation and return on the four winds of Heaven to bless the land with plenty.

This resolution did not pass, but Henry soon introduced a somewhat similar measure that was adopted by the Delegates after a

* When professor of law at William and Mary, the first college professorship of the kind in the country, it is said that the scholarly George Wythe used to cite to his students the last two paragraphs of this speech by Henry as a happy example of how to use figures of speech that "unite the beauty of decoration with the effect of argument."

majority had come around to his view, with results beneficial to Virginia as it struggled to build up its economy. For one thing, it enabled Virginians to dispose profitably of their vast surplus of tobacco, their principal money crop.

Another problem relating to finance came up. During the last years of the war, Virginia had paid her soldiers in certificates that, so it was promised, would later be redeemed at face value in cash. Many poor soldiers, distressed and in debt, needed money immediately, not in some unspecified future, and they fell a prey to speculators who began buying up their certificates at enormous discounts. Deciding that something had to be done to stop this exploitation of the soldiers' needs, Madison drafted a bill and showed it to Henry, asking if he would support it. Henry said yes, but as there was no further conversation about the matter then or later, Madison feared that Henry "had forgotten the circumstance."

When the bill was introduced, Madison looked "with an anxious eye" to where Henry sat, "upon which the latter arose and addressed the House." On this occasion, said Madison, Henry was "particularly eloquent," speaking in a voice that reminded him "of a trumpeter on the field of battle calling the troops to a charge." The "trumpeter" carried the House with him and the audience, too.

Sitting in the public gallery was a chief speculator in soldier certificates. In the great hush that fell after Henry's speech, this man exclaimed in a voice audible to all: "That bill ought to pass!"

And the bill did pass, unanimously, which often happened when Henry exerted his full powers in advocating a measure. As Washington once remarked, not altogether approvingly, all Henry had to do was to say, "Let this be Law, and it is Law." Jefferson and others kept bills they favored off the floor if they had reason to believe that Henry might speak against them. They would wait until he was "out of the way," as he was now and again because of recurring malarial fevers.

But Henry, even when present on the floor, was far from being always successful, experiencing strong opposition and several defeats on proposals he offered during these years. A troublesome problem continued to be the laws regulating religious and ecclesiastical affairs.

Up to the Revolution, as noted earlier, Virginia had a state-supported official church—the Church of England. No other had been tolerated during the first century of settlement. Later, when the reins were loosened a bit, ministers of Dissenter congregations—

Presbyterians, Baptists, Quakers, Methodists, and others—were allowed to preach, but only after they had applied and been granted a license to preach by the General Court, all of whom, Crown-appointed, were stout Anglicans. When Dissenter ministers declined to apply for a license, saying they had no need of one to exercise their right "to preach the word of God," and went on preaching, they were fined, or jailed, or both, as the law stipulated.

The law also stipulated that no marriage was "lawful" unless the ceremony had been performed by a properly ordained Anglican parson, or by a Dissenting minister holding a license. This law raised legal questions about inheritance, property rights, and other related matters. Shortly after independence, the Assembly had passed, with Henry's strong approval, an "act declaring what shall be a lawful marriage." This act declared that a marriage performed by any Dissenting minister was "lawful"; the law was made retroactive to validate all such marriages previously made.

At the same time, the Assembly exempted Dissenters from contributing to the support of the Established [Anglican] Church, and there was to be no more governmental interference with the "exercise of any mode of worship."

Henry was delighted with all this, even if it was only a start toward carrying out what he had put into his draft of the sixteenth article in the Virginia Declaration of Rights: "That all men are equally entitled to the free exercise of religion, according to the dictates of conscience. . . ."

Final comprehensive reform of the laws dealing with religious and ecclesiastical matters was slow in coming, being put off from year to year, in part because of the war, but largely because of delaying tactics by a small but still influential conservative group, led by eminent Anglican laymen, who wished as little reform as possible. The chief of this group was Edmund Pendleton, spokesman for the interests and patrician desires of the Tidewater lords. At the time of the Revolution, so Jefferson estimated, Virginia had a population of 400,000, almost half of whom were slaves. Of the 200,000 white freeholders, two thirds had become Dissenters by the time of independence, according to Jefferson. If so, the Anglican third still remained, as became obvious, a powerful group.

In 1779, while Henry was serving his third term as governor, Jefferson introduced in the House a broad and well-conceived measure entitled a Bill for Establishing Religious Freedom in Virginia. But little happened immediately on the fundamentals of the bill, partly because Jefferson could no longer actively work for the cause in the House, soon leaving the legislature on his election as governor to succeed Henry. After two years as chief magistrate, and a brief retirement from public affairs, Jefferson returned to the House and again began mustering support for his proposals.

Jefferson was greatly assisted in this by the petitions that continued to flow into the Assembly from Dissenter organizations urging absolute separation of Church and State. On the other hand, the Episcopal Church sought to retain as much as possible of the special status, property rights, and many privileges and perquisites it had enjoyed up to the Revolution as part of the State-sponsored and tax-supported Church of England.* Virginia Episcopalians sought a general tax for the support of religion, which would help pay the salaries of their parsons formerly carried on the tax rolls. They also sought an act allowing their church to become a corporate body under the civil law. Such an incorporation act would enable it to gain private title to public property–churches and chapels, parsonage houses and glebe lands–bestowed on it at taxpayers' expense under the old regime.

At the Assembly session in the spring of 1784, a bill for the incorporation of the Episcopal Church was introduced. But after two days of debate, the House decided to postpone consideration of the question till the next session. "Extraordinary as such a project was," wrote James Madison, "it was preserved from a dishonorable death by the talents of Mr. Henry." A bill to levy an "assessment"–euphemism for tax–for the "support of religion" had been prepared, but "the friends of the measure did not choose to try their strength in the House."

* From the beginning, Virginia had been, as remarked before, a part of the see of the Lord Bishop of London. All directives about doctrine, ritual, and important ecclesiastical affairs came from him. Theoretically, the churches in all the American colonies were under his jurisdiction and command. But the writ of the Lord Bishop did not run in many of the colonies–and certainly not among the Pilgrims and Puritans of New England whose ancestors had fled their homeland and staked their lives in the wilderness to get away from the prosecutions, persecutions, and what they denounced as the "abominations" of the Church of England. To them, that church was anathema; Anglican worship was not permitted among them for generations.

Right after independence, all ties with the Church of England were abruptly cut. Virginia Anglicans began organizing themselves as the Protestant Episcopal Church, retaining Church of England doctrine, ritual, and mode of worship except in a few particulars. For one thing, the prescribed form of morning and evening prayers no longer ended with the supplication: "O God save the King."

Meeting again in the fall of 1784, the Assembly passed a bill "for the incorporation of all societies of the Christian religion which may apply for the same," a bill which had the strong support of Henry, who introduced a measure "to incorporate the clergy of the Protestant Episcopal Church." No other church sought incorporation. Indeed, all were strenuously opposed to the whole idea of incorporation, for that would again bring the State into Church affairs.

Henry's was a faulty bill and had to be amended. It was changed to read that not merely the clergy of the Episcopal Church were to be incorporated, but its lay officers as well, such as vestrymen and others. In short, the church apparatus as a whole was to be incorporated. The bill, as broadened by amendment, passed the House by a vote of sixty-two to twenty-three, but was soon repealed.

This move of the Episcopal Church, assisted by Henry, to entrench itself behind civil authority was a grave error, hastening the day when it would be stripped of the last of its special privileges inherited from the old order.

On the matter of tax support for organized religion, the Episcopal Church again was the only one in favor, all others being very much opposed. Again, Henry took the Anglican view, a strange position for one who had written the "freedom of religion" article into the Virginia Declaration of Rights. With Henry taking the lead, the House adopted by a vote of forty-seven to thirty-two a report favoring "a moderate assessment for the support of the Christian religion," and named Henry as chairman of the committee to draft an appropriate bill for carrying out the recommendation.

The bill, largely Henry's handiwork, was given an educational twist to make it more palatable. It proposed a small levy on all taxable property for the support of "teachers" (ministers) of the Christian faith. Each taxpayer might designate the particular church or religious society to which he wished his money to go. Taxes raised from those not particularly interested in any church, or in religion at all, were to be used as a start toward establishing and maintaining free county public schools, none of which existed as yet, nor would for some time.

Quite apart from the questions of principle and policy involved, this scheme would have been an administrative nightmare. What amounts should go to whom? Fortunately, Henry's "offspring," in Madison's phrase, was stillborn.

It is doubly strange that Henry at this time should have advocated a new special religious tax, for he had just been pleading, successfully, against any immediate increase in regular taxes, arguing that "the people should have some repose after the fatigues and privations to which they had been subjected during a long and arduous struggle for Independence."

Henry's attitudes toward settling religious affairs in Virginia on a new foundation are difficult to account for. His more apologetic biographers argue that, if wrongheaded in the measures he sponsored, he was at least righthearted; that he feared a decline in "virtue" if church services were not held regularly with enforced public support; that he was, fundamentally, a deeply religious man.

This last is true, in a sense. Though never much of a churchgoer, preferring his own solitary meditations, Henry had become down the years increasingly interested in Christian theology and ethics, particularly as expounded by Lord Bishop Joseph Butler in his *Analogy of Religion, Natural and Revealed, to the Course and Constitution of Nature.*

This thoroughly Anglican work was aimed at reassuring believers and, hopefully, at silencing Deists and other freethinkers who, like Jefferson and many more in America, Britain, France, and elsewhere, were highly skeptical about miracles, pillars of fire, apparitions in the night, disembodied voices, and other manifestations of "revealed" religion, whether Christian or not.

Another volume Henry came to prize was *View of the Internal Evidence of Christianity,* a popular and shallow book by an English layman, Soame Jenyns, who had served in the House of Commons for some time, later becoming a member of the Board of Trade which the colonies had found to be such a nuisance.*

Henry had copies of Jenyns' book and Butler's *Analogy* printed at his own expense, and never drove the circuit of county courts without taking along copies. These he would give to friends, clients, and judges, "desiring them at the same time not to take him for a traveling monk." In his last years, as he became increasingly devout, he used to gather his family around him every Sunday evening and read passages from these books, or from Sherlock's *Sermons,* or from the Bible, before taking up his violin to lead them in singing an Anglican hymn or two.

But Henry's religious feelings and beliefs, whatever they were, do

---

* Jenyns is chiefly remembered for the terrific blasting he got from the great Dr. Samuel Johnson who reviewed in the *Literary Magazine* his *Internal Evidence* and his *Free Inquiry into the Nature and Origin of Evil.*

not explain or condone the want of political and philosophical judgment shown in the attitude he took in the long bitter struggle to achieve in Virginia a complete separation of Church and State. In that struggle he turned his back on his old friends the Dissenters—Baptists, Presbyterians, and others—by advocating what they had long fought and were most opposed to.

First introduced in 1779, Jefferson's comprehensive bill for establishing religious freedom had been left hanging for years. Finally, in 1785, at the persistent urging of the Dissenters, the bill came to a vote and was passed. The substance of the bill read:

> No man shall be compelled to frequent or support any religious worship or ministry whatsoever, nor shall be enforced, restrained, molested or burthened in his body or goods, nor shall otherwise suffer on account of his religious opinions or beliefs; but that all men shall be free to profess, and by argument to maintain, their opinions in matters of religion, and that the same shall in nowise diminish, enlarge, or affect their civil capacities.*

Henry did not participate in the final vote on Jefferson's sweeping reform because he had ceased being a member of the House, having again been chosen as governor, being elected "without competition or opposition." It would appear from this that his critics and opponents were only too happy to join in honoring Henry, for his elevation removed him from the floor of the House where his influence was enormous. Why Henry agreed once more to take a post with little power and of no particular significance remains a question. From the start he had been complaining about the "phantom" power of the governor in the Commonwealth.

---

* Jefferson was as proud of his authorship of this bill as of the Declaration of Independence. In his last years he expressed a wish to be remembered for three things. The simple stone shaft over his grave at Monticello bears this inscription which he composed:

> Author of the Declaration of American Independence
> of the Statute of Virginia for Religious Freedom
> and Father of the University of Virginia

Curiously, both Jefferson and John Adams died on July 4, 1826, the fiftieth anniversary of independence, for which both had worked so hard.

XXIV
Governor Again

. . . heartily tired of the bustle we live in here

—PATRICK HENRY

Henry was elected to serve his fourth term as governor late in 1784, succeeding Benjamin Harrison, who had served three consecutive terms and was therefore ineligible to succeed himself.

Before settling down in office, Henry returned for a time to his home in the remote Leatherwood country, there to arrange his private affairs and make plans to bring his family back with him to Richmond. While in the House, he had gone back and forth between Leatherwood and Richmond whenever a legislative session was called. But it was the duty of a governor to live in or near the capital the year round, which necessitated a change of residence. It may be that one reason why Henry accepted the governorship was that he was getting bored with the lonesome life at Leatherwood. Certainly, his sprightly young wife Dorothea would have welcomed a change from backwoods isolation to the bustle and pleasures of town life, even though Richmond was not yet much of a town.

Rather recently founded, it had been improved a bit since becoming the state capital in 1780. But there was not yet a capitol building, as in Williamsburg, to house the two legislative chambers and government offices, though a new State House was under construction. Government offices were placed in small rented buildings.

There was nothing to compare with the accommodations and social amenities offered by the Raleigh Tavern, Wedderburn's, Mrs. Purdie's, and other celebrated taverns and hostelries in old Williamsburg. Nor was there a Governor's Mansion. In want of any town house suitable to serve as the official mansion, the Henrys decided to live some fifteen miles west of Richmond, establishing themselves at Salisbury, an ample house, the pleasant seat of a 16,000-acre estate.

Just installed at Salisbury, Henry received a welcome letter. It came from an old friend, Richard Henry Lee, currently the president of Congress. Before and during the Revolution, Henry and Lee had been political allies and personal friends, usually seeing eye to eye on major matters. In the postwar period, however, they had frequent sharp clashes on issues. This caused an estrangement that neither of them liked. Lee took the first step toward breaking the ice, writing to Henry:

> We are placed now, I think, pretty nearly in the same political relation under which our former correspondence was conducted; if it shall prove agreeable to you to renew it, . . . I shall be happy to contribute my part.

Henry was delighted, replying immediately that resumption of their "friendly intercourse" would be not only a great personal pleasure, but of benefit to Virginia through their exchange of "so much advantageous information." A long letter of such information soon came from Lee, detailing his views on the many grave problems in national affairs as seen by him as head of Congress. Henry had expressed the hope that the renewal of their friendship and cooperation would continue "with no interruption," and so it did. The two worked closely together down the years, though they had differences of opinion about which they argued emphatically from time to time.

While Lee's was welcome, other letters coming to the governor about this time were not. One brought the sad news that his mother Sarah had died. She had had a great influence on Henry in his early years. After her husband's death a decade before, his widow Sarah disposed of their Mount Brilliant farm and went to live with her daughter Jane, wife of Patrick's friend from boyhood, Samuel Meredith. Informing Patrick of his mother's death, Meredith wrote:

"She has been in my family upwards of eleven years, and from the beginning to the end of that time, it most evidently appeared to me that it was one continued scene of piety and devotion, guided by such a share of good sense as rendered her amiable and agreeable to all who were so happy as to be acquainted with her.* Never did I know a Christian character equal to hers . . . What an honor it is to all those that claim descent from such a person. . . ."

Soon after this, Henry had occasion to write to a close friend and political supporter, his wife's cousin and Martha Washington's brother, Bartholomew Dandridge, to tell him:

> I heartily lament with you the death of Mr. Burbridge, so far as it is rational to lament the exchange of a bad world for one where sorrow never enters.
>
> This particular time is remarkable for the death of my near connections. My dear and ever beloved mother died six or eight weeks ago, my brother William two weeks, and my only surviving aunt ten days.
>
> Thus is the last generation clearing the way for us as we must shortly do for the next.

Within three months, his young friend Dandridge suddenly died, and also his mother, so that Henry and his wife, a Dandridge, had more personal losses to lament.

Henry, with many other Virginians, had long been interested in stimulating commerce in the state by improving and extending navigation on its larger rivers. He was a sponsor and shareholder in a dredging and canal project along the Roanoke River in southwestern Virginia.

Early in 1785, the Assembly chartered two canal companies—the Potomac and the James River—and voted to give fifty shares in each to General Washington, partly in acknowledgement of his many services, partly because he had long been interested in extending water traffic westward, but no doubt principally because it would be good business to have Washington's name listed among the sponsors and shareholders in these enterprises.

As governor, Henry wrote to Mount Vernon to inform Washington officially about this. In a long letter of explanation, Washington replied that he was both honored and embarrassed. On becoming commander-in-chief, he had told Congress, he said, that he would not accept any

* Sarah (Winston) Henry appears to have remained as charming as she was on the day long ago when, as "Widow Syme," she had so entranced that rich and experienced worldling, Col. William Byrd II, when he chanced to stop by for a visit at Studley Farm.

payment for his services, and it had become his "fixed determination . . . never to hold any other office under Government by which emolument might become a necessary appendage . . . Nor to accept of any pecuniary acknowledgement for what had passed." His mind, he said, had never swerved from that resolution.

"The Act, therefore, which your Excellency enclosed, is embarrassing to me. On the one hand, I should be unhappy if my non-acceptance of the shares should be considered as a slight of the favor (the magnitude of which I think very highly of) or disrespectful to the generous intention of my country. On the other hand, I should be equally hurt if motives of pride, or an ostentatious display of disinterestedness, should be ascribed to the action . . . whilst I am indulging the bent of my inclination by acting independent of rewards for occasional & accidental services." Washington concluded by asking Henry for his "frank & full opinion of this matter."

After further correspondence, Washington followed a suggestion made by Henry, asking the Assembly "to permit me to turn the destination of the fund vested in me from my private emolument to objects of a public nature." His request was granted. His shares and profits paid on them were to be held and distributed by Washington as directed "by deed during his life, or by his last will and testament." Washington later indicated his choices: the Potomac shares were to help found a projected national university in the District of Columbia; the James River shares went to the Liberty Hall Academy in Lexington (Virginia), soon renamed Washington Academy, later incorporated as Washington College and again incorporated in 1871 as Washington and Lee University.*

While corresponding with Washington about the canal company shares, Governor Henry was visited unexpectedly by a man having a novel idea about improving navigation—John Fitch, who had a proposition to make. He would build a vessel driven by a steam engine if he could find sufficient funds to finance the venture. Born in Connecticut, now a man in his early forties, Fitch had led a hard and luckless life as a watchmaker, as a gunsmith during the Revolution, then as a surveyor in the western wilds. Out of his surveying and travel notes, and from other studies, Fitch had drawn and engraved a useful map of the vast Northwest Territory.

Henry was deeply interested in the commercial opportunities offered by the invention of a steamboat. Against the anticipated sales

* The Lee being the great Confederate general, Robert E. Lee, who became president of the institution right after the Civil War.

of Fitch's map, which the state government would help promote, the governor on his own responsibility advanced the inventor £350 under a bonded promissory note. This note bore the provision that when and if Fitch had received the equivalent of "one thousand French crowns" from subscriptions for his map, his debt should be canceled if "the said Fitch, . . . within nine months after said subscriptions are received, . . . exhibits a full proof of the practicality of rowing a vessel by the force of a steam engine in the Commonwealth of Virginia . . . in a vessel of not less than one ton burthen."

Fitch went to work on his experiment. But as Henry's subsidy was not enough, he looked elsewhere for support. Two years later, in the summer of 1787, he successfully demonstrated on the Delaware at Philadelphia a forty-five-foot vessel driven by oars operated with steam power. He later launched larger steamboats that were even more successful.

But Fitch was ahead of his time. After many rebuffs and reverses both in this country and abroad, he took his life with poison in a small Kentucky tavern in 1798. Impoverished, discouraged, and desolate, he had written in his Journal not long before: "The day will come when some more powerful man will get fame and riches from *my* invention; but nobody will believe that poor John Fitch can do anything worthy of attention."

In the summer of 1807, twenty years after Fitch had demonstrated on the waters of the Delaware near Philadelphia his first successful steam-powered vessel, Robert Fulton's *Clermont,* a side-wheeler, took off from New York on a run up the Hudson to Albany, about 150 miles. The round trip took five and a half days, because of ceremonial stops along the way; the actual running time was about half that. Fitch had taken out patents on his steamboat, and later there were lawsuits about this. Fulton, it was charged, had gained unauthorized access to Fitch's papers, his studies and drawings, and had used them in developing his *Clermont*. However that may be, the first successful steamboat enterprise was on the Hudson, and not in Virginia waters, as Governor Henry had hoped in helping to finance such a venture.

As governor, Henry became deeply involved in another matter. By the peace treaty with Britain, the United States had been ceded, except for Spanish East and West Florida, all of the territory south of Canada from the Atlantic to the Mississippi, almost half a continent. By royal charters, early colonial grants, and Indian treaties, a number of states—Virginia, Pennsylvania, New York, Connecticut, and Massachusetts—had conflicting claims to parts of this vast and still sparsely settled territory. Land companies and other real estate promoters were anxious to obtain from these states a title to western lands so that they might exploit them. Speculators hoped to make a fortune by carving out of the wilderness farms and house lots to sell to pioneering settlers who, for the most part, were poor but hardy folk moving westward to acquire virgin soil in the hope of bettering their lot.

The states involved, after acrimonious bickering and tedious negotiation, finally agreed to cede their claims north of the Ohio River to the central government which was to protect and develop the territory for the benefit and account of all members of the Confederation. Congress soon created the Northwest Territory—a vast domain, still largely wilderness, extending from the Pennsylvania line west to the Mississippi, and from the Ohio River north to the upper Great Lakes.*

But in relinquishing the lands she claimed north of the Ohio, Virginia retained title to the land she held south of the river—a wide swath of territory stretching from the Atlantic, over the mountains, and through the Kentucky country to the Mississippi. North Carolina's boundaries also extended from the ocean, through the Tennessee country, to the Mississippi.

In 1784, North Carolina ceded the Tennessee country to the central government, on condition that Congress accept the cession within two years. This alarmed the growing settlements in the Tennessee wilderness. The pioneers there were convinced that Congress, with so many other pressing problems on hand, would not accept the cession within the time prescribed. Meantime, they would receive no care or protection from either North Carolina or the central government.

Consequently, the Tennessee settlers decided to set up a government of their own, the independent State of Franklin—inside the Confederation if accepted; outside, if necessity required.** This se-

---

* Out of this huge expanse were later carved the states of Ohio (1803), Indiana (1816), Illinois (1818), Michigan (1837), Wisconsin (1848), and a considerable part of Minnesota (1858)—a reminder of how recent has been a great part of American development. Relatively, our transcontinental empire was born only yesterday.

** The State of Franklin was short-lived. John Sevier, born in Virginia, was its governor. Tried for treason in North Carolina and convicted, he escaped. Later pardoned, he became the first governor of Tennessee when it was admitted as the sixteenth state of the Union in 1796.

cessionist movement gave ideas to settlers in Virginia's western lands. There were meetings in Kentucky about cutting off from Virginia, and from the Confederation as well, if there was no other way to assure better protection and obtain a larger voice in administering local affairs. Some in the trans-Appalachia counties talked of joining the new State of Franklin.

These separatist movements deeply disturbed Henry as governor. In regard to the Virginia secessionists, he recommended to the Assembly that it take "lenient measures in order to reclaim our erring fellow-citizens." At the same time he proposed a law, which passed, making it high treason to set up inside Virginia boundaries separate independent government without the express consent of the Assembly. The bill authorized the governor to call out the militia and take whatever other steps were necessary to suppress any such attempt with utmost rigor. It was one thing for the colonies to separate from Britain, but a spirit of separatism on United States soil was something else again, not to be tolerated.

To quiet western settlers, the Virginia Assembly decreed that the huge county of Kentucky should be divided into several smaller counties, each with its courthouse for the settlement of local legal and administrative matters, and that the whole area, once it had sufficient population, would be free to apply for admission as a new state of the Union,* a policy that Henry strongly supported.

As governor, Henry played a ceremonial part—a happy role for him—in honoring two men he highly admired. While he was still in the House, the Virginia legislature had appropriated funds by unanimous vote to have sculptures done of General Washington and the Marquis de Lafayette. Jefferson, who was our ambassador in Paris, was commissioned to engage a capable artist to carry out the work. Guided by his usual good taste and acumen, Jefferson approached Jean Antoine Houdon, one of the best-known sculptors of his day, who had already carved busts or statues of Catherine the Great of Russia, Molière, Diderot, Rousseau, Voltaire, Benjamin Franklin, and would later, at the command of Napoleon himself, do a statue of the Emperor in the nude, a curiosity still to be seen at Dijon.

Houdon was delighted with the idea of doing a life-size figure of Washington, so Jefferson informed Governor Henry, saying that Houdon "was so anxious to be the person who should hand down

---

* Kentucky was admitted as the fifteenth state of the Union less than a decade later, in 1792.

the figure of the General to future ages that, without hesitating a moment, he offered to abandon his business here, to leave the statues of kings unfinished, &c., to go to America to take the true figure by actual inspection and mensuration." Addressing him as "your Excellency," Jefferson asked Governor Henry to let him know if the ideas outlined in his letter varied in any point "from the wishes of the Executive or legislature." Jefferson was told by Henry to proceed along the lines he had laid out.

Arriving late in 1785, Houdon spent a few weeks at Mount Vernon in "mensurating" Washington and making a plaster bust of him which he could use as a model on his return to Paris. Two years later, the marble statue of Washington was completed and soon shipped to Virginia.

Meantime, Houdon had been working on two marble busts of the Marquis de Lafayette.* It was originally intended to present one of these marbles to the marquis. But there was a change in plans, and Governor Henry wrote to his friend that the bust intended for him was going to be a present from Virginia to the City of Paris. The gift was accepted and with fitting ceremony, placed prominently in the city's famed old municipal building, the Hôtel de Ville. The second bust, wrote Henry, was to be set up in the state capital near Washington's statue.

Expressing thanks for the "goodness" shown to him by Virginia, the marquis replied that the "situation of the other bust will be the more pleasing to me as . . . I shall be eternally by the side of, and paying an everlasting homage to, the statue of my beloved General." This bust by Houdon and his Washington statue have long stood, facing each other, in the rotunda of the State Capitol in Richmond.**

As his second consecutive term as governor (his fifth in the office) drew toward a close, Henry let it be known among his many friends and supporters in the Assembly that he did not wish "to stand in the nomination for the ensuing year." Warmly thanking the Assembly for the "past honours" conferred on him, he explained that "a variety of circumstances concur to render retirement necessary for me."

One circumstance was that he was tired of being governor, a largely

---

* Henry named one of his sons Fayette.

** Near the building, in Capitol Square, rises the Washington Monument, unveiled in 1858. On top of the sixty-foot column is a bronze statue of Washington on horseback. Around the wide stone base of the column stand bronze figures, nine feet tall, of Patrick Henry, George Mason, Thomas Jefferson, John Marshall, Thomas Nelson, and General Andrew Lewis.

ceremonial office with little power and influence. He wished to be back on the floor of the House where he could lift his voice in affecting the decision to be taken on a major national issue now boiling up. Also, he was worried about family finances.

As governor, Henry had performed his ceremonial duties well and in appropriate style. "With respect to his family, they were furnished with an excellent coach (at a time when these vehicles were not so common as at present)," said Spencer Roane, writing in 1814. "They lived as genteelly, and associated with as polished society, as any Governor before or since had done. He entertained as much company as others, and in as genteel a style,* and when at the end of two years he resigned his office, he had greatly exceeded his salary, and was in debt, which was one cause that induced him to resume the practice of law."

Just before he left office, Henry had written to his sister Anne that he and his wife were "heartily tired of the bustle we live in here. I shall go to Hanover to land I am like to get from Gen. Nelson; or if that fails, towards Leatherwood again. My wife has five very fine and promising children"—Dorothea Spotswood, Sarah Butler, Martha Catherine, Patrick, and Fayette.

Of his six children by his first marriage, most were no longer living at home. His three daughters had married well and had comfortable homes of their own. But Henry still had to provide for the support and education of his younger sons. These he had placed in Hampden-Sydney College, a Presbyterian institution about eighty miles southwest of Richmond in Prince Edward County, near the hamlet of Kingsville.

Now fifty, often ill, in debt, having a large and growing young family, Henry had reason to be concerned about increasing his income. He was not poor, by any means. He owned much developed and undeveloped land, many slaves, and had other assets, but none negotiable at the moment. His greatest asset remained his brilliance as a trial lawyer.

On resigning as governor, Henry did not, as he had first planned, go back to Hanover County, which was home territory for him, nor did he return to live at distant Leatherwood. Rather, he established himself in Prince Edward County where he bought a 1,700-acre farm for £2,100, paying for it in slaves and trade of other lands.

* It is curious that no guest left an account or even a revealing note about any dinner party or other social affair at Henry's whether in his early or late years.

Henry chose this spot, where he was to live for six years, for several reasons. First, it was near the Prince Edward County Courthouse at Farmville, and law business in this and neighboring counties was certain to be livelier than in remote and sparsely settled Henry County where Leatherwood lay. Second, Henry would be close to his sons who were attending Hampden-Sydney College not many miles away.

Shortly after the Henrys moved to Prince Edward County, a friend and neighbor stopped by. In the course of the conversation, Henry talked frankly about his money situation and the debts that worried him.

"Go back to the bar," said his friend, "your tongue will soon pay your debts. If you promise to go, I will give you a retaining fee on the spot." This he did, paying him £5, the first income Henry had received from the law since suspending his practice in 1774, more than a decade before.

But Henry was not retiring from the political world. He soon became deeply and passionately engaged in debate on a question as important as any in our history—a debate that strikingly drew forth his full powers.

XXV
The Philadelphia Document

Mr. Henry's disgust exceeds all measure . . .

—JAMES MADISON

The United States, as organized under the Articles of Confederation, had somehow managed after a long line of reverses to win the Revolution and independence. That seemed almost a miracle at the time, to be attributed more, perhaps, to the sheer incompetence, both political and military, of the British administration under Lord North, than to the "flaming Spirit of 1776."

During the war, with energies concentrated on achieving victory in the field, there had been little or no disposition to advocate a change in the structure of the national government. But now that peace had come and urgent daily pressures were relieved, a growing number came to feel that it was time something were done to better the operations of the central government by expanding its powers and responsibilities. As set forth in the Articles of Confederation, the Constitution was a weak and rickety structure, obviously needing repair and perhaps some additions.

Authority centered in Congress, which was at once the legislature and the executive of the nation. In its executive functions, Congress operated largely through standing committees and special committees named to deal with specific matters. But there was no single chief executive responsible for seeing that policies and directives were carried out. Congress had a president, to be sure, elected from session to session. But he was little more than the presiding officer, speaker of the house; besides, presidents were changed frequently, occasionally from year to year.

All states, whether large or small, had an equal vote in Congress—one state, one vote. Many felt that this was unfair; that smaller states carried a disproportionate weight in decisions. For want of strong and balanced power in national affairs, deliberations of Congress came to be regarded by many as so inconsequential that now and again—sometimes for weeks on end—no business at all could be conducted for want of a quorum of states—seven for ordinary business, nine for major policy matters. Vital questions were left hanging as Congress went on debating issues year after year, without coming to any decision.

The weakness of the central government made itself painfully evident in many areas. For one thing, Congress had no authority to regulate and control interstate commerce, or foreign commerce in important respects. To protect their farmers and infant industries against "foreign" competition, the semisovereign states* were busily erecting more and ever higher tariff barriers against one another.

Only Connecticut-made hats could be sold in Connecticut, where a flourishing trade in felt toppers had been established in Danbury, known down to our day as "the Hat City." New York levied duties on firewood brought in from Connecticut, on vegetables from New Jersey. Other states placed similar levies on imports of anything produced outside their boundaries.

Forgetting his impassioned plea for free trade—"Fetter not commerce," he had said. "Let her be free as air"—Patrick Henry turned provincial and proposed that Virginia prohibit bringing into the state—no matter what the outside source—any pork, beef, distilled liquor, butter, cheese, tallow, or tallow candles, and that heavy duties be imposed to discourage the import of coal, iron, and cordage. The Assembly did not go to the length that Henry proposed but, after some compromises to conciliate various interests, raised considerably the tariffs on strong drink and many other items.

Trade with foreign nations presented a different but rather similar problem. The country, to increase both its export and import trade,

---

* The basic clause in the Articles of Confederation read: " . . . each state retains its sovereignty, freedom, and independence."

had great need of negotiating advantageous commercial treaties with Britain, Holland, France, Spain, and other countries. Under the Articles of Confederation, Congress had the right, theoretically, to negotiate such treaties. But practically, the right was useless. As European diplomats asked, what was the point of negotiating a commercial treaty with the central government so long as individual states could exercise their right to tax and regulate foreign trade as they pleased?

South Carolina, for instance, levied a general import duty of 2.5 per cent on foreign goods, with a much higher rate for certain articles. Massachusetts prohibited the export of any goods on British ships, and doubled the tonnage duty on goods brought in on other than American ships. Similar discriminatory laws in regard to duties, port fees, and other charges were enforced in New York, Pennsylvania, Rhode Island, New Hampshire, Maryland, and North Carolina.

Another problem was basically commercial. At the approach of the Revolution, and during it, laws had been passed relieving American debtors from legal obligations to pay the money they owed merchants and others in Britain. By the terms of the peace treaty, these laws were to be repealed. Congress recommended such action to all the states, but few immediately responded.

Charging violation of the peace treaty, Britain took a firm stand, declaring that the question about collection of private debts had to be settled before she would evacuate her military-trading posts in the interior—at Oswego, Niagara, Detroit, Vincennes, Michilimackinac, and other garrison points on United States soil. These points were centers of agitation and intrigue, with British traders and military officers stirring up the Indians to resist the ever increasing westward migration of Americans. All of these posts still flying the British flag were thorns in the flesh of the Union.

Another of the Confederation's disabilities, perhaps the greatest, was Congress' want of authority to raise any revenue directly for the support of the central government in carrying out its scattered functions. When Congress passed an appropriation bill for a specific purpose, all it could do was to request the states to contribute their allotted share of the general assessment. As states did not like taxing their own people for general purposes, it is no wonder that many of them were slow in paying.

In 1781, Congress asked the states for $8,000,000 to meet emergency needs. At the end of three years, less than $1,500,000 of this assessment had been paid in. On occasion, as New Jersey did in

1786, a state flatly refused to contribute a penny toward carrying out a Congressional decision of which it disapproved. As a consequence, in want of ready money, the central government was often delinquent in meeting its debts and obligations, which hurt American credit and prestige. It seemed to a growing number on both sides of the Atlantic that a young nation unable to pay its domestic and foreign bills when due could not long endure.

Hoping to bring some order into the Confederation's chaotic fiscal affairs, Congress created early in 1781 the office of Superintendent of Finance, naming to that post Robert Morris of Pennsylvania. Born in England, brought to this country by his family when in his early teens, Morris rose to become a partner in the firm of Willing & Morris, a Philadelphia countinghouse (bank), one of the country's largest and strongest.

Hailed as "financier of the Revolution," Morris initiated economies and straightened out tangles in the country's fiscal affairs. He succeeded in obtaining, on very shaky security, loans from France and other countries. He organized the Bank of North America to bolster public credit. He raised the $1,400,000 that enabled Washington to undertake the campaign that led to American triumph at Yorktown.

When funds in the national Treasury were low, as was often the case, Morris raised money on personal notes, for his credit was better than the government's. When he stepped down from office late in 1784, he left in the Treasury not a staggering deficit, as almost everybody anticipated, but a surplus. It was only $21,000, a trifling sum, but still a surplus.* This offered a gleam of hope, but did nothing to change the basic disabilities of the Confederation.

In 1784, while in the Virginia House of Delegates, Henry expressed serious concern about the weakness of the central government. He saw "ruin inevitable" unless something were done to give that government "compulsory process" under which it could collect the revenue owed it by delinquent states; Virginia should set "a bold

---

* The Founding Fathers, in their naïveté about the mysteries of higher finance, could not possibly have comprehended how a national government, as ours today, can continue to operate on accumulating deficits of billions year after year. Or why the ceiling on the national debt had to be raised recently (1967) to well over $300,000,000,000 so that the government might issue more paper —greenbacks, Treasury notes, bonds, and other IOUs—to pay its current bills.

Some are still as much mystified by this as the Founding Fathers would have been.

example" by proposing that Congress be given such compulsory power. In considering the general problem, Henry talked particularly with two colleagues in the House, James Madison and Joseph Jones.

"I find him strenuous for invigorating the federal government," wrote Madison, "though without any precise plan." The three of them agreed that Madison and Jones "should sketch some plan for giving greater power to the federal government," and Henry would "support it from the floor." Nothing immediately came of this initiative.

Later, early in 1786, Virginia took the lead in suggesting a convention of all the states to consider the whole question of interstate commercial relations. Nine states agreed to the proposal, but when the convention met at Annapolis some months later, only five states were represented–Virginia, Delaware, Pennsylvania, New Jersey, and New York. Realizing that little could be accomplished under the circumstances, the delegates–there were only a dozen of them–appointed Alexander Hamilton of New York to draft an address calling upon the states to send commissioners to a new convention to be held in Philadelphia on the second Monday in May, 1787.

This Convention was to discuss not only commercial problems but all other matters required "to render the constitution of the Federal Government adequate to the exigencies of the Union." But almost five months passed before Congress cautiously endorsed the plan, expressing the opinion that it was "expedient" to hold a convention "for the sole and express purpose of revising the Articles of Confederation and reporting to Congress and the several legislatures such alterations and provisions therein."

Virginia was among the first to act on the proposed Constitutional Convention and five days after Henry had stepped down as governor, announcing his intention to retire to private life, the Assembly elected a delegation. Listed in order of the number of votes each received, the delegates were Washington (unanimous), Patrick Henry, Edmund Randolph,* John Blair, James Madison, George Mason, and George Wythe.

Notified of his election by Governor Randolph, Henry did not immediately reply, waiting more than two months before writing to the governor: "It is with much concern that I feel constrained to decline acting under this appointment." Henry's seat was offered to

---

* Who had succeeded Henry as governor. Jefferson was not on the list because he was abroad, being ambassador to France, a post he held for four years.

a former governor, Thomas Nelson, who declined to accept because of ill health, and then to Richard Henry Lee, who also declined, the seat finally going to a respected physician, one of Jefferson's friends, Dr. James McClurg. Washington, too, had at first declined his appointment, but was prevailed upon by friends to change his mind.

Henry's decision not to serve in the Convention seemed "ominous" to Madison and others wishing to fashion a stronger central government. Governor Randolph, for one, refused to accept "no" as Henry's final answer. "I have essayed every means to prevail on him to go" to the Convention, he told Madison, "but he is peremptory in refusing" on the ground of being "distressed in his private circumstances."

It soon became evident that Henry was "distressed" by something much more than his private cares. He sniffed in the wind the smell of some unsavory political business.

Two years earlier, in 1785, Don Diego de Gardoqui had arrived as Spain's envoy to the country and came bringing some tempting offers that hopefully might open the way for negotiating a mutually profitable trade treaty. Americans were particularly interested in settling one bothersome question—navigation rights on the lower Mississippi River.

For most of its length, the river was the boundary between American and Spanish territories, and inhabitants in both navigated its waters freely. But Spain held both banks of the river for several hundred miles above its mouth on the Gulf of Mexico. From New Orleans, a thriving river and ocean port, the Spanish controlled all shipping coming into the river and passing out of it. They had a territorial right to do so and, as usual in such cases, made the most of it, favoring Spanish commerce by imposing restrictions, levies, and tolls on foreign shipping.

This pained Americans, particularly those with interests higher up the river. These wished free and unhampered navigation all the way to the Gulf. Otherwise, settlement and development of the then American West would be discouraged. It would be much easier and cheaper to float its produce down the river and out into the Gulf than to cart it laboriously eastward over the mountains.

Gardoqui had come from Madrid with strict instructions that, in negotiating a trade treaty, he was not to yield an inch on Spain's rights along the lower Mississippi. In authorizing John Jay, Secretary of Foreign Affairs, to negotiate with Gardoqui, Congress strictly instructed him that he was "particularly to stipulate the right of the

United States . . . to free navigation of the Mississippi." As things stood, it was scarcely surprising that secret negotiations went on for more than a year with nothing settled.

Then came a turn that caused widespread alarm and threatened to split the Union in two. To break the deadlock in negotiations, Secretary Jay recommended to Congress that his instructions be changed. Congress went into secret session and by a vote of seven to five, after bitter debate, decided that Jay might "forbear" in pressing the Mississippi issue. The vote on the forbearance question divided along sectional lines, with the New England and Middle States in favor,* while the Southern states were opposed—particularly, Virginia and North Carolina which had western territories along the Mississippi.

At the same time, Congress revoked an order that no treaty was to be concluded until the text had been submitted to Congress for consideration. On this new basis, negotiations with Gardoqui were resumed, again in private. But reports of what was going on soon leaked out. In the summer of 1786, when his last term as governor was running out, Henry received a firsthand report in a very long letter and postscript from his young friend James Monroe, writing from New York where Congress was sitting. Monroe began by saying that he wished he could write in code, but the Virginia delegation had lost its "cypher," so that he would have to risk his "communication without that cover." Detailing the "intrigue" used by Jay to have his instructions changed, Monroe exploded:

> This is one of the most extraordinary transactions I have ever known, a minister negotiating expressly for defeating the object of his instructions, and by a long train of intrigue and management seducing the representatives of the states to concur in it.

With the support of seven states—not the nine required to conclude a treaty—Jay was working to obtain trade concessions from Spain, "upon condition on our part of a forbearance of the use of the Mississippi for twenty-five or thirty years." Nor was this the only subject of consequence to which he wished to call Henry's attention:

> Certain it is that committees are held in this town of Eastern

---

* The seven voting in favor were New Hampshire, Massachusetts, Rhode Island, Connecticut, New York, New Jersey, and Pennsylvania, all of whom were interested in promoting Atlantic seaboard trade.

> men, and others of this state, upon the subject of a dismemberment of the states east of the Hudson from the Union, and the erection of them into a separate government. To what lengths they have gone, I know not, but have assurance as to the truth of the above position, with this addition to it, that the measure is talked about in Mass. familiarly, and is supposed to have originated there. . . .

Though a break of the Union should be avoided at all costs, Monroe went on, "yet I do consider it as necessary on our part to contemplate it as an event which may possibly happen . . . It should be so managed (if it takes place) either that it should be formed into three divisions or, if into two, that Penna., if not Jersey, should be included in ours."

Monroe assured Henry that his information was "founded on authentic documents" and expressed a hope that "these intrigues are confined to a few only, but by these men I am assured they are not." In saying that he wished very much to have Henry's "sentiments upon these important matters," Monroe added:

> You will necessarily consider this as under an injunction of secrecy and confide it to none in whom the most perfect confidence cannot be reposed. If any benefit may result from it, I should have no objection to your presenting it to the view of the [Governor's] Council. Of this, you will judge.

As governor, Henry evidently confided the substance of Monroe's letter not only to his Council, but to others as well, for the Virginia Assembly soon expressed a strong unanimous opinion about the Spanish business:

> *Resolved,* That the common right of navigating the river Mississippi and of communicating with other nations through that channel ought to be considered as the bountiful gift of Nature* to the United States as proprietors of the territories watered by the said river and its eastern branches, and as moreover secured to them by the late revolution.**

The next resolution, stronger than the first, declared that a sacri-

---

* A quite far-fetched application of the doctrine of "Natural" rights.

** This was not true; the Revolution had "secured" no rights for Americans in Spain's territory at the mouth of the Mississippi, or in Spanish territories elsewhere.

fice of the rights of any one part of the Union to the "supposed or real interests" of another part would be "a flagrant violation of justice, a direct contravention of the end for which the federal government was instituted. . . ."

Therefore, the resolutions concluded, the Virginia delegates in Congress should be instructed "in the most decided terms" to oppose any attempt made "to barter or surrender the right of the United States to the free and common use of the river Mississippi." Such barter or surrender would be "a dishonorable departure" from the basic principle of the Confederation, would provoke the "just resentments and reproaches of our western brethren whose essential rights and interests would be thereby sacrificed and sold." The whole business tended to undermine the Union itself by "destroying that confidence in the wisdom, justice, and liberality of the Federal Councils which is so necessary at this crisis."

It was in the shadow of these developments that Henry decided not to go to the Constitutional Convention at Philadelphia. Whether it would have been better if he had chosen to go is a question. Madison surmised—rightly, it appears—that Henry's motive was a desire to remain free and uncommitted, so that he could take what stand seemed best to him on whatever proposals came out of the convention. Madison, writing from Richmond, told Washington:

> I am entirely convinced from what I observe here that unless the project of Congress for ceding to Spain the Mississippi for twenty-five years can be reversed, the hopes of carrying this State into a proper federal system will be demolished. Many of our most federal leading men are extremely soured by what has already passed.
>
> Mr. Henry, who has been hitherto the champion of the federal cause, has become a cold advocate, and in the event of an actual sacrifice of the Mississippi by Congress, will unquestionably go over to the opposite side.

In another letter at this time, addressed to Jefferson in Paris, Madison wrote: "Mr. Henry's disgust exceeds all measure, and I am not singular in ascribing his refusal to attend the convention to the policy of keeping himself free to combat or espouse the result of it, according to the result of the Mississippi business, among other circumstances."

Writing again to Jefferson a little later, Madison said that he despaired of creating a stronger central government "at the present crisis," that he hoped only for "commercial reform," that he was not even hopeful about that. The situation was serious, he explained:

> You will find the cause in a measure now before Congress, . . . a proposed treaty with Spain, one article of which shuts the Mississippi for twenty or thirty years.
>
> Passing by the other Southern states, figure to yourself the effect of such a stipulation on the Assembly of Virginia, already jealous of Northern politics . . .
>
> Figure to yourself its effect on the people at large on the Western waters who are impatiently awaiting for a favorable result to the negotiations with Gardoqui, and who will consider themselves sold by their Atlantic brethren.
>
> Will it be an unusual consequence if they consider themselves absolved from every federal tie, and court some protection for their betrayed rights?*

Another advocate of a stronger central government, John Marshall, informed a friend at this time that "Mr. Henry, whose opinions have their usual [i.e., overpowering] influence, has been heard to say that he would rather part with the Confederation than relinquish the navigation of the Mississippi."

Several weeks behind schedule, the Constitutional Convention held its first session in Philadelphia late in May, 1787. The opening had to be delayed because so many delegations took their time about coming, evidently feeling no great urgency about the meeting. Not all states were represented. Rhode Island, radical and agrarian in its general views, ignored the Convention, regarding it as a trap set by large landed proprietors and rich conservative urban families to advance their special interests.

The delegates, in the main, were rather young men, most of whom had yet to make a name for themselves–and many never would. The members' average age was forty-four. Out of the younger group came a number of the most influential leaders at the Convention, notably –James Madison, aged thirty-six; Alexander Hamilton of New York, thirty-two; Charles Pinckney of South Carolina, forty-one; Gouverneur Morris of New York, thirty-five.

The Convention included some stalwarts of the Revolution: George

---

* The people "at large on the Western waters" were talking (1) of their own independent concerted assault to drive the Spanish from the lower Mississippi, or (2) of coming to some separate accommodation with them regardless of what Congress did.

Washington, aged fifty-five; Benjamin Franklin, now in his eighties, chief executive of Pennsylvania and the Convention's oldest member; George Mason and George Wythe of Virginia; Robert Morris, recently the Confederation's Superintendent of Finance, and the learned James Wilson, both of Pennsylvania; John Dickinson, formerly of Pennsylvania, now of Delaware; Roger Sherman of Connecticut, a tart shrewd Yankee, once a shoemaker by trade, democratic in his views, an influential member of the First Continental Congress and a signer of the Declaration of Independence; and John Rutledge, active in the initial Continental Congresses and South Carolina's first governor after independence.

Other "old standards," for various reasons, were not present: Patrick Henry, as noted; his friend Richard Henry Lee, who followed Henry in declining to serve; Thomas Jefferson, who was in Paris as ambassador; John Adams, ambassador in London; John Jay of New York, who as Secretary of Foreign Affairs was busy negotiating about the Mississippi and other matters with the Spanish minister, Gardoqui; Sam Adams and John Hancock of Massachusetts.

On a very rainy Friday morning, May 25, 1787, the Constitutional Convention finally got down to work with only seven states—a bare majority—represented. Five more delegations would soon arrive. Washington was elected unanimously to be president of the Convention and, though not a parliamentarian, presided very well, with skill and tact. He was evenhanded in his rulings from the chair and imperturbable even in the sharpest clashes of opinion on points of order and procedures of debate. Everybody trusted the cool judgment of "old Stone Face," as some called him without any want of affection or respect.

Having organized itself and chosen its officers, the Convention decided to sit behind closed doors. All of its proceedings were to be kept as secret as possible. Nothing was to be said about them publicly. No member was to be a source of news about what had been discussed, or who had said what on any issue, or how the vote had gone on particular questions. This pledge of secrecy was well kept. Armed sentries were placed around the State House and in the corridor by the locked doors behind which the Convention was sitting.

On one occasion, a delegate lost the notes he had been taking on an important matter. Found outside Convention Hall, the notes were turned over to Washington who kept them in his pocket till the end of the day's meeting. When a motion to adjourn was made, Washington rose as chairman and spoke rather angrily:

> Gentlemen, I am sorry to find that some one Member of this Body has been so neglectful to the secrets of the Convention as to drop in the State House a copy of their proceedings, which by accident was picked up and delivered to me this morning. I must entreat Gentlemen to be more careful lest our Transactions get into the News Papers, and disturb the public repose by premature speculations.
>
> I know not whose Paper it is, but there it is [throwing it down on the table]; let him who owns it take it!

With that, Washington bowed, picked up his hat, "and quitted the room with a dignity so severe that every Person seemed alarmed." It is almost gratuitous to add that no one claimed the "Paper."

Learning of the secrecy rule, Jefferson wrote from Paris to denounce it as abominable. The people of the country had the right to know what was being done at a meeting where their delegates were discussing and deciding matters of vital concern to all. But Jefferson's friend and disciple, young James Madison, one of the Convention's most active members, defended the secrecy provision in making a point that seems wise under the circumstances. At a time when men were groping and feeling their way toward solutions for many complicated problems, trying to reconcile sharp conflicts of class and sectional interests, there would be more freedom of discussion, argued Madison, if delegates could exchange ideas and debate them off the record, so to speak.

In its first major action, the Convention decided not to devote its time, energy, and thought to amending the Articles of Confederation, but rather to designing a whole new constitutional framework, having come to the opinion "that a national government ought to be established consisting of a supreme Legislative, Judiciary, and Executive."

Reflecting the views of the larger states, Virginia submitted a plan drafted largely by Madison. It provided for a president, a supreme court and inferior United States courts, and a legislature of two chambers. In both chambers, state representation would be based on population.

Objecting to this, New Jersey proposed another plan. It spoke for the smaller states, insisting that in at least one legislative chamber all states should have an equal vote, as in Congress under the Articles of Confederation. Connecticut offered a compromise and, after spirited debate, the Convention hammered together, in a remarkably short time, a new frame of government that has weathered well the strifes and strains of almost two centuries in a rapidly changing world.

The smaller states won their point; each state was to have equal representation–two seats–in the United States Senate. Members of this body were to be elected for six-year terms on a rotating schedule, with each state deciding how its senators should be chosen.

Larger states got what they wanted in having representation in the lower house based on each state's white population, plus three-fifths of its slave population–a provision which gave Southern slave-holders disproportionate weight in the House of Representatives. All members of the House stood for election by popular vote every two years.

Given ample powers, the sole responsible executive head was to be a president, elected every four years by a cumbersome Electoral College system. Provision was made to establish a United States supreme court, with subsidiary circuit and district courts. Congress was to have the authority to raise revenue for national purposes, and to regulate both interstate and foreign commerce.

When in final form, a copy of the proposed constitution was duly engrossed, and delegates asked to sign it. Of the forty-two members present, three refused to do so–Elbridge Gerry of Massachusetts, and two Virginians, the veteran George Mason and young Governor Edmund Randolph, the latter pronouncing the document "odious." The Convention sent the engrossed copy to Congress, which decided to transmit copies to the state legislatures. These were to call special conventions to ratify or reject the new constitutional plan.

As soon as he returned from Philadelphia to Mount Vernon, Washington sent copies of the plan to influential friends. One of the first went to Patrick Henry with a short but friendly note, in which Washington remarked that he was sending the plan without making any observations about particular points:

> Your own judgment will at once discover the good and the exceptionable parts of it . . . I wish the constitution which is offered had been more perfect; but I sincerely believe it is the best that could be obtained at this time. And as a constitutional door is opened for amendments hereafter, the adoption of it under the present circumstances of the Union is in my opinion desirable.

Henry took a month to ponder the document before replying to thank Washington for sending a copy, and to express his high appreciation of all that Washington had done in "the arduous Business of the late Convention." Having made a deferential bow, Henry went on:

> I have to lament that I cannot bring my mind to accord with the proposed Constitution. The concern I feel on this account is really greater than I am able to express. Perhaps mature reflections may furnish me reasons to change my present sentiments into a conformity with the opinions of those personages for whom I have the highest reverence.
>
> Be that as it may, I beg you will be persuaded of the unalterable regard & attachment with which I shall ever be, dear Sir,
>
> Your obliged & very humble Servant,
>
> P. Henry

This exchange of letters, though friendly enough, at least formally, cooled for a time the warm personal relations and the shared political views that had existed between the two men for more than two decades, ever since 1765 when Henry first took a seat in the House of Burgesses and, as the youngest and newest member, offered his Stamp Tax Resolutions, which Washington supported and highly praised.

Among American leaders of great influence, Henry was not alone in casting a critical eye at the proposed new national constitution. In his letter to Henry, Washington had admitted that the constitution as drafted left much to be desired. But nothing better could be obtained under the circumstances, he argued. Obvious imperfections could later be corrected under the provision for making amendments. In his attitude Benjamin Franklin was, to say the least, ambivalent and ambiguous, remarking:

> I agree to this Constitution with all its faults, if they are such, . . . because I expect no better, and because I am not sure that it is not the best.

Jefferson, being in Paris as our ambassador there, did not participate directly in the debate. But he was keeping a sharp eye on developments at home and had serious misgivings about much of what was going on there. He agreed that the Articles of Confederation needed to be strengthened, extended, and amended.

But why, he asked, had the Convention at Philadelphia assumed the authority—which it did not have—to scrap the Confederation entirely and set out on the uncharted course of writing a whole new constitution for the infant republic. As much good could have been accomplished if three or four provisions had been added to the Articles of Confederation, "the good old and venerable fabric which should have been preserved, even as a religious relic."

And why the extreme secrecy about the proceedings at Philadelphia? As if the people were not entitled to know what had been said and done there by the delegates whom they had chosen to speak for their various and often conflicting views and interests!* And why the great rush in pushing for ratification? The electorate should not be asked to adopt or reject the proposed constitution at the drop of a hat, so to speak. The country was at peace with the world and moving along reasonably well, as well as could be expected under the circumstances. There was no sudden emergency, no great crisis demanding immediate attention.

If it were deemed desirable to make a massive shift in the nation's foundations and on them hammer together a whole new framework of government, why not spend a little time in examining the design, considering alternatives, exploring all possibilities?

After the subject had been thoroughly explored and discussed throughout the country, would it not then be a good idea to issue a call for a second national constitutional convention which could review and improve the work of the first? Patrick Henry was already of this opinion.

Soon after the Philadelphia convention issued its document, a long series of articles and essays—in all, more than seventy of them—began appearing in New York newspapers in praise of the proposed constitution and urging prompt ratification. The articles pointed to the acknowledged defects of the Confederation, stressed the need of a strong national government based firmly on representative republican principles, and that had been provided for.

The essay series was signed by one "Publius," but it soon trans-

---

* Few details about the course of discussion and decision at Philadelphia were known until more than a half century later, not till 1840, with the publication of the elaborate notes James Madison had made at the Convention and kept secret, having decided that his notes were not to be published till after his death.

The official Journal of the Convention had been published previously, some twenty years before, in 1819. But the Journal was not very informative, being rather cursory in its reporting, with few illuminating details about the clashes of opinion on the floor and the political horse-trading that resulted in the compromises that were reached.

pired that Publius was fifty-one parts Alexander Hamilton, twenty-nine parts James Madison, and five parts John Jay. The newspaper articles, plus another eight essays, were collected in book form and quickly published in two volumes as *The Federalist,* which became the Bible of those favoring ratification.

Madison sent a copy to his friend Jefferson in Paris. The latter was greatly impressed, praising the *Federalist* as the "best commentary on the principles of government ever written." But he still had some serious reservations about the constitution the *Federalist* was advocating. He declined, however, to take sides with the anti-Federalists. He did not wish to have a party label pinned on him. As he told a friend at this time, "I never submitted the whole system of my opinions to the creed of any party whatever, in religion, in politics, or in anything else where I was capable of thinking for myself. If I could not go to heaven but with a party, I would not be there at all"—a rather curious remark by one who soon founded a major political party that is still going strong.

In October, 1787, about a month after the Philadelphia Convention adjourned, the Virginia legislature met in Richmond. Henry took his seat in the House of Delegates as a representative of Prince Edward County where he was presently living. The main item on the agenda was the issuance of a call for the election of delegates to a state convention which would decide whether Virginia chose to ratify or reject the Federalist constitution.

Some suspected that Henry might make a move to block such a call, but their fears were groundless. Henry highly favored the holding of a convention of popularly elected delegates. In the campaigns for the nomination and selection of delegates, there would be the widest possible public discussion of the questions at issue, and in that field Henry was confident that, as always, he could hold his own.

Virginia was in no hurry about holding its convention, putting off its opening date for more than six months. This gave both Federalists and their opponents plenty of time to marshal and line up their forces. Henry took the lead in encouraging and organizing the Antis, with such success that it alarmed Madison. As chief architect of the Federalist plan, Madison did not wish to see his brainchild knocked in the head in Virginia, and perhaps elsewhere. In Virginia, "the first raptures in favor of the constitution were excessive. Every town resounded with applause." But now the tide was turning, as Madison noted with deep concern:

> What change may be produced by the united influence and exertions of Mr. Henry, Mr. Mason, and the Governor [Edmund Randolph], with some pretty able auxiliaries, is uncertain . . .
>
> Mr. Henry is the great adversary who will render the event precarious. He is, I find, with his usual address, working up every possible interest into a spirit of opposition.

Federalists charged Henry with "excessive zeal" in electioneering, but this was *ex parte* criticism. They were being quite as zealous, but in a different and more genteel manner. While Henry was addressing large crowds of the "common sort" on courthouse greens, in roadside taverns, and elsewhere, the Federalists were going quietly about visiting the big houses to make certain of the support of friends and numerous relatives, most of whom were men of affluence and influence, long active in state and local affairs–judges, lawyers, merchants, large landowners.

Henry well knew from experience the power of such economic, professional, and family connections, particularly in Tidewater and the older counties, but he was sanguine. In a letter to a friend in New York, where the Antis were very strong under the leadership of George Clinton, who was serving his eleventh year as governor, Henry wrote:

> It is a matter of great consolation to find that the sentiments of a vast majority of Virginians are in unison with those of our northern friends. I am satisfied 4/5 of our inhabitants are opposed to the new scheme of government. Indeed in the part of this country lying north of James River, I am confident 9/10 are opposed to it.

Henry's estimate may have been high, but there can be no doubt that a large majority of Virginians were opposed to the new scheme of government. But the election of delegates to the state constitutional convention did not reflect this.

"Strange as it may seem," wrote Henry, "the members in Convention appear equal on both sides, so that the majority, which way soever it goes, will be small. The friends & seekers of power have with their usual subtlety wriggled themselves into the choice of the people by assuming shapes as various as the faces of the men addressed on such occasions."

On the first Monday in June, 1788, the convention convened in

Richmond, meeting in the largest auditorium in town, the new Academy, built as part of a planned American-French college, a project later abandoned. The hall was not large enough to accommodate at one time the many people who came from all parts of Virginia to follow with eager attention the proceedings that would shape the future of the state and the nation, and the vital interests of all.

On the floor of the convention were 170 delegates, elected by eligible voters. As in choosing members for the House of Delegates, the election had been conducted along county lines, as elections had been in Virginia almost from the founding of the old House of Burgesses in 1619. At the constitutional convention, each of the eighty-four counties, regardless of size or population, was equally represented with two delegates. This gave disproportionate weight to the older, richer, but now smaller and less populous counties in Tidewater and the lower Piedmont, where "aristocrats" had their big houses and large ancestral estates.

However that was, voters in each county had had the opportunity to hear and assess the arguments of the Federalist and Anti candidates, and decide which of them should be sent to the convention to represent the county's majority view.*

By the time the Virginia convention met, eight states had accepted what shall hereafter be called the Philadelphia document. It is improper to call it "the constitution." As yet, it was nothing of the sort. It was merely a proposal, a proposition, and there was spirited opposition to it in a number of states, including two of the largest and strongest, Virginia and New York. If these two voted against the proposition, it seemed very doubtful that the plan for a federated union could be put into effect, no matter what the other states did.

Delaware had been the first to assent to the proposition, thereafter styling itself "the First State." Its convention voted unanimously for acceptance, pleased with the provision that Delaware, one of the smallest and weakest states, would have in the United States Senate representation equal to that of the biggest and richest states. This provision was also responsible to a considerable degree for bringing about favorable action by conventions in New Jersey, Georgia, South Carolina, Maryland, and Connecticut.

In Pennsylvania, by devious means and some very forceful arm-

---

* There were two noncounty delegates—one for the town of Williamsburg, another for Norfolk. This was in accord with a traditional pattern, for each of the towns had long held a seat in the lower legislative chamber.

twisting, the Federalists of Philadelphia and smaller commercial towns, though representing only a minority view in the state, blocked Anti-Federalist moves for amendments and delay, and succeeded at length in having the state convention accept the proposed constitution by a vote of forty-six to twenty-three.

In the Massachusetts convention it was estimated that the Federalists were outnumbered four to three, but won over some of the opposition by agreeing that, in the act of ratifying the Philadelphia document, the convention should strongly recommend the immediate adoption of amendments by the new government. This move satisfied Sam Adams, who had been very dubious about the whole business, and swung the convention to ratification, though by a very narrow margin, 187 to 168.

New Hampshire had held a convention, with Anti-Federalists in control. The Federalists, facing defeat, persuaded the convention to recess for four months, on the pretext that a small state like New Hampshire should wait to see what the larger states were doing.

The Rhode Island legislature, controlled by the Antis, declined to call for a state convention and decided instead to hold a popular referendum. Angry about this change in recommended procedure, Federalists boycotted the referendum, with the result that Rhode Islanders in a large turnout voted more than ten to one against ratification. Anti sentiment was strong in North Carolina, but no action had yet been taken there.

With eight states having ratified, another was needed before the new scheme of government could go into effect, and it appeared that the vote in Virginia would be pivotal. The Old Dominion might become the ninth state to ratify, but there was no certainty about that. The question would be decided only after weeks of sharp brilliant debate. Nowhere was the Philadelphia document as critically examined and searchingly analyzed as in Virginia.

Most of the outstanding men in the state had seats in the Virginia convention when it met in the Academy at Richmond. Among the Federalist leaders were such seasoned stalwarts as Edmund Pendleton, George Wythe, John Blair, and George Nicholas, and such younger ones as James Madison, John Marshall, Bushrod Washington (the general's nephew), and General Henry ("Light Horse Harry") Lee, a hero of the Revolution, later the father of General Robert E. Lee.

Besides Henry, who was chief and most active member of the

group, the Anti leaders included the great and highly respected George Mason and his brother Thomson, Benjamin Harrison (a member of the First Continental Congress, signer of the Declaration of Independence, and former governor of Virginia), Colonel William Grayson (earlier an aide-de-camp to General Washington, later one of the state's two representatives in the first session of the United States Senate), Judge John Tyler, and James Monroe, now just thirty, who months before had written from New York to warn Henry of the talk going on among prominent New Yorkers and New Englanders about the desirability of breaking the Union and splitting it into North and South, with each following its own interests.

Richard Henry Lee, who had published strong arguments against ratification, was not at the convention, having declined to run as a delegate because he was ill—not that he was actually ill, but he had found that Richmond always made him ill. If Lee had been at the convention, his mere presence, his incisive argument, his Ciceronian eloquence, his personal charm and wide acquaintance among the delegates would have greatly aided the Anti cause.

Two other eminent Virginians were absent. Jefferson was still at the French Court as ambassador. Washington had not stood for election as a delegate to the convention, preferring to stay home at Mount Vernon and exercise his enormous influence from there. He had already become something of a *pater familias* not only in Virginia but throughout the country, and his every pronouncement was pondered. After a two days' visit at Mount Vernon, a friend reported that he had never seen Washington "so keen for anything . . . as he is for the adoption of the new scheme of government."

Washington had already struck the Antis a mighty blow. The latter, as a main line of strategy, were seeking to put off a vote on immediate ratification by advocating that the Philadelphia document, after full discussion in all the states, should be placed before a second national constitutional convention for consideration of the many amendments that Virginia and a number of states desired. Let there be an improved draft of a new scheme of government. In reply to a letter about this from his friend Charles Carter, a Virginia Grandee and ardent Federalist, Washington wrote:

> There is no alternative between the adoption of the constitution and anarchy. Should one state [Virginia], however important it may conceive itself to be, or a minority of the states, suppose that they can dictate a constitution to the majority,

> . . . they will find themselves deceived. Opposition to it is addressed more to passion than to reason.
>
> If another federal convention is attempted, the members will be more discordant than the last. They will agree upon no general plan.
>
> The constitution or disunion is before us. If the first is our choice, a constitutional door is open for amendments in a peaceable manner, without tumult or disorder.

No alternative "between the adoption of the constitution and anarchy . . ." It was either immediate ratification, or "tumult and disorder." These were strong words.

It seems fairly obvious that Washington's letter opposing those calling for another federal convention was written with an eye to publication. At any rate, it was published, and was widely read and discussed throughout the country, having a great impact upon those who had not yet made up their minds about ratification. Certainly, if the alternative were order or chaos, then they were for ratification, whatever their reservations.

Federalists had the strength to organize the Virginia convention. As president, they elected the venerable, imposing, and elegant Edmund Pendleton who, as chancellor, held the highest judiciary post in the state. Pendleton was a skilled experienced parliamentarian and a very able and persuasive debater–Jefferson once declared him to be the ablest man he had ever met in debate.

Pendleton and Henry had often been adversaries down the years, in political halls and in the courts, and now in the Academy they would have another resounding clash. Though formally polite, Henry disliked Pendleton for his conservative views and attitudes, and had never forgiven him for the part he had played in having Henry displaced as commander-in-chief of Virginia military forces as hostilities with Britain began.

XXVI
Anti-Ratification

Where is the Bill of Rights?
—PATRICK HENRY

With Pendleton presiding, the Virginia convention opened with a clash on a matter of organization and procedure. The Federalists had arranged for one David Robertson and his assistants to take notes on the proceedings in shorthand. Henry and other Antis were on their feet immediately.

Why this innovation? they asked. It had always been the practice at such conventions for the secretary and his staff to keep the minutes, and that was sufficient. The Antis suspected that the "shorthand gentlemen" were Federalist sympathizers, as they were, and not to be trusted. They might give a "fatal stab to a gentleman of the House from a perversion of his language." On a close vote, Robertson and his shorthanders were accepted.

After other preliminaries had been settled, George Mason rose and was the first to get the floor to speak on the main business. The new scheme of government should be subjected to the closest scrutiny. This subject, he said, "ought to obtain the freest discussion, clause by clause, before any general previous question be put; nor ought it to be precluded by any other question."

This proposal for clause-by-clause consideration of the Philadelphia document pleased Pendleton, Madison, and other Federalist leaders, and they happily assented to it. It gave them an advantage; they could play for time. What they had most feared was a broad frontal attack on the document as a whole, and that was not long in coming. Said Henry in the first of a number of brilliant general assaults, in a speech that deeply affected the members of the convention and the people in the crowded galleries:

> The public mind, as well as my own, is extremely uneasy at the proposed change of government . . . I wish to be thoroughly acquainted with the reasons for this perilous and uneasy situation, and why we are brought hither to decide on this great national question. . . .
>
> A year ago, the minds of our citizens were at perfect repose. Before the meeting of the late federal Convention at Philadelphia, a general peace and a universal tranquility prevailed in this country; but since that period, they are exceedingly uneasy and disquieted . . . If our situation be thus uneasy, whence has arisen this fearful jeopardy? It arises from this fatal system; it arises from a proposal to change our government . . .
>
> Sir, give me leave to demand, What right had they to say *We, the people?* Who authorized them to speak the language of *We, the people,* instead of *We, the states?* States are the characteristics and the soul of a confederation. If the states be not agents of this compact, it must be one great consolidated national government of the people of all the states.*
>
> I have the highest respect for those gentlemen who formed the [federal] Convention . . . But, sir, on this great occasion, I would demand the cause of their conduct. Even from that illustrious man [Washington] who saved us by his valor, I would have a reason for his conduct . . . That they exceeded their power is perfectly clear . . .
>
> The federal Convention ought to have amended the old sys-

* This was a sensitive point, and a telling argument. There was a widespread fear, particularly among the common people, that the new scheme would result in one great "consolidated" government that would intrude into not only state but local affairs. If ratification had been put to a nationwide popular vote, there is every reason to believe by the evidence that it would have been defeated. Henry was speaking for the popular side, for the majority of the people. The Federalists had to spend a lot of time in denying that a "consolidated" government could possibly result.

tem; for that purpose they were solely delegated. The object of their mission extended to no other consideration.*

This speech by Henry, delivered with logic and with such intense but controlled emotion, had a tremendous effect both on the convention floor and in the galleries. The Anti cause was beginning to soar and might well triumph.

The next speaker was Governor Edmund Randolph. He was young, tall, handsome, elegant in dress, gracious in manner, and a good speaker. There was great suspense in the convention hall as he rose, for no one knew what he was going to say. As one of the Virginia delegates at Philadelphia, the governor, along with his colleague George Mason, had refused to sign and thereby endorse the plan for a new government, denouncing the plan as "odious." The proposed constitution should not be accepted until it had been amended at a second national convention.

Washington and Madison had been courting the governor, urging the necessity of immediately adopting the proposed constitution as it was, without previous amendments. It was rumored that the governor was wavering in his stand. But the Antis were confident. They were still counting heavily on Randolph, and the Randolph name always counted in Virginia affairs.

After a long and rambling introduction to explain the motives behind what he was about to say, Randolph announced that he had changed his mind about immediate ratification. He would vote for it. It was too late to consider calling a second national convention to amend the proposed constitution. It had to be accepted as it stood. Any delay would cause "inevitable ruin to the Union." He had refused to sign the document at first and "if the same reasons operated on my mind, I would still refuse," he concluded. "But as I think that those eight states which have adopted the Constitution will not recede, I am a friend of the Union."

---

* Speeches by Henry and others, as reported, were approximations of what was said. Shorthand had not yet developed into the skill it is today. The "shorthand gentlemen" at the convention did not attempt a *verbatim* report of everything that was said. Rather, they reported the lines of argument, the special points that were made, but their notes did manage to convey something of the style of the various speakers, picking up and preserving many of their more graphic phrases.

On one occasion, the reporter became so entranced with what Henry was saying that he lifted his pen and just sat there, failing to take notes, so that there is quite a gap in Henry's speech as recorded and later published.

Henry and all of the Antis were surprised and shocked. So were their many adherents in the crowded galleries where there was much murmuring and muttering, and not a few angry exclamations. "Young Arnold!" the usually gentle George Mason remarked acidly in an audible voice. "Young Arnold!" he repeated more loudly—another Benedict Arnold whom the enemy had seduced and taken over.

To counter the stunning blow of Randolph's "defection,"* Mason immediately rose and directed a spirited attack on a principal clause in the proposed constitution—the power of direct taxation. This power, by itself, would inevitably create a consolidated government that would quickly submerge, and in the end extinguish the state governments. This power should be restrained, argued Mason. If it were, he would withdraw his objections to this part of the constitution. The amendment of this clause, he said, "is with me a *sine qua non* of adoption. I wish for such amendments, and such only, as are necessary to secure the dearest rights of the people."

As chief architect of the constitution and the most ardent advocate of its immediate adoption, Madison felt called upon to speak. He made a few general remarks which were of no consequence. Then, saying that the hour was growing late, he made a motion—which was passed—that further discussion should be postponed "to a more convenient time." Federalist leaders wished to hold a conference on how best to answer Henry and Mason, and decide who should undertake this.

Anti leaders were also anxious to hold a meeting to consider their strategy and tactics. It had not been a good day for them. Randolph's unexpected switch of position had knocked a prop from under them. But they were not too discouraged.

"Though we are alarmed, we do not despond," wrote one of them, Colonel William Grayson. "The district of Kentucky is with us & if we can [win] over the four Counties which lye on the Ohio between the Pennsylvania line & Big Sandy Creek [in what is now West Virginia], the day is our own."

---

* The point cannot be proved, but it seems probable that Randolph and his influence provided the extra few votes that enabled the Virginia Federalists to win by a narrow margin on ratification.

In any case, the Federalists deeply appreciated Randolph's "change of mind," and rewarded him for it. President Washington appointed him as our first United States Attorney General and as our second Secretary of State, upon Jefferson's resignation.

The next day, with the convention sitting as Committee of the Whole, President Pendleton asked George Wythe to take the chair so that he could go to the floor and speak from there. Everybody expected Madison to resume the speech he had started the day before. All eyes were on Madison's seat, but he was not there. He later reported himself ill. This may have been so.

But it is more probable that Madison's was a "strategic" illness. Federalist leaders, it would appear, had decided that Madison was not the man to attack and overturn the arguments of Henry and Mason, and counteract their overpowering eloquence. With his grasp of the theory of government, with his clarity of thought and expression, Madison could well have answered the Henry and Mason arguments. But he was not an orator. Besides, he was a short man, having to stand on tiptoe to be seen over the high rostrum in convention hall. His voice was thin, often squeaky. Federalist leaders had decided, evidently with Madison agreeing, that another should deliver their thunder.

That is why Pendleton had asked George Wythe to take the chair and had moved down from the dais to take a seat up front on the convention floor. Now almost seventy, an impressive and respected figure, always an effective speaker, Pendleton had been chosen as the Federalist champion to knock down Henry and Mason if he could.

Some years before, Pendleton had been thrown by a horse and suffered severe injury to his hip and a leg. For a year or more he was laid up at home and often doubted whether he could ever walk again. Though his injuries left him badly crippled, he trained himself to get around on crutches. As he was a tall heavy man, it was very difficult for him to move about at all. In view of his age and infirmities, none had expected that he would undertake to be a chief Federalist spokesman in the debate on the floor. But he had so chosen.

As soon as the day's session opened, he struggled to his feet, friends handed him his crutches so that he could stand, and Pendleton began a long and well-wrought speech, one of the major speeches of his life. Addressing himself first to Henry, he said:

> My worthy friend has expressed great uneasiness in his mind and informed us that a great many of our citizens are also extremely uneasy at the proposal of changing our government; but that a year ago, before this fatal system was thought of, the public mind was at perfect repose.

Pendleton denied this. What was the situation of the country before the meeting of the convention at Philadelphia?

> Our general government was totally inadequate to the purpose of its institution; our commerce decayed; our finances deranged; public and private credit destroyed; these and many other national evils rendered necessary the meeting of that Convention. . . .
>
> What has created the public uneasiness since? Not public reports, which are not to be depended upon, but mistaken apprehensions of danger, drawn from observations on government which do not apply to us. . . .
>
> We are perfectly free from sedition and war; we are not yet in confusion; we are left to consider our real happiness and security; we want to secure these objects; we know they cannot be attained without government . . .
>
> There is no quarrel between government and liberty; the former is the shield and protector of the latter. The war is between government and licentiousness, faction, turbulence, and other violations of the rules of society. . . .

Pendleton was beside the point here. Henry and Mason were not contending that there was a quarrel between government and liberty. They were contending that the new scheme of government would curtail the liberties of Americans. They were not advocating anarchy, but a better form of government than proposed. Pendleton went on to make a telling point against Henry, who had more than once said, "I own myself a democrat." Henry had objected to the phrase "We, the people," in the draft of the constitution, insisting that it should read "We, the States." Said Pendleton:

> Permit me to ask the gentleman who made this objection, who but the people can delegate powers? Who but the people have a right to form government? The expression is a common one, and a favorite one with me . . . If the objection be that the Union ought not to be of the people, but of the state governments, then I think the choice of the former very happy and proper. What have the state governments to do with it?

This was special pleading of a very high order. The people had had very little to say directly in the selection of delegates to the Philadelphia convention. The delegates had been elected by the state legislatures, the members of which had been chosen by an electorate rather narrowly limited by property and other qualifications. Pendleton was being something of a demagogue—he often implied that Henry was one—in suddenly professing his love of "the people" and praising the new scheme of government as more or less their work which they would doubtless accept. Pendleton had always preferred dealing with the rich and well-born, with those in power, and he was subtly doing it now.

Pendleton went on to reply to Henry's contention that the Philadelphia convention had exceeded its authority. That was not so. The convention had broad powers to remove all defects in government. Its members, in considering "all the defects in our general government," were not confined to any particular plan.

Were they deceived? This was the proper question at the moment. The question was between the new scheme of government and the Confederation. "The latter is no government at all," said Pendleton. "It has been said that it has carried us through a dangerous war to a happy issue." But it was not the Articles of Confederation that carried the country through. It was the sense of common danger, the concerted effort inspired by the slogan, "United we stand, divided we fall." The proposed constitution preserved and strengthened the bonds of union. Those opposing the constitution as drafted and seeking an amended substitute were "grasping at feathers."

Addressing himself to both Henry and Mason, Pendleton denied that the constitution would result in a consolidated government. What is the nature of such a government? One with sole and unlimited powers. The government proposed was not such. There was a division of powers between the executive, the legislative, and the judiciary, with each having a check on the others. The government would act only on nationwide concerns, and not interfere in state and local matters. The strength of the states would be increased, for the national government would have to depend upon the states for its existence.

Anxious to answer Pendleton, Henry was immediately on his feet to gain recognition from the chair. But Chairman Wythe, a determined Federalist, failed to "see" him. He looked the other way and gave the floor to another ardent Federalist, General Henry Lee, whose views on the constitution were directly opposed to those of his elder brother Richard Henry Lee.

Still rather young, a dashing hero of the Revolutionary War, tall and handsome, composed and engaging in manner, General Lee had a pleasant voice and was an effective speaker. In line with Federalist strategy, which evidently was not only to knock down Henry's arguments but to disparage him as a public figure, Lee proceeded to attack Henry personally in a tone and manner that few others would have dared. Having extolled Henry's "brilliant talents" in a mock-serious way, he remarked:

> On so important an occasion, and before so respectable a body, I expected a new display of his powers of oratory. But instead of proceeding to investigate the new plan of government, the worthy character informs us of horrors which he felt, of apprehensions in his mind, which made him tremblingly fearful of the fate of the Commonwealth.
>
> Mr. Chairman, was it proper for him to appeal to the fears of this House? The question before us belongs to the judgment of this House. I trust he is come to judge, and not to alarm. I trust that he and every other gentleman in this House comes with a firm resolution coolly and calmly to examine, and fairly and impartially to determine.

Eager to answer this sarcastic speech, Henry rose immediately and this time got the floor, to deliver one of the most eloquent speeches of his career. Speaking without notes, he held everyone in the convention hall spellbound for hours as he critically examined the questions at issue. Though the rule had been adopted that the constitution was to be discussed clause by clause, Henry ignored that rule and ranged the document as a whole, as some Federalists had been doing. Referring to the remarks by General Lee, Henry said:

> Mr. Chairman, I am much obliged to the very worthy gentleman for his encomium. I wish I was possessed of talents, or possessed of anything, that might enable me to elucidate this great subject. I own, sir, I am not free from suspicion. I am apt to entertain doubts. I rose, on yesterday, not to enter upon the discussion, but merely to ask a question which had arisen in my mind. When I asked that question, I thought the meaning of my interrogation was obvious.
>
> The fate of America may depend on this question. Have they said, "We, the States"? Have they made a proposal of a compact between states? If they had, this would be a confederation; it is, otherwise, most clearly a consolidated government.

The powers of such a consolidated government, Henry went on, would be enormous, highly dangerous, quite ruinous to the rights of states and the liberties of individuals. "The sovereignty of the States will be relinquished . . . The rights of conscience, trial by jury, liberty of the press, all your immunities and franchises, all pretensions to human rights and privileges, are rendered insecure, if not lost, by this change so loudly talked of by some, so inconsiderately by others." The proposed constitution did not contain a Bill of Rights, and "a Bill of Rights is indispensably necessary," said Henry.

"I trust that gentlemen, on this occasion, will see that the great objects of religion, liberty of the press, trial by jury, interdiction of cruel punishments, and every other sacred right are secured before they agree to that paper." The constitution was quite explicit on the powers to be given to the new government. But in regard to civil rights and privileges, there was "an ambiguity which is very astonishing! . . . Guard with jealous attention the public liberty. Suspect everyone who approaches that jewel . . . Consider what you are about to do . . . Take longer time in reckoning things."

Many nations were groaning under "intolerable despotism" because of "negligently suffering their liberty to be wrested from them." Federalist speakers were talking of grave dangers the country faced unless the constitution was adopted forthwith, to which Henry replied:

> I ask, where is that danger? I see none. Other gentlemen have told us within these walls that the union is gone, or that the union will be gone. Is this not trifling with the judgment of their fellow-citizens? Till they give us the ground of their fears, I will consider them as imaginary. I rose to make inquiry where these dangers were; they could make no answer; I believe I never shall have that answer.

Remarking that the only danger to the nation would be the adoption of the new scheme of government without prior amendments, Henry turned a critical eye on the presidency. The powers given to that office were too strong, and would be subject to abuse. Jefferson shared this view, having suggested that there be rotation in that office, that a president having served four years should be ineligible for re-election so that no man could build up a personal vested interest in continuing as chief of state. Henry was impassioned here:

> The Constitution is said to have beautiful features; but when I come to examine these features, Sir, they appear to me horri-

> bly frightful. Among other deformities, it has an awful squinting —it squints toward monarchy. And does not this raise indignation in the breast of every true American? Your president may easily become king . . . Where are your checks in this government?
>
> Your strongholds [control of the army and the purse] will be in the hands of your enemies. It is on a supposition that our American governors shall be honest that all the good qualities of this government are founded; but its defective and imperfect construction puts it in their power to perpetuate the worst of mischiefs, should they be bad men.
>
> And, Sir, would not all the world, from the eastern to the western hemispheres, blame our distracted folly in resting our rights upon the contingency of our rulers being good or bad?
>
> Show me that age and country where the rights and liberties of the people were placed on the sole chance of their rulers being good men without a consequent loss of liberty . . .
>
> If your American chief be a man of ambition and abilities, how easy is it for him to render himself absolute! The army is in his hands and if he be a man of address, it will be attached to him, and it will not be a subject of long meditation with him to seize the first auspicious moment to accomplish his design . . .
>
> I would rather infinitely—and I am sure most of this convention are of the same opinion—have a king, lords, and commons than a government so replete with such insupportable evils.
>
> If we make a king, we may prescribe the rules by which he shall rule his people, and interpose such checks as will prevent him from infringing on them. But the president, in the field with his army, can prescribe the terms on which he shall reign as master, so far that it will puzzle any American ever to get his neck from under the galling yoke.

What if the people wished to get rid of such a master and bring him to trial for his derelictions in office? How could this be done? There was no way of doing it. The people would be powerless. Could he not, as commander-in-chief of all armed forces, beat down every opposition? "The army will salute him monarch.* Your militia will

* The fear of monarchy was not chimerical. There was a great deal of monarchical talk throughout the country, especially among the rich and well-born. A group of discontented army officers had already gone so far as to propose

leave you and assist in making him president, and fight against you [at the order of the commander-in-chief]. And what have you to oppose this force? What will then become of you and your rights? Will not absolute despotism ensue?"

As Henry warmed to this subject, his oratory soared to an extraordinary height as he went on to depict, in graphic and moving detail, all of the many disasters that would befall the country under such a despotism. With all eyes fixed on him, there was not a sound in convention hall except Henry's resonant and persuasive voice as it rose and fell. There was breathless silence, no movement at all, when Henry stopped for one of his long dramatic pauses as if he were searching his mind for just the right singing and stinging phrases he would use next. By all accounts, even by those most strongly opposed to him and his views, Henry's effort here was magnificent and truly inspired with the fire of genius.

The effect of his words, his voice, his gestures, and his manner of speaking was overpowering–so overpowering, in fact, that this was one of the occasions on which the shorthand reporter (a Federalist) became so enthralled in listening to Henry that he laid down his pen and neglected to take notes. As a consequence, we know very little but the general tone and tenor of Henry's remarks on this point. The reporter, to repair the gap in his copy, picked up his pen and inserted this short sentence: "Mr. Henry strongly and pathetically expatiated on the probability of the President's enslaving America, and the horrid consequences that must result."

Henry went on to attack other parts of the new scheme of government. The United States Congress, both Senate and House, could be a rubber stamp in the hands of an ambitious president. Members of Congress could set their salaries as high as they pleased. "I suppose, if they be good men," said Henry, "their own delicacy will lead them to be satisfied with moderate salaries. But there is no security for this."

Congress was to be authorized to pass all laws necessary to carry into effect the many strong specific powers granted to the national government. This specification of powers would, in practice, mean

---

directly to Washington that he make himself king–a proposal that Washington angrily denounced as fraught with the "greatest michiefs."

Soon after the new Constitution went into effect, John Adams, having moved far to the right of his early democratic views, suggested that the chief executive be addressed as "His Majesty, the President."

little or nothing. Under the pretense of putting a specific power into effect, Congress could do almost anything it pleased.

There was another ambiguity. Congress was to make public its proceedings only "from time to time." They could hold back publication so that the people would not learn what was going on in time to prevent an "ambuscade" of their liberties.

There would be a clash in jurisdictions between the state courts and the federal judiciary which was to consist of a United States supreme court and as many inferior courts as Congress saw fit to establish. This would provide a rich source of patronage for hungry politicians. There would also be a rich source of patronage in the appointment of revenue officers, tax collectors, and other federal agents who would swarm over the country like a cloud of locusts.

Madison had said, in speaking of the nature of the new government, that he conceived it to be of "a mixed nature. It is, in a manner, unprecedented. We cannot find one express example in the experience of the world—it stands by itself. In some respects, it is a government of a federal nature; in others, it is of a consolidated nature." One of Madison's supporters, Francis Corbin, suggested that it would be best to call it "a representative federal government," without any reference to consolidation. Henry was withering in his scorn about this:

> This government is so new it wants a name. I wish its other novelties were as harmless as this. We are told that . . . it is without example—that it is national in this part, and federal in that part, etc. We may be amused, if we please, by a treatise on political anatomy. In the brain, it is national; the stamina are federal; some limbs are federal, others national . . . It is federal in conferring general powers, but national in retaining them . . .
>
> What signifies it to me that you have the most curious anatomical description of its creation? For common purposes of legislation, it is a great consolidation of government.
>
> You are not to have the right to legislation in any but trivial cases. You are not to touch private contracts. You are not to have the right of having armies in your own defence. You cannot be trusted in dealing out justice between man and man. What shall the states have to do? Take care of the poor—repair and make highways—erect bridges—and so on and so on!
>
> Abolish the state legislatures at once! What purpose should

> they be continued for? Our legislature will indeed be a ludicrous spectacle—180 men, marching in solemn farcical procession, exhibiting a mournful proof of the lost liberty of their country, without the power of restoring it.
>
> But, Sir, we have the consolation that it is a mixed government!—that is, it may work sorely on your neck. But you will have some comfort by saying that it was a federal government in origin.

To gain support for immediate adoption, the Federalists kept hammering away on the theme that it was damaging to delay, there was no need for prior amendments, that there was "a plain easy way" to amend the constitution later. "When I come to contemplate this part, I suppose that I am mad, or that my countrymen are so," said Henry. "The way to amendment is, in my conception, shut. Let us consider this plain easy way."

Citing particulars, Henry pointed out that the way might be plain, but certainly was not easy. For adoption, a proposed amendment required the concurrence of three fourths of the states. This meant that four of the smallest states, having not a tenth of the population of the country, could defeat even the most desirable amendment.

> Is this, Sir, an easy mode of securing public liberty? It is, Sir, a most fearful situation when the most contemptible minority can prevent the alteration of the most oppressive government, for it may, in many respects, prove to be such. Is this the spirit of republicanism? . . . of democracy?

Against the argument that eight states had adopted the new plan and Virginia had perforce to follow, Henry declared "that if twelve and a half states had adopted it, I would with manly firmness and in spite of an erring world reject it."

What should Virginia do? She should notify all states that she would never ratify the plan unless there were prior amendments. There was good reason to believe the adopting states would yield. Virginia's move would promote unity, not disunity, and then all would be well. "I speak the language of thousands," Henry said in defending his critical views. "But, Sir, I mean not to breathe the spirit nor utter the language of secession."

Henry's long, eloquent, witty, humorous, impassioned, and argumentative speech had a noticeably marked effect upon all in convention hall. As there had been in his audience a breathless silence when he was speaking, so now there was a prolonged silence as he sat down. Men looked at one another, questioningly. Perhaps the great dangers that Henry had so vividly and convincingly pictured lay just around the corner.

Next day, to blast Henry and counter his arguments point by point, the Federalists brought up their big guns—Madison, Randolph, and George Nicholas. These managed to monopolize the floor most of the day so that the Antis could not speak except to ask a question or raise a point of order.

Repeating his former arguments, Madison spoke with his usual lucidity. His appeal to logic, while rather convincing, did not stir his hearers and left them cool, if not cold. His speech was no match for Henry's. Governor Randolph warmly advocated immediate adoption of the constitution, which he had earlier denounced publicly in strong terms. At the Philadelphia Convention, he had made a motion, which was defeated, "that the State conventions should be at liberty to amend, and that a second convention should be holden to discuss the amendments which should be suggested by them."

This was exactly what Henry was advocating. As Randolph went on, for the third time, to explain his change of position, Henry became very annoyed and impatient, and rose to say:

> The honorable member will not accuse me of want of candor when I cast in my mind what he had given to the public and compare it to what happened since. It seems to me very strange and unaccountable that that which was the object of his execration should now receive his encomiums. Something extraordinary must have operated so great a change in his position.

Henry had been twitting Randolph on his startling change of mind. His insinuations that there was more in it than met the ear and eye made Randolph very angry. Losing his temper, he replied:

> I find myself attacked in the most illiberal manner by the honorable gentleman. I disdain his aspersions and insinuations. His asperity is warranted by no principle of parliamentary decency nor compatible with the least shadow of friendship. If our friendship must fall, let it fall like Lucifer, never to rise again.

Henry got the floor to say that he had no desire to offend anybody, that if he had done so, he was sorry. He was merely doing his duty in asking for information of interest to the public. Randolph then said that he was "relieved" by what Henry had said, and "that were it not for the concession of the gentleman, he would have made some men's hair stand on end by the disclosure of the certain facts."

Henry replied that if Randolph had anything to say about him, let him say it and disclose his "certain facts." Randolph did not, and went on with his elaborate self-defense. He probably knew that his "facts" were mere gossip, for the two men had been good friends for years, until the question of the constitution came up. If Randolph had been certain of his facts, he would have broken off with Henry long before.

On another occasion, later in the session, Henry had a head-on clash with George Nicholas, another of the Federalist leaders. Nicholas was the son of Henry's old friend Robert Carter Nicholas, who had been one of Henry's law examiners and had later turned over to Henry his very lucrative practice in the General Court. George Nicholas, now in his early thirties, was a pugnacious man. He was short, square, and bulky, with an enormously fat neck. It was said of him that he looked like "a plum pudding, with legs to it."

However he looked, young Nicholas was an able advocate and debater, skilled at political in-fighting and capable of delivering a knockout punch. He swung at Henry what he hoped would be a lethal blow. Objecting to something Henry had said, Nicholas declared that there were some in the convention who had "come by large possessions" in a manner that was "not easy to account for." This jibe was obviously directed at Henry, who immediately got the floor to ask if Nicholas meant anything personal.

"I mean what I say, Sir," shouted Nicholas, and "if such conduct meets the contempt of that gentleman, I can assure him it meets with an equal degree of contempt from me." Nicholas added that Henry had made remarks "which ought not to have come from one gentleman to another," and went on with his speech. When he sat down, Henry was on his feet again to protest:

> If the gentleman means personal insinuations—or to wound my private reputation—I think this an improper place to do so . . . I can tell how I came by what I have. . . . I have what I hold in right, and in a just manner.*

It was a very angry altercation. When Chairman Wythe did noth-

* Both Henry and Nicholas had speculative holdings in western lands, in Kentucky particularly.

ing to intervene and smooth things over, Pendleton got up on his crutches and came over to quiet Henry and Nicholas, urging that they "should investigate the subject calmly, and in a peaceable manner."

It had seemed, for a moment, that a challenge for a duel might be issued. While there had been no duels in Virginia for some years, one was still possible. If a duel had ensued and been fought with pistols, Henry would not have had much to worry about. Having been always "fond of his gun," he was a crack shot and could scarcely have missed "plum pudding" Nicholas. But if fought with other weapons, such as rapiers or swords, Henry would have been greatly disadvantaged against his burly opponent.

Though he was only in his early fifties, Henry looked much older than his years. His recurrent malarial fevers and other ailments had taken their toll. He was frail and more stoop shouldered than ever. Yet in the long debate on the new constitution, the supreme effort of his life, he showed no want of physical strength and stamina. He carried by far the largest load on the Anti side of the argument.

In his *Patrick Henry* (1898), a good short biography, the scholarly Moses Coit Tyler noted that on only five days of the convention did Henry fail to take the floor. On one day, he made three speeches; on another, five; on another, eight. In one of his speeches he was on his feet talking continuously for more than seven hours. The report of debate in the Virginia convention was later published by Jonathan Elliot, in a volume of 663 pages. Henry's speeches take up "nearly one quarter of the entire book"—about 160 pages. At the convention, certainly, Henry evidenced no want of energy, information, learning, or imagination. His powers of body and mind were still at his command.

In the course of debate, Henry brought up an issue which the Federalists hoped could somehow be evaded—the negotiations going on with Count Gardoqui, the Spanish envoy, about navigation rights on the lower Mississippi. Spain wished to close such navigation to Americans for twenty or more years in exchange for a treaty that would give to New England shipping and fisheries a favorable market in Spain and in her large American possessions.

In the Continental Congress, seven states, all of them northern, had favored accepting such a treaty, which was regarded by Virginia and North Carolina as an abject surrender and ruinous to their interests. Both extended westward to the Mississippi—Virginia through the Kentucky district, North Carolina through what became the state of Tennessee. The southern states did not wish to be sold down the river as they well might be, said Henry.

This argument had a profound effect, as noted in a letter that Madison wrote that night to the great silent chief of the Federalists at Mount Vernon, General Washington:

> Appearances at present are less favorable than at the date of my last. Our progress is slow, and every advantage is taken of the delay to work on local prejudices of particular sets of members. British debts, the Indiana claim, and the Mississippi are the principal topics of private discussion and intrigue, as well as of public declamation . . .
>
> There is reason to believe that the event may depend on the Kentucky members, who seem to lean more against than in favor of the constitution. The business is in the most ticklish state that can be imagined.
>
> The majority will certainly be very small on whatever side it may finally lie, and I dare not encourage much expectation that it will be on the favorable side.

Now began what was called "scuffling for the Kentucky votes." There were fourteen of them, almost all of whom had been elected as Antis. On June 23, after three weeks of debate on the new constitution, clause by clause and in general, it became apparent that a final vote was approaching. It was also apparent that the vote would be very close. A swing of five or six votes would decide the question. Before the vote on ratification, Henry rose to offer a motion:

> *Resolved*, That previous to the ratification of the new Constitution . . . a declaration of rights, asserting and securing from encroachment the great principles of civil and religious liberty, and the unalienable rights of the people, together with amendments to the most exceptionable parts of the said Constitution of government, ought to be referred by this Convention to the other states . . . for their consideration.

All in convention hall, both delegates and audience, realized that this was the critical and decisive vote. If Henry's motion passed, ratification would be long delayed and, in the end, probably defeated. If the motion was lost, prompt ratification was virtually assured.

The clerk was ordered to call the roll—alphabetically, by counties, as had been the custom in the old House of Burgesses, a practice retained by its successor, the House of Delegates.

"Accomac County," the clerk intoned. The delegation was split —one vote for, one against. Albemarle County—its two delegates, George Nicholas and his brother Wilson Cary, were against. Amelia and Amherst Counties were in favor, Augusta was against, Bedford was for. Henry's forces took an early lead, with a vote of twenty-five to twelve. The Federalists picked up strength and with almost half of the convention delegates counted, the vote was tied, at forty to forty. It was again tied at sixty to sixty, and again at sixty-nine to sixty-nine. The Antis moved up to eighty votes, but the Federalists were two votes ahead.

The Federalist strategist and floor manager, Edmund Pendleton, could now relax. Only six more votes were to be cast, and he knew they were "safe"—General Henry Lee and Bushrod Washington, from Westmoreland County; his good friends and fellow jurists, John Blair and George Wythe, from York; Attorney General James Innes, of Williamsburg; and a delegate from Norfolk. Henry's motion, the most important in the convention, was lost by a vote of eighty-eight to eighty, a small margin.

As debate drew to a close, George Mason had expressed grave concern that there would be popular resistance and violent disorders if the convention adopted the Philadelphia document as it stood, without prior amendments. The Federalists pretended to be greatly shocked by this, but they, too, had good reason to fear resistance and civil disorders. They well knew that the majority in the Virginia legislature, and the majority of the people, did not favor immediate adoption. Henry had made his position clear:

> I beg pardon of this House for having taken up more time than came to my share, and I thank them for the patience and polite attention with which I have been heard.
>
> If I shall be in a minority, I shall have those painful sensations which arise from a conviction of being overpowered in a good cause.
>
> Yet, I will be a peaceable citizen. My head, my hand, my heart shall be free to retrieve the loss of liberty, and remove the defects of that system, in a constitutional way.
>
> I wish not to go to violence, but will wait with hopes that the spirit which predominated in the Revolution is not yet gone,

> nor the cause of those who are attached to the Revolution yet lost.
>
> I shall therefore patiently wait in expectation of seeing that government changed so as to be compatible with the safety, liberty, and happiness of the people.

On June 25, 1788, after more than three weeks of pointed and sometimes acrimonious debate, George Wythe's motion for adoption of the new plan of government came to the floor, and the clerk was ordered to call the roll. The division was much the same as on Henry's motion. There were eighty-nine votes for immediate adoption, seventy-nine against—one Anti had shifted to the Federalist side.

Though the Antis had lost in their determined battle to prevent the proposed constitution from being accepted unless amended, they won a main point. Almost everyone in the Virginia Constitutional Convention agreed with them that the new scheme of government needed to be amended immediately. Along with a notification that the Constitution had been approved, the convention sent to the Continental Congress "sundry amendments" on which the new United States Congress should take action without delay, "after being considered in the mode prescribed in the Constitution."

The "sundry" amendments contained a bill of rights, based on Virginia's celebrated Declaration of Rights, passed in 1776, drafted largely by George Mason, with an article on religious liberty added by Henry. The Virginia Convention also strongly recommended serious and immediate consideration of twenty other amendments to and revisions of the new Constitution. To hold their votes, Madison and other Federalist leaders had promised that, once the new government was instituted, they would press hard for constitutional amendments as fast as possible—a promise that Madison carried out.

Those at the convention assumed that their action there had made Virginia the ninth state to ratify, making up the requisite number of states needed for adoption of the Constitution. A few days previously, however, New Hampshire had ratified, becoming the ninth state to join the new plan of Union, so Virginia became the tenth. The vote in New Hampshire had been close, fifty-seven to forty-seven, and obtained only by simultaneous adoption of twelve proposed amendments.

About a month later, after a fierce struggle between Governor George Clinton and Alexander Hamilton, the Federalists in New York, helped greatly by the action taken in Virginia and New Hampshire, finally mustered just barely enough strength to carry the day for ratification by a vote of thirty to twenty-seven. But the New York convention insisted that a bill of rights should be incorporated in the Constitution and also proposed thirty-two specific amendments.

Two states—Rhode Island and North Carolina—did not immediately join the Union, and neither suffered any of the dire consequences that the Federalists had been talking about in their argument for the need of immediate ratification. North Carolina stayed out for more than a year, and Rhode Island for almost two years, until May, 1790, when a state convention finally ratified grudgingly. Rhode Islanders were still of a divided mind about the "beauties" of the Constitution, for the vote in the convention was very close—thirty-four for, thirty-two against.

On the day the convention in Richmond adjourned *sine die,* a group of Antis met in town to discuss what to do next. Henry was asked to join them, and to preside, which he did. There was some talk among them that, with the aim of increasing pressure for amendments, steps should be taken to delay setting up the machinery necessary for the operation of the new government. Henry argued strongly against this and advised his friends to return home and start working hard for the election of good solid Antis to the state legislature and in the upcoming Congressional elections.

Henry campaigned actively both for himself and his friends, and when the Virginia legislature next convened, four months after ratification, Antis were in firm control, with Henry as their leader, dominating the whole session. His influence had not been diminished in the slightest by his defeat on ratification. It was at this time that Washington complained in a letter to Madison:

> The edicts of Mr. Henry are enregistered with less opposition by the majority of that body [the legislature] than those of the Grand Monarch are in the parliaments of France. He has only to say let this be law, and it is law.

One of the first orders of business was for the Assembly in joint session to elect two United States senators. Friends proposed to Henry that he run for the Senate, but he declined. The Antis chose their candidates carefully—the veteran Richard Henry Lee and a younger man of ability and spirit, William Grayson. Henry took the unusual step of making the nominating speech for each of them. The Federalist candidate was Madison, who had been the mastermind of the Federalists at both the Philadelphia and the Richmond conventions, and who had increased his prestige enormously with his tireless work and his brilliant analytical mind, which was "a logic box," said one.

Madison was defeated, Lee and Grayson winning by comfortable margins, so that the Antis had a considerable triumph. They would have two eloquent and powerful spokesmen in the upper house of Congress. After his defeat, Madison decided to run for the lower house of Congress. Henry did his best to defeat him. It was well for Henry and for the country that he did not succeed, for Madison went on to play a major role in pushing for the adoption of the constitutional amendments that all Antis and perhaps a majority of Federalists desired.

Having engineered the election of Lee and Grayson, Henry turned to another matter of the deepest concern to him. How to go about arranging things so that a second national convention would be called as soon as possible to rectify the admitted faults in the now ratified Constitution?

In the House of Delegates, sitting as Committee of the Whole, Henry offered a lengthy and strong resolution on the need for speedy action. The Virginia legislature should take a hand in forwarding this. The people were uneasy about "their great and unalienable rights as freemen" and the sooner "the public apprehensions are quieted, and the [federal] government is possessed of the confidence of the people, the more salutary will be its operations, and the longer its duration. The cause of amendments we consider as a common cause . . . The slow forms of Congressional discussion and recommendation, if indeed they should ever agree to any change, would, we fear, be less certain of success" than calling a second national constitutional convention. The Virginia legislature should invite other states to join her in appealing for such a convention.

Federalists shuddered. This, above all things, they wished to avoid. They feared that another convention would open old wounds and inflict new ones, that the real aim of Henry and other Anti leaders was to wreck the Constitution, that they would be less interested in rectifying it than in tearing it apart, clause by clause.

A motion was made to substitute a vague and much weaker resolution than Henry's. After lively and prolonged debate, Henry's was adopted as originally drafted by him. A letter from the General Assembly immediately went out to all the states enclosing a copy of Virginia's application to Congress for the immediate call of a convention, "of deputies from the several states, with full power to take into their consideration the defects of this Constitution that have been suggested by the state conventions, and to report such amendments thereto as they shall find best suited to preserve our common interests and secure to ourselves and our latest posterity the great and unalienable rights of mankind."

In the often heated exchanges during the debate on the resolution, Henry was boldly attacked and sarcastically ridiculed both as a public figure and as a person by young Francis Corbin, an ardent Federalist, son of the last receiver-general. It was from the receiver-general, it will be remembered, that Henry, by his unauthorized armed march on Williamsburg, had extracted more than £300 in compensation for the gunpowder that Lord Dunmore had surreptitiously removed one midnight from the Magazine in Williamsburg.

The Corbins, rich and one of the older families, were Tories before and during the Revolution. But as they remained quiet and passive, not offering any obstruction to the Patriot cause, they were not molested, and their properties were not confiscated or looted as were those of many Tories. As hostilities developed, to keep him from becoming involved, young Francis Corbin had been sent abroad to study, spending most of his time in England, leading a very gay and pleasant life during the war years, for the Corbins had high social connections in London and at Court.

Young Corbin, personable and elegant, with courtly manners and a fluent tongue, had since returned to Virginia to establish a law practice and enter politics. As he sat in the House of Delegates listening to debate, he felt that he had heard enough from Henry and decided that he would silence him by a clever attack that would knock him flat.

In the course of debate on his move for amendments, Henry had said that he regarded his opinions as nothing if they were opposed to those of his constituents, that he was ready and willing, "at all times and on all occasions, to bow, with the utmost deference, to the majesty of the people."

Corbin picked up this last phrase and played on it rather well and amusingly in his long speech. He denied that the people were uneasy and anxious for amendments. They felt their "great and unalienable rights" were sufficiently secured by the Constitution. Contrary to what Henry contended, the people were at peace and wished to get on with their work without any more agitation.

"And yet," said Corbin, "the gentleman tells us he is ever ready and willing, at all times and on all occasions, to bow to the majesty of the people." Saying this with a flourish, the speaker made a deep and elaborate bow, and went on:

> The gentleman has set himself in opposition to the will of the people throughout the whole course of this transaction. The people approved of the Constitution. The suffrage of their constituents in the last convention proved it. The people wished, most anxiously wished, the adoption of the Constitution as the only means of saving the credit and honor of the country, and producing the stability of the union. The gentleman, on the contrary, had placed himself at the head of those who opposed adoption.
>
> And yet [accompanied with another flourish and mocking bow], the gentleman is ever ready and willing, at all times and on all occasions, to bow to the majesty of the people. . . .

As Corbin went on, he emphasized every main point he made against Henry by ending it with another flourish and a deep bow, making thirteen of them. Toward the end of his speech, he slanted off to make a more personal attack on Henry's political character and his appearance.

> It is of little importance whether a country is ruled by a despot, with a tiara on his head, or by a demagogue in red cloak, a caul-bare wig, . . . although he should profess on all occasions to bow to the majesty of the people.

With gestures and flourishes, spoken in a pleasant voice, Corbin's was an effective polemical speech, though many of its assumptions and assertions were extremely dubious, if not demonstrably false. The Federalists, though with some notable exceptions, smiled and were pleased with the speech. Henry, for once, had been put in his place.

The Antis and all of Henry's many friends were, of course, infuriated. To make a personal derisive attack on a man of Henry's years and stature, "the Noble Patriot," who had been the "idol of the country" for more than two decades, seemed the worst of bad taste, almost a sacrilege, a green-with-envy evidence of party venom.

When Corbin sat down and was congratulated by friends around him, he was very pleased with himself. But this feeling did not last long. During his speech, Henry had sat quietly, making no notes, making no interruptions or interjections, as he might well have done and been entitled to do. At times, he seemed scarcely to be paying attention to what was being said. He was probably composing in his mind what he would say to give young Corbin a tongue-lashing and humiliation he would never forget. As Corbin quickly discovered, it would have been wise for him to have had a second thought about engaging in verbalistics with a master of the art. After a pause with no one asking for the floor, Henry rose to reply, speaking slowly and gently as he did at the beginning of his every speech:

> Mr. Speaker: I am a plain man, and have been educated altogether in Virginia. My whole life has been spent among planters and other plain men of similar education who have never had the advantage of that polish which a Court alone can give, and which the gentleman over the way has so happily acquired.
>
> Indeed, Sir, the gentleman's employments and mine, in common with the great mass of our countrymen, have been as widely different as our fortunes. For while that gentleman was availing himself of the opportunity which a splendid fortune afforded him of acquiring a foreign education, mixing among the great, attending levees and Courts, basking in the beams of royal favor at St. James' and exchanging courtesies with crowned heads, I was engaged in the arduous task of revolution, and was probably as far from thinking of acquiring those polite accomplishments which the gentleman has so successfully cultivated as that gentleman then was from sharing in the toils and dangers in which his unpolished countrymen were then engaged.
>
> I will not, therefore, presume to vie with the gentleman in those courtly accomplishments of which he has just given the House so agreeable a specimen. Yet such a bow, as I can make, shall be ever at the service of the people.

Henry could make as graceful a bow as anyone. But at this point he decided to play the "unpolished" American and made a bow so deliberately awkward, so clumsy, and so comic that it brought a roar of laughter from the House. With not a trace of a smile, with no rancor in his tone of voice, Henry went on calmly, making a few more "unpolished" bows, to pound the now flushed and writhing Corbin deeper into his seat, and to win a large majority for his motion on amendments.

Shortly after this, on January 7, 1789, all ratifying states except

New York* chose their delegates to the Electoral College. The electors were named by joint legislative sessions in some states; by popular vote in others. While elections to the First Congress were proceeding, the college met in New York City, the temporary capital. As almost everybody hopefully anticipated, Federalists and Antis alike, General Washington was elected President, with sixty-nine votes; the vote was unanimous. With thirty-four votes, John Adams became Vice-President. On April 30, 1789, Washington was sworn into office on the balcony of Federal Hall, on Wall Street at the corner of Broad in New York. Meantime, the members of the First Congress had assembled, and the Senate and the House had organized themselves for the work ahead.

In setting up his administration, Washington surrounded himself with very able and distinguished lieutenants, two of them being Virginians—Jefferson, as Secretary of State, and Edmund Randolph, as Attorney General. Having first offered the post to Robert Morris of Pennsylvania, Washington named Alexander Hamilton of New York as Secretary of the Treasury, and chose one of his favorites, General Henry Knox of Massachusetts, to be Secretary of War. John Jay of New York was appointed as Chief Justice of the U. S. Supreme Court, to consist of six members.

The nation was now in business under new management, and what a business it has turned out to be—the largest, wealthiest, and also most expensive business in the history of the world. In comparison with the operations of our proliferating governmental apparatus, our largest business corporation is a mere pigmy, and a baby pigmy at that.

Federal government expenditures alone are currently (1967) running at the fantastic and dizzying height of more than $130 billions a year!—with $70 billions of that going to war and preparations for war, euphemistically called "defense." We have grown big, even Gargantuan, in all kinds of ways. Federal budget experts calculate that, for the year 1967 alone, the national Treasury will run a deficit of $29 billions. To slow the flow of red ink, if not red blood, the administration has proposed a 10 per cent surcharge on federal income taxes for the coming year.

Ah, the wonders of growth and "progress," the beauties of "scientific" management.

---

* Because of political squabbles between Antis and Federalists, who were still bitterly fighting, New York failed to name delegates to the Electoral College.

XXVII
To Red Hill

. . . a pleasant spot

—PATRICK HENRY

In 1791, when it came time to elect a new House of Delegates, Henry announced that he was not running for re-election. His constituents in Prince Edward County earnestly and insistently pleaded with him to change his mind, but Henry could not be dissuaded. He intended to retire from public life, he said. He would devote his time and energies to his personal affairs that now so sorely needed attention after his many years in public office, where his salaries scarcely paid family expenses. A friend visiting about this time noted in his diary:*

> Go . . . to Colonel Patrick Henry's, spend the balance of the day, and take dinner with him . . . What a weight of worldly concerns rests upon this old man's shoulders. He supports it with strength and fortitude, but nature must sink under the load ere long. His head now blossoms for the grave, his

---

* Quoted from *Patrick Henry* by William Wirt Henry, who had seen and made use of a manuscript diary kept by Richard N. Venable, a lawyer, one of Henry's neighbors.

> body bends to mingle with its kindred dust, but his fame shall remain and grow like the tall oak of the forest. . . .

But Henry was not as weighed down as all that, though he had a large household to care for. His six children by his first wife Sarah Shelton had grown up and been off on their own, but his oldest and favorite daughter, Martha (Patsy), had recently lost her husband, John Fontaine, and returned with four children to live with the Henrys. By his second wife, Dorothea, he now had more than a half dozen children, the oldest in her middle teens, and more were to come till there were eleven of them (two died as infants or in their early years). On the death of his sister Anne Christian, Henry became guardian of her only son and provided for him. Altogether, Henry was directly responsible for the well-being of some fifteen persons, and he did well in shouldering the burden, even though he was tired and frequently ill.

"Go back to the law," a friend had advised him in 1786 when Henry stepped down as governor, announcing that he did not wish to be nominated for a third term. "Your tongue will pay your debts," his friend had said, and it did. It not only paid his debts but, within a short time, made him a fortune—not a great fortune, but large enough to relieve him of financial worries. Even during his intense activities to block immediate ratification of the Constitution, he found what time he could to practice law.

Clients from all over the state eagerly sought his services in civil suits, in Chancery cases, in criminal trials. Because of his prestige and his prowess, particularly as a trial lawyer, he could and did ask large fees. In involved cases, he required his clients to engage other lawyers to handle, under his supervision, the preparation of briefs and tedious legal preliminaries of the case. Henry would appear and take charge when the case came up for trial in court.

Two of the wealthy Carter clan, Charles and Robert of Nomini Hall, went to law about their conflicting claims to a 12,000-acre tract and to the rents that had been collected there for years. Robert Carter wrote to Henry asking him to be his counsel. Henry declined. He was not well, he told Carter, and he could not face the long trip from Prince Edward County to Leesburg, where the trial was to be held. Henry added:

> The importance of the case, added to the voluminous nature of the papers & proceedings in it, would call for long & close study to comprehend them fully. . . . And when I put together

> every consideration, I find that the money I should charge you would amount to so large a sum as to give you ground perhaps to think me mercenary, or even rapacious.

Carter pleaded with Henry to change his mind, and the latter finally agreed to act. Opposing counsel was Edmund Randolph, with whom Henry had recently clashed so sharply at the Virginia constitutional convention. At Leesburg, wrote Randolph after the trial, "I was confronted with Mr. Henry, and for three days we lay alongside of each other, with our best cannon in action." It was a diverting scene, thought Randolph, who added:

> My client, Charles Carter, must have been defeated if a single point of four had gone against him. . . . In three points, the court were unanimously against Mr. Henry; on the fourth, he had a bare majority.
>
> Thus being mortified with defeats, and willing to disguise under the name of a compromise, he proposed that his client, Robert Carter, should surrender 6,000 acres of land, and £450. To this I agreed, knowing that two of the four points were in strictness by no means in our favor.

An arrangement had been made that if the case were won, Robert Carter would pay Henry 400 guineas; if lost, 100 guineas. Henry had not won the case, but he had not lost it, either. He had effected a compromise that saved his client 6,000 acres of good land and a large sum of money. For his semi-victory, Henry thought himself entitled to a fee of 200 guineas. Carter was one of the richest of the Virginia Grandees, but Henry had to dun him repeatedly before he finally got paid.

Many stories about how sharp and smart Henry was as a lawyer have come down to us. Most of these stories have no doubt been stretched in the telling and retelling. One of them goes like this: a man had stolen a hog and dressed it before he was suspected and indicted. He came to ask Henry to defend him.

"Did you walk away with that shoat?" Henry inquired.

"I don't like to say."

"Out with it!"

"Yessir."

"Have you got the carcass?"

"Yessir."

"You go home, you wretch; cut the pig lengthwise in half,

and hang as much of it in my smokehouse as you keep in yours." Henry won an acquittal, concluding his argument by turning to the judge and saying:

"Your Honor, this man has no more of that stolen shoat than I have. If necessary, I'd kiss the Bible on that."

But enough of what may be called "legal" jokes. Why is it that so many of them are so unfunny, and why do they so often turn on some "smart" bit of sharp practice, or equivocation, or chicanery, or worse? Is it because of the nature of the calling?

Henry's biggest case in these years, and perhaps of his career, concerned a question about debts Virginians owed to Britons under contracts signed in pre-Revolutionary days. Could British creditors or their assignees go to court to force payment of these debts? The issue concerned many people, involved very large sums of money, and had been politically disturbing in the country ever since peace was signed in 1783.

The question covered very broad ground, involving difficult and abstruse points in many fields of law—municipal, state, national, and international. In 1777, Virginia had passed an act of sequestration making it lawful for anyone owing money to a British subject to pay that debt, in whole or in part, into the state Treasury, from which he would receive a receipt discharging him from so much of the debt as was paid.

Two years later, Virginia passed an act of forfeiture declaring that all British property in the state should be "deemed to be vested in the Commonwealth." And another law in 1782, declaring that no debt originally due to a British subject "should be recoverable in any court of this Commonwealth," though the debt might be assigned to a citizen of the state who could take legal action under certain circumstances.

An article in the Treaty of Paris ending the war with Britain stated explicitly that all debts owed to creditors of either country by citizens of the other were to be validated and made collectible by law, no matter what legislation had been passed during the heat of the war. The Continental Congress, having no power to enforce this, could only urge the states to do something, each in its own way, about the British debts. The states were in no hurry about this, and did little or nothing. Was this a violation of the treaty?

Britain regarded it as such and refused to evacuate Niagara, Detroit, and other western forts and posts until a way for collecting British debts was assured. Was this a violation of the treaty? And if both were, which violations occurred first, the American or British? This was really an academic question, but it was lengthily argued.

Now, with the new Federal Constitution in force, British merchants had high hopes of collecting at last the large debts owed them for so long. The Constitution made all treaties in force, such as the 1783 peace treaty with Britain, and treaties subsequently negotiated the supreme law of the land, invalidating any state legislation that contravened them.

In 1790 with the opening of the first Federal district court in Richmond, British merchants and other British creditors filed a large number of suits against their individual Virginia debtors, who were numerous, many being of high station. Trial of the suits was put over to the next year. The debtors, as theirs was a common cause, banded together and jointly engaged Henry as their chief counsel. Associated with him were young John Marshall, now rapidly rising to the top of his profession, and Virginia Attorney General James Innes, an experienced lawyer and persuasive advocate. The plaintiffs, the creditors, also pooled their interests and engaged four able lawyers to prepare and argue their case.

Henry took great pains in preparing for the upcoming trials. He read and studied everything he could on the many points at issue. On one occasion he sent his grandson, twenty-year-old Patrick Henry Fontaine, who was studying law with his grandfather, on a journey of sixty miles to obtain a copy of Vassal's *Law of Nations*. From this book, and dozens of others, he made quotations and "with the whole syllabus of notes and heads of arguments, he filled a manuscript volume more than an inch thick, and closely written." Bound in leather, the volume was small enough to be "convenient for carrying in his pocket."

On his Prince Edward estate, Henry had built an office a little distance from the house, and here he spent a large part of every working day. In front of the office was a walk shaded by a fine line of black locusts. Henry used the walk as a favorite place to stroll and meditate whenever the weather was good.

While working on the British Debts case, Henry paced frequently up and down this walk, "with his notebook in his hand, which he often opened and read," and "from his gestures, while promenading alone in the shade of the locusts," it was evident that he was committing to memory what he wished to say at the trial. Henry's speeches were not always as unrehearsed as they appeared to be, though he never wrote out and read a set speech, and often spoke without notes.

But the British Debts case was different, requiring minute and accurate preparation of citations and precedents. As the day of the trial drew near, Henry shut himself up in his office for three days. During that time he did not see any of his family; a servant brought him his meals which Henry took from him at the door.

The British Debts case came to trial at Richmond in November, 1791, with a panel of three judges sitting. Counsel for the plaintiffs took up all of the first day with their motions and arguments. As it was known that Henry would speak the next day, the chamber in the courthouse was early filled to capacity, with an overflow crowd pushing to get in. The legislature was meeting at the time, and so many members came to hear Henry that no legislative business could be done in want of a quorum. There was a profound "listening silence" as Henry rose to speak slowly and softly:

> I stand here, may it please your Honors, to support, according to my powers, that side of the question which respects the American debtor. I beg leave to beseech the patience of this honorable court because the subject is very great and important, and because I have . . . these numerous observations which have come from opposing counsel to answer. . . .
>
> Sir, there is a circumstance in this case that is more to be deplored than that which I have just mentioned, and that is this: these animosities which the injustice of the British nation hath produced, and which I had well hoped would never again be the subject of discussion, are necessarily brought forth. The conduct of that nation, which bore so hard upon us in the late contest, becomes once more the subject of investigation.
>
> I know, Sir, how well it becomes a liberal man and a Christian to forget and to forgive . . . injuries done us as individuals. But when to the character of Christian you add the character of patriot, you are in a different position . . . If your enemy smite one cheek, turn the other to him. But you must stop there. You cannot apply this to your country . . . When you consider injuries done to your country, your political duty tells you of vengeance.
>
> Forgive as a private man, but never forgive public injuries. Observations of this nature are exceedingly unpleasant, but it is my duty to use them.

This appeal to patriotism, though quite irrelevant to the facts at issue, visibly moved his audience, as Henry knew it would. Having created the mood he wished, he held the floor for three days as he went on elaborating his argument, the gist of which was: that under international law and other law, Virginia had every right to pass the legislation she had adopted about British debts during the Revolution, and that such legislation was still valid.

No decision on the case was taken at this session of court. A second hearing was held in May, 1793, a year and a half later. Again the court chamber in Richmond was filled to overflowing. The case was deemed of such importance that the three judges on the bench included the Chief Justice of the U. S. Supreme Court, John Jay, and an associate Supreme Court Justice, James Iredell.

A spirited twenty-year-old, John Randolph, later well known as the brilliant but eccentric John Randolph of Roanoke, came to the courtroom early and obtained a seat right up front where he could overhear what the judges were saying among themselves. Randolph left a vivid picture of the scene.

John Jay knew Henry and had heard his eloquent addresses at the First and Second Continental Congresses. Justice Iredell had never heard Henry speak. Turning to Iredell and pointing to Henry, Jay said, there is "the greatest of orators." Iredell was dubious after looking at Henry who seemed to be old and feeble, wrapped up in mufflers and "resting his head on the bar." Eager to hear what Henry had to say, the Bench asked him to proceed with his argument and gave him the floor. Henry had not planned to speak at just this moment, but he did not demur and made the most of a dramatic opportunity.

Lumbering to his feet, Henry said that it was too great a hardship "to put the laboring oar into the hands of a decrepid old man, trembling, with one foot in the grave, weak in his best days, and far inferior to the able associates by him." Randolph realized he was putting on an act to gain sympathy and attention.

As Henry went on and warmed up, his pace became that "of a first-rate, four-mile racehorse, sometimes displaying his whole power and then taking up again." As Henry approached the end of his speech, he "got up to full speed, and took a rapid view of what England had done when she had been successful in arms, and what would have been our fate had we been unsuccessful."

> The color began to come and go in the face of the Chief Justice, while Iredell sat with his mouth and eyes stretched

> open, in perfect wonder. Finally, Henry arrived at his utmost height and grandeur. He raised his hands in one of his grand and solemn pauses.*

Thunderous applause exploded in the courtroom. "Gracious God!" exclaimed Justice Iredell. "He is an orator indeed!" Later, alluding to Henry, Iredell wrote: "I shall as long as I live remember with pleasure and respect the arguments I have heard in this case. They have discovered an ingenuity, a depth of investigation, and a power of reasoning fully equal to anything I have ever witnessed, and some of them have been adorned with a splendor of eloquence surpassing what I ever felt before."

Even Jefferson, usually so critical of Henry's abilities and knowledge as a lawyer, was impressed and said of him on this occasion, rather grudgingly:

> I believe he never distinguished himself so much as on the question of British debts . . . He had exerted a degree of industry in that case totally foreign to his character and not only seemed, but had made himself really, learned on the subject.**

While conducting his very remunerative law practice, Henry was at the same time investing in more speculations in western lands and watching closely the properties he already owned. The comfortable fortune he built up in these later years came largely from his real estate operations. It was still possible to obtain huge tracts of unsettled public lands for almost nothing. Henry used great discrimination in his selection of such tracts and was able to sell or exchange them at a considerable profit.

A few of his speculative land deals did not turn out so well. Henry bought a tract along the Tennessee River in lands which the Creek Indians had ceded to Georgia by treaty in 1783. Still a powerful tribe, the Creek were harassing settlers moving westward and kept the region in turmoil by waging war on neighboring tribes. Seeking allies to help them check ever increasing encroachments by land-

---

* In later years, recalling this speech and others, John Randolph of Roanoke said of Henry: "He was Shakespeare and Garrick combined."

** Later, with Henry not participating in the proceedings, the Virginia debtors lost their case. The Federal courts, reversing an earlier decision, held that British creditors could sue for the collection of their debts on the ground that the 1783 peace treaty was still in force, that it was therefore the supreme law of the land under the new Constitution, which annulled whatever acts Virginia had passed previously, even though she had been sovereign—or semi-sovereign—at the time.

hungry American settlers and speculators, the Creek had established relations with Spanish headquarters in New Orleans.

In 1790, in the hope of pacifying the Creek, President Washington invited their great chief Alexander McGillivray to a parley in New York. The chief was received with great ceremony, and he and Washington soon drafted a treaty that was adopted.

The Creek were promised a liberal annuity; the lands they had ceded to Georgia under duress were restored to them; Chief McGillivray was given the rank and pay of a brigadier general in the United States Army. For their part, the Creek promised to be "under the protection of the United States, and of no other nation whatsoever," which referred to their dealings with Spain.

Henry was furious, for the large tract along the Tennessee which he had bought lay in the extensive territory that had been taken from Georgia and returned to the Creek. He wrote letters to the governor of Georgia and prominent leaders of the state, criticizing the high-handed "assumptions of power" by the federal government.

They were just such assumptions, he said, that he had feared all along. He was not disposed "to bow down before the threats of power . . . It is a deception to urge that encroachments from the American government are not dangerous. In fact, they are more to be dreaded at this particular time in our own government than from any other quarter. No foreign power can annoy us. . . ."

If precedents like this treaty were allowed to stand, "it is but too easy to see the fatal examples they will furnish for a repetition of the like or greater mischiefs. There is therefore no doubt remaining of the propriety of doing everything which becomes patriots to rescue your country [Georgia] from the calamities which must ensue from the present effects & future mischiefs of this treaty. If you demand what is to be done, I own myself at a loss to answer; but I will give you my present thoughts, unmatured as they are."

First, a "decent but spirited" protest should be sent to the federal government, "stating your right to the territory & deducing it from the Crown of England down to the present time . . ." Indian affairs were handled much better under the British government, being directed by "men of sufficient understanding from the respective colonies" who superintended and guarded "the interests of all concerned." The Continental Congress followed that policy. "Instead of dismembering states, guaranteeing countries, and paying tribute to Indians, they gave peace, assigning them lands to live & hunt upon, &c." Henry did not mention that the Indians were not at all pleased with the restricted "assignments" given to them for the use of lands that belonged to them.

"A dispassionate candid statement of facts, addressed to every state in the Union, seems to me necessary," Henry went on. "The particulars of the injury you suffer are not known to many persons in the states distant from yours. The whole matter should be fairly explained to the world at large. How else can you be redressed? . . . Will you pardon, Sir, the freedom of my expressions. My real concern for the prosperity of your country [Georgia] is my only motive."

Henry was stretching it a bit here, for later in the same letter he admitted his personal interest in the matter. "Endeared as Georgia is to me by the hope of being possessed of valuable property within her limits, & where I fondly hoped to fix my posterity, I shall anxiously await the result of affairs at this session of your Assembly."

Whether Henry seriously contemplated removing himself and his family to the wilds along the Tennessee is uncertain, but it is doubtful that he did. He was making a play to enlist the fullest possible support for his hope of possessing the "valuable property" he had bought in the Creek country. The Georgia authorities, both the legislature and the governor, strongly protested the treaty with Chief McGillivray, but to no avail.

Another speculation in Georgia real estate turned out even worse, and led to some ill-founded criticism of Henry on the part of those who wished to defame him—ill-founded criticism that has been repeated by some biographers and historians who did not bother to discover the facts of the matter.

In 1789, seeing that Georgia was disposed to sell the unsettled lands she held to the west as far as the Mississippi, Henry and some friends organized the Virginia Yazoo Company, naming it for the Yazoo River, a tributary of the Mississippi. The company drew up a petition and approached the Georgia legislature, which approved it and granted the company a large tract along the Yazoo. The price was $93,740, to be paid in two years "in the currency of the State, or any liquidated debts against the State."

The company began buying up Georgia debt certificates and, within the time limit, handed these to the State Treasurer in full payment for the tract. But the Treasurer refused to accept them, for the legislature had meantime ruled that he was to accept payments only in gold, silver, and paper currency, and not in debt certificates.

Matters rested thus till 1794, when the company sent an agent to Georgia with a petition urging the legislature to carry out the contract made in 1789. The agent found the legislature engaged in selling not only the Virginia company's tract but an additional huge area to several newly organized land companies—the Georgia Company, the Georgia Mississippi Company, the Upper Mississippi Company, and the Tennessee Company. For $500,000, these companies acquired a vast empire of 35,000,000 acres in what is now northern Alabama and Mississippi. The price for the empire worked out at a little more than a cent an acre.

There was an immediate outcry from the people in Georgia. With this "scandalous deal" as the main issue, a new legislature was elected, and it proceeded immediately to look into what had been done at the previous session. Upon investigation, it found that very many of the legislators voting for the gigantic land grab had been personally interested in the deal, and had engineered the "Yazoo Fraud." The legislative transfer of the 35,000,000 acres was rescinded, and all documents of sale on these acres were ordered to be burned in front of the State House, which was done with great ceremony and celebration.

Henry and his partners in the Virginia Yazoo Company now decided to file suit against the State of Georgia in the United States Supreme Court to assert their claim to the large tract for which they had successfully negotiated in 1789, but which had been subsequently sold to other companies. Counsel was appointed to prepare and prosecute their case. But it never came to a hearing, for it was stopped by the adoption of the Eleventh Amendment to the Constitution which declares that a state cannot be sued by citizens of another state, or by citizens of a foreign nation.

Far from being involved in and profiting from the Yazoo Fraud, as is often carelessly and erroneously stated, Henry and his partners in the Virginia Yazoo Company lost the tract they claimed because of that fraud.

In general, however, Henry did very well with his investments and speculations in land. After his two youthful dismal failures as a country merchant and storekeeper, he had learned the ways of the world and become an astute man of business, with a sharp eye for bargains. As was said of Henry by his son-in-law Spencer Roane, "He could buy or sell a horse, or a Negro, as well as anybody, and was peculiarly a judge of the value and quality of lands." It was on this peculiar judgment that he built the considerable fortune that the members of his numerous family inherited.

In 1794, Henry gave up the practice of law. For some thirty-five years, except for a break during the Revolution, Henry had been riding the circuit, in fair weather and foul, from one county courthouse to another, wherever he had business pending. In early years, he had journeyed on horseback; in more recent years, in a stick gig, a light two-wheeled carriage, usually with no top, drawn by a single horse. All this traveling Henry found exhausting, and no longer felt himself up to it.

On retiring as a lawyer, Henry sold his 16,000-acre farm in Prince Edward County–no doubt at a profit–and moved southwestward into Campbell County, where he had bought, along the Staunton River, a large estate called Long Island, named for an island in the river. He soon sold Long Island on buying another large estate about twenty miles down the river, naming it Red Hill because of the color of the soil. Here Henry spent the remaining years of his life, with few excursions that took him more than a mile or two from home.

Henry's last years, except for recurrent illnesses, appear to have been happy ones. He did not miss the excitement of clashes with opposing counsel in courtrooms, or with political adversaries in legislative halls or in public meetings. Henry had always been, at heart, a family man.

"In every relation, as a husband, father, master, and neighbor, he was entirely exemplary," wrote his son-in-law, Judge Spencer Roane, who was quite objective about Henry and could at times be very critical of him. "As to the disposition of Mr. Henry, it was the best imaginable. I am positive that I never saw him in a passion, nor apparently out of temper. Circumstances that would have highly irritated other men had no visible effect on him; he was always cool and collected." Roane added:

> No man ever vaunted less of his achievements than Mr. Henry. I hardly ever heard him speak of [his] great achievements . . . As for boasting, he was entirely a stranger to it unless it be that in his latter days he seemed proud of the goodness of his lands, and I believe wished to be thought wealthy. It is my opinion that he was better pleased to be flattered as to his wealth than as to his great talents. . . .

Shortly after the adoption of the Constitution, Henry had been attacked in a most abusive and scurrilous way in a series of articles signed by one "Decius"—probably written by George Nicholas and his friends, with whom Henry had violently clashed at the Virginia Constitutional Convention, almost leading to a duel. Decius not only castigated Henry's conduct at the convention but "slandered his character by various stories hatched up against him. These pieces were extremely hateful to all of Mr. Henry's friends and, indeed, to a great portion of the community," said Roane.

> I was at his house in Prince Edward during the thickest of them. . . . He evinced no feeling on the occasion, and far less condescended to parry the effects on the public mind. It was too puny a contest for him, and he reposed upon the consciousness of his own integrity. . . .
>
> With many sublime virtues, he had no vice that I knew or ever heard of, and scarcely a foible. I have thought, indeed, that he was too much attached to property—a defect, however, which might be excused when we reflect on the largeness of a beloved family, and the straitened circumstances in which he had been confined during a great part of his life.

Henry enjoyed his secluded retirement at Red Hill, which was a pleasant spot. The large frame house there stood on a knoll overlooking the Staunton River and the broad rich meadows and fields lying in the bottom lands on either side of the river. In the distance to the west could be seen the Peaks of Otter along the Blue Ridge. It was unspoiled and lovely country, such as Henry had always preferred since his youngest years when growing up at Studley Farm.

Henry had always been an early riser, and continued to be. Before sunrise on clear mornings, in spring, summer, and fall, when the air was cool and filled with birdsong and the lowing of cattle, Henry would walk out to a high point looking down on the fields along the river and give "orders and directions to his servants at work a half mile distant from him," recalled his grandson, Patrick Henry Fontaine, who lived these years with the Henrys.

> The strong musical voices of the Negroes responded to him. During this morning exercise, his enunciation was clear and distinct enough to be heard over an area which ten thousand could not have filled, and the tones of his voice were as melodious as the notes of an Alpine horn.

Having made his Alpine call, Henry would return to the house, pick up his Bible to read, and sit down at the table to wait for breakfast. As the members of his large household appeared—his wife, their many sons and daughters, and grandsons and granddaughters by other marriages—he would greet each of them, even the tiniest, with a cheerful "Good morrow."

After breakfast, if the weather were good, he would go out of doors and sit under one of the high trees shading his lawn, from which he could see the beautiful valley spread out below. Not only in the mornings but in the evenings he would sit under the trees, "with his chair leaning against one of their trunks and a can of cool spring water by his side, from which he took frequent draughts. Occasionally, he walked to and fro in the yard from one clump of trees to another, buried in revery, at which time he was never interrupted. . . . His great delight was in conversation in the society of his friends and family, and in the resources of his own mind."

Henry was always "the most sociable of men," as Jefferson and others noted, and many visitors came to Red Hill to enjoy his open hospitality and the charm of his company. He liked to talk with all kinds of people, no matter what their station in life, from the highest to the humblest, and once observed that he had never talked with anyone without learning something.

Henry was a wonderful conversationalist, being at once an engaging raconteur and a good listener (a rare combination), and out of his long experience in the courts and public assemblies he had fascinating tales to tell—some of them serious, but quite as many of them witty and amusing, which sent his company into gales of laughter.

There was no "front" or ceremony at Red Hill. When distinguished visitors arrived to talk with Henry, they "not infrequently caught him lying on the floor with a group of little ones [his youngest children and his grandchildren] climbing over him in every direction, or dancing around him with obstreperous mirth, to the tune of his violin, while the only contest seemed to be who could make the most noise." When in a serious mood, he would talk, but only confidentially to particular friends, about those with whom he had been associated in public life. He had "strong prejudices" here, both for and against:

> He had the highest opinion of George Mason's talents, patriotism, and republican principles.* He considered him as a man

* Mason, for his part, held Henry in the highest esteem, writing, as noted earlier: "He is by far the most powerful speaker I ever heard. . . . But his eloquence is the smallest part of his merit. He is, in my opinion, the first man upon this continent as well in abilities as public virtues. . . ."

well acquainted with the interests of the people, and warmly attached to the liberty of his country. A cordial friendship existed between them.

Of R.H. [Richard Henry] Lee, he did not think quite so well, and they were very often opposed to each other. Yet they coalesced on great questions, as that of independence and opposition to the Federal constitution.* He was very fond of John Tyler as a warmhearted patriot and an honest sensible man. . . .

As to Mr. Madison, he considered him in 1783–4 as a man of great acquirements, but too theoretical as a politician, and that he was not well versed in the affairs of men. This opinion increased in the convention of 1788. He was astonished that Madison would take the constitution, admitting its defects, . . . and he believed him too friendly to a strong government and too hostile to the governments of the States. . . . Henry's prejudice against Madison always remained in some degree, and to this may possibly in some measure be ascribed his alleged secession from the Republican Party,** now headed by Madison, toward the close of his life.

Guests at Red Hill enjoyed good food cooked and served in a simple manner, without any frills. Almost all of the things brought to the table came from the farm: vegetables from the kitchen garden, fruit from the orchards, homemade preserves, fowl and eggs from the chicken yard, meats from the smokehouse–beef, veal, hams, bacon, mutton, lamb, and venison on occasion. Though not much of a trencherman, Henry relished good "honest" dishes. When Jefferson returned after his years in Paris as our ambassador there, he brought back recipes for many elaborately made and elaborately served French delicacies and put his cook to work on them, extolling the merits and pleasures of French cookery. "What's the matter?" Henry once asked rather sardonically. "Isn't roast beef now good enough for him?"

Though those entertained at Red Hill were doubtless offered wines and drinks made of rum and whisky, Henry never had a taste for "strong waters," or the fruit of the vine. In a day of very heavy drink-

---

* During these years Henry lost both of these old friends. Mason died in 1792, Lee in 1794. The older generation of Revolutionary leaders was passing, which must have put some thoughts in Henry's mind.

** Henry's "secession" from the Republican Party will be discussed shortly.

ing among Virginians, Henry was notably abstemious. The increase of drunkenness during and after the Revolution had disturbed him and led him to ponder means of checking it. His grandson Fontaine tells us:

> He thought that the introduction of a harmless beverage, as a substitute for distilled spirits, would be beneficial. To effect this object, he ordered from his merchant in Scotland a consignment of barley seed, and a Scotch brewer and his wife to cultivate the grain, and make small beer. To render the beverage fashionable and popular, he always had it on his table while he was governor during his last terms, . . . and he continued its use, but drank nothing stronger.

Henry's reading in his leisure at Red Hill seems to have been largely confined to the Bible and to theological works on the tenets of Christianity by Archbishop Tillotson, Bishop Butler, and the Reverend Sherlock, all of them Church of England divines. A neighbor came for a visit one day and found Henry reading his Bible. "This book is worth all the books that were ever printed," said Henry, holding up the opened Bible, "and it has been my misfortune that I have never found time to read it with the proper attention and feeling till recently. I trust in the mercy of Heaven that it is not yet too late."

Henry was particularly impressed with the published sermons of Sherlock, which had dispelled, he said, all of his "doubts of the truth of Christianity." On Sunday evenings he would read one of Sherlock's sermons to his family gathered about him, "after which they all joined in sacred music, while he accompanied them on the violin."

As his father was an Anglican, Henry had been baptized in what was then the Church of England* by his uncle, the Reverend Patrick Henry, rector of St. Paul's Parish. Though he befriended and greatly helped the Baptists, Quakers, Methodists, and other Dissenters in the days before 1776, when they were being violently persecuted by bigoted neighbors, Henry was never converted to their doctrines. He remained an Anglican all his life.

But however religious he became in his later years, he was never an active churchman. There is no record of his ever having been a regular communicant in any church. He took communion occasion-

* Which became the Protestant Episcopal Church when the ties with Britain were cut. The new church retained the credo and the liturgy of the old, as noted before, except for the elision in prayers of "God save the King."

ally in the church near home or in those that were convenient when he was on the road from court to court. Henry evidently preferred his private meditations to formal church services.

Jefferson more than once marveled how Henry knew so much when he read so little. He all but suggested that Henry had never read anything but his law books, but Henry must have read much more than was generally known. From allusions in his speeches it is evident that Henry had read wisely and widely in the histories of ancient Greece and Rome, and of England and Virginia.

And what Henry read, he knew, storing in his most retentive memory the points of interest and of use to him. There is no indication that he was familiar with Shakespeare, which was a pity. He would have delighted in the poet's singing verse and his strong declaratory rhetoric. But he had read other works of high merit, and he remembered them.

On one occasion Henry and other notables had been invited by Edmund Randolph to have dinner and stay the night at his country house. After dinner, the company sat conversing, no doubt with a bottle of good port going around the table. Richard Henry Lee began talking about and expatiating on the genius of Cervantes, especially as shown in *Don Quixote*. Lee's conversation often tended to become a monologue, as this one did, and it went on and on. The hour was getting late. After a while, Henry rose from the table, sauntered to the mantelpiece at the end of the room, walked slowly back and, standing near Lee, interrupted him gently.

"But, Sir, you have overlooked in your eulogy one of the finest things in the work."

"What is that?"

"It is that divine exclamation of Sancho: 'Blessed be the man that first invented sleep; it covers one all over like a cloak.' "

Lee looked up, caught the point, wound up his discourse and the company, "in good humor," went yawning to bed.

XXVIII
Last Years

. . . I shall never more appear in a public character . . .

—PATRICK HENRY

During his retirement years at Red Hill, Henry was not, except on one notable occasion, politically active. But he kept a close watch on events at home and abroad. In the light of such events, his political opinions began to change.

Though the foremost leader of those opposed to ratifying the Philadelphia document without prior amendments, Henry had accepted his defeat gracefully, announcing that he would not proceed to violence, that he would work for amendments by constitutional means. Henry, Mason, Richard Henry Lee, and many more in Virginia and all the states sincerely believed that amendments could not, or at least would not, be made by such means. Once the Constitution was adopted, it would remain set, hard and rigid, with no additions or subtractions.

But Henry and others of like mind were mistaken. Due wholly to the pressure of the Anti-Federalists and to the widespread popular dissatisfaction which that pressure reflected, the First Congress, prodded by Madison,* took up the subject of amendments and adopted twelve of them. These were submitted to the states, which in 1791 adopted ten of them—which became known as our national Bill of Rights, being largely based on Virginia's celebrated Declaration of Rights, adopted in June, 1776, before the signing of the Declaration of Independence.

Though they did not wholly meet the objections of the Anti-ratificationists, the ten amendments satisfied Henry who began to shift in his attitude toward the Constitution and toward the Washington administration—just when he shifted is not clear, but it must have been in Washington's first administration.

That Washington had been elected as the first President gave Henry assurance that the great powers of that office would not be stretched or abused. Henry had long had the highest admiration and respect for Washington's integrity of character and soundness of judgment. Among the great leaders assembled in Philadelphia for the First Continental Congress in 1774, Henry had said of Washington that though he had no pretensions to eloquence, he was "a man of more solid judgment and information than any man on that floor."

Henry had worked with John Adams in having Washington named as commander-in-chief of the Continental Army and as virtual President of the United States from 1775 to 1783. Henry was one of the first to alert Washington about the machinations of the Conway Cabal which sought in 1777 to displace General Washington as commander-in-chief after a series of severe military reverses. Henry no doubt voted for Washington when he was elected for his second term as President in 1792, with John Adams again as Vice-President.

Foreign affairs now began to disturb American politics, as they have so often in the past and increasingly so in recent years. The entire Western World was shaken to its foundations by the great French Revolution which began on July 14, 1789, when angry Parisians stormed and tore down the prison in the center of the city, the Bastille, hated symbol of the centuries-old oppressions of the semi-feudal *ancien régime*. Except for the crowned heads of Europe and their courtiers, the Revolution was generally welcomed as a breath of fresh air, a beacon of hope—indeed, as the harbinger of the millennium.

Shouts of *liberté, egalité, fraternité* echoed over the Continent, in

* Madison personally took the view that amendments were not necessary, but that as so many were clamoring for amendments, it would be politic for the Federalists to give in and silence that clamor by adopting amendments.

the British Isles, and across the Atlantic. Shortly after the fall of the Bastille came the creation of a great national army independent of King Louis XVI, the Declaration of the Rights of Man, the destruction of the entire semi-feudal establishment, the abolition of titles of nobility, and the march on Versailles by Parisian *poissardes* (fishwives) who triumphantly led a supposedly invincible monarch back to Paris as a captive.

Europe's oldest and most resplendent absolutism had fallen, and the English people, reported the *Annual Register,* "were universally disposed to congratulate its ancient rival upon the dawn of its liberty." The Revolution, exclaimed Charles James Fox, a young Whig leader, was the greatest and best event that had ever happened in the world. It was a time of boundless enthusiasm. The young poet William Wordsworth, in Paris at the time, later recalled with a quickening of the pulse those days when

> Not favoured spots alone, but the whole earth,
> The beauty wore of promise.

The brilliant English essayist and critic, William Hazlitt, also recalled those days: "A new world was opening to the astonished sight. Scenes, lovely as hope can paint, dawned on the imagination, visions of unsullied bliss lulled the senses and hid the darkness of surrounding objects, rising in bright succession and endless gradations, like the steps of the ladder that was once set up on earth and whose top reached to heaven. Nothing was too mighty for this new begotten hope, and the path that led to human happiness seemed as plain as the pictures in *Pilgrim's Progress* leading to Paradise."

Tom Paine, having returned to England from America, where he had been very shabbily treated after many great services to the Patriot cause, hastened to Paris to greet and congratulate his friend Lafayette, whom he had met and come to admire during the American Revolution, in which both had served with high distinction.

As there was no American ambassador in Paris at the moment, Jefferson having left for home to become Secretary of State, Lafayette, a leader of the moderates in the new regime, having been made commander-in-chief of the reorganized French army, received Paine as the official representative of the United States. To Paine, Lafayette handed the key to the Bastille and asked him to forward it, as he did, to President Washington as a gift from the now liberated French people.

Paine would soon publish his *Rights of Man,* a most explosive work that had a greater popular political impact than any book of its day, and is still worth reading, for Paine was a phrasemaker. A thoroughgoing republican since the days of the American Revolution, Paine declared that kings were all cheats and impostors who lived by war and human butchery. When wearied with their play, they "sit down to rest and call it peace." An hereditary ruler was as absurd as an hereditary poet. Men were monarchs who did not have "the capacities of a village constable."

Men had "natural, inalienable rights—to liberty, property, security, and resistance to oppression." Any government worthy of the name was something more than a glorified police force. It held the welfare of the community in its hands. It had a duty to the weak and the poor. These should be helped, Paine proposed, by old age pensions and maternity benefits, and all should be enlightened by a free compulsory system of education. This could be hoped for only in a popularly based republican form of government.

Sir Horace Walpole spoke the minds of most aristocrats in finding Paine's work "the most seditious pamphlet ever seen but in open rebellion."

Paine's pen had much the same appeal and force as Henry's tongue. Both men had a plain, simple, and direct style, often pell-mell in its pace, piling climax upon climax. Both were masters at commanding the emotions. It was said of Henry that he could make his listeners laugh or cry at will. Without any literary embroidery or flourishes, Henry and Paine could drive a point home by unerringly hitting the nail squarely on the head, telling men what they were eager to hear, and in their own language.

As the French Revolution began, even the most conservative saw no cause for alarm. In Britain, for example, King George III was pleased and smiled at the ironic fate of his fellow monarch; he was getting more or less what he deserved for having given aid to the American "rebels"—aid that contributed to the fiscal problems that had led Louis XVI into serious troubles.

To cynical British diplomats, French liberty meant little. But it mattered a great deal to them that France, as a world power, "was quite out of line, and not worthy to be reckoned as a friend or a foe." The Revolution, in shattering France, had removed Britain's historic imperialist rival.

Edmund Burke, who would soon violently denounce the Revolution and all of its works, declared in the House of Commons early in 1790, that he had looked at the map of Europe and where France had been, there was only a void. It would be safe therefore to cut British military expenditures materially. When Mirabeau heard of Burke's remark, he pronounced it *"une grande sottise . . . ce vide est un volcan."*

Mirabeau was certainly a better prophet than Burke, as the latter soon discovered to his utter horror. As the volcano went on erupting with ever greater violence, this caused a split in American public opinion. Like the British, Americans at first had been generally sympathetic with the struggle of the French people to gain equality of rights and abolish the "trappings" of monarchy and of an indolent, corrupt, and callous aristocracy that enjoyed, with its titles, exceptional rights and powers by reason of birth and of inherited wealth deriving from institutions going back to the Middle Ages and even before. France was being updated, which was good.

But then came the proclamation of the French Republic in September, 1792, followed by the execution of Louis XVI, of Queen Marie Antoinette, and of a number of counterrevolutionary leaders who had been conspiring with the crowned heads of Europe to organize an armed force to restore the monarchy and the whole of the *ancien régime.*

After extreme provocations in the form of armed interventions against her, the French Republic declared war on Britain, Holland, and Spain early in 1793. This opened a new epoch that led through the Napoleonic wars down to the Battle of Waterloo in 1814 more than twenty years later.

France's declaration of war against Britain and other powers in 1793 injected the French Revolution and all that it stood for into American politics. There was a large group, with Jefferson as a chief spokesman, that was pro-French—but perhaps more anti-British than pro-French. This group began organizing what they called Democratic clubs for the discussion of political theories, principles of government, and current issues.

Watching with growing concern the increasingly bitter strife between the pro-French and the pro-British parties, President Washington issued early in 1793 a neutrality proclamation (though not using the word "neutrality"), in which he pointed out that the country was at peace with both Britain and France and warned Americans not to commit hostile acts against any of the belligerent powers.

From being an ardent Federalist, Madison had moved over into the pro-French Republican party and under the name of "Helvidius" strongly denounced the neutrality proclamation. Speaking for the pro-British Federalists and signing himself "Pacificus,"* Alexander Hamilton defended the proclamation and the President's right to issue it on his own initiative, which the Republicans denied.

Then arose another issue which plagued American politics for years. Contrary to the peace treaty of 1783, Britain was still holding Niagara, Detroit, and other strong posts in the western United States, on the ground that legal obstacles had been placed in the way of recovering pre-Revolution debts owed to British merchants and of compensating Loyalists for their property which had been confiscated.

In 1793, by Orders in Council, the British aggravated the situation by interfering with all neutral shipping, insisting upon their own definition of contraband and their own rules of the sea. American vessels were stopped, searched, and seized; American seamen were imprisoned and even pressed into British service. The two countries were close to war.

To negotiate a settlement, President Washington named a staunch pro-British Federalist, John Jay, Chief Justice of the United States Supreme Court, to act as a special envoy in London. The treaty that Jay negotiated was generally thought to be a giveaway. Even Washington found it unsatisfactory. After extended debate, the Senate finally accepted the treaty, but the Republicans in the House attempted to block its enforcement by denying appropriations for the purpose. The House asked to see all the papers relating to Jay's treaty, but President Washington refused to submit them, asserting his executive prerogative, setting an important precedent.

During these years Henry had not been talking publicly about national policies and issues. As he had long before proclaimed, "I own myself a democrat," the Democratic-Republican party expected him to take his stand on their side. On the other hand, the Federalist party had reason to think that he might not.

Federalists had begun courting Henry early in 1793, when the Governor of Virginia, General Henry Lee, had suggested to President Washington that Henry's great influence might be brought to the support of the administration if he were named to a major post. Washington agreed. On his return to Virginia, Lee talked with Henry "very freely and confidentially." Lee found Henry nursing a deep wound to his pride.

---

* Hamilton was anything but pacific. He had long been advocating an immediate declaration of war against France to stop the spread of ideas that might result in "anarchy and civil disorder."

In 1791, while on a journey to the South, President Washington had passed through Prince Edward County where Henry was then living. Washington had not stopped for a visit, and it was later reported to Henry that the President on his journey had more than once said that he regarded Henry as "a factious, seditious character."

Henry was "deeply and sorely affected" by this, Lee reported to Washington. "It is very much to be regretted," Lee added, "for he is a man of positive virtue as well as transcendent talents, and were it not for his feelings . . . , I verily believe he would be found among the most active supporters of your administration. Excuse me for mentioning this matter to you. I have long wished to do it in the hope that it will lead to a refutation of the sentiments entertained by Mr. Henry."

In a letter marked "private" and dated August 26, 1794, Washington replied to Lee, denying that he had ever said anything disrespectful of Henry. Some malicious men were putting words in his mouth and circulating rumors to create general discord and enmity.

> Under this head may be classed, I conceive, what it is reported I have said of Mr. Henry . . . It is evident, therefore, that these reports are propagated with evil intentions, to create personal differences.
>
> On the question of the Constitution, Mr. Henry and myself, it is well known, have been of different opinions. But, personally, I have always respected and esteemed him.
>
> Nay, more, I have conceived myself under obligations to him for the friendly manner in which he transmitted to me some insidious anonymous writings that were sent to him in the close of the year 1777, with a view to embark him in the opposition that was forming against me at that time.*

Washington recalled to Lee the conversations they had had about Henry, and some of the questions discussed. First, could Henry "be induced to accept any appointment under the general government?" Lee believed so, but said he could not be sure. What if Henry proved "to be inimical to it?" asked Washington. "The wound the government would receive by his refusal, and the charge of attempting to silence his opposition by a place, would be great."

---

* Referring to the unsigned letters, later discovered to have been written by Dr. Benjamin Rush of Philadelphia, in which the latter sought Henry's support for a move being contemplated to oust General Washington as commander-in-chief. Henry immediately forwarded the letters to Washington.

Second, Lee was of the opinion that Henry would not accept any office that would make residence at the seat of government essential. This limited possibilities. Washington and Lee agreed that if an appointment were offered, Henry could not be expected to accept "anything short of one of the great offices." Washington then came to the point with Lee:

> What is it then you have in contemplation that you conceive would be relished? And ought there not be a moral certainty of its acceptance?
>
> This being the case, there would not be wanting a disposition on my part, but strong inducements on public and private grounds, to invite Mr. Henry into any employment under the general government to which his inclination might lead . . .

Lee informed Henry of the relevant parts of Washington's letter, and this broke the ice. An offer of appointment soon came. Secretary of State Edmund Randolph wrote to Henry signifying the President's wish that Henry "act in the character of envoy extraordinary to the Court of Madrid on the business of the Mississippi navigation"—a business in which Henry had long been interested. Henry replied that a variety of circumstances prevented him from accepting the appointment:

> The importance of the negotiation & its probable length in a country so distant are difficulties not easy to reconcile to one at my time of life. But to these are added others which leave me no room to hesitate.
>
> Whilst I sincerely regret the causes which compel me to decline the honor intended me, I cannot forbear to express my highest obligations to the President for his favorable sentiments . . .

The next year, in 1795, a vacancy occurred in Washington's Cabinet with the resignation of Secretary of State Edmund Randolph who was under the shadow of charges later disproved. The office of Attorney General was also open due to death. Washington, as he complained, was encountering great difficulties "in finding out, and prevailing upon, fit characters to fill offices of importance." He had already offered the office of Secretary of State to three persons, all of whom declined. Then the President thought of Henry as a possibility. After some political consultations with two Virginia friends and trusted Federalists, John Marshal and Edward Carrington, the latter forwarded to Henry a letter from Washington.

Henry doubtless knew, wrote Washington, "that the office of State is vacant, and no one can be more sensible than yourself of the importance of filling it with a person of abilities, and one in whom the public would have confidence." Washington candidly admitted that the office had been offered to others, but added that he would have offered it first to Henry except for his conviction that the latter would not accept. This was not quite true. In any case, the recent conversation with General Lee had caused Washington to change his mind:

> I need scarcely add that if this appointment could be made to comport with your inclination, it would be as pleasing to me as I believe it would be acceptable to the public. With this assurance, and with this belief, I make you the offer of it.
>
> My first wish is that you would accept it; the next is that you would be so good as to give me answer as soon as you conveniently can, as the public business in that department is now suffering for want of the Secretary.

Washington assured Henry that the chief aim of his administration was to comply strictly with all engagements, domestic and foreign, but to keep the United States free from political connections with foreign nations and thus be independent of them and under the influence of none.

> In a word, I want an *American* character that the powers of Europe may be convinced we act for *ourselves,* and not for others. This in my judgment is the only way to be respected abroad and happy at home, and not by becoming the partisans of Great Britain or France . . .
>
> I am satisfied these sentiments cannot but be otherwise than congenial to your own. Your aid therefore in carrying them into effect would be flattering and pleasing . . .

Henry agreed with Washington's views, but again declined appointment. To disobey a call to the country's service when made by "her venerable chief" would be a crime, he said, unless there were "the most substantial reasons" for doing so:

> My domestic situation pleads strongly against a removal to Philadelphia, having no less than eight children by my present marriage, and Mrs. Henry's situation* now forbidding her ap-

* She was evidently pregnant again. After this child, there would be two more, the last of them dying at birth a year before Henry's death.

> proach to the small pox, which neither herself nor any in our family ever had.
>
> To this may be added other considerations arising from loss of crops and consequent derangement of my finances. And what is of decisive weight with me, my own health and strength, I believe, are unequal to the duties of the station you are pleased to offer me . . .
>
> Permit me to add that, having devoted many years of the prime of my life to the public service and thereby injured my circumstances, I have been obliged to resume my profession and go again to the Bar at a time of life too advanced to support the fatigue of it.* By this means my health has been injured.
>
> When these things are considered, may I hope for your favorable judgment on the motives by which I am actuated? . . .

Federalists, in their courtship of Henry, were certainly nothing if not persistent. Another call soon came to Henry. The President had named John Rutledge of South Carolina to be Chief Justice of the United States Supreme Court. The Senate refused to confirm Rutledge's appointment, which left that high and important office vacant. Washington immediately asked General Lee to find out if Henry would be willing to take the post. Writing posthaste, Lee urged his friend Henry to say yes:

> For your country's sake, for your friends' sake, for your family's sake, tell me you will obey a call to it. You know my friendship for you, you know my circumspection, and I trust you know, too, that I would not address you on such a subject without good grounds.
>
> Surely no situation better suits an individual than that will you—you continue at home [except] when on duty—change of air and exercise will add to your days.
>
> The salary excellent and the honor very great. Be explicit in your reply.

Two weeks later, Washington complained to Lee that he had heard nothing from him about the Henry business. This "is em-

* Henry was stretching it a bit here. He had given up his general law practice several years before, though he may still have been handling a few cases, but for settlement out of court. Henry had addressed a jury or a bench of judges for the last time.

barrassing in the extreme," wrote Washington, "for not only the nomination of Chief Justice, but an Associate Judge and Secretary of War, is suspended on the answer you were to receive from Mr. Henry." Besides, the Supreme Court would be sitting within three weeks and, "for particular reasons, the bench ought to be full."

Nothing more was heard about this matter, but Henry did not become Chief Justice, no doubt having declined the offered appointment, because as he had explained before, he did not wish to leave his more or less secluded manner of life at Red Hill.

Learning how hard the Federalists were trying to bring Henry over to their side, the Democrats were uneasy. Jefferson soon termed Henry "the great apostate"; others called him a "turncoat." Sneered Jefferson in a letter to James Monroe in 1796: "Most assiduous court is paid to Patrick Henry. He has been offered everything which they [the Federalists] knew he would not accept. Some impression is thought to have been made on him, but we do not believe it is radical. If they thought they could count on him, they would run him for their vice president." Writing years later, after Henry's death, Jefferson even more sharply criticized Washington, Lee, and Henry:

> General Washington flattered him by an appointment to a mission to Spain, which he declined, and by proposing to him the office of Secretary of State on the earnest solicitation of General Henry Lee, who pledged himself that Henry would not accept it, for General Washington knew that he was entirely unqualified for it and, moreover, that his self-esteem had never suffered him to act as second to any man on earth.
>
> I had this fact from information, but the mission to Spain is of my own knowledge because, after retiring from office as Secretary of State, General Washington passed the papers to Mr. Henry through my hands.

Henry's political views and affiliations at this time are best summarized in his letter to a daughter, Elizabeth Aylett, written in the summer of 1796:

> As to the reports you have heard of my changing sides in politics, I can only say that they are not true. I am too old to exchange my former opinions which have grown up into fixed habits of thinking.
>
> True it is, I have condemned the conduct of our members in Congress because, in refusing to raise money for the purpose of the British treaty, they in effect would have surrendered our

> country, bound hand and foot, to the power of the British nation . . . The treaty is, in my opinion, a very bad one indeed*. . . .
>
> These sentiments I did mention in conversations in Richmond and perhaps others which I don't remember. But sure I am, my first principle is that from the British we have everything to dread when opportunities of oppressing us shall offer.
>
> It seems that every word was watched which I casually dropped, or wrested to answer party views. Who can have been so meanly employed, I know not. Nor do I care, for I no longer consider myself an actor on the stage of public life. It is time for me to retire, and I shall never more appear in public character unless some un-looked-for circumstance shall demand from me a transient effort not inconsistent with private life, in which I have determined to continue.

Henry expressed deep concern that President Washington, "our old commander-in-chief," was being so "abusively treated; nor are his long and great services remembered as any apology for his mistakes in an office to which he was totally unaccustomed." Even Washington, usually so placid and unruffled, was very upset by the bitter and often vicious attacks being made upon him. He was being misrepresented, he complained, "in such exaggerated and indecent terms as could scarcely be applied to a Nero—to a notorious defaulter—or even to a common pickpocket." Henry, in the letter to his daughter Betsy, expressed concern about something else:

> Amongst other strange things said of me, I hear it said by the deists that I am one of their number and, indeed, that some good people think I am no Christian. This thought gives me much more pain than the appellation of Tory, because I think religion of infinitely higher importance than politics; and I find much cause to reproach myself that I have lived so long and have given no decided proofs of my being a Christian. . . .
>
> What is there in the wit and wisdom of the present deistical

---

* This observation is revealing. If Henry had accepted appointment as Secretary of State, he would have been obliged to defend and implement the British treaty which was generally regarded as a rather stupid sellout and deplored in almost all American circles. Henry's dislike of the treaty was an unspoken consideration in his decision not to accept the appointment.

> writers or professors that can compare them with Hume, Shaftsbury, Bolingbroke, and others?* Yet these have been confuted, and their fame decaying, insomuch that the puny efforts of Paine are thrown in to prop their tottering structure? . . .

In 1794–95, Tom Paine published his *Age of Reason,* an attack on revealed religion and on ecclesiastical establishments in general and on the Bible and Christian establishments in particular. A typical 18th century deist in his views, Paine held that "all religions are in their nature mild and benign," but only when quite separated from political systems. Paine's views outraged Henry and, according to family tradition, he sat down to write a reply to the *Age of Reason.* But coming upon a volume entitled *Apology for the Bible,* written by Bishop Watson of Llandaff in Wales, Henry gave up his project and destroyed his manuscript. This was unfortunate for posterity, for it has deprived us of the only long and sustained composition to come from Henry's hand.

After his famed "Farewell Address," President Washington stepped from office, having announced that he would not be a candidate for re-election. After some maneuvering, the Federalists united behind John Adams to succeed him; Jefferson was the Republican candidate. It was a bitterly contested election, with wild charges and mean insinuations being broadcast by both parties. In the Electoral College, Adams received seventy-one votes and became President; with sixty-eight votes, Jefferson became Vice-President.**

Far from quieting the public agitation stirred up by fierce political partisanship, the election accentuated the strife. In their war against Britain and other powers, the French were interfering with American commerce and shipping, and insulted an American ambassador by refusing to receive him. The British were also interfering with American commerce and shipping, but the Federalists were disposed to overlook that. Led by Hamilton, the strong pro-British

---

* From this comment it is evident that at some time Henry had read David Hume and other religious skeptics.

** Under Electoral College procedure established originally and which was then still in force, the candidate receiving the most votes became President, and the runner-up became Vice-President. This accounts for the anomaly of Adams being teamed with his arch-enemy Jefferson; politically, the two were poles apart, and also personally estranged. It was not until the 1804 Presidential election that the voting procedure was changed to what it has since remained—a ballot for the Presidency, a separate ballot for the Vice Presidency.

faction among the Federalists began calling for a declaration of war against "revolutionary" France.

President Adams did not favor this course, wishing to better relations with France if he could. To explore possibilities, he sent a commission of three "Ministers Extraordinary" to Paris under instructions to do their best to secure a treaty of commerce and friendship. Negotiations broke down, in part because of what became known as the XYZ Affair, and early in 1798 the President reported to Congress the failure of the mission.

The cry for an immediate declaration of war against France grew louder. Adams opposed this action, saying that if war came, it would have to come from France. The President and Congress, however, took immediate steps to strengthen the national defense. Washington was named commander-in-chief of the military forces, with Alexander Hamilton second in command as inspector general. A Navy Department was organized. Increased revenues were to be raised by loans and higher taxes. Congress terminated the treaty of alliance signed with France in 1778. Undeclared naval warfare, though on a minor scale, broke out between the two countries.

If the Adams administration had contented itself with these sensible and reasonable defense measures, it would have spared the country a grave crisis. But the Federalists, under mounting criticism, became panicky and lost their heads, spying a French spy under every bush and regarding the Republican opposition with its Democratic societies as little more than an arm of the French Jacobin clubs.

In the summer of 1798, the Federalists in control of Congress pushed through that body the notorious Alien and Sedition Acts —the worst legislation ever passed by Congress with the exception of the measures adopted during the anti-Communist hysteria of the 1940s and 1950s, measures that the Supreme Court has been knocking down, one by one, as unconstitutional and in clear violation of the provisions of the Bill of Rights.

Among other things, the Alien and Sedition Acts gave the President the power to deport from the country any alien deemed dangerous to the public peace and safety, or suspected of "treasonable or secret" inclinations. The Acts made it a high misdemeanor, punishable by fine or imprisonment or both, for persons to enter into "unlawful" combinations to prevent execution of national laws, or to aid or attempt "any insurrection, riot, unlawful assembly, or combination." Anyone convicted of publishing "any false, scandalous, and malicious writing" about the Federal administration, Congress, or the President could be fined not more than $2,000 and imprisoned for not more than two years. Not only were these acts bad in themselves, but they were enforced in a very high-handed partisan manner. Of the twenty-five persons prosecuted under the Sedition Act, ten were convicted, all being leading Republican writers, editors, and printers.

The Federalist acts were plainly aimed at intimidating and silencing the opposition, and the Republicans accepted the challenge. With Jefferson and Madison in the lead, they attacked the Alien and Sedition Acts as unnecessary, despotic, and unconstitutional. Of more moment, they quickly rallied their forces in the Virginia and Kentucky legislatures and succeeded in securing adoption of two historic documents—the Kentucky Resolutions, drafted by Jefferson, and the Virginia Resolutions, framed by Madison. Both sets of resolutions were passed by large majorities, signifying wide popular support.

These resolutions, in brief, invoked the compact theory of the Constitution. The federal government had been delegated certain powers, and when it exceeded them, as in the Alien and Sedition Acts, each state had "an equal right to judge for itself, as well of infractions as of the mode and measure of redress." When infractions occurred, the states were "in duty bound to interpose for arresting the progress of the evil."

To the argument that the Supreme Court had the sole authority to determine constitutionality, the resolutions replied that the "sovereign" states had the right to judge, too, and that "nullification . . . of all unauthorized acts done under color of that instrument [the Constitution] is the rightful remedy."

Here was the first reasoned statement of the doctrine of nullification. For the moment, however, the doctrine remained purely theoretic, not being applied. Both Virginia and Kentucky declared their firm attachment to the Union, and neither took any steps to nullify the Alien and Sedition Acts, or to interfere with their enforcement.*

In view of his long strong resistance to despotic measures, one would expect that Henry immediately took a stand on the Alien and Sedition Acts. But he did not at first, saying nothing publicly. He did not give his endorsement to the acts; indeed, close friends reported that he regarded the acts as unconstitutional, agreeing with

* But when Jefferson became President a few years later, his Republican administration immediately repealed the obnoxious acts or allowed them to lapse. Jefferson pardoned all editors and printers convicted under the acts, and Congress returned to them the fines they had paid, plus interest.

Jefferson, Madison, and many more on that. But neither did Henry condemn and oppose the acts as repressive and extreme. His attitude appears to have been best summarized in his remark that as Congress had passed the laws, Congress could repeal them, but that he was not going to lend himself to any public agitation for repeal. The times were too tumultuous and dangerous.

But on a related matter, Henry had very strong and decided opinions. He thoroughly disapproved of the nullification resolutions engineered by Jefferson and Madison. He would not and could not support the Republican position here. In a recent letter to his daughter Betsy, he had denied the charge that he was "changing sides." But now he did, openly becoming a Federalist, even standing as a party candidate.

Early in 1799, with elections coming up, Henry received a letter from Washington, written from Mount Vernon and marked "confidential." It was a long letter detailing Washington's great anxieties about what was happening in the country, particularly the threat of civil war, and making an appeal to Henry:

> It would be a waste of time to attempt to bring to the view of a person of your observation and discernment the endeavors of a certain party among us to disquiet the public mind with unfounded alarms, to arraign every act of the administration, to set the people at variance with their government, and to embarrass all its measures.
>
> Equally useless would it be to predict what must be the inevitable consequences of such a policy if it cannot be arrested. Unfortunately—and extremely do I regret it—the State of Virginia has taken the lead in this opposition. . . .

The people of Virginia, Washington believed, were in general well affected to the government and to the Union. Why was it then that the Republicans could capture the state legislature and pass their nullification resolutions? It was because the "most respectable and best qualified characters among us do not come forward."

> I come now, my dear Sir, to the object of my letter, which is to express a hope and an earnest wish that you will come forward at the ensuing elections (if not for Congress, which you may think would take you too long from home) as a candidate for representative in the General Assembly of this Commonwealth . . .
>
> Your weight of character and influence in the House of Delegates would be a bulwark against such dangerous senti-

> ments as are delivered there at present. It would be a rallying point for the timid, and an attraction for the wavering.
>
> In a word, I conceive it to be of immense importance at this crisis that you should be there, and I would fain hope that all minor considerations will be made to yield to the measure.

With Henry, as he read this appeal and pondered his decision, it was not a question of yielding to "minor considerations." Primarily, it was a question of his strength and failing health. In answering a letter about this time, Henry declared that he was so tired and ill that he could scarcely write.

Even so, in response to Washington's plea, he decided to enter the lists once more, announcing that he would run as a Federalist candidate for a seat in the Virginia legislature, there to represent Charlotte County where now he lived.

On election day, Henry appeared at the polling place, the Charlotte County courthouse, having been driven in his carriage from Red Hill, about twenty miles away. Learning that Henry was to speak, a large crowd had gathered. Many had never seen Henry or heard him speak, and were anxious to do so. Classes at Hampden-Sydney College in neighboring Prince Edward County were dismissed so that faculty and students could attend the occasion.

When Henry stepped out of his carriage, many people crowded around him and followed him as he walked to the porch of the tavern that stood across the road from the courthouse. Seated on the porch, he talked with some old friends till time for him to speak.

When it came time, he got up from his chair "with difficulty and stood somewhat bowed with age and weakness." He was pale and his voice, as he began to speak, was "slightly cracked and tremulous." But shortly, as he warmed to his theme, there occurred "a wonderful transformation of the whole man," according to the account of one who was present and standing very near Henry:*

> He stood erect; his eye beamed with a light that was almost supernatural; his features glowed with the hue and fire of youth; and his voice rang clear and melodious with the intonations of some grand musical instrument whose notes filled the area and fell distinctly and delightfully upon the ears of the most distant of the thousands gathered before him.

---

* The quotations above and the paragraph below come from reminiscences reportedly told in conversation forty years later by John Miller, one of the Hampden-Sydney students who attended the Charlotte meeting.

It is not known exactly what the respected "old war horse" said on this occasion. The speech was not taken down, and no one appears to have taken notes while the speech was being delivered. But a number of prominent men who were present later wrote or spoke about what they remembered of Henry's last public address. Their accounts more or less agree.

According to one of these, Henry began by saying that the nullification resolutions adopted by the Virginia legislature had filled him with apprehension and alarm. They had planted thorns upon his pillow, and had drawn him from the happy retirement in which he had hoped to pass, in quiet, his remaining days.

Virginia had overstepped her authority in daring to challenge the validity of federal laws. Such opposition, if carried out, would necessitate military enforcement, which might well lead to civil war. And that would lead to foreign alliances, with the result that Americans would be subjugated by the foreign powers called in. Virginians should pause and take thought before they rushed into a position from which there could be no retreat.

Referring to the debate on the adoption of the Constitution, Henry said that he had seen with regret the unlimited power over the purse and the sword granted to the national government. His arguments against this had been overruled, however, and now it was necessary to submit to the constitutional exercise of that power.

> If I am asked what is to be done when a people feel themselves intolerably oppressed, my answer is ready—overturn the government!
>
> But do not, I beseech you, carry matters to this length without provocation. Wait at least until some infringement is made upon your rights, and which cannot otherwise be redressed. For if ever you recur to another change, you may bid adieu forever to representative government. You can never exchange the present government but for a monarchy. If the administration has done wrong, let us all go wrong together.*

At this point Henry paused, clasped his hands, and began swaying his body from side to side. His listeners began swaying from side to side as Henry picked up again:

> Let us trust God and our better judgment to set us right

---

* This anticipated President Lyndon B. Johnson's ideas about the desirability of "consensus." Let us all, without a murmur, jump through the hoop and into the fire together.

> hereafter. United we stand, divided we fall. Let us not split into factions which must destroy that union upon which our existence hangs. Let us preserve our strength for the French, the English, the Germans, or whoever else shall dare invade our territory, and not exhaust it in civil commotions and intestine wars.

Henry concluded by saying that, if elected, he would do his utmost "to allay the heart-burnings and jealousies which have been fomented in the state legislature."

The next speaker was one of Henry's great admirers, young John Randolph, but who, on this occasion, was "constrained to differ from him *toto coelo.*" Randolph was running as Republican Democratic candidate for Congress from the district.

Before Randolph rose to speak, Henry left the platform and retired to a room in the tavern where he might rest, having asked a friend to report to him any of Randolph's remarks that might require an answer. Reports on Randolph's arguments were made to him, but Henry did not reply. He was unable to do so, for he was in a state of near collapse.

Assisted to his carriage, Henry was driven home to Red Hill. Counting of the votes revealed that he had been elected, but he did not take his seat in the House of Delegates. Indeed, he never again stepped foot out of his house at Red Hill, being confined to bed for weeks. As his ailments grew worse, he called for a physician and old friend, Dr. George Cabell, who came down from Lynchburg, about forty miles away, and remained with Henry to the end.

"Dear Patsy," he wrote to his oldest daughter and favorite child, Martha Fontaine, "I am very unwell, and have Dr. Cabell with me." On this news, Patsy and others of his family in the neighborhood hastened to Red Hill. They found Henry "sitting in a large old-fashioned armchair in which he was easier than upon a bed." Members of the family living in or beyond Richmond did not come because of the sudden death of Henry's daughter, Anne Roane, while on a visit with a sister. It was decided that Henry should not be told about Anne's sudden death because the shock might be too great.

Dr. Cabell diagnosed Henry's latest and most painful ailment as intussusception—in simple terms, a blockage of the bowels. Early in June, 1799, two months after the Charlotte meeting, Dr. Cabell decided that as all other medication had failed, he would have to prescribe something more drastic and handed Henry a vial of liquid mercury.

"I suppose, Doctor, this is your last resort," said Henry.*

"I am sorry to say, Governor, that it is. Acute inflammation of the intestines has already taken place, and unless it is removed, mortification will ensue if it has not already commenced, which I fear."

"What will be the effect of this medicine?" asked Henry.

"It will give you immediate relief, or . . ."

"You mean, Doctor, that it will give relief or will prove fatal immediately?"

"You can live only a very short time without it, and it may possibly relieve you."

"Excuse me, Doctor, for a few minutes," said Henry, as he drew his silken skull cap down over his eyes and prayed. Dr. Cabell left the house and, in tears, threw himself down on the lawn under a tree.

Regaining control of himself, Cabell returned and found Henry sitting in his old chair, quietly watching his fingernails turn blue.

Henry soon began to lose consciousness and, after a short time of quiet breathing, died. The date was June 6, 1799, little more than a week after his sixty-third birthday.

As he had requested, Henry was buried with simple ceremony at the foot of his sloping garden at Red Hill. Later, a large marble slab was laid on the ground to mark the grave. This gravestone, still there, bears this inscription carved long ago.

"His fame his best epitaph."

There is a deep irony here. His fame has gone into almost total eclipse. Henry has been relegated to limbo, where he does not belong.

Everyone knows his "give me liberty or give me death" phrase, but little else about Henry, what he accomplished and what he failed to accomplish, his strength and his faults, and the many forces, both personal and general, that enabled him to emerge unheralded from the back country to play such an important role in founding the nation and shaping its beginnings.

As one of the greatest of the Founding Fathers, as the one who "gave the first impulse to the ball of Revolution" and almost overnight became "the Noble Patriot," our first national hero, "the idol of the country" in his day, Patrick Henry deserves to be better remembered and more highly honored by his countrymen than he has been for generations.

---

* Details on Henry's death scene come from a narrative by his grandson, Patrick Henry Fontaine, who was living at Red Hill at the time. Fontaine no doubt "made up" most of the quoted conversation, dramatizing his vivid remembrance of the scene and the gist of what was said there.

Appendix A

Henry's biographers, all of them obviously proper gentlemen, sedate and most genteel, also more than a bit moralistic, have stretched themselves to tenuous and rather ridiculous lengths in trying to "explain" Henry's barkeeping days—as if tending bar *per se* were the grossest of improprieties and, if not a mortal, at least a venial, sin, crying out for apology and Christian forgiveness.

Wrote William Wirt (1817):

> He [Henry] seems to have spent the greatest part of his time [while studying and first practicing law] . . . with his father-in-law, Mr. Shelton, who then kept the tavern at Hanover Courthouse. Whenever Mr. Shelton was from home, Mr. Henry supplied his place in the tavern, received the guests, and attended to their entertainment.
>
> All this was very natural in Mr. Henry's situation, and seems to have been purely the voluntary movement of his naturally kind and obliging disposition.
>
> Hence, however, a story has arisen that, in the early part of his life, he was a barkeeper by profession. The fact seems not to have been so; but if it had been, it would certainly have redounded much more to his honour than to his discredit. . . .

Moses Coit Tyler (1888):

> . . . his father-in-law [Shelton] had become the keeper of a tavern in Hanover; and for the next two or three years, while he [Henry] was rapidly making his way as a general practitioner of the law in that neighborhood, Patrick seems *occasionally* [italics mine] to have been a *visitor* [!!] at this

> tavern.* It was in this way, undoubtedly, that he sometimes acted as host, especially in the absence of his father-in-law—receiving all comers, and providing for their entertainment. . . .

W. W. Henry (1891):

> As Patrick's grandson, W. W. Henry chose to make no mention of his grandfather's stay and activities at the tavern, which was one way of avoiding what he obviously regarded as a "moral" problem.

George Morgan (1907):

> View the bar-keeping story as we may, it is allowable to conclude that Patrick would have been a scurvy fellow indeed had he not helped John Shelton.

Robert Douthat Meade (1957):

> Taverns were operated by some substantial gentlemen of the Piedmont, . . . and liquor was served as a matter of course. John Shelton had various interests, and was apparently trying hard to maintain his own and his son-in-law's family. Patrick, a repeated failure and living with his wife and children at Shelton's tavern, would have been most ungrateful not to have helped with the guests when needed. There is a difference between lending a hand to his generous father-in-law and being "originally a barkeeper."

All of which is pretty silly, and gratuitous. His bartending days never bothered Henry. Indeed, he obviously found them pleasant, amusing, even exciting at times.

Gregarious and very sociable, always a fascinated and shrewd observer of human traits and behavior, fond of lively conversation, sharp repartee, and good rousing argument, he must have enjoyed the rough, often profane, and occasionally obscene give-and-take of conversation at the bar in Shelton's backwoods tavern.

And Virginians of the day, by all accounts, were masters of the profane and obscene. Many a native and many a "foreigner" noted that in the Old Dominion even the most polished and otherwise conventional "gentlemen" could scarcely speak a sentence without uttering an oath or some (then) unprintable scatological expletive or adjective.

---

* Henry and his family lived in the tavern from 1757 to 1766, and again from 1768 until 1771, when Henry bought and established himself and family on his large Scotchtown estate.

Appendix B

Not long after the stamp tax debate, a story began going the rounds in certain circles that the Stamp Tax Resolutions had not been written by Henry, but by George Johnston of Fairfax County and/or John Fleming of Cumberland, both of whom were able and experienced Burgesses, men of established position.

Years later, when at sword's point with Henry politically, James Madison became curious about this story, perhaps thinking he could turn it against Henry, and wrote to ask Edmund Pendleton "where the resolutions proposed by Mr. Henry *really* originated." It is not known what Pendleton replied, for his letter has been lost. Madison also wrote to Jefferson on the same subject. Jefferson, who had been on the scene and behind the scenes at the time of the debate, informed Madison that the story about Johnston-Fleming authorship of the resolutions was based on "mere rumor."

It would seem that it should have been evident from the start that the story was most unlikely. If Johnston and Fleming had written the Stamp Tax Resolutions, why did they not present them themselves? If they had some reason for not doing so, it is beyond belief that these two seasoned veterans in public affairs would have chosen as their spokesman and the champion of their cause the newest, rawest, and youngest member of the House, as yet scarcely known to most of the Burgesses.

For reasons unexplained, some historians and biographers seem to have a compulsive obsession to denigrate Henry and belittle his achievements at every opportunity. A recent example of this occurs in *Williamsburg: Seat of Empire* by Carl Bridenbaugh, who, after a rather slurring account of Henry's part in the stamp tax debate, goes on to talk about the "Fleming-Henry resolutions."

There is no reason whatever to doubt Henry's statement that, by himself, he wrote the resolutions that sparked the Revolution.

Appendix C

It is curious that no one else who heard the debate–neither Jefferson, nor any of the members of the House–ever recalled hearing "henery" beg to be pardoned for what he had said. Almost half of the Burgesses were hostile to Henry and everything he stood for, and would have been only too happy to report that their cries of treason had forced Henry to back down and apologize. But none of them so reported.

Yet some academic historians and popular lecturers, wishing to spice up stale scripts, have seized upon the French traveler's remarks to represent Henry as suddenly turning tail and retreating from his forward position. This is an absolutely false picture, as shown by the fact that Henry persevered and persuaded the House to adopt all of the five resolutions he brought to the floor on May 30.

After his "treason" speech, Henry may have said something–though none but the Frenchman recalled it–with the aim of taking some of the sharpness off what he had said. After all, he was not proposing to raise a one-man revolt against the King. He had no desire to arouse the fears of the timid; they should be quieted. No one knew better than Henry the necessity of persuading, by one means or another, the hesitant to step forward to the limits of their courage, and not be frightened.

One thing in the Frenchman's account is almost certainly mistaken, due perhaps to his difficulty in understanding spoken English, particularly in a lively loud debate. According to his account, Henry said, in "begging pardon," that he was ready "to show his loyalty to his majesty King G. the third at the Expense of the last Drop of his blood." Henry cannot conceivably have said anything like that. He had long passed the point where unquestioning loyalty to the Crown was his guiding star–that was for tradition-bound Grandees.

Appendix D

Robert Pleasants, one of Henry's many Quaker friends in Virginia, sent him a copy of a book against slavery, well written and cogently reasoned, a collection of tracts by Anthony Benezet of Philadelphia, a Quaker and a pioneer in the Abolitionist movement. Owner of a large plantation along the James, Robert Pleasants had educated his Negro slaves and then freed them, at a cost to him of £5,000. Wrote Henry to his friend Pleasants:

Hanover
January 18, 1773

Dear Sir:

I take this opportunity to acknowledge the receipt of Anthony Benezet's book against the Slave Trade. I thank you for it.

It is not a little surprising that the professors of Christianity, whose chief excellence consists in softening the human heart, and in cherishing and improving its finer feelings, should encourage a practice [slavery] so totally repugnant to the first impressions of right and wrong.

What adds to the wonder is that this abominable practice has been introduced in the most enlightened ages. Times that seem to have pretensions to boast of high improvements in the arts and sciences and refined morality, have brought into general use, and guarded by many laws, a species of violence and tyranny which our more rude and barbarous, but more honest, ancestors detested.

Is it not amazing that at a time when the rights of humanity are defined and understood in a country, above all others, fond of liberty, that in such an age and country we find men professing a religion the most humane, mild, gentle, and generous, adopting a principle as repugnant to humanity as it is inconsistent with the Bible and destructive to liberty. Every thinking honest man rejects it . . .

> Would anyone believe I am a master of slaves of my own purchase! I am drawn along by the general inconvenience of living here without them.
>
> I will not, I cannot justify it. However culpable my conduct, I will so far pay my *devoir* to virtue as to own the excellence and rectitude of her precepts and lament my want of conformity to them.
>
> I believe a time will come when an opportunity will be offered to abolish this lamentable evil. Everything we can do is to improve it, if it happens in our day. If not, let us transmit to our descendants, together with our slaves, a pity for their unhappy lot and an abhorrence of slavery.
>
> If we cannot reduce this wished-for reformation to practice, let us treat the unhappy victims with lenity. It is the furthest advance we can make toward justice . . .
>
> I know not when to stop. I could say many things on the subject, a serious view of which gives a gloomy perspective to future times.

A "gloomy perspective" indeed! Problems arising from slavery are still with us in very acute form two centuries later.

Appendix E

There were two fiscal officers in the colony—the treasurer, elected by the House of Burgesses, who had charge of collecting and dispensing all monies raised in Virginia by taxes and other levies authorized by the General Assembly for strictly provincial purposes; and a receiver-general, appointed by the King, who was responsible for all Crown revenues arising from quitrents, customs duties, and other imposts.

Receiver-General Corbin was a staunch Loyalist-Royalist. But as he was not an active Tory, he was allowed to live in peace through the Revolution.

It is an interesting footnote that Corbin and his wife had long been almost totally estranged. She lived at one end, and he at the other end of their massive house, almost a hundred yards long, about the size of a modern football field. Regularly, once a year, Corbin ordered his coach and four brought around and was driven in great style to the other end of the house, where he paid a formal call and had tea with his wife. That ended communication for a year. Both liked this arrangement, and they appear to have lived happily ever after.

Appendix F

Many years later, when he was seventy-four, John Taylor of Caroline, Pendleton's protégé, then serving in the United States Senate, told John Quincy Adams one day that at the Staunton session, Henry persuaded the House to go into secret session and there proposed that Virginia "should be the first to submit to Great Britain in order that she might obtain the most favorable terms."

Taylor's story is preposterous on the face of it. The House Journal records no such meeting. During the bitter political fighting among Virginians in the late 1780s and the 1790s, many blasts were directed at Henry by his enemies. Yet not one of them so much as hinted at Henry's alleged attempt to have Virginia "sell out" to the British.

Yet certain historians have picked up the story and repeated it almost as a fact, rather than as a figment of the imagination of a feeble old man, wasted in body and mind, who died a few months later.

Perhaps the most judicious comment on the story was made by James Madison when he heard it: "It is difficult to resist the positive testimony of Colonel Taylor as to the intention of Mr. Henry to give up the contest with Great Britain. But is it not more difficult to resist the extreme improbability of the fact?"

Appendix G

Jefferson was still smarting under the implied vote of censure leveled against him by the Assembly for his acts as governor, "a wound on my spirit which only will be cured by the all-healing grave," feeling so aggrieved that he declared he was through with holding public office. He had taken his "final leave of everything of that nature," he announced. "I have retired to my farm, my family and books, from which I think nothing will evermore separate me."

Many of his closest friends were highly critical of his announced retirement, including James Madison: "Great as my partiality is to Mr. Jefferson, the mode in which he seems determined to revenge the wrong he received from his country does not appear to me to be dictated either by philosophy or patriotism. It argues, indeed, a keen sensibility and strong consciousness of rectitude. But his sensibility ought to be as great towards the relenting as the misdoings of the [Virginia] Legislature"—which had just dropped the proposed inquiry into Jefferson's administration.

Index